Institutions in Transition

Institutions in Transition

Land Ownership, Property Rights, and Social Conflict in China

PETER HO

OXFORD
UNIVERSITY PRESS

OXFORD
UNIVERSITY PRESS

Great Clarendon Street, Oxford OX2 6DP

Oxford University Press is a department of the University of Oxford.
It furthers the University's objective of excellence in research, scholarship,
and education by publishing worldwide in

Oxford New York

Auckland Cape Town Dar es Salaam Hong Kong Karachi
Kuala Lumpur Madrid Melbourne Mexico City Nairobi
New Delhi Shanghai Taipei Toronto

With offices in

Argentina Austria Brazil Chile Czech Republic France Greece
Guatemala Hungary Italy Japan Poland Portugal Singapore
South Korea Switzerland Thailand Turkey Ukraine Vietnam

Oxford is a registered trade mark of Oxford University Press
in the UK and in certain other countries

Published in the United States
by Oxford University Press Inc., New York

First published 2005

British Library Cataloguing in Publication Data
Data available

Library of Congress Cataloging in Publication Data
Data available

Typeset by Newgen Imaging Systems (P) Ltd., Chennai, India
Printed in Great Britain
on acid-free paper by
Biddles Ltd., King's Lynn, Norfolk

ISBN 0–19–928069–X 978–0–19–928069–8

1 3 5 7 9 10 8 6 4 2

For 'DD' Zhao Heng, my love and guide

Foreword

A book examining China's land policies and their socio-economic impact on rural society should not go unnoticed. First of all, because it addresses issues that have risen to the surface in modern China as we witness it today. Second, because this volume appears to be the first of its kind devoted entirely to the subject of the institutional design of land property rights in China. And finally, because it is a book written with an eye for much detail and with an extraordinary understanding of the political, social, and legal developments which have taken place in China in recent years.

Frankly, I am not surprised to find that a book with these merits is written by Peter Ho. I have had the privilege of being assisted by him while serving during two consecutive terms in office as a minister in the Dutch government, each time benefiting from his skills as an interpreter during my various official visits to China. From 1997 onwards Peter accompanied me on those visits and facilitated my discussions with my Chinese counterparts.

It was during one of those visits when Peter served as my official interpreter that I discussed the subject of land reform in China with the Chinese Minister for Foreign Affairs, Tang Jiaxuan. During a gathering of the Asia Europe Meeting (ASEM) that took place in Berlin in the spring of 1999, we discussed the role of China in the world. Tang Jiaxuan and I agreed then that it was not a matter for discussion whether China would have a major impact on global developments and international relations, but only when this would happen. I added, however, that there were still many hurdles to be taken by China.

The adequate protection of human rights and the establishment of a truly free society, for one. To see China develop into a liberal democracy where people can speak their minds and worship their gods, where they can live without the fear of arbitrary arrest and torture: that is not only in the interest of the Chinese citizens. It is in the interest of the whole world community. Chris Patten, the former and last British Governor in Hong Kong, said it right: 'Societies that treat their own people intolerably, governments whose own laws are a farce, are bad and potentially dangerous neighbours.' Proper and fair laws, a strong rule of law, should therefore be part and parcel of a strong and prosperous China with an important role in international relations. Land property rights, the reform of the Chinese land market, should be covered by those laws, just as civil rights and political liberties should.

Especially in the light of China's recent entry into the World Trade Organization (WTO), it is important that China introduces all necessary reforms to accompany its transition to a market-based and open economy. Reform of its land market, which has lagged behind for many years, should be part and parcel of them. There are several reasons why the momentum generated by China's WTO membership should be seized to take the necessary measures in the area of land ownership.

First, the land in China is highly fragmented. This is due in large part to rural unemployment and the fact that millions of farmers are tied to their land in order to maintain their livelihoods. This land fragmentation hampers mechanization and large-scale agricultural activities, thereby endangering rural development as a whole. This problem could be partly overcome by establishing a free land market, allowing for the exchange and transfer of plots of land.

The second reason why land reforms are necessary is that current land property rights are unclear and uncertain. Land has not been adequately registered and no systematic cadastre has been developed. This enhances the problem of poor land and spatial planning. Land is used in inefficient and improper ways: desertification, deforestation and industrial pollution by agro-industries are common problems. Moreover, the lack of a cadastre also impedes foreign land investment since land cannot be used as collateral. This might have a negative impact on overall economic development in China. Foreign investors, including those from the European Union, are unlikely to consider private Chinese industries as reliable partners unless they have secure land tenure. Potential investors will therefore feel obliged to look for ways to reduce the investment risks caused by unclear land rights. China's WTO membership will only make this problem more apparent and increase the need for appropriate reform measures in China.

With his extensive research and analysis on the subject, Peter Ho therefore provides an important contribution to the process of reform in China and to its further development as a major player in the world market. The reform of the Chinese land market is spurred on by the gradual opening of the Chinese economy. The design and implementation of the appropriate measures will prove challenging for both Chinese and international researchers, policy makers and legislators. As Peter Ho makes amply clear in this volume, it is, however, one challenge that can and should not be circumvented.

Jozias van Aartsen
Former Minister of Foreign Affairs of The Netherlands
Former Minister of Agriculture of The Netherlands

Acknowledgements

The person who has seen this book maturing, the research questions continuously changing, yet who has always given me the necessary support and advice (at times hard to accept, nevertheless seldom unjustified), is Mark Selden. I would like to thank him for countless discussions about rural development and Chinese politics, for being my intellectual sparring partner, friend, and 'walking encyclopaedia'.

Someone else without whom this research would have never been realized is Gao Guiying, my cheerful and sharp-witted counterpart at the Ningxia Academy of Social Sciences. She accompanied me on all my fieldtrips, lived with me—like Mao Zedong—in a cave dwelling, placated grumpy local officials and Party cadres with her 'ping-pong diplomacy', and never failed to arrange any interview I asked for because of her extensive network of *guanxi*. The time we spent in the countryside, far removed from running tap water and television, but living a life of relative peace and simplicity, has become one of my cherished memories and an abode where I love to hide. I could not mention Gao Guiying without mentioning Shi Wenzheng of the University of Inner Mongolia. His path-breaking book on China's grassland law turned out to be the serendipity for my research: who owns China's land? I will always admire and respect him for his extensive knowledge on land rights, and for being my teacher in the true Chinese sense of a *laoshi*. And then there are so many others who have advised me, helped me to order my thoughts, or were simply there to bear with my changing moods. Without them this book would have never been as it lies in your hands today.

I will name them here in alphabetical order, and please forgive me if I have forgotten anyone: the series editors Frank Dikötter and Phil Deans for their pleasant and efficient support during the revision process; Richard Edmonds for his faith in and unlimited support for this manuscript—indeed, his warm and positive reaction to my first article on the topic gave me the idea and strength to write this book; Jim Harkness for all the information he gave me about the Four Wastelands Auction Policy and the 'environmental scene' in Beijing; Ji Kunqi and all the others of the Ningxia Science and Technology Commission; Jeroen de Kloet, and well, both he and I know what he meant to me during the ups and downs of my moods, which were sometimes related to the research and sometimes not; Lai Cunli of the Zhejiang Academy of Social Sciences, who made me aware of the vanguard role Zhejiang Province plays in the reform of China's property rights system; Li Weimin of the Chinese Academy of Agricultural Sciences; Liu Ruihua, who as the mayor's wife showed me how *guanxi* can make the difference between a fine of $US2,000 and $100 and saved my university a lot of bucks; Ma Yaocheng and his family for their warmth and hospitality during the year that I lived in their cave dwelling—I still regret the chicken he had slaughtered for me and Guiying—in addition, I would also like to mention his daughter who literally saved my life during what might have been my last night, spent on a Chinese *kang*; Hein Mallee for the talks on forest and wasteland, the beer and good Japanese food in Beijing, and—not to forget—his generous support for the panel on land rights in China, hosted at the Second International Convention for Asia Scholars, Berlin, 9–12 August 2001; the participants of the aforementioned panel, in particular Frank Pieke, Vivienne Shue, and Wang Weiguo; the rangeland specialists Tony Banks, Robin Mearns, and John Morton for their specialized comments on pastoralism; Ni Dongfa, with whom the one interview I had was worth more than a hundred with others; Jan-Michiel Otto for sharing with me his expertise on law and administration in developing countries and navigating me through the intellectual pitfalls of the writing process; Tony Saich for all the old China hands in different fields he brought me into contact with, for the intellectual and logistical support for my research even when time was tighter than tight, and for offering me a place to stay when I was to my horror suddenly branded an 'illegal alien' in China; Qu Futian, for bringing me into contact with the people at the Directorate General of Land Titling of the Ministry of Land Resources; Eduard 'Ward' Vermeer, for all his open advise and generous support; and, of course, the two anonymous referees for their helpful comments on the manuscript.

I would also like to express my heartfelt thanks to all the farmers and officials who willingly answered all my nitty-gritty questions, who lodged me, and gave me their hospitality and their confidence. I have tried to capture some of their lively spirit and harsh life on tape to broadcast over radio to people here in the Netherlands, yet failed to help the village that asked me for it. That thought is mine to struggle with. Of the officials I would particularly like to mention Li Sheng, Director General at the Ministry of Agriculture; and the two Deputy Directors General for Land Titling at the Ministry of Land Resources, Wang Guanghua and Zao Long, as well as Dai Guangcui and Zhang Lei of the State Bureau of Forestry. Lastly, there are my parents, who fled from peril and violence to bring us—the children—to a safe and stable haven, and my sister Wenny, who as the only true forester in our family and with her knowledge of the development world has helped me out more than once; and, of course, Zhao Heng, my Significant Other, who made me fall in love with a country, culture and language, and forms the roots of this research.

This research was funded by the Research School for Asian, African and Amerindian Studies (Research School CNWS) of Leiden University, the EU-China Research Fellowship Fund (ECRFF) of the European Commission, and the Netherlands Organisation for Scientific Research (NWO). Several chapters of this book are based on earlier articles that were published by *The China Quarterly*, *Development and Change*, and *The Journal of Peasant Studies*.

Peter Ho
Groningen, February 2005

Contents

List of Figures

List of Tables

List of Plates

List of Abbreviations

CCP	Chinese Communist Party
FAO	Food and Agriculture Organization
KMT	Kuomintang
NGO	Non-governmental organization
NOAA	National Oceanic and Atmospheric Administration
NPC	National People's Congress
NZTFS	Nongyebu Zhengce Tigai Fagui Si
PRC	People's Republic of China
RFGW	Renda Fazhi Gongzuo Weiyuanhui
RMB	Renminbi
WTO	World Trade Organization
ZRJGDDY	Zhongguo Renmin Jiefangjun Guofang Daxue Dangshi Yanjiushi
ZTGZBW	Zhongguo Tudi Guanli Zonglan Bianji Weiyuanhui

Introduction

Land is the source of all material wealth. From it we get everything that we use or value, whether it be food, clothing, fuel, shelter, metal, or precious stones. We live on the land and from the land, and to the land our bodies or our ashes are committed when we die. The availability of land is the key to human existence, and its distribution and use are of vital importance.

(R. Rowton Simpson, *Land Law and Registration*)

The idea for this book came in a flash. The problems that confront the Chinese peasant are diverse: Muslim Hui farmers in Ningxia trying to prevent the shifting sands from engulfing their crops; rural residents on the outskirts of Beijing who resort to legal action as they suffer from the dust and noise of an illegal coal-processing plant; herders in Inner Mongolia fighting off invaders who destroy their pasture in search of valuable medicinal herbs; and villagers in Zhejiang who have been bought out their homes to make way for an expanding city. At a certain time it dawned on me that many of the problems I witnessed in rural China today were actually the expression of something more fundamental: the control over land. This became the driving question for my research.

Whenever I went to a village, a rural enterprise, or a mosque I would start my investigation with a simple question: 'Who owns the land?' It struck me time and again how the same plot of land could be owned by as many different persons and legal entities as the question was put to. A farmer would give a completely different answer from a township cadre, while the cadre's reply would be anything but consistent with the view of a provincial official. How could it be that such an easy and basic question resulted in such a myriad of replies? It was then that I knew I had stumbled on to something big, something which its availability—in the words of Rowton Simpson—is 'the key to human existence'.[1] But *how* big it was and *how many* years it would take me to uncover the entire minefield of paradoxes and ambiguities I did not know when I started studying herders and livestock farmers in 1993.

Analysing Institutional Change, Credibility and Property Rights

This monograph examines institutional change in China by focusing on the shifts in institutional arrangements that surround one of mankind's most basic resources: the land off which he lives. The analysis attempts to answer the question of what institutions since Land Reform and up to the era of economic reform have generated the current dynamics of the Chinese rural economy and society. This will be done by reviewing the institutions of various types of rural land—cropland, grassland, forest,

[1] R. Rowton Simpson, *Land Law and Registration* (Cambridge: Cambridge University Press, 1976), p. 3.

and wasteland—with an occasional detour into urban land. In the study of institutional change, I will distinguish two different analytical levels: the national and the local (leaving aside the meso level of analysis). The local level consists of the echelon of the street-level bureaucrats[2] who are in direct contact with the populace at the grass roots, as well as the administrative tiers that govern them. In the Chinese context this can include the township, the county, and the prefecture.

Throughout this volume two theoretical concepts will form a leitmotiv: 'institutions' (or institutional arrangements) and 'property rights'. The term 'institution' is here *not* broadly construed as pertaining to 'the rules of the game in a society or, more formally, . . . the humanly devised constraints that shape human interaction', as defined by Nobel Prize winner Douglass North.[3] Instead, the notion is used in a narrower sense referring to institutional arrangements embodied in promulgated policies, formal laws and customary rules, and the state administration. I regard societal and economic phenomena—such as farmland loss, improper land use and management, and lagging investments in land resources—as affected by and affecting institutions, rather than the institution as an underlying factor of a higher order. In conceptualizing institutional change one easily ends up with a 'chicken and egg' dilemma: what came first, the chicken of institutions or the egg of changes in socio-economic conditions?

The issue is more complicated than that: using China's transitional economy as a case study, I will argue that institutions both *drive* and are *subject to* the evolutionary process of socio-economic change. It follows that, if neither institutions nor socio-economic conditions are favourable to socio-economic change, reforms of property rights are likely to fail. This is not sufficient for the policy-maker who, in the process of 'institutional engineering', wants to know at what point in time new institutions must be created to guide socio-economic change, and to what extent socio-economic conditions dictate the set-up of institutions. There is no fixed answer to these questions, as institutions and socio-economic parameters are both caught up in a fluid and dynamic process of change.

[2] The term 'street-level bureaucrat' was first introduced by Michael Lipsky. See Michael Lipsky, 'Street-level Bureaucracy: The Critical Role of Street-Level Bureaucrats', in Jay Shafritz and Albert Hyde (eds.), *Classics of Public Administration* (Belmont: Wadsworth Publishing Company, 1992).

[3] Douglass North, *Institutions, Institutional Change and Economic Performance* (Cambridge: Cambridge University Press, 1990), p. 3. For sociologists, the term 'institution' refers to an agreement system that organizes some general aspects of group life. As Babbie writes: 'An institution is a relatively stable and integrated set of symbols, beliefs, values, norms, roles and statuses relating to some aspect of social life.' E. R. Babbie, *Sociology: An Introduction* (Belmont: Wadsworth, 1980), p. 114. Economic institutions are thus agreement systems that organize the production and distribution of goods and services. One of the major figures in the institutional school of economics is Commons, who clarified the institution thus: 'Sometimes an institution seems to be analogous to a building, a sort of framework of laws and regulations, within which individuals act like inmates. Sometimes it seems to mean the "behavior" of the inmates themselves.' J. R. Commons, *Institutional Economics* (Madison: University of Wisconsin Press, 1961), p. 69. There is a wide body of literature available on institutional change and the relationship between institutions and economic behaviour. One of the earliest influential articles on the topic was written in 1955 by C. J. Wolf, 'Institutions and Economic Development', *American Economic Review*, Vol. 45 (1955), pp. 867–83.

Not a very reassuring thought; and, indeed, throughout this volume I will demonstrate that deferring reform of institutions when socio-economic conditions call for change, or creating institutions at the 'wrong' time, has inherent dangers: the eruption of social conflict as villagers' rights to land are trampled; the rise of a new class of impoverished, landless peasants; and the destruction of natural resources due to short-term exploitation. As I have argued elsewhere, another pitfall in the institutional design by the state is the creation of a so-called 'empty institution'. In such cases, the new institution remains nothing more than a paper agreement or a hollow shell with little effect on social action.[4] And indeed, in this book a poignant example of this will be given in the account of China's grassland policy.

On the other hand, we will also see that at critical moments a 'hands-off' approach by the state has allowed for the emergence of institutions that are widely perceived by social actors as credible. In fact, the state's deliberate choice to shroud certain institutions in a mist of indeterminacy—what I have termed 'intentional institutional ambiguity'—is in many ways the key to understanding the success of China's rural reforms. Note that, following Diermeyer et al., I have consciously opted to refer to the 'credibility' of institutions instead of to the more fashionable concept of 'trust'.[5] Whereas scholarly discussions about trust focus more on the relations of trust between social actors[6]—whether face-to-face 'thick' interpersonal trust or networks of social capita—I would like to draw attention to the nature of *institutions* and the way in which they are *perceived* by social actors. Put differently, 'trust' relates more directly to the social actor, whereas 'credibility' puts more emphasis on the institution itself.

Most studies of land property rights in China have focused on the socio-economic parameters. However, if we ever want to understand the inner workings of institutional change and their relation to socio-economic conditions, we must start by examining the very nature of institutions over time. In the academic literature the words 'institutions' and 'property rights' are frequently used side by side, even to the point that the distinction between them becomes blurred.[7] In particular, when social

[4] For a further discussion of the notions of 'empty' and 'credible' institutions, see Peter Ho (ed.), *Developmental Dilemmas: Land Reform and Institutional Change in China* (London and New York: Routledge, 2005).

[5] Daniel Diermeyer, Joel M. Ericson, Timothy Frye, and Steven Lewis, 'Credible Commitment and Property Rights: The Role of Strategic Interaction between Political and Economic Actors', in David L. Weimer (ed.), *The Political Economy of Property Rights: Institutional Change and Credibility in the Reform of Centrally Planned Economies* (Cambridge: Cambridge University Press, 1997), p. 20.

[6] See, for instance, William Mishler and Richard Rose, 'Trust, Distrust and Skepticism: Popular Evaluations of Civil and Political Institutions in Post-Communist Societies', *Journal of Politics*, Vol. 59 (1997), pp. 418–51; and David W. Lovell, 'Trust and the Politics of Postcommunism', *Communist and Post-Communist Studies*, Vol. 34 (2001), pp. 27–38.

[7] Property rights and institutions are brought together in a single analysis in the study of so-called common property or common pool resources. See Elinor Ostrom, *Governing the Commons: The Evolution of Institutions for Collective Action* (Cambridge: Cambridge University Press, 1990); Larry L. Kiser and Elinor Ostrom, 'The Three Worlds of Action: A Metatheoretical Synthesis of Institutional Approaches', in: Elinor Ostrom (ed.), *Strategies*

scientists define property rights as a 'social relation'[8] the two terms blend into one. To be analytically clear, a property right is an institution, but an institution is not necessarily a property right. Moreover, the concept of property rights is here understood in the Demsetzian or common law tradition as a 'bundle of rights'.[9] Instead of the civil law definition of 'ownership' as an absolute and all-inclusive right,[10] property can include—with temporal and geographical variations—such rights as use, alienation, usufruct, access, management, and the right of way. However, the attentive reader will note that I do use the word 'ownership' in addition to 'property right', particularly in the first few chapters on the national policies on cropland, grassland, forest, and wasteland. This is a conscious choice, as I will demonstrate in Chapter 1 that the concept of ownership as an all-inclusive right describes more appropriately than the notion of a 'bundle of rights' the Chinese state's *envisaged* legal and political context for land tenure.

At this point, I touch on the second pivotal question that underlies this volume: who owns and controls rural land? Three critical issues will be addressed: first, the main constraints and inconsistencies in the current institutional framework of land property rights; second, the socio-economic impact on rural society of national policies for agricultural land (cropland), forest, grassland, and wasteland; and third, the possible alternatives or improvements in land tenure that could lead to a socially acceptable, ecologically sustainable, and economically viable use of land resources.

This research draws on ample Chinese sources, including the minutes of the NPC's Standing Committee and Legislative Affairs Work Committee; the officially solicited opinions of central and local state institutions, mass organizations, and relevant experts; the interpretations of laws released by the NPC, various departments, and people's courts; and the training and reference material for rural land administration cadres (including grassland and forest). In addition, fieldwork was carried out in different periods from 1993 to 2001. A total of over 150 interviews were conducted with central, provincial, and local officials, as well as farmers and pastoralists in Beijing, Zhejiang (Longquan and Yiwu County), Inner Mongolia (Wuyuan and Zunge'er Banner), and Ningxia (Tongxin, Yanchi, Guyuan, and Pengyang County). The fieldwork also included a quantitative survey, which covered a total of 284 farm households selected from twenty natural

of Political Inquiry (London Sage Publications, 1982); and Norman Nicholson, 'The State of the Art', in Vincent Ostrom, David Feeny, and Hartmut Picht (eds.), *Rethinking Institutional Analysis and Development: Issues, Alternatives and Choices* (San Francisco: ICS Press, 1988).

[8] Hoebel cited in Hann: 'Property, in other words, is not a thing, but a network of social relations that governs the conduct of people with respect to the use and disposition of things.' C. M. Hann, 'The Embeddedness of Property', p. 4.

[9] See also Harold Demsetz, 'Toward a Theory of Property Rights', *American Economic Review*, Vol. 62 (1967), pp. 347–59.

[10] See Van den Bergh on the notion of ownership in modern civil law. Govaert C. J. J. Van den Bergh, 'Property versus Ownership: Some Cursory Notes', in Joep Spiertz and Melanie G. Wiber (eds.), *The Role of Law in Natural Resource Management* (The Hague: VUGA, 1996), p. 172.

villages in Ningxia.[11] The counties and villages have been chosen to represent regions that differ ecologically (hilly forest, fluvial plains, arid steppe, and semi-arid loess area) and socio-economically (inland poverty regions versus wealthier coastal regions with ample off-farm employment, and dry and irrigated agricultural areas versus (semi)pastoral areas).

China's Land Rights in a Nutshell

The study of land rights in China is one of the most fascinating issues of scholarly research. Why so? Because it involves one of mankind's most fundamental resources: land. In addition, due to its fundamental nature it is the area in which the state's struggle to shape new institutions for a market economy is most pronounced. And lastly, it is an extremely complicated and sensitive question touching directly on the collectivist past during which the land ownership structure was turned upside-down and land theft was common, as a result of which land titles can hardly be traced today.

Few of us can truly fathom the magnitude of China's social experiment in moving an economy based on centralist and socialist structures to one that is equipped for the complexities of the free market. When does the central government need to actively intervene in society and when does it need to exert restraint? How much do laws and policies need to prescribe a national model and how much space should be allowed for regional variation and experimentation—surely a question of relevance for a country with the size and diversity of China? There are no clear-cut answers to these questions. The economics and politics of transition are a dynamic process in which intervention and restraint, centralization and decentralization, interact and alternate with each other. And we will see *how* by focusing on institutional change in land property rights.

The history of land policy in the People's Republic is in many ways also a chronicle of twentieth-century China. With the promise of 'land to the tiller' Mao Zedong built his rural power base, which brought him victory over the Nationalist forces in the late 1940s. Land Reform encompassed a wide range of issues, from ownership and tenancy to rents and debts. It had a profound impact on Chinese society: with the overthrow of the rural elite, the entire power structure was turned upside-down. In addition, Land Reform heralded the end of the legal and customary property rights structure as it had existed up to the late imperial and republican era. The timing and intensity of Land Reform differed in time and place. In the 1930s Land Reform in the old revolutionary base areas, such as the Jiangxi Soviet and the Shaan-Gan-Ning Border Region, was carried out with the least possible social disruption. Middle and rich peasants were allowed to keep part of their land holdings, whereas expropriated landlords were allocated sufficient land to make a living. Yet, in the politically laden atmosphere directly after the Second World War, Land Reform quickly took a radical

[11] The villages are: Shangyuan, Xiamaguan, Xigouzi, and Guankou, Tongxin County; Xiawangzhuang, Shangwangzhuang, Ma'erzhuang, Guankou, and Shangjijuan, Yanchi County; Qianwa, Liwa, Xintang, Xiaoshigou, Lanyuan, and Guanting, Guyuan County; Changcheng, Shanzhuang, Xiaosi, Niuzui, and Chenzhuang, Pengyang County.

turn, costing the lives of many rich peasants and landlords. It was not until a speech by Mao in 1948 that a moderate stance was taken once more.[12]

The second period of great changes in ownership and control over land began with the establishment of the Higher Agricultural Production Cooperatives in 1956. Thereafter private land ownership was effectively abolished, leaving land in the hands of the state or the collective. Until decollectivization in the mid-1980s, there were basically only two factors making for change in land policies: the level of collective ownership and the extent of freedom in private land use. The disaster of the Great Leap Forward (1958–62) forced the central leadership to decentralize land ownership from the commune to the production team. This was laid down in Party regulations promulgated in 1962 (the Sixty Articles). Freedom in the private use of land shifted with the political winds. Before 1958, when rural China was overnight organized into huge administrative units—the people's communes—farmers were allocated small plots of collective land for their own use (the so-called *ziliudi*). Depending on the region, farming was more or less privatized, with managerial responsibilities vested in the household. Individual farm households negotiated contracts under which they had to deliver grain quota to the state at low fixed prices. The surplus grain produced above the quota could be sold freely at private markets.[13] These privileges were rescinded twice (and subsequently reinstalled) during the leftist extremism of the Great Leap Forward and the Great Proletarian Cultural Revolution (1966–76).[14]

The Plenum of the 11th Central Committee of the Communist Party in December 1978 marked the beginning of the economic reforms and the end of collectivism. Following regional experiments, the Household Contract Responsibility System was introduced in the early 1980s, and with it a return to private, family-based farming was made. Initially the national government allowed farm households a land-lease period of five years, which was extended to fifteen years in 1984. The bumper harvest of 1984 (surpassing a total grain production of 400 million tons) silenced all doubt within the conservative faction of the central leadership. It also provided sufficient legitimacy for the contract responsibility system in forestry, animal husbandry, and fishery. To safeguard stable tenure, the lease term was extended to thirty years in 1993.[15] As most contracts

[12] For more information on Land Reform in China, see also Richard Madsen, 'The Countryside under Communism', in Roderick MacFarquhar and John K. Fairbank (eds.), *Cambridge History of China, The People's Republic, Part 2: Revolutions within the Chinese Revolution 1966–1982* (Cambridge: Cambridge University Press, 1991), p. 624; Jack Gray, *Rebellions and Revolutions: China from the 1800s to the 1980s* (Oxford: Oxford University Press, 1990), pp. 266–7; and Victor D. Lippit, *Land Reform and Economic Development in China: A Study of Institutional Change and Development Finance* (White Plains, NY: International Arts and Sciences Press, 1974), pp. 98–100.

[13] The grain procurement system of 'unified purchase and supply' was established in the autumn of 1953.

[14] Madsen, 'The Countryside under Communism', pp. 647–8. For a local account of the swings in privatization and recentralization of the control over land, see for example Anita Chan, Richard Madsen, and Jonathan Unger, *Chen Village under Mao and Deng*, 2nd edn. (Berkeley: University of California Press, 1992), pp. 19–27.

[15] Yuk-shing Cheng and Shu-ki Tsang, 'Agricultural Land Reform in a Mixed System: The Chinese experience of 1984–1994', *China Information*, Vol. 10, No. 3/4 (1995/6),

expired at the end of the 1990s, the 1986 Land Administration Law was revised in 1998 to provide the legal basis for the 'second round of lease' (*di'erlun chengbao*). In contrast to the first round at the time of decollectivization, authorities were required to issue farmers individual, standardized, and notarized contracts during the second round of lease (see Appendix E and Appendix F).

The 1998 Revised Land Administration Law stipulated the exact term of the lease: thirty years. In practice, however, local authorities felt that this term was insufficient for land resources that needed longer-term investments than agricultural land, such as forest, grassland, and wasteland. After discussions within the National People's Congress (NPC) it was decided that more detailed regulations should be drafted. For this reason, the 2002 Rural Land Contracting Law defined that 'the lease term for grassland can be 30 to 50 years, for forest land 30 to 70 years, and for forest land with special trees and shrubs the lease term can be extended after approval by the forest administrative departments of the State Council'.[16] The latter stipulation was to account for the lease of wasteland for which no national laws were effective.

The land lease system replaced the centralist command-and-control commune system and privatized agricultural operation. After more than two decades of reform, China's economy appears to many as having decisively turned to the capitalist development path. Yet, of the three means of production, only capital and labour have been privatized, while land ownership is still firmly in the hands of the state and the collective. The central government's decision to maintain the Marx-Leninist principle of state and collective ownership implied that the secret hopes of former owners or their descendants for an eventual return of expropriated land holdings were dashed. What did change over the period of reform is the entity of collective ownership. Following decollectivization, the people's commune and its subordinate administrative units the production brigade and team—were replaced by the township, the administrative village, and the natural village or villagers' group. How scholars conceptualized and analysed these various shifts in the ownership and control over land is the subject of the following section.

Land Loss and Economic Growth: Some Scholarly Perspectives

Since the introduction of the Household Contract Responsibility System in China, a stream of writings about rural land policies and management have been published by Western social scientists. These can be divided into categories of research on the loss of agricultural land[17] and

p. 44; Erwin M. Reisch, 'Land Reform Policy in China: Political Guidelines and Tendencies', in Eduard B. Vermeer (ed.), *From Peasant to Entrepreneur: Growth and Change in Rural China* (Wageningen: Pudoc, 1992), pp. 15–16.

[16] Hu Kangsheng (ed.), *Zhonghua Renmin Gongheguo Nongcun Tudi Chengbaofa Shiyi* [Legal Interpretation of the Rural Land Contracting Law of the People's Republic of China] (Beijing: Falü Chubanshe, 2002), p. 174.

[17] See for example Robert Ash and Richard L. Edmonds, 'China's Land Resources, Environment and Agricultural Production', *The China Quarterly*, No. 156 (December

investigations into the relation between land tenure and use (in terms of cultivation, management, and investment). The majority of the latter studies have focused on issues of cropland tenure.[18]

Research on agricultural land loss is motivated by concern over China's ability to achieve food security without relying on massive grain imports. In 1995 Lester Brown shocked the Chinese government with his prediction that the People's Republic would face critical food shortages in the future.[19] Despite substantial agricultural growth generated predominantly by increased use of chemical fertilizers, land is still one of the basic inputs in farm production. From the viewpoint of the government, the average area of farmland per capita is low: only one-third of the world average.[20] The situation is aggravated by substantial losses in arable land due to rapid urbanization, industrialization, and environmental problems (soil erosion and desertification). The official figures mention a decrease of 4 per cent in the total arable area over 1978–96: an annual loss of 218,000ha.[21] There is a strong economic case for regional agricultural specialization and cash crop cultivation to enable higher grain imports. But the government is committed to grain self-sufficiency for strategic considerations.

Brown's thesis is highly contested by scholars on several grounds. First, the full impact of farm-land loss on food security is difficult to assess as the total area is unknown due to significant under-reporting in official statistics in the range of 25–50 per cent; second, Brown did not address the issue of the capacity of land for increased agricultural productivity, while the greater part of China's land actually produces well below its potential; third, it is uncertain *what* land is lost. In this respect, Ash and Edmonds have rightly drawn attention to the need for a qualitative assessment of land losses in relation to the remaining area of arable land. Most valuable is their observation that 'structural change within the agricultural sector [transfer of crop land into forestry, animal husbandry and aquaculture]

1998), pp. 836–79; Vaclav Smil, 'China's Agricultural Land', *The China Quarterly*, No. 158 (June 1999), pp. 414–29.

18 James Kai-sing Kung and Shouying Liu, 'Farmers' Preferences regarding Ownership and Land Tenure in Post-Mao China: Unexpected Evidence from Eight Counties', *The China Journal*, No. 38 (July 1997), pp. 33–64; Shouying Liu, Michael R. Carter and Yang Yao, 'Dimensions and Diversity of Property Rights in Rural China: Dilemmas on the Road to Further Reform', *World Development*, Vol. 26, No. 10 (1998), pp. 1789–806; Wei Hu, 'Household Land Tenure Reform in China: Its Impact on Farming Land Use and Agro-Environment', *Land Use Policy*, Vol. 14, No. 3 (1997), pp. 175–86. The research on urban land touches on a similar topic: the relation between property rights and the construction industry. See Anthony Walker, *Land, Property and Construction in the PRC* (Hong Kong: Hong Kong University Press, 1991); Jean Chen and David Wills, *The Impact of China's Economic Reforms upon Land Property and Construction* (Aldershot: Ashgate, 1999). For an excellent introduction on land ownership in China from the 1950s until the early 1990s, see Mark Selden and Aiguo Lu, 'The Reform of Landownership and the Political Economy of Contemporary China', in Mark Selden (ed.), *The Political Economy of Chinese Development* (Armonk, NY: M. E. Sharpe: 1993).

19 Lester Brown, *Who will Feed China? Wake-up Call for a Small Planet* (New York: Norton, 1995).

20 Compared with a country with a strong export-oriented agricultural sector but with a much lower land per capita ratio, such as The Netherlands, it can be seen that taking the world average as the standard is irrelevant.

21 See also Ash and Edmonds, 'China's Land Resources', p. 838.

itself has made by far the most significant contribution to such losses, accounting for . . . well over half of the shrinkage of China's cultivated acreage . . . '.[22]

The academic issue for the relation between (crop)land tenure and use revolves around the question frequently asked by neo-liberal economists: can the present land tenure system—under conditions of socio-economic and demographic change, and strong control by the lessor (rural collective)—provide the lessee with sufficient economic incentives to ensure economic growth? In other words, can the institutional layout of land property rights acquire sufficient credibility in the eyes of social actors to guarantee stable and sustained economic development? I will show that in the case of cropland tenure the answer to this question is positive. In order to fully comprehend the theoretical and practical background of this question, some additional explanation is needed. China's chosen path of Land Reform is unique in scale and ambition among the (ex)socialist states: a government-owned and controlled land market that prohibits private ownership and a free land market, but with the ideological compromise of paid lease and transfer of use rights.[23] In conceptualizing development, some scholars deem competitive markets, free individuals, and civil and political liberties protected by 'the rule of law' critical preconditions for stable economic growth. Private property rights are part and parcel of these preconditions, which constitute the 'liberal democratic' development model. Studies that show the rise of states based on liberal democratic principles[24] reinforce the dominance of this view. Typically, the communist world formed the major challenge to liberal democracy and its emphasis on private property. In the various stages of societal development from a capitalist, to a socialist, to a fully communist society, as conceived by Marx, the issue of property rights was prominent in socialist states. In the process of creating an egalitarian society based on communist principles, private property was outlawed or severely restricted, and replaced by state or collective property.

However, after fierce debates over property rights in the 1970s and 1980s, the dramatic fall of the Soviet Union once more bolstered the ascendancy of private property throughout the world. As Hann writes:

> Property became a very prominent issue after the collapse of communism in the Soviet bloc in 1989–91. Most post-communist governments and their Western advisers were ideologically committed to a very pure version of the liberal model.

[22] See Ziping Wu and Alan W. Kirke, 'An Assessment of Some Key Chinese Agricultural Statistics', *China Information*, Vol. 9, No. 1 (Summer 1994), p. 42–76; Smil, 'China's Agricultural Land', p. 414; Ash and Edmonds, 'China's Land Resources', p. 847. The general academic consensus is now that long-term farmland loss remains a matter of serious concern. However, future research will surely need to provide more detailed qualitative assessments of land losses.

[23] This situation very much resembles the Vietnamese system. See also Anita Chan, Benedict Kerkvliet, and Jonathan Unger, *Transforming Asian Socialism: China and Vietnam Compared* (Rowman and Littlefield: Lanham, 1999).

[24] According to Samuel Huntington, the percentage of formally democratic states grew from 25% in 1973 to 68% in 1992. Cited in Adrian Leftwich, *Democracy and Development* (Cambridge: Polity Press, 1996), p. 3.

They then found themselves in the awkward situation of having to design and enforce structures that were generally supposed to evolve 'naturally'. Ministries of Privatization were set up to expedite the transfer of ownership rights away from the state, a step seen as indispensable to 'systemic transformation'.[25]

But the impressive economic growth rates that China has achieved over the past two decades seem to defy the need for privatization of land ownership. Under the ideological rubric of a 'socialist market economy with Chinese characteristics', the central government subscribes to an alternative model of development that ensures long-term economic growth *without* abandoning the principle of state and collective land ownership.

Many problems still beset the rural land lease system. Due to the unclear property structure and a low level of legal awareness, villagers are uncertain about the rights they enjoy to land. For example, many farmers still believe that they, rather than the collective, own the land on which their houses are built.[26] A major concern of the Chinese authorities and scholars is the powerful control of the lessor over cropland rights. The contract is often no more than a paper agreement because collectives can appropriate and redistribute leased land whenever they deem it necessary. On the other hand, redistribution of land is a bare necessity in response to demographic change. In land-scarce regions the collective faces strong social pressure from the community to uphold a more egalitarian land allocation, which leads to frequent readjustment of cropland.[27] Since the 1980s the implementation of the Household Contract Responsibility System for cropland has been closely monitored by the Communist Party Central Policy Research Office. In its 1997 nationwide survey of 271 observation villages, it was found that 80 per cent of them had readjusted the leased plots since the introduction of the land lease system (of which 66 per cent had done so twice or more).[28] Liberal economists believe that tenure insecurity will prove harmful to China's economic growth.

[25] C. M. Hann, 'The Embeddedness of Property', in C. M. Hann (ed.), *Property Relations: Renewing the Anthropological Tradition* (Cambridge: Cambridge University Press, 1998), p. 18. In the introduction, Hann provides an excellent overview of the recent anthropological theories and literature on property relations.

[26] The confusion is caused by the term 'family plot' or 'private plot' (*ziliudi*), which was introduced in the early 1960s. By this term is meant that a small plot of land can be used for personal needs. However, land ownership remains with the collective.

[27] Based on research in Sichuan Province, Pennarz observed a more even distribution of resources, stricter land use regulations, and a stronger commitment to strive for common interests in land-scarce (with high population pressure) as opposed to land-abundant regions. See Johanna Pennarz, *Collective Land Ownership and Sustainable Agriculture: Perspectives on the Diversity of Land Use Rights in China*, Room Document No. 2 (Paris: Workshop on Agricultural Policies in China, OECD Headquarters), 12–13 December 1996.

[28] Huimin Wang, 'Dangqian Nongcun Tudi Chengbao Jingying Guanli de Xianzhuang ji Wenti' ['The Present Situation and Problems facing the Management and Administration of Rural Land Lease'], *Zhongguo Nongcun Guancha*, No. 5 (1998), pp. 56–7. In the Central Policy Research Office's 1991 survey, all 274 villages had readjusted land: 20.1% readjusted once, 25.9% twice, 30.7% three times, 12.8% four, 2.9% five, and 7.6% six times or more. Nongcun Guding Guanchadian Bangongshi (ed.), *Quanguo Nongcun Jingji Dianxing Diaocha Shuju Huibian, 1986–1990* [A Compilation of Data from the National Rural Survey, 1986–1990] (Beijing: Zhonggong Zhongyang Dangxiao Chubanshe, 1992), p. 437.

The reality is more messy. Government and academic studies have shown that the majority of farmers actually support the redistribution of contracted cropland in response to changes in family size.[29] In the absence of sufficient alternative off-farm employment, the Chinese farmer is 'tied' to his land as a source of basic social security. And the redistributions ensure that each farmer has access to this social security. It is at this point that one might suspect a direct correlation between the perceived credibility of institutions in the eyes of social actors and the socio-economic function that these institutions perform at a given time and place. In addition, these findings, combined with the negative experiences of corruption and economic stagnation that accompanied the 'shock therapy' of privatization in ex-socialist states, have given rise to an alternative view of the role of property rights in development. Rather than privatization as a precondition for development, it is thought that the structure of property rights is actually the outcome of societal evolution. In this respect, privatization can proceed only gradually, guided by the proper socio-economic and legal conditions.[30] Oi and Walder have retorted that 'while these arguments are appealing on intellectual grounds, the earlier failure of such evolutionary reforms in Hungary justified skepticism about calls for gradual reform'.[31] However, recent research carried out by Liu, Carter, and Yao furnishes empirical evidence on the relation between changes in property rights and the level of socio-economic development in China. They demonstrate that the privatization of cropland lease extended furthest in regions where land is of modest economic importance because of ample off-farm employment or relatively abundant land per capita.[32]

These are crucial findings as they support two main economic arguments. First, it seems futile to talk about reforming the property rights structure if socio-economic conditions do not permit it; and second, the hidden unemployment of the rural population is one of the great issues that must be solved in the near future if China's agriculture is ever going to be commercialized. What Liu, Carter, and Yao have left aside, however, is the central question of the institutional arrangements under which privatization occurred. Unless that question is answered first, one cannot hope to meaningfully address the relation between property rights and socio-economic development. That question will be the focal point of this monograph.

[29] See Wang, 'Present Situation and Problems', p. 57; Nongcun Guding Guanchadian Bangongshi (ed.), *A Compilation of the National Rural Survey*, p. 329; and Kung and Liu, 'Farmers' Preferences', p. 34.

[30] See Peter Murrell, 'Can Neoclassical Economics Underpin the Reform of Centrally Planned Economies?', *Journal of Economic Perspectives*, Vol. 5, No. 4 (1991), pp. 59–76; David Stark, 'Recombinant Property in East European Capitalism', *American Journal of Sociology*, No. 101 (1996), pp. 993–1027; David Stark and Lászlό Bruszt, *Postsocialist Pathways: Transforming Politics and Property in East Central Europe* (Cambridge: Cambridge University Press, 1998).

[31] Jean C. Oi and Andrew G. Walder, 'Property Rights in the Chinese Economy: Contours of the Process of Change', in Jean C. Oi and Andrew G. Walder (eds.), *Property Rights and Economic Reform in China* (Stanford: Stanford University Press, 1999), p. 2.

[32] Liu, Carter, and Yao, 'Dimensions and Diversity of Property Rights', p. 1803.

Structure of the Book

In contrast to the idea of the liberal democratic development model that tenure insecurity hampers economic growth, there is ample empirical evidence that the *current* tenure system of agricultural land or cropland (excluding forest, grassland, and wasteland) is credible and socially accepted by the state and the rural populace. Predicated upon this premise, Chapter 1 seeks to explore the institutional arrangements that have made this possible. For this purpose, the chapter starts with a broad review of the national policy and law-making process that dictates property rights for cropland, grassland, forest, and wasteland. It is argued that the restraint which the central government exercised in leaving land rights ambiguous—the creation of 'intentional institutional ambiguity'—offers the greater part of the explanation of why the tenure system for cropland functions.

The argument is supported by demonstrating the occurrence of intentional institutional ambiguity in four areas: (*a*) the legal structure of land ownership; (*b*) the registration of land titles; (*c*) the organizational reform of the Ministry of Land Resources; and (*d*) the establishment of a market for rural land lease. In addition, Chapter 1 attempts to unravel the complex issue of rural land ownership in China. Rural land ownership was in principle vested in the lowest collective level: the production team. However, during the period of reform land ownership by the natural village, the successor of the production team, was no longer clear. There is an inherent danger in the natural village's unclear land ownership: in economically developed regions where land prices are booming due to real estate development, higher administrative levels might misuse ambiguous property rights to expropriate land. Farmers are confronted with forced evictions and relocation to 'modern apartment buildings in the city' in the name of economic progress. The focus in Chapter 1 on national policy and law-making has left one critical issue unaddressed: why has collective land ownership become unclear even though it was stipulated in Party regulations? This will be the starting point for the second chapter.

To answer this question, Chapter 2 descends from the national level to the grass roots. Through an analysis of several (translated and strongly revised) legal cases on land disputes, it is shown that the natural village—in its capacity as the production team—exercised no real power over land, even though it enjoyed formal land ownership. Instead, control over land ownership resided with the commune and higher administrative levels (the county and above). This implied that, in the case of land requisition, the natural village could not adequately defend its interests in the land. It is argued that there are three main reasons for this. The first is the incoherent legal framework and the absence of the rule of law during the collective period. As a result, land was frequently requisitioned from the team and brigade for the sake of economic development without formal procedures being followed. The second is the lack of a nationwide land cadastre. At the time of decollectivization, when the national government launched the first attempt at land registration, the natural village was not included. Problematic in this respect is the validity the state accords to historical land claims. According to law, all claims based on evidence that predate Land Reform in the 1950s have no legal force. However, the two main events that had an impact on the land holdings of the natural village—Land Reform and the Four Fixes Movement of 1962—generally did not provide a sound basis for a land registry. The third reason why the natural village could not adequately defend its interests in the land is the problems the state has in recognizing customary land rights. This issue is of particular importance in the minority regions, where the fluid nature of traditional access rights to land and the nomadic way of life are frequently misunderstood by the (local) government. However, customary rights are not restricted to the minority regions alone. Where the rural populace has opened up land on its own accord without state intervention, claims to land will naturally arise so long as the unofficial custody over land lasts—be it by planting trees or reclaiming waste for agriculture. The general problem with customary rights is their unwritten character, which makes it difficult to render them in statutory law. From another perspective, the recognition problem boils down to a confrontation between two different worlds: a society that in the midst of industrialization and commercialization strives to implement 'the rule of law', and a traditional agrarian society dominated by the 'rule by man'.

Like the Household Contract Responsibility System for agricultural land or cropland, the pasture contract system is infected with a certain degree of intentional institutional ambiguity, though from a different source. In Chapter 3 I demonstrate that one of the main reasons for the failure of national grassland policy and the pasture contract system is an institution that does not suit the current socio-economic parameters: the grassland law. I will argue that this law is a classic example of what in the sociology of law is termed a 'symbol law' and what I would describe as an 'empty institution'. The 'empty institution' incorporates rules that have not yet been widely accepted in society, yet in such way that these can have no real impact on the behaviour of social actors. An empty institution generally arises from a compromise over sensitive political issues. It satisfies the faction that opposes its creation because it is generally ineffective; but the policy-makers striving for its establishment have at least seen their rules incorporated in the created institution—be it a new law, a state department, or the specific layout of land ownership. The grassland law reflects a political compromise over the core of grassland rights: the distinction between state and collective property. In contrast to agricultural land ownership, grassland—and for that matter forest and wasteland too—is state-owned unless collective title can be proven. As there is no legal basis to prove collective title, the state generally considers grassland as its property. This is particularly a problem in the vast pastoral areas inhabited by nomadic peoples, as their transhumance and flexible use of grasslands make collective title difficult to establish. In addition to traditional herder communities, the rural collectives have over time come to regard the grassland they use as their own. The murky property rights structure of grasslands that fails to recognize common property regimes is one of the major factors that have led to the failure of national grassland policy and the pasture contract system.

In Chapter 4, I argue that, compared with agricultural land tenure, the forest tenure system is far from socially acceptable and credible, for three reasons. The first is the nature of the resource itself. Forest management is characterized by slow returns, difficulty in excluding others from its use, high transaction costs, and possible externalities. Second, unlike agricultural land, which serves as a basic means of social security for the greater part of the rural populace, forest is exploited as a sideline. As a result, the use and valuation of forest might be different from those of agricultural land. Finally, the laws that govern forest tenure are different from those governing agricultural tenure. Whereas agricultural land is in principle owned by the collective, forest is owned by the state unless the contrary is proved.

The low credibility of forest tenure is expressed in bad management practices and the high incidence of social conflict. Improper management leads to forest degradation and the loss of forest through illegal conversion to non-forestry land. The latter phenomenon reached such proportions that the central authorities called a halt on all forest reclamation projects in 1998. However, the statistics demonstrate that, in the areas where illegal reclamation was widespread before the halt, the frequency of illegal forest conversion has not decreased. Forest disputes have been a particular problem since forest registration started in the early 1980s. At this point, several issues touched upon in the second chapter are elaborated on with particular reference to forest tenure. The registration of forest is seriously hampered by the present legal framework, which provides no consistent guidelines for the handling of customary claims and claims by the rural communities. In addition, the claims that predate collectivization are extremely complicated because of the innumerable expropriations that occurred afterwards. This question has long been ignored or denied in China because of its sensitivity. How these reshuffles of land—often merely cover-ups for ordinary theft—affect forest administration today is uncertain, but that it does is beyond doubt. Chapter 4 includes two cases that illustrate the complexity involved in the recognition of customary and historical forest claims.

Chapter 5 deals with wasteland and related policies. As a natural resource, wasteland falls somewhere in between forest and grassland—in the ecological sense as well as in terms of its administration and property rights structure. China still has vast areas of undeveloped, marginal lands that are prone to erosion. In order to exploit these resources, the central government launched the so-called Four Wastelands Auction Policy. This policy was hailed as a breakthrough in land management, which would open up undeveloped land resources, improve the ecological environment, and increase farmers' income. The wastelands policy might spawn great changes in land tenure, not only because the auctions commercialize wasteland rights at an unprecedented scale but also because they close the so-called rural–urban divide. Social groups that in the past were barred from access to rural land can now obtain land use rights through auctions. These involve urban cadres and entrepreneurs, state organizations, companies, and even foreign investors. It was hoped that the commercialization and privatization of wasteland rights would result in a cost-efficient allocation and development of this marginal resource. Yet policy-makers and scholars also warned of the danger of rising rural poverty and the emergence of a class of landless farmers. This chapter will analyse the societal impact of the Four Wastelands Auction Policy and examines its relative importance in the reform of China's land tenure system. For this purpose, the chapter draws on village case studies undertaken in the Ningxia Hui Autonomous Region. The central argument here is that the wastelands policy did not—and for the foreseeable future most likely will not—play its proclaimed role in the reform and commercialization of land rights, because both the institutions and the socio-economic conditions do not permit such changes. Even worse, in the particular case of Ningxia the auctions were a complete failure and stirred up widespread grievances among the rural populace.

Forest, grassland, and wasteland share certain similarities: they are generally marginal natural resources with long-term economic returns, while, in the Chinese context, society places a high demand on them. This can easily result in the squandering of the resource and increased rural poverty. The theory of common property, whose notions and premises are specifically dealt with in Chapter 6, suggests that such natural resources are managed in a more cost-effective and ecologically sustainable manner by a community of users. However, the overall trend of property rights reform in China is towards nationalization or semi-privatization through the household lease system, intensified by policy-makers' fear that common use and ownership will lead only to free-riding and environmental degradation. The flooding of the Yellow River in 1998 and the sharp increase in sand storms over the past few years have shown that current natural resource policies have serious drawbacks. For this reason, experimentation with alternative land tenure arrangements, other than nationalization and privatization through lease, is essential. Such experimentation is particularly important when one considers the high costs of supervising vast, nationalized nature reserves, and the problems in implementing the lease system for forest, wasteland, and grassland. In a review of two village case studies on community-based pasture management, Chapter 6 discusses the political implications, possibilities, and limitations of common property arrangements for natural resource management, with particular reference to grassland. We will see that common property regimes are not a panacea for natural resource management. At times, regional conflicts over natural resources overwhelm the ability of the village community to manage the resource in a sustainable manner. This becomes painfully clear through the eruption of fierce battles over medicinal herbs.

The book concludes with a review of current developments in, and the debates on, land ownership and property rights. The final chapter argues that intentional institutional ambiguity has yielded important gains in land tenure reforms, but that further deferring the clarification, protection, and registration of collective land ownership will lead to social instability. In this respect, particular attention is paid to the draft proposal for the new Property Law, published in April 2001, which contains important stipulations for rural land ownership.

1
The Credibility of Agricultural Land Tenure, or Why Intentional Institutional Ambiguity Might Work

In many cases land leases are issued by the administrative village, while the land belonged to the natural village in the past. It is like the ownership rights to land have been silently stolen from the natural village and vested in a level higher . . . Yet, to date there are not many conflicts, because farmers are not well imbued with the idea of 'property'. But problems are sure to arise in the future . . .

(Sheng Li, oral communication, 1999)

Readjustments, Fragmentation: Land as a Means of Social Security?

The statement in the epigraph by a senior official within the Ministry of Agriculture aptly captures one of the most sensitive issues confronting the Chinese state: rural land ownership. Rural China has witnessed profound and, at times, erratic shifts in the ownership and control of land. During the rule of the nationalist government (1912–49), land tenure consisted on the one hand of communal and customary rights vested in landlords and nobles, religious institutions, and village communities, and on the other of statutory land rights grafted on to a German and Japanese civil law tradition. Almost a century later, China is left with a socialist legacy: a state-dominated land rights system with a burgeoning private land lease market and numerous unresolved land issues from the past. Over such a long period of major changes in land tenure, policy-makers and scholars may ask themselves: where has the Chinese land rights system come from, where is it presently, and where might it be going to? It is uncertain whether and how many rights such as the sale and transfer of use rights, mortgage, and ownership can be enjoyed, partly because they have not been defined in law and partly because, even if defined, they are not adequately protected by the state. It is therefore no wonder that many Chinese and Western observers have noted that China's land rights structure is opaque and ambiguous.[1]

In the wealthier and coastal regions, rural land is coming under increasing pressure due to the rapid commercialization and urbanization over the past decades. Real estate development has led to agricultural land losses while the transfer of rural labour to the non-agricultural sector has enabled a diversification in land use and rights. It is important to understand the ambiguities in the institutional framework of the land tenure system and the reasons why it is ambiguous, because they determine such crucial issues as the legitimacy of historical claims to land, the legal space

[1] See, for example, Wei Hu, 'Household Land Tenure Reform in China: Its Impact on Farming Land Use and Agro-Environment', *Land Use Policy*, Vol. 14, No. 3 (1997), p. 179.

in which disputes between the state, the collective and the individual are settled, and the overall functioning of the land tenure system.

The latter issue touches on the crucial concept of 'confidence in the system' or, in the words of Diermeyer et al., the 'fundamental question of property rights: Do economic and political actors believe that property rights are credible?'[2] Unlike academic debates on 'trust' that put more emphasis on the relations between social actors, Diermeyer's concept of 'credibility' directs the scholarly gaze towards the nature of the institution and its relation with social actors.[3] Most institutional theories hold not only that institutional structure is a function of rational choice or intentional design but also that the particular choice of institutional design has a direct impact on performance and on the credibility of institutions to actors. Throughout this chapter, we will see that the central state's choice to allow local, informal institutions a certain space for existence rather than formalizing them through national laws is the fundamental explanation of such institutions' credibility and successful functioning. We saw in the Introduction that frequent reallocations in cropland are still part and parcel of China's current land tenure system. Many economists and social scientists fear that tenure insecurity will lead to low investments in, and eventually a squandering of, land resources. At the same time, however, many studies have found that land readjustments in response to demographic changes have actually been supported by the rural populace ever since the late 1980s. According to the 1987 survey of the Central Policy Research Office, 80.6 per cent of the 10,679 households (40 per cent of the total observation households) believed that their contract land had to be expanded if household size increased.[4] In a renewed survey in 1997 the Central Policy Research Office found that 62.8 per cent of the sample villages still advocated redistribution of cropland.[5] Similar findings were furnished by Kung and Liu. In a survey of 800 households in

[2] Daniel Diermeyer, Joel M. Ericson, Timothy Frye, and Steven Lewis, 'Credible Commitment and Property Rights: The Role of Strategic Interaction between Political and Economic Actors', in David L. Weimer (ed.), *The Political Economy of Property Rights: Institutional Change and Credibility in the Reform of Centrally Planned Economies* (Cambridge: Cambridge University Press, 1997), p. 20.

[3] See, for example, William Mishler and Richard Rose, 'What Are The Origins of Political Trust? Testing Institutional and Cultural Theories in Post-Communist Societies', *Comparative Political Studies*, Vol. 34, No. 1 (2001), pp. 30–63.

[4] Unfortunately, there are no similar figures at the village level. See Nongcun Guding Guanchadian Bangongshi (ed.), *Quanguo Nongcun Jingji Dianxing Diaocha Shuju Huibian, 1986–1990* [A Compilation of Data from the National Rural Survey, 1986–1990] (Beijing: Zhonggong Zhongyang Dangxiao Chubanshe, 1992), p. 329; James Kai-sing Kung and Shouying Liu, 'Farmers' Preferences regarding Ownership and Land Tenure in Post-Mao China: Unexpected Evidence from Eight Counties', *The China Journal*, No. 38 (July 1997), p. 34.

[5] Of the 36.1% of farmers who opposed land redistributions, 46.7% thought their villagers' committee could safeguard a policy of stable land lease, 22.9% said that land was abundant and uneven land distribution would not incite social conflict, 17.1% said that income from land was no longer important because of alternative employment opportunities, and 13.3% stated that land distribution was too cumbersome and they were unwilling to redistribute after the first time. See Huimin Wang, 'Dangqian Nongcun Tudi Chengbao Jingying Guanli de Xianzhuang ji Wenti' ['The Present Situation and Problems facing the Management and Administration of Rural Land Lease'], *Zhongguo Nongcun Guancha*, No. 5 (1998), p. 57.

four provinces, they discovered that 62 per cent of the respondents preferred the village policy 'that periodically reassigns land among farm families in response to changes in the composition of their families'.[6] Moreover, the assumption that insecure land rights would lead to bad management practices proved to be far from straightforward. In a study of 135 households, Kung and Cai show that the 'allegation of farmers neglecting to preserve the soil fertility of their contracted plots is wholly unfounded'.[7] The above findings lend strong support to the notion that cropland tenure is widely perceived by social actors to be credible.

More importantly, the agricultural land lease system fulfils an important role as a social welfare net for the vast surplus of rural labour. The egalitarianism of land readjustments do result in an extreme fragmentation of the land, which inhibits a farming operation with greater economies of scale. At present, the average area of cultivable land per capita of rural households is a mere 0.10ha.[8] However, researchers on agricultural development have rightly pointed out that, when alternative risk-spreading mechanisms such as insurance, storage, and rural credit are unavailable or more costly, land fragmentation might persist as a risk-avoiding strategy.[9] And China is no exception, as land readjustments ensure that farmers have access to rural land, and thus a basic living. As the agricultural expert Wen Tiejun remarked: 'If you talk about land being a means of social security for the farmers, you are actually speaking about its dual function: it is a means of production, as well as a security for farmers' livelihood.'[10] For these reasons, one can safely assume that the agricultural land or cropland lease system—in spite of its frequent readjustments—*is* credible and accepted by the authorities as well as by the rural populace under present socio-economic conditions. Simultaneously, this also implies that the land lease system's credibility might erode or that the system as a whole might change as socio-economic parameters change. New developments in the wealthier provinces are already testimony to this. In these regions an increasing number of farmers are finding employment outside the agricultural realm. As farmers work elsewhere, contract land is either directly sub-leased to others or returned to the village collective, which then sub-leases the land to fewer farmers or even companies. As a result, a farming operation emerges with larger economies of scale and longer-term lease rights as land reallocations are no longer necessary.

For example, in Jianli County (Hubei Province) the farmers working outside agriculture numbered 220,000 in 2001, which is 49 per cent of the

[6] See, for example, Kung and Liu, 'Farmers' Preferences regarding Ownership', p. 34.

[7] See James Kai-sing Kung and Yong-Shun Cai, 'Property Rights and Fertilizing Practices in Rural China: Evidence from Northern Jiangsu', *Modern China*, Vol. 26, No. 3 (July 2000), pp. 276–308.

[8] National Bureau of Statistics (ed.), *China Statistical Yearbook 2003* (Beijing: Zhongguo Tongji Chubanshe, 2003), pp. 6, 97.

[9] See also Neil Charlesworth, 'The Origins of Fragmentation of Land Holdings in British India: A Comparative Examination', in Peter Robb (ed.), *Rural India: Land, Power and Society under British Rule* (London: Curzon Press Ltd., 1983); Brian W. Ilbery, 'Farm Fragmentation in the Vale of Evesham', *Area*, Vol. 16 (1984), pp. 159–65.

[10] Tiejun Wen, quoted in Ke Deng, 'Tudi Neng Baozhang Nongmin Shenme?' ['What can Land Guarantee for the Farmer?'], *Nanfang Zhoumo* (14 June 2001), p. 3.

total rural labour force. They left behind 520,000mu (35,000ha)[11] of arable land—one third of the county's total area of arable land—which was subsequently sub-leased. Remarkably, in most cases the original lessee has to pay the new tenant a fee to work his land, as agriculture is less profitable! This fee could amount to 300 renminbi (RMB)[12] per mu.[13] These developments also forced the central government to rethink its land policy. Whereas its former 1997 policy guaranteed a land lease of '30 years no change' under all circumstances, the Chinese government now realized that tenure security should not be an aim in itself, but made dependent on specific local conditions.[14] In other words, a certain degree of flexibility in the term of lease should be made possible, yet without weakening the legal position of the lessee.[15] To this end, article 25 of the draft version of the 2002 Rural Land Contracting Law was changed to allow for the transfer of land rights back to the village collective or to other legal persons, but on the specific condition that consent from the lessee had been obtained.[16]

This chapter will investigate which institutional arrangements at the national level have led to the current credibility of the agricultural land tenure system. For this purpose, I will sketch the evolutionary process of the national policy and law-making that shaped China's post-collective institutional framework for agricultural land or cropland rights, with occasional reference to forest, grassland, and wasteland. This is done by reviewing how the state's intentions—expressed during the political debate and embodied in laws and policies—have changed over time.

[11] A mu covers about one-fifteenth of a hectare.

[12] One RMB is worth about one-eighth of a US dollar. The renminbi is pegged to the dollar.

[13] Guangming Huang, 'Xin Tudi Geming' ['The New Land Revolution'], *Nanfang Zhoumo* (14 June 2001), p. 1.

[14] Zhonggong Zhongyang Bangongting, Zhonggong Zhongyang Bangongting, Guowuyuan Bangongting guanyu Jinyibu Wending he Wanshan Nongcun Tudi Chengbao Guanxi de Tongzhi [Notice by the Central Secretariat of the CCP and the Secretariat of the State Council on the Further Stabilization and Perfectioning of the Contract Relations of Rural Land], No. 16 (1997); Article 14, Revised Land Administration Law, in Weilan Fang (ed.), *Zhonghua Renmin Gongheguo Tudi Guanlifa' Shiyong Jianghua* [A Practical Discussion of the 'Land Administration Law of the People's Republic of China'] (Beijing: Zhongguo Minzhu Fazhi Chubanshe, 1998), p. 208.

[15] The 2002 Rural Land Contracting Law also broke with the past in another respect: it sought to increase the legal security of women's rights to land. Married or divorced women and widows have less access than men to land. For this purpose, the Rural Land Contracting Law has defined several new regulations. For more information on this topic, see Zongmin Li and John Bruce, 'Gender, Landlessness and Equity in Rural China', in Peter Ho (ed.), *Developmental Dilemmas: Land Reform and Institutional Change in China* (London and New York: Routledge, 2005).

[16] In the draft law, article 25 reads: 'during the term of lease, the lessor cannot take back contract land'. In the law effective since March 2003, this now reads: 'during the term of lease, the lessor cannot take back contract land', but 'if the lessee has settled in a town, the management right of his contract land can be retained or the management right to his contract land can be legally transferred, according to the wishes of the lessee' and 'if the lessee's entire family has moved to the city and changed to an urban residence registration, the lessee needs to return the contracted agricultural land or grassland to the lessor ... The lessor must give appropriate compensation for the investments and increase of productivity of the contract land.' See Hu Kangsheng (ed.), *Zhonghua Renmin Gongheguo Nongcun Tudi Chengbaofa Shiyi* [Legal Interpretation of the Rural Land Contracting Law of the People's Republic of China] (Beijing: Falü Chubanshe, 2002), p. 174.

In writing this chapter, I have made three conscious choices: first, to concentrate the analysis on policy and law-making while leaving aside the process of implementation as much as possible;[17] second, to focus on the national level; and third, to study the relation between institutional arrangements and, based on research cited above, the assumed credibility of agricultural land or cropland tenure.

The following considerations precede these choices. First, the policy and law-making process that led to the current layout of China's land rights system is an extremely complex yet little-researched issue. It therefore deserves to be dealt with in its own right. The impact of the national land rights system at the grass roots will be demonstrated through an analysis of court cases in Chapter 2. Second, the national legal-political framework for land rights underlies many of the problems that are encountered at the grass roots. In order to comprehend what is happening at the village level, one cannot avoid analysing national land policies and laws. Third, although the land rights system is an integral component of the rural economy, it is but one of many. To answer meaningfully Jean Oi and Andrew Walder's broader question of what institutional arrangements can contribute to 'an invigorated rural economy',[18] the role of the industrial sector *and* the layout of land property rights should be brought together in a single analysis. But that remains an issue for future exploration.[19]

It will be argued that institutional indeterminacy is the lubricant on which the system runs: the ambiguity of legal rules allows the agricultural land tenure system to function at the *current* stage of economic reforms. Moreover, this institutional indeterminacy is partly the result of efforts by the central leadership to create leeway for reacting to societal developments. For this reason, I speak of 'intentional institutional ambiguity' as upheld by the state.[20] The deliberate nature of the institutional ambiguity

[17] This is difficult to achieve, because policy and law-making are, in fact, entwined with the implementation process in an evolutionary cycle. See also Merilee S. Grindle (ed.), *Politics and Policy Implementation in the Third World* (Princeton: Princeton University Press, 1980), pp. 7–8.

[18] Jean C. Oi and Andrew G. Walder, 'Property Rights in the Chinese Economy: Contours of the Process of Change', in Jean C. Oi and Andrew G. Walder (eds.), *Property Rights and Economic Reform in China* (Stanford: Stanford University Press, 1999), p. 2.

[19] There are obvious similarities between the property rights of (rural) enterprises and land. For example, Keith mentions the imprecise definition of the collective enterprise and the masquerading of private enterprises as collective entities (the so-called 'red hats'). He also warns that 'the sorting out of contemporary property rights can have potentially explosive political and social consequences'. See Ronald C. Keith, *China's Struggle for the Rule of Law* (New York: St Martin's Press, 1994), pp. 137–41. Oi and Walder's 'Property Rights in the Chinese Economy', cited above, is one of the latest works on property rights in industries. Another interesting article on this topic is by Pei Xiaolin, 'Township-Village Enterprises, Local Governments, and Rural Communities: The Chinese Village as a Firm during Economic Transition', in Eduard B. Vermeer, Frank Pieke, and Woei Lien Chong (eds.), *Cooperative and Collective in China's Rural Development: Between State and Private Interests* (New York: M. E. Sharpe, 1998).

[20] I am aware that the term 'intentional' suggests that the Chinese state is consciously reacting to societal developments rather than 'muddling through'. See also Charles Lindblom, 'The Science of "Muddling Through"', in Jay M. Shafritz and Albert C. Hyde (eds.), *Classics of Public Administration*, 3rd edn (Belmont: Wadsworth Publishing Company, 1992); and Charles Lindblom, 'Still Muddling, Not Yet Through', *Public Administration Review*, Vol. 39 (November/December 1979), pp. 517–37.

becomes apparent in the ownership shifts of collective land. Although land ownership was vested in the lowest collective level (the production team) during the period of the people's communes, ownership by its successor (the natural village or villagers' group) is no longer clear in the era of reform. First of all, the term 'collective' is intentionally kept vague in the law out of fear of widespread large-scale social conflict. It is thus uncertain which collective level actually holds the title to land. Second, the first national collective land registration in Chinese history has halted at the most crucial level: that of the original owner, the production team.

I will demonstrate that in the course of ownership shifts there is a significant danger that the collective ownership rights of villagers may be trampled on. In the economically developed coastal regions, local authorities tend to appropriate collective ownership rights in order to facilitate land planning and urban construction. The intentional institutional ambiguity upheld by the central government is gratefully made use of to force through such operations. In this respect, institutional ambiguity, rather than lending credibility to institutions, could actually become a potentially explosive source of future social conflict. This points to the critical need to consider institutions against the backdrop of history and space instead of as fixed in stone. In short, institutional arrangements that worked at a given point in time might no longer work a decade later. Last, but certainly not least, in the course of the analysis I will address one basic question: who is the legal owner of rural land? In this context, the term 'ownership' is deliberately used instead of 'property'. In the following section, it will be argued that in the Chinese legal and political setting the modern civil law concept of ownership as an absolute and supreme right is more appropriate than Demsetz's notion of property as a 'bundle of rights'.[21] The chapter is thematically organized and examines four critical issues in the political debate over rural land rights: (*a*) land ownership, discussed in three separate subsections: the confrontation between state institutions and between collective institutions, and the state versus the collective; (*b*) the registration of land ownership titles and the creation of a cadastre; (*c*) the reform of the Ministry of Land Resources (*Guotu Ziyuanbu*)—the institution responsible for land administration; and (*d*) the establishment of a market for land leases.

Land Ownership: 'Bundle of Rights' or 'Absolute and Supreme'?

When one considers land ownership titles in China, it is best to talk about 'ownership' rather than 'property'. Anthropologists have long argued against the modern civil law concept of ownership as the absolute and supreme right[22] because of its ethnocentric baggage. Instead, the common

[21] See also Harold Demsetz, 'Toward a Theory of Property Rights', *American Economic Review*, Vol. 62 (1967), pp. 347–59.

[22] However, as Sonius has rightly remarked: '. . . absolute ownership does not exist and has never existed. Ownership has always (in Justinian law as well) been restricted by all kinds of regulations which, in the general interest or in the interest of others, deprived the owner of part of his absolute power over the object.' See H. W. J. Sonius, *Introduction to*

law definition of property as 'a bundle of rights' or its more abstract notion as a 'social relation'[23] is preferred. Conceptualizing ownership as property allows for more analytical flexibility to cope with the variations in land rights encountered during cross-cultural research. However, as demonstrated below, Chinese land ownership conforms more to the theorems of modern civil law:

> Ownership is the supreme right, there can be no rights which would not be contained in ownership. Ownership is abstract: its content cannot be described by enumerating single powers, and none of these powers needs to be legitimized specifically, or related to an acceptable social purpose. Ownership is absolute: apart from what the law expressly forbids the owner may do whatever he likes, he can exclude everybody else from influencing the goods, everybody else is obliged to abstain from breaching his ownership rights, the owner is the supreme ruler over his goods.[24]

The fundamental principle of land rights in China is the identification of the state (and, less so, the collective) as the absolute owner. All other rights are derived from this.[25] The full logic of China's land ownership is reflected in a passage from a textbook for land administration cadres: 'China practises the system of public ownership for land. According to laws and regulations, the nature of land rights can be divided into: the collective ownership to land, the use right to state-owned land, the use right to collectively owned land, and other real rights.'[26] Note that state ownership is *not* listed separately as a right. The term only appears in the phrase 'the use right to state-owned land'.

The implications are clear: state ownership is a given and need not be established as such, in contrast to the rights of collective ownership and use, and other real rights. Therefore, the law makes no stipulations on the assessment of title in state-owned land except for forest, grassland, and fisheries. Moreover, the ownership of state land is a constant and the state is free to allocate state-owned land to any legal person it wants to. One can obtain the use right to state land through non-taxed transfer (common in the past), transfer by paying a premium or tax, or lease. The ownership of collective land, however, can be changed into state ownership if the proper

Aspects of Customary Land Law in Africa: As compared with some Indonesian Aspects (Leiden: Universitaire Pers Leiden, 1963), p. 19.

23 Hann cites Hoebel for a textbook anthropological definition: 'Property, in other words, is not a thing, but a network of social relations that governs the conduct of people with respect to the use and disposition of things.' C. M. Hann, 'The Embeddedness of Property', in C. M. Hann (ed.), *Property Relations: Renewing the Anthropological Tradition* (Cambridge: Cambridge University Press, 1998), p. 4.

24 Govaert C. J. J. Van den Bergh, 'Property versus Ownership: Some Cursory Notes', in Spiertz and Wiber (eds.), *The Role of Law in Natural Resource Management*, p. 172.

25 As Mark Selden and Aiguo Lu noted: 'The state alone—all levels of state administration and state agencies—enjoys wide rights of eminent domain which permit it to purchase and sell use rights as well as transfer rights.' Mark Selden and Aiguo Lu, 'The Reform of Landownership and the Political Economy of Contemporary China', in Mark Selden (ed.), *The Political Economy of Chinese Development* (Armonk, NY: M. E. Sharpe, 1993), p. 190.

26 Hu Cunzhi (ed.), *Tudi Dengji Lilun yu Fangfa* [Theory and Methods of Land Registration], Vol. I (Beijing: Zhongguo Nongye Chubanshe, 1998), p. 12.

procedures for land requisition are followed.[27] In particular during the early period of reform, the self-perception of local governments as holding absolute land ownership sometimes failed to ensure that proper requisition procedures were followed. The legal dispute described below in the section 'the state versus the collective' is a case in point.

What is the dividing line between state land and collective land? According to the 1982 Constitution, natural resources such as waters and streams, forest, mountains, grassland, and wasteland are state-owned, unless defined by law as collectively owned. This means that the burden of proof for the ownership title to natural resources lies with the collective and not the state. By contrast, suburban and rural land (including the 'private plots' or *ziliudi/shan* for villagers) are collectively owned unless state ownership has been proved. Urban land is by definition state-owned; there can be no urban land owned by the collective.[28] The structure of land ownership seems relatively clear: in principle, natural resources and urban land are state-owned, while suburban and rural land are collectively owned. Yet the economic reforms have exposed many weaknesses in this legal structure that can lead to frequent social conflict.

There are three main kinds of land ownership dispute. First, conflicts between state institutions: for example, is military land being used by a ministry also its possession? And what about land used by local government? Indeed, which level of government is entitled to represent land ownership? Second, conflicts generated by the confrontation between rural collectives: for instance, is the natural village as the successor of the team still the basic unit of land ownership? Can a brick factory owned by a township collective own the land on which it is built? And finally, disputes arising from the confrontation between the state and the collective: what happens to the ownership of rural land included within expanding cities? Is wasteland reclaimed by villages owned by the state or collectively? The consequences of such confrontations are dealt with in the following three subsections. It has to be borne in mind that the discussion along these three dimensions is not absolute: there are various possible land ownership disputes that simultaneously apply to state–state, state–collective, and collective–collective interactions.

State versus state conflicts. Ownership disputes following the confrontation between state institutions revolve around the question: who represents the state? In the years after the communist state was established, the authorities nationalized certain land resources.[29] All urban land was

[27] For the theoretical background of Chinese state and collective ownership, see Hu Cunzhi, Theory and Methods of Land Registration, Vol. I, pp. 211–40. Definitions for taxed and non-taxed transfer of state land are given in n. 80.

[28] Articles 9 and 10 of the Constitution, see Zhongguo Falü Chubanshe (ed.), *Zhonghua Renmin Gongheguo Xianfa* [The Constitution of the People's Republic of China, 4 December 1982] (Beijing: Zhongguo Falü Chubanshe, 1999), p. 8. These articles have been unchanged during the three revisions of the Constitution in 1988, 1993, and 1999. The 1986 and 1998 Land Administration Law follows the Constitution's stipulations on ownership.

[29] Articles 16 and 18 of the 1950 Land Reform Law, in Jianhong Sun (ed.), *Tudi Quanshu Shiwu Zhinan* [Practical Compass on Land Titles] (Beijing, Zhongguo Dadi Chubanshe: 1998), p. 109. Later included in the 1954 Constitution, see also Chapter 2.

defined as state-owned, whereas forest, grassland, and wasteland were nationalized in so far as no collective title could be proved. As we will see in the subsection on state–collective conflicts, the latter rule is at the root of many land disputes, as collective titles often cannot be furnished. In disputes between state institutions, conflicts arise from the fact that the concept of the state as owner was not specified in law. Figure 1 shows that the state consists of four administrative levels ranging from the national state to the county. One of the main underlying causes of the recent great losses in arable land is the illegal and indiscriminate sale of land for construction by local governments. In the wealthier and coastal regions the value of land has risen steeply, as a result of which local governments are enticed to sell state-owned land to the ever-expanding cities. In a speech to the NPC in 1986, Xiang Zhongyang, the former Deputy Minister of Agriculture, was the first to call attention to this problem. Since the late 1990s, the problem of arable land loss has received the highest political priority and has become one of the driving arguments for revising the 1986 Land Administration Law.[30]

'Overcoming local protectionism' was regarded critical in halting arable land loss. For this reason, the drafters of the Revised Land Administration Law favoured a strong recentralization of land policies.[31] For the first time, the law now states that 'the ownership right of state-owned land is exercised by the State Council as representative of the state'. In practice state ownership should be exercised by the Ministry of Land Resources (also stipulated in law).[32]

To end all possible confusion, the NPC Legal Affairs Work Committee (hereafter Legal Committee) issued a formal legal interpretation of the revised law. The Legal Committee stated that 'the various levels of local government are not the representative for the ownership of state-owned land. They have no right to deal with state-owned land without authorization . . .' It also added that 'the right to profit from state-owned land belongs to the central people's government'.[33]

With these new stipulations, the source of conflicts between central and local government has in principle been removed. It implies that from

[30] Zhongyang Xiang, 'Guanyu "Zhonghua Renmin Gongheguo Tudi Guanlifa (Cao'an)" de Shuoming' [Explanation on the 'Land Administration Law of the People's Republic of China'], speech at the 15th Session of the Standing Committee of the 6th National People's Congress, 15 March 1986, p. 2. A notice on the protection of arable land (CCP Document 1997/11) jointly promulgated in 1997 by the Communist Party Secretariat and the State Council demonstrates that land loss is still regarded as an urgent problem.

[31] Renda Fazhi Gongzuo Weiyuanhui (RFGW) (ed.), *Zhonghua Renmin Gongheguo Tudi Guanlifa Shiyi* [An Interpretation of the Land Administration Law of the People's Republic of China] (Beijing: Falü Chubanshe, 1998), p. 68.

[32] The law reads: 'The responsible department for land administration of the State Council [the Ministry of Land Resources] is uniformly charged with the management and supervision of the nation's land.' See Articles 2 and 5, Revised Land Administration Law, in Fang (ed.), A Practical Discussion of the 'Land Administration Law of the People's Republic of China', p. 207.

[33] The last stipulation on the state's right to profit is a principle. For practical reasons, however, the state 'can entrust local people's governments and state-owned companies to exercise this right' as the Legal Committee states. RFGW (ed.), An Interpretation of the Land Administration Law, p. 37.

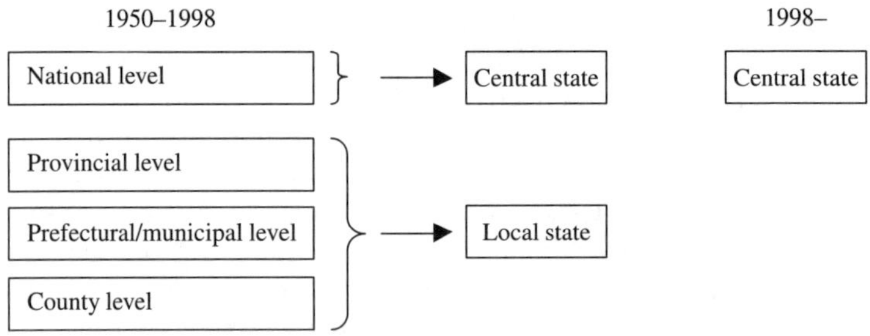

Figure 1: **Changes in ownership of state land (urban land, forest, grassland, and wasteland) since 1950.**

Source: Author.

1998 onwards, all urban land, as well as the forest, grassland, and wasteland that was nationalized or not proved to be collectively owned, is by law owned by the central state. The changes in the structure of state land ownership are depicted in Fig. 1. Whether the Revised Land Administration Law is actually able to effectively stop the illegal appropriation of land by local government remains to be seen.[34] The foregoing stipulations are part of a larger scheme to concentrate and consolidate the supreme and absolute right of ownership in the hands of the central state and the collective. Throughout this chapter we will see that this is a recurring theme in China's land administration.

In the case of forest, grassland, and wasteland there is actually a second source of state–state conflicts: those resulting from the fragmented nature of land administration (see also the section on the reform of the Ministry of Land Resources). Forest is in principle administered by the State Forestry Bureau (former Ministry of Forestry), grassland by the Ministry of Agriculture, and wasteland by both depending on the ecological definition used ('grassy forest' or 'forested grassland'). In addition, the Ministry of Land Resources is responsible for all land resources, be it forest, grassland, or wasteland. To make things worse, each state organ is entitled to issue forest, grassland, wasteland, or land ownership and use permits (they are generally issued by the relevant subordinate institutions at the county level). It needs little imagination to see that this easily results in chaos and unsustainable use of natural resources. In a formal request to the NPC, the

[34] Note that the issue of illegal land expropriation was one of the reasons that the Constitution was revised in March 2004 and the Land Administration Law five months later. The revision comprised a single change (the Land Administration Law is left unchanged in all other areas) relating to the distinction between 'expropriation' (*zhengshou*) and 'requisition' (*zhengyong*). 'Expropriation' now refers to the state appropriation of collective land for national projects (such as roads, railways and bridges) whereby land ownership is transferred to the state. 'Requisition' refers to the temporary, compulsory lease of collective land to the state for the public benefit; in this case, *no* transfer of ownership takes place as the property rights are in principle returned once the lease expires. This distinction means that it is legally possible to appropriate collective land without changing ownership rights. It is a matter for future research to assess whether this recent revision amounts to a merely cosmetic change or will be truly effective in halting illegal land expropriation.

Heilongjiang Forestry Bureau noted:

The sharp contradictions of forest titles are unfavourable for forest protection. The province . . . has issued forest permits, but the greater part of forest has been occupied by individuals, townships, village collective economic organizations and local governments, which in some cases have also been issued land permits. . . . The Land Administration Law should bring the forest and land permits in line with each other.[35]

Collective versus collective conflicts. The issue that was most hotly debated by the NPC during the revision of the Land Administration Law did not concern state ownership but rather collective ownership. In present-day China the term 'collective' is an enigma, which has resulted in fierce disputes between collectives, and between the state and collectives. To understand how the confusion over such a crucial term arises it is necessary to delve into history.

The current format of collective ownership is the direct heritage of collectivization and the commune system. The former people's commune consisted of three echelons: the commune, the production brigade, and the production team. In response to the disastrous results of the Great Leap Forward, ownership of the means of production—agricultural fields, farm animals, implements, and so forth—was refashioned on three levels of ownership. Between 1959 and 1962, the central leadership wavered between the production brigade and the production team as the basic holder of land ownership and accounting. Mao wanted more control over land and strongly advocated vesting ownership in the brigade. However, more moderate factions argued that farmers would not feel sufficiently responsible for the land if the team—in practice, the natural village—did not hold ownership. After three years of debate, in September 1962 the Eighth National Party Congress finally adopted the revised draft of the Work Regulations for the Rural People's Communes, popularly known as the Sixty Articles. In the Sixty Articles, the team was identified as the primary accounting unit and the owner of land:

All land within the limits of the production team is owned by the production team. . . . Collective forest, water resources, and grassland are all owned by the production team.[36]

[35] 'Remarks on the "Land Administration Law (Revised Draft)" by Relevant Departments, Several Experts and Grassroots Units of Heilongjiang Province', in RFGW (ed.), An Interpretation of the Land Administration Law, p. 352.

[36] For a detailed description of the central leadership's discussion on the level of collective land ownership, see Peter Ho, 'The Clash over State and Collective Property: The Making of the Rangeland Law', *The China Quarterly*, Vol. 161 (March 2000), pp. 247–9. See also Chinese Communist Party (CCP), 'Nongcun Renmin Gongshe Gongzuo Tiaoli—Cao'an' ['Work Regulations for the Rural People's Communes—Draft Version'] 3/1961, in: Zhongguo Renmin Jiefangjun Guofang Daxue Dangshi Yanjiushi (ZRJGDDY) (ed.), *Zhonggong Dangshi Jiaoxue Cankao Ziliao* [Reference and Educational Material on the History of the CCP], Vol. 23 (Beijing: Guofang Daxue Chubanshe, 1986), p. 454; CCP, 'Nongcun Renmin Gongshe Gongzuo Tiaoli Xiuzheng Cao'an' ['Revised Draft of the Work Regulations of the Rural People's Communes'], 27/9/1962, in ZRJGDDY (ed.), Reference and Educational Material on the History of the CCP, Vol. 24 (Beijing: Guofang Daxue Chubanshe, 1986), pp. 141–2.

For more than two decades, the Sixty Articles would be the basic document defining the land ownership structure of the rural collectives (see also Fig. 2).

By the early 1980s, the communes had been dismantled. Apart from regional differences, generally the township/town (*xiang/zhen*) replaced the commune, the administrative village (*xingzhengcun*) replaced the brigade, and the natural village (*zirancun*) or the villagers' group (*cunmin xiaozu*) replaced the team.[37] The critical question is: what happened to the status of the team as the primary owner of rural land? The outline of collective land ownership is laid down in the Revised Land Administration Law as follows:

> The land owned by the farmers' collective is by law owned by the farmers' collective of the village, and managed and administered by the village collective economic organization or the villagers' committee;[38] what is already owned by more than two rural collective economic organizations of the farmers' collective is managed and administered by each of these rural collective economic organizations or the villagers' groups;[39] what is already owned by the farmers' collective of the township (town) is managed and administered by the rural collective economic organization of the township (town).[40]

The law employs quite elaborate formulations to define collective ownership. However, it seems that the law did not alter the ownership structure of the communes. In other words, the villagers' group (or natural village) that succeeded the production team is still the primary owner of land, apart from that already owned by the commune and brigade before the proclamation of the Sixty Articles in 1962. But appearances are deceptive. A closer reading of this passage reveals that ownership by the former team

[37] There are exceptions to this description because of regional differences and historical changes in the size of administrative units. Following the demise of the communes, generally an administrative village administers several natural villages, while the natural village administers several villagers' groups. However, to add to the confusion, the natural village can coincide with the administrative village, and the villagers' group with the natural village. Such situations could emerge if the former commune consisted of two levels instead of three. As also written in article 2 of the Sixty Articles: 'The organization of the commune can consist of two levels: the commune and the team; but it can also consist of three levels: the commune, the production brigade and the production team.' See CCP, 'Nongcun Renmin Gongshe Gongzuo Tiaoli Xiuzheng Cao'an' [Revised Draft of the Work Regulations of the Rural People's Communes], 27/9/1962, in ZRJGDDY (ed.), Reference and Educational Material on the History of the CCP, Vol. 23, p. 137. Note also that the term 'natural village' is not an official legal term, although it is still frequently used in Chinese official and unofficial texts. An illustration of the confusing situation over the villagers' group and the natural village is given in Chapter 6; see the village description of Xiawangzhuang and the accompanying text in the footnote.

[38] The Organic Law stipulates that 'the villagers' committee is established in accordance with the villagers' situation of residence, number of population, and the principle of facilitating the self-government of the masses. The establishment, abolition, and adjustment of the limits of the villagers' committee is proposed by the people's government of the township, minority township and town, and reported for approval to the county people's government after debate and consent of the villagers' congress.' Article 8, *ibid.*, p. 2.

[39] Defined thus: 'in accordance with the villagers' situation of residence, the villagers' committee may establish several villagers' groups, the villagers' group leader is elected by the villagers' group congress.' Article 10, *ibid.*, p. 2.

[40] Articles 8 and 10, Revised Land Administration Law, in Fang (ed.), A Practical Discussion of the 'Land Administration Law', p. 208.

is no longer clear: indeed, collective ownership has not been defined at all.[41] As with state ownership, the crux lies in the question: who is legally entitled to ownership?

According to the Revised Land Administration Law the 'farmers' collective' (*nongmin jiti*) or the 'collective economic organization' (*jiti jingji zuzhi*) are entitled to land ownership, whereas the 'collective economic organization of the township (town)', the 'villagers' committee' (*cunmin weiyuanhui*), and the 'villagers' group' are entitled only to the right of management and administration. However, as there is no law that defines the farmers' collective or the collective economic organization,[42] it is unclear whether the institutions that manage and administer land also hold ownership. To quote a Chinese scholar:

> Although the law stipulates that the village farmers' collective is the owner, it does not define the organization or structure that represents the village farmers' collective. By law the village collective economic organization and the villagers' committee have only managerial and administrative rights, which does not necessarily imply that they can legally represent and exercise the ownership of the owner or reap the profits from ownership.[43]

The shifts that occurred in the ownership of collective land from the 1962 Sixty Articles to decollectivization in the mid-1980s are shown in Fig. 2.

The vague definition of the collective was taken up during the NPC debates on the Revised Land Administration Law. In fact, Li Boyong, the Vice-Chairman of the NPC Legal Committee, acknowledged that the

[41] Although the interpretation of the NPC Legal Committee makes several important clarifications, it does not solve the fundamental problem as the term 'collective' is still left undefined. The legal interpretation makes three stipulations. First, the stipulation that 'the land owned by the farmers' collective is by law owned by the farmers' collective of the village' means that this land is 'owned by the farmers' collective of the administrative village'. Second, the stipulation that 'what is already owned by more than two rural collective economic organizations of the farmers' collective' means that 'if land prior to the reforms belonged to more than two production teams, their land is now still owned by each of these rural collective economic organizations or the villagers' groups equivalent to the former production teams'. Third, the stipulation that 'what is already owned by the farmers' collective of the township (town)' means that 'the land of the people's commune . . . after its transformation into the township/town still belongs to the farmers' collective of the township/town'. RFGW (ed.), An Interpretation of the Land Administration Law, pp. 65–6.

[42] Neither term is defined in law. Article 5 of the Organic Law states only that 'the villagers' committee must respect the power of decision-making of the village collective economic organization in executing economic activities according to the law'. Zhongguo Falü Chubanshe (ed.), *Zhonghua Renmin Gongheguo Cunmin Weiyuanhui Zuzhifa* [The Organic Law on the Villagers' Committee of the People's Republic of China], 4 November 1998 (Beijing: Zhongguo Falü Chubanshe, 1998), p. 2.

[43] Feng Xu, 'Gufen Hezuo yu Nongye Tudi Zhidu Gaige' ['Shareholding Cooperatives and the Reform of the Agricultural Land System'], *Nongye Jingji Wenti*, No. 5 (1998), p. 22. Xu does not mention the right of management and administration of the villagers' group. The reason is that his article was written before the Revised Land Administration Law became effective and this right had not yet been stipulated in law. A similar line of argument can also be found in Zuhui Huang and Yinyin Chen, 'Nongdi Chanquan Jieguo he Wo Guo de Jiating Nongye' ['The Structure of Property Rights of Agricultural Land and China's Household Agriculture'], *Nongye Jingji Wenti*, No. 5 (1998), p. 19; and Cunxue Wang, Xiangcong Ma, Mingchuan Huang, and Sheng Li, 'Nongye Falü Tixi Jianshe Jiben Wenti' ['Fundamental Problems on the Construction of a Legal System for Agriculture'], *Faxue Yanjiu*, Vol. 18, No. 6 (1996), p. 72.

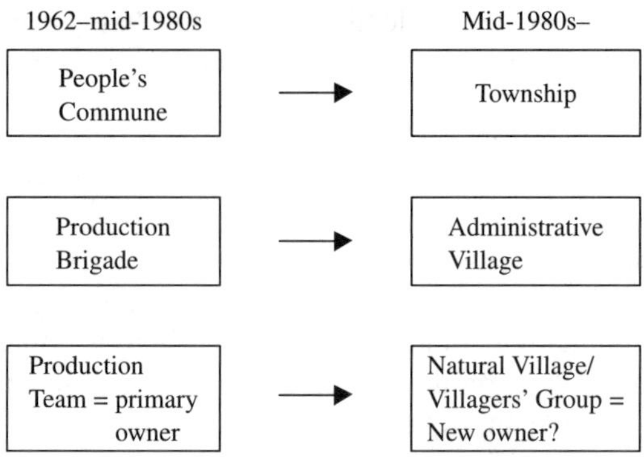

Figure 2: **Changes in ownership of collective land (all rural land not proven state-owned).**

Source: Author.

regulations on collective land ownership should be changed because 'delegates of the NPC Standing Committee remarked that it is unclear who represents the land ownership . . . of the farmers' collective'.[44] Yet on this point the revised law is essentially similar to the 1986 Land Administration Law. One can ask why this issue is so sensitive. Why does the central government attempt to intentionally cover up the nature of collective land ownership?

Legal indeterminacy is a major feature of the current Chinese land rights structure. But, more importantly—and here we touch on the central argument—a great deal of this ambiguity is *intentionally* sustained by the central leadership. There are several reasons why the central leadership does so. As we will see in more detail in Chapter 2, the production team was incapable of effectively protecting its interest in land even though it held formal land ownership. In the name of economic development, land was frequently expropriated illegally from production teams by higher administrative levels (the brigade, commune, or local government) without proper financial compensation. With the communes dismantled, it is, however, still impossible to return stolen land to the original owners because of the long-term use of and substantial investments made in the land. On the other hand, the rising value of land also means that those expropriated become increasingly aware of their former claims over land. Should the ownership structure of the communes be continued after decollectivization, the natural village or villagers' group would have the legal means to pursue these claims. And this in turn would give rise to an outbreak of widespread social conflict over land.

By intentionally keeping collective ownership vague, the state hopes that in the course of socio-economic and legal development the conflicting

44 Boyong Li, *Quanguo Renda Falü Weiyuanhui guanyu 'Zhonghua Renmin Gongheguo Tudi Guanlifa (Xiuding Cao'an)' Shenyi Jieguo de Baogao* [Report on the Results of the Review of the 'Land Administration Law of the People's Republic (Revised Draft)' by the Law Committee of the National People's Congress], Speech at the 4th Session of the Standing Committee of the 9th National People's Congress, 24 August 1998, p. 3.

claims to land by the various collective levels (the natural village/villagers' group, administrative village, and township/town) will eventually be resolved. The reader might retort that, despite all the conflicting rules, it remains remarkable that there is such a 'relative rarity of conflicts', as Dicks remarked about China's legal system.[45] However, the fact that the collective ownership structure is highly explosive is beyond any doubt. It is all there in the words of the official quoted in the epigraph of this chapter: 'It is like the ownership rights to land have been silently stolen from the natural village and vested in a level higher.' The practice of the Household Contract Responsibility System actually confirms the official's suspicions. In the lease of agricultural land the administrative village (under the supervision of the township) usually acts as the formal lessor, rather than the villagers' group or natural village. The 1997 survey of the Central Policy Research Office found that 60.5 per cent of the land was leased by the administrative village.[46] Moreover, the right to the redistribution of land in response to changes in household size is by law reserved to the institutions of the administrative village (the villagers' committee and the villagers' delegates) rather than the natural village.[47]

The opinions of officials and scholars differ widely on this sensitive issue. During the NPC debates on the Revised Land Administration Law, some championed granting ownership to the administrative as well as the natural village. As the comments by the Central Policy Research Office to the NPC read: 'Now that the commune has been changed into the township/town, the brigade into the villagers' committee, and the team into the villagers' group, there is no longer any collective economic organization. To vest the collective ownership of land in the villagers' committee and the villagers' group is more attuned to reality.'[48] On the other side of the spectrum, we find radical proposals that boil down to the requisition of land from the natural village. From the angle of Zhejiang Province: 'Some towns have already abolished the limits of the natural village (villagers' group). . . . If we allow ownership to the villagers' group, town and village planning will be difficult to implement, which will hinder economic growth.'[49] To regain control over land administration, it is proposed that 'the Land Administration Law changes the three-level

[45] Anthony R. Dicks, 'Compartmentalized Law and Judicial Restraint: An Inductive View of Some Jurisdictional Barriers to Reform', in Stanley B. Lubman (ed.), *China's Legal Reforms* (Oxford: Oxford University Press, 1996), pp. 90, 102. Dicks attributes this to the 'judicial restraint' exercised by central and local state institutions.

[46] The villagers' group accounted for 32.3%, the township for 1.1%, and other categories for 3%. See Wang, 'Present Situation and Problems', p. 56.

[47] Or *cunmin daibiao*. See article 14, Revised Land Administration Law in Fang (ed.), A Practical Discussion of the 'Land Administration Law', p. 209.

[48] 'Remarks on the "Land Administration Law (Revised Draft)" by Relevant Central Departments and Mass Organizations', in RFGW (ed.), An Interpretation of the Land Administration Law, p. 338. Vesting land ownership in the villagers' group is also advocated by the authors of 'Remarks on the "Land Administration Law (Revised Draft)" in Letters sent by Some Experts, Scholars, Jurists and Researchers', in RFGW (ed.), An Interpretation of the Land Administration Law, p. 395.

[49] 'Remarks on the "Land Administration Law (Revised Draft)" by Relevant Units and Personnel of Zhejiang Province', in RFGW (ed.), An Interpretation of the Land Administration Law, p. 366.

ownership of collective land into a two-level ownership' (*sic*). In other words, 'the ownership right to collective land of the villagers' group is not stipulated, or the three-level ownership is uniformly administrated by the [administrative] village'.[50] Abolition of land ownership by the villagers' group naturally would facilitate land registration and spatial planning, as there are only around 740,000 administrative villages. However, it would also entail the expropriation of land from almost 1.5 million natural villages,[51] with unknown consequences for social stability.

The Zhejiang proposal is extremely important. Due to its high level of socio-economic development, Zhejiang Province is in the vanguard of Land Reform and experiments with alternative land tenure forms. Local governments use the institutional ambiguity maintained by the central authorities in attempting to impose a land rights structure that abolishes land ownership with the natural village as the basic unit. In the rush for real estate development there is a high risk that the collective ownership rights of villagers will be violated. In particular, as the villagers' group and the villagers' committee have not been established as legal owners, they lack the power to represent the farmers' collective ownership. The scholar Xu Feng remarks that 'if the villagers' committee is mandated by all villagers, it is eligible to be the owner of land', but 'in reality the villagers' committee has become an extension of the political power of the township/town . . . as a result of which the collective ownership of farmers is often difficult to realize and farmers cannot enjoy the rights and interests of the collective'.[52] To protect villagers' interests, it is therefore imperative that the central government lifts the veil of institutional ambiguity and articulates the legal nature of collective ownership.

State versus collective conflicts. The vague nature of collective ownership also gives rise to conflicts between the state and collectives. These conflicts generally arise in two situations: at the interface of rural, collective land with urban state-owned land; and at the interface of state-owned forest, grassland, and wasteland with customary collective forest, grassland, and wasteland.

The Revised Land Administration Law stipulates that land of the 'city's urban area' (*chengshi shiqu*) is state-owned, while land of the 'city's suburbs' (*chengshi jiaoqu*) belongs to the collective. This is not fixed in stone. Due to continuous urban expansion through construction, much of the formerly collective land has been subsumed within the limits of the city. In the rush for real estate development, collective land and sometimes entire collectives have been sold or appropriated *without* formal change of land ownership titles. Cadres seeking to gain from their terms of service approve the construction of factories, office blocks, and apartment buildings on agricultural land, which opens up large opportunities for

[50] 'Remarks on the "Land Administration Law (Revised Draft)" by Relevant Units and Personnel of Zhejiang Province', in RFGW (ed.), An Interpretation of the Land Administration Law, p. 366.

[51] National Bureau of Statistics, *China Statistical Yearbook* (China Statistical Press, Beijing, 1999), p. 379.

[52] Xu, 'Shareholding Cooperatives and Reform', p. 22.

corruption.[53] On the other hand, the position of township and village leaders as the legal holders of collective ownership is unclear, while cadres often make decisions to sell land in their private capacity. In the end, villagers are confronted with forced eviction from their land, as corrupt cadres have sold it for more profitable uses. De jure land that is illegally sold to cities by the village collective remains collectively owned. For these reasons NPC delegates proposed that the Land Administration Law be revised and the terms 'urban area' and 'suburbs' redefined. These proposals foundered, however, because they required a revision of the Constitution.[54]

State–collective conflicts arise at the interface of state-owned forest, grassland, and wasteland and customary, collectively owned forest, grassland, and wasteland. However, since these conflicts raise quite different issues than for cropland, they will be discussed in more detail in the separate chapters on forest, grassland, and wasteland. Suffice it here to give a brief account of the background of this type of ownership dispute. There is frequent friction between the state and the collective over forest, grassland, and wasteland in long-term use by the collective, caused by the specific formulation of the respective Land Administration, Forest, and Grassland Laws. They stipulate that forest, grassland, and wasteland are by law state-owned *unless* collective ownership is proved. And this is where the snag is: there is generally no legal title of collective ownership for these natural resources, and if titles ever existed they were often lost during socio-political upheaval.

Once reclaimed and in use, forest, grassland, and wasteland were over time claimed by customary, and thus generally unwritten, land rights. This accounts for the common village woods used for forest by-products and firewood collection in Guizhou and Yunnan,[55] as well as for the forests and

[53] See David Zweig, 'The "Externalities of Development": Can New Political Institutions Manage Rural Conflict?', in Elizabeth J. Perry and Mark Selden (eds.), *Chinese Society: Change, Conflict and Resistance* (London: Routledge, 2000).

[54] Article 10; Zhongguo Falü Chubanshe (ed.), *The Constitution of China*, (China Legal Press, Beijing, 1996), p. 8; article 8, Revised Land Administration Law, in Fang (ed.), A Practical Discussion of the 'Land Administration Law', p. 208; and RFGW (ed.), An Interpretation of the Land Administration Law, pp. 58–9. There is also confusion about the distinction between the terms 'city' and 'urban area'. According to the interpretation of the Legal Committee, 'city' must be read as the 'municipality directly under the central government, city or town according to the administrative and organizational setup by the state'. In contrast, 'urban area' must be understood as the built-up area, and not the planned construction area as suggested by the City Planning Societies of Beijing and Hunan. See 'Remarks on the "Land Administration Law (Revised Draft)" in Letters sent by Some Experts, Scholars, Jurists and Researchers' in RFGW (ed.), An Interpretation of the Land Administration Law, p. 395. In addition, the Legal Committee has proposed that a better legal definition be made of the terms 'land used for agriculture', 'land used for construction', and 'unused land'. Boyong Li, *Quanguo Renda Falü Weiyuanhui guanyu 'Zhonghua Renmin Gongheguo Tudi Guanlifa (Xiuding Cao'an)' chubu Shenyi Qingkuang de Huibao* [Report on the Preliminary Review of the Situation on the 'Land Administration Law of the People's Republic (Revised Draft)' by the Law Committee of the National People's Congress], Speech at the 3rd Session of the Standing Committee of the 9th National People's Congress, 24 June 1998, p. 3.

[55] See, for example, Emily T. Yeh, 'Forest Claims, Conflicts and Commodification: The Political Ecology of Tibetan Mushroom-Harvesting Villages in Yunnan Province', *The China Quarterly*, Vol. 161 (March 2000), pp. 264–78.

pastures in frontier areas such as Heilongjiang, Inner Mongolia, and Xinjiang. After land reform, the settler villages in existence at the frontier before 1949 suddenly found themselves included in state reserves without recognition of their land ownership. Ironically, the government-supported reclamation schemes of the communist state repeated history, as the land reclaimed and leased out to settlers and village colonies during and after the collective period (1956–78) was never titled either.[56]

Land Registration: Assessing the Boundaries of Ownership

Under the present legal framework the county and higher administrative levels[57] are charged with the assessment of land ownership titles, as well as with the issue of permits for the use of state land and the ownership of collective land.[58] In contrast to urban land, forest, grassland, and other natural resources that are in principle state-owned, the burden of proof for the title of rural land lies with the state. That is, rural land is—in principle—collectively owned. The only task for the state is to determine and register the title to land. Here the problems start, because rural land was never systematically registered, whereas the majority of land ownership titles that were issued were lost during the political campaigns after Land Reform.

In theory, land registration begins with the formation by the County Bureau of Land Administration of a Leading Group in which representatives of relevant departments and local governments participate. Under the Leading Group, a Land Assessment Team is set up, which is responsible for executing the actual land registration.[59] Land registration consists of five stages: (*a*) land declaration to the relevant authorities by the owner or user; (*b*) examination of the land title; (*c*) verification of the title; (*d*) registration in the cadastre; and (*e*) issue of the permit. The most important stage is the examination of the land title, which includes the assessment of land rights (collective ownership, use right of collective land, use right of state land, and other real rights) and the land survey (geographical location, boundaries, land use and quality, and so forth). Together with the owner and user, the Land Assessment Team collects all necessary statistical data, documents, and maps on the land title. (For an illustration of a land title assessment of two villages and a record of disputed land, see respectively Appendix A and Appendix B.)[60]

[56] See, for example, Emily T. Yeh, 'Forest Claims, Conflicts and Commodification: The Political Ecology of Tibetan Mushroom-Harvesting Villages in Yunnan Province', *The China Quarterly*, Vol. 161 (March 2000), p. 352. For problems about land ownership titles of grassland and wasteland, see also Wenzheng Shi, *Caoyuan yu Caoye de Fazhi Jianshe Yanjiu* [Research of the Construction of a Judicial System for Rangeland and Pastoralism] (Hohhot: Neimenggu Daxue Chubanshe, 1996), p. 43.

[57] The term '*Xianji yishang*' in the Land Administration Law refers to the administrative levels starting from the county and higher.

[58] Article 11, Revised Land Administration Law in Fang (ed.), A Practical Discussion of the 'Land Administration Law', p. 208.

[59] This team works in close unison with the Township Land Management Station and village officials.

[60] For reasons of space I have given only a brief overview of the land registration procedures. They are described in detail in Hu Cunzhi, Theory and Methods of Land Registration, Vol. I, pp. 94–143.

The boundary assessment and conflict resolution at all administrative levels down to the township/town is not, as might be expected, carried out by the Ministry of Land Resources but by the Ministry of Civil Administration.[61] The boundary assessment of farmers' collectives at the village and lower administrative levels is the responsibility of local people's governments and the land administration departments. The influence of the Ministry of Civil Administration is uncertain in this respect. The national land registration of farmers' collectives was executed from 1984 until the late 1990s,[62] but stopped at the level of the natural village! This is of major importance, as the natural village and villagers' group are the de facto inheritors of collective land ownership since the demise of the people's communes. With this move, the central state once again consciously supports institutional ambiguity, as when it leaves collective ownership undefined in law.

Even at the administrative village level, land registration has run into quite a few problems due to the state's intentional institutional ambiguity. The terms 'farmers' collective', 'collective economic organization', and 'villagers' committee' are often confounded by cadres.[63] Together with the vague distinction between state and collective land, this created a great deal of confusion in the establishment of a nationwide cadastre. For instance, in an administrative village in Inner Mongolia land ownership title was granted to a primary school and a brick kiln (see Appendix C and Appendix D).[64] A senior economist in the Institute of Land Policy of the Ministry of Land Resources indignantly claimed that vesting land ownership in a school or brick kiln was 'absolutely illegal' because it was not a 'collective economic organization'. Only if officially registered with the Department of Industry and Commerce can an institution be regarded as a collective economic organization and entitled to land ownership.[65] Restricting the right of ownership to the collective economic organization is bound to create problems, as other collective institutions such as village infirmaries, temples, and mosques will in the future surely claim the land they are built on.[66]

[61] See 'Xingzheng Bianjie Zhengyi Chuli Tiaoli' [Regulations on the Handling of Administrative Border Disputes], in Neimeng Xingzheng Quhua Bianjie Lingdao Xiaozu (ed.), *Xingzheng Quhua, Tiaochu Bianjie Zhengyi Wenjian Xuanbian* [A Compilation of Documents on the Handling of Boundary Disputes and Administrative Divisions] (Hohhot: Restricted Circulation, 30 August 1990), pp. 141–9.

[62] The period for the boundary assessment of the administrative villages differs among provinces and regions. For example, in Inner Mongolia the work was completed during 1984–92, and in Ningxia during 1984–98 (Shi Wenzheng, oral communication, 1999).

[63] For the present legal definitions, see nn. 39 and 40.

[64] A collection of land ownership certificates was obtained from villages in Inner Mongolia during the 1999 fieldwork. However, for reasons of space they have not been included in this chapter. Unfortunately, cadres were unwilling to provide such certificates for Ningxia and Zhejiang.

[65] Confusingly, the same official stated that the villagers' committee is not a collective economic organization, albeit entitled to land ownership, because it is considered a 'self-governing organization' (*zizhi zuzhi*). Jian Xu (oral communication, 1999). The illegality of granting ownership to this school was also confirmed by the Deputy Director of the Real Estate Consultative Center of the Ministry of Land Resources, Xianbin Chen (oral communication, 1999).

[66] In Ningxia, for example, the land of a mosque is by Islamic law regarded as *waqf*, which 'is a form of charitable endowment, similar to the modern concept of trust. It entitles any kind of private property–buildings, land, or wells–to be constituted as inalienable public estate.'

One of the main problems that severely hampers land registration is the extreme fragmentation of authority in land administration and policy-making. The central state is desperately trying to recentralize land administration into a single state institution, the Ministry of Land Resources. However, as will be demonstrated in the following section, the results of this undertaking are mixed.

The Ministry of Land Resources: From Fragmentation to Centralization

Typical of the problems with land administration in China are the current *and* postponed organizational reforms of the Ministry of Land Resources. The structure of land management is in flux as it moves from fragmented authority to centralized administration. What is presently administered by various institutions was formerly the sole jurisdiction of the (abolished) Ministry of Internal Affairs (*Neiwubu*).

China set up the Ministry of Internal Affairs in 1949 on the lines of the Nationalist model of unified land administration. It included the Department of Land Administration, responsible for rural and urban land matters. In the mid-1950s this system was abolished and land administration was dispersed over authorities administering urban, rural and other land resources. Today, urban land is administered by municipal government institutions, the Land Administrative Agency or Real Estate Administration Agency, while rural land falls under the jurisdiction of the Ministry of Land Resources. Other land (and water) resources fall under a wide variety of institutions such as the State Forestry Bureau and the Ministries of Agriculture, Water Resources, Railways, Communications, National Defence, and Civil Affairs.[67]

We noted above that the lack of coordination between the different institutions issuing land permits led to great confusion about land ownership titles, especially in forest, grassland, and water resources. To solve this problem, some NPC delegates proposed to broaden the legal scope of the Land Administration Law so as to determine ownership titles of land resources stipulated under the Forest Law, Grassland Law, and Fishery Law. This would be a major step towards the unification of land

Peter Ho, 'Rangeland Policy, Pastoralism and Poverty in China's Northwest: Ningxia Province in the Twentieth Century', Ph.D. dissertation (Leiden University: Leiden, 1999), p. 55; Pieter W. Germeraad, *Open Space in Human Settlements: The Lesson from the Islamic Tradition* (Wageningen: Germeraad, 1990), p. 33. One of the best explanations of Islamic Law (Shari'a) and *waqf* is given (in Dutch) by Ruud Peters, 'Het Recht—Recente Ontwikkelingen' ['The Law: Recent Developments'], in Jacques Waardenburg (ed.), *Islam: Norm, Ideaal en Werkelijkheid* (Antwerpen: Standaard Uitgeverij, 1984), pp. 292–310.

[67] Their respective responsibilities are forest, grassland, land for railways, land for roads and waterways, water resources, military land, and the determination of administrative boundaries and boundary conflict resolution. Han Wang and Jingming Yao, 'Neiwubu Jigou ji Zhineng' ['The Functions and Structure of the Ministry of Internal Affairs'], *Zhongguo Minzheng*, No. 1 (1999), p. 35; Xinhua Liu (ed.), *Xin Tudi Guanlifa Quanshu* [Encyclopedia of the New Land Administration Law], Vol. I (Beijing: Zhongguo Wujia Chubanshe, 1998), pp. 169–70; Jen-Kai Liu, 'The Main National Leadership of the PRC', *China Aktuell* (July 1998), pp. 2–5.

administration in China. The Legal Committee replied that the principle of unified land management should be defined in law, but added:

> The administrative system which defines in law the definition of titles and issue of permits for forest, grassland and fisheries . . . was formed over many years. Under the present circumstances it is still effective. The main aim to revise the Land Administration Law this time is to reinforce the protection of arable land. Should we change the administrative system and revise the currently effective, relevant laws, it will pose complex problems; at this time it is too difficult to solve.[68]

The very name of the Land Administration Law implies a postponed restructuring of land management. When the law was first drafted in the early 1980s it was originally meant to concentrate the authority of all land resources in one state institution and a single 'mother law' (*mufa*): the 'Land Law'. However, fearing intensified inter-departmental strife, the NPC Legal Committee recommended that the name be temporarily changed to 'Land Administration Law' and its legal scope restricted until it had gained more practical experience in 'the planning, consolidation and development of the nation's land'.[69] Nevertheless, numerous signs point to a gradual centralization of land administration.

First, in 1998 the former State Land Administration, the Ministry of Geology and Mineral Resources, the State Bureau of Marine Resources, and the State Topography Bureau merged into a newly established Ministry of Land Resources. At the same time, the Ministry of Forestry was downgraded to a bureau directly under the State Council.[70] The organizational reforms at the central level meant a significant strengthening of the institutions charged with land matters. The implications for the provincial and lower levels are still unknown.[71] The law leaves the options open by stipulating that such matters are decided according to regulations of the State Council. But these still need to be drafted.[72] Second, the Revised Land Administration Law concentrated power in the hands of the central leadership by granting the State Council authority over state land ownership and use by central state institutions. According to the Legal Committee 'this is a relatively large revision' as it 'facilitates the unified control over land resources of central state institutions . . . and prevents the loss of state land resources through corruption and the unauthorized handling of use rights by departments'.[73] Finally, the old quota system was replaced by

[68] Li, Preliminary Review of the 'Land Administration Law', p. 2.

[69] RFGW (ed.), An Interpretation of the Land Administration Law, p. 50.

[70] Zou Xiaoyun, a senior economist within the land planning division of the Ministry of Land Resources claimed that there were rumours that the Bureau of Forestry might again be upgraded to a ministry. The background of this is the sandstorms that swept over Beijing in the spring of 2000. They were caused by the increasing desertification in the north-west. In reaction, Premier Zhu Rongji placed natural resource management high on the political agenda with a policy of giving up agriculture in favour of forestry and animal husbandry (*tuigeng huanlin, huanmu*) (oral communication, 2000).

[71] The question is whether the local equivalents of the central departments will merge into one provincial Bureau of Land Resources or other institutions charged with urban land matters will be included.

[72] Article 5, Section 2, Revised Land Administration Law in Fang (ed.), A Practical Discussion of the 'Land Administration Law', p. 207.

[73] Articles 2 and 11, Revised Land Administration Law in *ibid.*, pp. 207–8; RFGW (ed.), An Interpretation of the Land Administration Law, p. 68.

a hierarchical approval system for land use planning. Under the new system the State Council has the final say in land use planning. Such centralization attracted criticism from NPC delegates and ministries: 'It is imperative that the right for approval is drawn to the centre, but the rules of the draft are too centralized, which makes them difficult to implement.' In response, the Legal Committee allowed the prefecture and the county to exercise limited authority.[74]

Land Use and Lease: Wavering between Ideology, the Market, and Social Stability

What the Chinese authorities are attempting to do as part of their reform policy is to shift the boundaries of definition, such that the right to use and transfer property rights falls under the now much broader heading of commodities (and therefore tradeable), and not means of production.[75]

In present-day China land ownership by the state and collective is an ideological given. For this reason, the 'socialist market economy' in rural areas can be realized only by commercializing the rights to land use and lease. In this policy arena, however, the clash between Marx-Leninist tenets and the reality of the reforms is striking. Land policy-making strongly resembles a trial-and-error process accompanied by intentional institutional ambiguity to facilitate political manoeuvring. The ambiguity results in a great deal of confusion about the officially condoned land property arrangements, but it also allows a certain degree of experimentation by local cadres.

In the course of the economic reforms, a market has emerged in use rights to state-owned (in fact urban) land. In general, state-owned land can be developed and leased for real estate and agricultural purposes. As for rural, collective land, the Household Contract Responsibility System has moved beyond its initial confines and farmers can in principle sub-lease and transfer their contracts provided that land use is limited to agriculture. In addition, since 1999 leasing by individuals and units outside the collective has become possible.[76] However, practices like sub-lease and transfer are rare in most of China.[77] In addition, the pricing of rural land is still an

[74] Articles 21:4 and 44:3, Revised Land Administration Law in Fang (ed.), A Practical Discussion of the 'Land Administration Law', pp. 211–12; Li, Preliminary Review of the 'Land Administration Law', p. 3.

[75] Anthony Walker, *Land, Property and Construction in the PRC* (Hong Kong: Hong Kong University Press, 1991), p. 61.

[76] Provided that approval of two-thirds of the villagers' congress or delegates has been obtained. Article 15, Revised Land Administration Law in Fang (ed.), A Practical Discussion of the 'Land Administration Law', p. 208.

[77] Several terms are often mistakenly used as synonyms for the 'transfer of use rights': *huabo*, *churang*, *zhuanrang*, and *zhuanbao*. *Huabo* is non-taxed land transfer to companies and institutions that invest in land development at the first-level market (state-monopolized). The period for this varies from forty to seventy years. Unlike in the past, the state now attempts to levy tax or a premium on land transfer, which is then called *churang*. *Zhuanrang* refers to the second-level market in which use rights are transferred to land users. *Zhuanbao* is sub-lease without the farmer ceding the rights to land. A good introduction on the theoretical background to China's land use market is provided in Kewei Ma (ed.), *Tudi Dacidian*

ideological taboo which inhibits an economically efficient exchange of land use rights. In this respect, the 'rural land market' is a far cry from its urban parallel.

The 'land market' as it exists in China today has come a long way. The revision of the Constitution in 1988 legitimized land rent and transfer under a 'valued use system' (*youchang shiyong zhidu*) and heralded the first major land policy change since decollectivization.[78] In the same year, the State Land Administration argued for the implementation of a valued use system for state *and* collective land, for three reasons: (*a*) to realize an efficient and sustainable use of land resources; (*b*) to secure for the state and collective the benefits from land holdings through land tax or a premium (rent for the entire lease term); and (*c*) attracting (foreign) investment in land and real estate.[79] The valued use of rural land boils down to the free transfer, rent and mortgage of land in and outside the agricultural realm. However, at that time the Legal Committee feared that the valued use system might destabilize rural land lease and proposed that 'the law temporarily makes no stipulations, in order to conduct further investigation and gain more experience'.[80]

The debate on this issue flared up again in the late 1990s, during the presentation of the draft for the Revised Land Administration Law, With many others, the Zhejiang Land Administration Bureau argued: 'The scope of the valued land use system for state land is too small . . . and should be extended to collective land. In fact, valued land use is already practised for collective land.' But the NPC Legal Committee reiterated its official stance of the late 1980s, with the result that the valued use system is restricted to state-owned land.[81] The reason for this is that the central government fears the rise of a new class of impoverished and landless farmers should rural land rights become freely tradable. The 61 per cent of the Chinese population registered as rural residents[82] represents widespread hidden unemployment in the countryside. For those millions of peasants active in the agricultural sector, the minuscule plot of land (0.14ha per capita in 1998)[83] they till is also a basic security.

The valued use of rural land is an opaque area in which economically more developed regions have often taken liberties not (yet) defined in law.

[The Great Dictionary on Land] (Changchun: Changchun Chubanshe, 1991), pp. 93, 183, 891, 988; and Walker, *Land, Property and Construction in the PRC*, pp. 38–44.

78 Article 10, Zhongguo Falü Chubanshe, *The Constitution of China*, p. 8; and in the same volume Article 2 of the Bill of Amendment, p. 42.

79 RFGW (ed.), An Interpretation of the Land Administration Law, p. 39.

80 Jianqing Lin, *Quanguo Renda Falü Weiyuanhui Dui 'Zhonghua Renmin Gongheguo Tudi Guanlifa Xiuzheng'an (Cao'an)' de Shenyi Jieguo de Baogao* [Report on the Results of the Review of the 'Revised Amendment of the Land Administration Law of the People's Republic (Draft)' by the Law Committee of the National People's Congress], Speech at the 5th Session of the Standing Committee of the 7th National People's Congress, 23 December 1988, p. 1.

81 RFGW (ed.), An Interpretation of the Land Administration Law, p. 366; Li, Preliminary Review of the 'Land Administration Law', p. 6; Article 2, Revised Land Administration Law in Fang (ed.), A Practical Discussion of the 'Land Administration Law', p. 207.

82 Of a total of 1.28 billion people in 2002, 60.9% were registered as rural population. See National Bureau of Statistics (ed.), *China Statistical Yearbook 2003*, p. 97.

83 *Ibid.*, p. 390.

For example, some village collectives let land to companies for agriculture or land improvement that, strictly speaking, transgresses the current boundaries of national law. Similarly confusing is the mortgage of use rights. The mortgage of state-owned land use rights is allowed by the central government, although it is not sanctioned in law.[84] A typical borderline case is the mortgage of wasteland. According to a notice by the State Council 'those who buy [wasteland] use rights, have the right to inherit, transfer, mortgage and shareholding management'.[85] According to the Constitution, wasteland is state-owned unless proven to be collective property.[86] Here we encounter a well-known problem discussed earlier. The greater area of wasteland is de jure state-owned only because collectives have failed to establish title to the land they have long used and invested in. But this does not prevent the collectives from laying customary claim to wasteland. It can therefore happen that collectives mortgage the use right of wasteland claimed by customary right, a practice that is prohibited by higher authorities that regard wasteland as state-owned. This hampers the development of a rural land market. In a submission to the NPC, Sichuan Province proposed to include the mortgage of collective land use rights in the Land Administration Law, but to no avail.[87]

The current trend of the rural land lease system is geared to stabilizing farmers' contracts and limiting—or, at least, not extending—the valued use of land outside the agricultural realm. The protection of farmers' legal interests has become common ground for policy-makers. During the NPC Standing Committee discussion on the Revised Land Administration Law in June 1998, delegates argued that 'the revised draft does not make sufficient stipulations . . . on the protection of farmers' contract right; this needs to be completed'.[88] In this respect, the new law breaks with the past in two respects: (*a*) it reiterates the policy of 1997, which in principle guarantees a land lease of '30 years no change';[89] and (*b*) it curtails the

[84] See the legal interpretation of the NPC Legal Committee. RFGW (ed.), An Interpretation of the Land Administration Law, p. 41.

[85] Article 6, Secretariat of the State Council, 'Zhili Kaifa Nongcun 'Sihuang' Ziyuan Jin Yi Bu Jiaqiang Shuitu Baochi Gongzuo de Tongzhi' [Notice on the Control and Development of the Rural 'Four Wastelands' Resources and the Intensified Strengthening of Soil and Water Conservation], in Zhongguo Falü Nianjian Bianji Weiyuanhui (ed.), *Zhongguo Falü Nianjian 1997* [China Legal Yearbook 1997] (Beijing: Zhongguo Falü Nianjianshe, 1997), pp. 425–6.

[86] See article 9, Zhongguo Falü Chubanshe (ed.), *The Constitution of China*, p. 8. Note that wasteland is mentioned only as such in the Constitution. It is not defined as a separate natural resource in other laws. It is therefore unclear whether wasteland should be handled according to the Forest Law or the Grassland Law. It is the cause for frequent strife between the Bureau of Animal Husbandry under the Ministry of Agriculture and the State Bureau of Forestry. See Peter Ho, 'The Wasteland Auction Policy in Northwest China: Solving Rural Poverty and Environmental Degradation?', in Peter Ho, Jacob Eyferth, and Eduard B. Vermeer (eds.), 'Rural Development in Transitional China: A Special Issue', *Journal of Peasant Studies*, Vol. 30, Nos. 3/4, (April/July 2003), pp. 121–59.

[87] 'Remarks on the 'Land Administration Law (Revised Draft)' by All Provinces, Autonomous Regions and Municipalities directly under the Central Government', in RFGW (ed.), An Interpretation of the Land Administration Law, p. 381.

[88] See Li, Preliminary Review of the 'Land Administration Law', p. 6.

[89] Zhonggong Zhongyang Bangongting, Zhonggong Zhongyang Bangongting, Guowuyuan Bangongting guanyu Jinyibu Wending he Wanshan Nongcun Tudi Chengbao Guanxi de Tongzhi [Notice by the Central Secretariat of the CCP and the Secretariat of the

power of the villagers' committee through the stipulation that leased land can be redistributed only if the approval of two-thirds of the villagers' congress or delegates has been obtained. A senior official of the Ministry of Agriculture commented: 'What the central government ultimately aims for is granting farmers the right to lease in perpetuity (*yongdianquan*). Because what will happen after 30 years? The lease will be extended for another 30 years, then another 30 years, and so on infinitely.'[90] Thus, the 'second round' of lease for which the 1998 Revised Land Administration Law provided the legal basis is the first in a long series. The second round was important as it was for the first time that farmers were issued individual, standardized, and notarized contracts. Nationwide, the contracts consisted of two parts: the contract (held by the village collective) and a small booklet (kept by the farmer, see Appendix E and Appendix F). In each village, the second round was ratified by the Village Representatives Congress and set out in a formal resolution.

What Makes the System Tick?

In the academic debate on states in transition, some argue for radical privatization of property rights while others maintain that privatization needs gradual guidance in keeping with the socio-economic and legal conditions. The People's Republic of China seems to defy the former argument. Of the three means of production—land, capital, and labour—the first is still firmly in the hands of the Chinese state and the collective. At the same time, research is finding increasing evidence that the current agricultural land tenure system, with its frequent readjustments in response to demographic change, is found to be credible by the rural populace. In fact, the readjustments fulfil an important role as a social safety net for the vast surplus of rural labour. Moreover, the impressive economic growth that began, and continues to be rooted, in the rural sector lends support to the idea that the privatization of land is actually not a *conditio sine qua non* for stable and sustained economic development. One may wonder what underlying institutional arrangements have led to this situation.

As land tenure touches on the very foundations of the Chinese state, striking the right balance between ideology and socio-economic reality is a tricky task for the central leadership. The question is how far privatization can proceed before corrupting the Marx-Leninist principles of state and collective land ownership. Land policy-making is, therefore, an alternation between restraining practices that exceed legal boundaries and giving space to experimentation by formulating intentionally unclear policies and laws. Throughout this chapter, I have argued that this 'intentional

State Council on the Further Stabilization and Perfectioning of the Contract Relations of Rural Land], No. 16 (1997); Article 14, Revised Land Administration Law, in Fang (ed.), A Practical Discussion of the 'Land Administration Law', p. 208.

[90] Sheng Li (oral communication, 1999). The official view fits in with the recent Chinese academic discussion on transforming the right to lease into a real right. See, for example, Su Chen, 'Tudi Chengbao Jingying Wuquanhua yu Nongdi Shiyongquan Zhidu de Queli' ['Changing the Contract Right to Land into a Real Right and the Establishment of a System for Agricultural Land User Rights'], *Zhongguo Faxue*, Vol. 3 (1996), p. 89.

institutional ambiguity' is what makes the agricultural land tenure system tick under the current socio-economic conditions. The argument was substantiated by reviewing four critical issues in the political debate over land administration with particular reference to rural land: (*a*) the right of ownership; (*b*) registration of land ownership titles; (*c*) the reform of the Ministry of Land Resources; and (*d*) the establishment of a market for lease and use rights.

To the question 'who owns the land?' no unequivocal answer is possible. The lack of clarity on state ownership springs from the dispersal of authority in land administration over various ministries. Clarifying state ownership is therefore closely linked to the organizational reform of the Ministry of Land Resources. In order to streamline land administration, the national government advocates centralization, which generates inter-departmental conflicts. Although the NPC Legal Committee regards unified land administration as the ultimate aim, it has ruled that its implementation should be postponed. This explains the contradictory formulation in the Revised Land Administration Law that stipulates unified land administration while leaving intact the separate management of forest, grassland, and fisheries.

A similar decision was taken for collective land ownership. To avoid an escalation of land disputes between the various levels of the rural collective, the law embodies an intentionally vague definition of collective ownership. This, in turn, has seriously impeded the execution of land registration. To date, the land titles of collective institutions at the administrative village and higher levels have been assessed without the eruption of widespread social conflict. But this is only because land registration halted at the most sensitive level, that of the original owner of collective land: the natural village. It testifies to the government's caution in Land Reform. In response to economic change, land rent and value principles were included in the Constitution in the late 1980s, opening the way for the free transfer of land use and lease rights. But in this area too the central government exercised considerable restraint. In the course of reform, the right to lease in perpetuity has materialized as a viable option in the eyes of the state. From an outright ban on the commercialization of land rights before 1988, the central government has gradually moved to 'valued use' of urban land, while the transfer of rural land rights remains in a legal twilight zone.

This chapter has given a detailed account of the past and present institutional framework, which is essential for understanding institutional change and the present agricultural land tenure system. On the basis of China's relatively successful economic performance over the past two decades, the farmers' support for an agricultural lease system that includes frequent reallocations, and the absence of widespread social conflict that challenges the current structure of agricultural land ownership, we may conclude that this institutional framework *is* credible and acceptable to the state and rural society today. But for how much longer can the central state postpone clarifying the nature of collective ownership, or centralizing the extreme fragmentation in land administration and policy-making?

Land registration has stopped at the level of the original owner as no decision could be taken on whether to register or expropriate 1.5 million natural villages. Either decision will give rise to strong social tensions. We can already witness the disadvantages of the state's deliberate institutional indeterminacy. Rapid urbanization and the frenzy for real estate development in the wealthier and coastal regions has led to a boom in land values. As a result, corrupt village cadres are eager to sell village land that is not sufficiently protected by law. At this point, there is a high risk that intentional institutional ambiguity will harm villagers' interests. To secure villagers' rights, it is critical that the central leadership takes the lead in clarifying the legal boundaries of the land administration system. The Chinese government is faced with the responsibility for shaping the future institutional framework for land policy and administration, and for guaranteeing its social credibility.

2
Why the Village Has No Power: Land Ownership Disputes and Customary Tenure

You cannot rely on law to rule the majority of the people; for the majority of the people you have to rely on cultivating [the right] habits. . . . I took part in establishing the Constitution, but I do not remember it. Every one of our [Party] resolutions is a law; when we hold a meeting, that's law too.

(Mao Zedong, 1958)[1]

What Happened to the Team's Land?

In Chapter 1 it was argued that the current tenure system for agricultural land is credible and accepted by the authorities and the rural populace, and the institutional arrangements that have made this possible were explored. For this reason, the chapter concentrated on policy and law-making at the national level, leaving aside the process of implementation at the grass roots. It was argued that the restraint that the central government exercised in leaving land rights ambiguous—the creation of 'intentional institutional ambiguity'—is the main explanation of how the agricultural land tenure system functions. It is important to realize that the central state's actions sanctioned and perpetuated rather than created the present indeterminacy of land rights. But one critical issue was left unaddressed: why has collective land ownership become unclear even though Party regulations stipulated that land is owned by the lowest collective level, that is, the production team? This is the starting point of the present chapter.

But first it would be helpful to make some clarifications about the unit of land ownership in China. It is important to remember that the natural village has been, and continues to be, the basic unit of land ownership from Republican times to the present. The 'natural village', however, is a traditional concept and—as Feuchtwang noted—refers to 'villagers' senses of what is local and long-standing, whatever the documented evidence of actual continuity'.[2] The term does not appear in modern Chinese law, even though it is frequently used in official and unofficial texts. For reasons of tax administration, both the Republican and Communist governments attempted to delimit village boundaries, leading to the frequent redrawing

[1] Stuart R. Schram, 'Mao Tse-tung's Thought from 1949–1976', in Roderick MacFarquhar and John K. Fairbank (eds.), *Cambridge History of China: The People's Republic, Part 2: Revolutions within the Chinese Revolution 1966–1982* (Cambridge University Press, Cambridge, 1991), p. 51.

[2] A good description of the difference between traditional and state concepts related to place is given by Stephan Feuchtwang, 'What is a Village', in Eduard B. Vermeer, Frank Pieke, and Woei Lien Chong (eds.), *Cooperative and Collective in China's Rural Development: Between State and Private Interests* (New York: M. E. Sharpe, 1998), pp. 47, 59–60, 61–6 (about the administrative village).

of village boundaries, renaming of villages, and merging of hamlets into larger territorial units. Collectivization with a three-tier system of basic administration—the people's commune, the production brigade, and the production team—and decollectivization in the mid-1980s have complicated the situation. With exceptions due to shifts in administrative units and regional differences,[3] the commune has become the present township/town (*xiang/zhen*), the brigade the administrative village (*xingzhengcun*), and the team the natural village (*zirancun*) and villagers' group (*cunmin xiaozu*). Note that the brigade and the administrative village are administrative units controlling natural villages, yet are simultaneously natural villages themselves. As such they claim ownership to land within the traditional village borders, which will be demonstrated in this chapter.[4]

To return to our central question: why has collective ownership become unclear even though it was clarified in Party regulations? I will argue that, although the natural village—in its capacity as the production team—held formal land ownership, it possessed no real power over land. Instead, control over land ownership rested with the commune and higher administrative levels (the county and above). This implied that, in the event of land requisition, the natural village was unable to safeguard its interests in the land its inhabitants lived on and tilled. There are three main reasons for this.

The first is the incoherent legal framework and the absence of a rule of law during the collective period (1956–78). As we will see, in the drive for economic development land was frequently requisitioned from the team and brigade without any formal procedures being followed or proper compensation provided. In many cases, the word of higher-level cadres was law: once their approval was secured—and that could take the form of oral commitments—economic projects such as the construction of a silk farm, water reservoirs, or plantations could proceed. In addition, under collectivism the legal framework was weak and inconsistent. For land requisition, the only formal rules in existence were the Measures on Land Requisition for State Construction proclaimed by the State Council on 6 January 1958. These measures were in effect during the entire collective period and were replaced only in 1982, with the State Council's Administrative Regulations for Land used for Building Construction in Villages and Towns and the Regulations for Land Requisition for State Construction. The 1958 measures had been proclaimed before the establishment of the people's communes and pertained to land requisition for state projects

[3] For example, such exceptions occurred if the former commune consisted of two levels rather than three. As also written in article 2 of the Sixty Articles: 'The organization of the commune can consist of two levels: the commune and the team; but it can also consist of three levels: the commune, the production brigade and the production team.' See CCP, 'Nongcun Renmin Gongshe Gongzuo Tiaoli Xiuzheng Cao'an' ['Revised Draft of the Work Regulations of the Rural People's Communes'] 27/9/1962, in Zhongguo Renmin Jiefangjun Guofang Daxue Dangshi Yanjiushi (ed.), *Zhonggong Dangshi Jiaoxue Cankao Ziliao* [Reference and Educational Material on the History of the CCP], Vol. 23 (Beijing: Guofang Daxue Chubanshe, 1986), p. 137.

[4] There is to date no evidence that administrative villages also claim ownership to the larger territory under their jurisdiction, which includes several natural villages.

土地房產所有證

山東省土地房產所有證

慶雲縣第三區 張牌 村居民

依據中國人民政治協商會議共同綱領第二十七條保護農民已得土地所有權之規定確定本戶全家 人所有土地共計 可耕地 非耕地 段 畝 分 釐 毫 房產共計房屋 間地基 段 畝 分 釐 毫均作為本戶全家 人私有產業有耕種居住典賣轉讓贈與等完全自由任何人不得侵犯特給此証

計開

土地							房產		
坐落	種類	畝數	四至	長寬尺度	附屬物	備考	坐落	種類間數	地基畝數

縣長

一九五一年四月一日發

Plate I: **A private land and house ownership certificate issued during Land Reform to a certain farmer Zhang Yunqing of Zhangpai Village, Qingyun County, Shandong Province, dated 1 April 1951.**

alone. As a result, the few stipulations about the 'cooperatives' (*hezuoshe*) did not take into account land requisition from and within the commune.[5]

Second, China has never established a nationwide land cadastre. The central government's first effort in this direction at the time of decollectivization did not include the natural village, the basic unit of land ownership. In the history of the People's Republic there were two important events that had an impact on the land holdings of the natural village: Land Reform in the 1950s and the Four Fixes Movement (*Si Guding*) in 1962. The Supreme Court and the Ministry of Land Resources still consider these two events the basis for the assessment of land title.[6] However, Land

[5] Articles 8 and 9 of the '1958 Measures on Land Requisition for State Construction'. See Hongyi Xiang (ed.), *Tudi Quequan Shiyong Shouce* [A Practical Manual for the Assessment of Land Title] (Beijing: Zhongguo Dadi Chubanshe, 1996), p. 110.

[6] See, for example, the review of the Supreme People's Court on 'The Use of Policies and Laws for the Land Dispute between the Villagers' Committee and the Villagers' Group'

Reform and the Four Fixes Movement did not provide a sound basis for a national cadastre. During Land Reform villagers had been issued with land titles, but not on a systematic basis (see Plate I). In addition, an unknown number were lost or destroyed in the subsequent years of political and social upheaval. The name of the Four Fixes Movement refers to the granting of permanent ownership of labour, land, animals, and tools to the production team in 1962. Its formal basis was provided by the Sixty Articles.[7] In principle, the team's land was supposed to be surveyed and registered as it had gained ownership, but, again, this never occurred.

The final reason for the villages' lack of control over land is related to the recognition of (historical) customary rights. As in other developing countries, Chinese village communities face a great challenge in having their customary land rights recognized by the state as they are generally unwritten.[8] On a different level, the problem of recognition pertains to a cultural confrontation: between a rapidly industrializing society moving towards the rule of law and an agrarian society based on a tradition of the 'rule by man'.[9] The academic controversy over the term 'customary law' reflects the intangibility and fluidity of customary tenure. Motion defined customary law as 'unwritten law established by long usage'[10] but that immediately gives rise to the question: how long is long?

In England, custom has legal force only if it has existed for so long that 'the memory of man runneth not to the contrary'. Curiously, the limit of human memory was fixed at the date of the accession of Richard I in 1189.[11] In the Chinese context such an arrangement is bound to be contested if only because of the very *recent* shifts in land ownership. The

and the 'State Land Administration's 1989 Regulations on the Assessment of Land Ownership and Use Rights', in Xiang (ed.), Manual for the Assessment of Land Title, pp. 293, 312–15. The 1989 Regulations take 1962 as the standard. This is the year when the Four Fixes Movement was carried out, for which the Sixty Articles provided the formal basis.

[7] Note that the original idea of the Four Fixes was to grant the production team permanent use , but not ownership, of labour, land, animals, and tools. Article 18 of the 1961 draft of the Sixty Articles states: 'The production brigade must give labour, land, animals and tools in fixed [permanent] use to the production team and have these registered.' Article 17 stipulated that 'all land . . . within the limits of the production brigade is owned by the production brigade'. By the time the revised draft of the Sixty Articles was finally issued by the Central Party Committee on 27 September 1962, the team had been given land ownership. See also 'Nongcun Renmin Gongshe Gongzuo Tiaoli Cao'an' ['Draft of the Work Regulations for the Rural People's Communes'], March 1961 in Zhongguo Renmin Jiefangjun Guofang Daxue Dangshi Yanjiushi (ed.), Reference and Educational Material on the CCP, Vol. 23, p. 454.

[8] A large body of literature is available on this issue, captured under key words such as 'common property resource management', 'common pool resources', and 'legal pluralism'. See, for example, Daniel W. Bromley, *Making the Commons Work: Theory, Practice and Policy* (San Francisco: Institute for Contemporary Studies Press, 1992); Elinor Ostrom, *Governing the Commons: The Evolution of Institutions for Collective Action* (Cambridge: Cambridge University Press, 1990); and Joep Spiertz and Melanie G. Wiber (eds.), *The Role of Law in Natural Resource Management* (The Hague: VUGA, 1996). A recent and interesting study on land rights in Surinam from the colonial period until today is *The Rights of Indigenous Peoples and Maroons in Suriname* (Copenhagen: International Work Group for Indigenous Affairs, 1999) written by the jurists Ellen-Roos Kambel and Fergus MacKay.

[9] The Chinese discussion on the 'rule by man' is described in Ronald C. Keith, *China's Struggle for the Rule of Law* (New York: St Martin's Press, 1994), p. 12.

[10] A. W. Motion cited in R. Rowton Simpson, *Land Law and Registration* (Cambridge: Cambridge University Press, 1976), p. 220. [11] *Ibid.*, pp. 220–1.

spontaneous and government-supported colonization of land provides an illustration. A major obstacle to the establishment of a cadastre during the Republican era and period of the People's Republic was so-called 'ripe wasteland' (*shuhuang*)—reclaimed and abandoned or untaxed 'black land'. In the regions that had suffered turmoil from armed conflict and natural disasters, peasants were forced to leave their land. When peace and social order were restored, the land was reclaimed, either spontaneously because former or new owners started to till the land or under large government reclamation schemes. However, the reclamation of abandoned land was not without problems. As the Ningxia Province[12] Reclamation Head Office reported: 'reclamation is relatively easy to extend... But procedures [to regain ownership rights] will be extremely difficult. It is feared that this cannot be done overnight.'[13] The recolonized land frequently failed to enter the tax registers, which certainly did not imply that the new settlers and villages did not claim ownership to it.

A general problem with the recognition of customary land tenure is the state's misconception of its nature and frequent denial of its existence. In traditional rural societies, land was generally regarded as belonging commonly to the social group, be it a tribe, village, lineage, or family. In addition, such communal belonging is hard to define in terms of Western (civil) law: the recordable, absolute, and all-inclusive right of ownership.[14] It is for this reason that anthropologists introduced the concept of property as a 'bundle of rights' or the more abstract notion of a 'social relation'.[15]

No better illustration of the conflict between Chinese state and customary law can be imagined than the legal predicament of forest, grassland,

[12] At the time Ningxia Province was one of China's typical frontier regions as it was much larger in size than at present and encompassed great parts of Inner Mongolia (former Suiyuan Province) and Gansu.

[13] A detailed account of land reclamation in a frontier region is given in Peter Ho, 'The Myth of Desertification at China's Northwestern Frontier', *Modern China*, Vol. 26, No. 3, pp. 359–66 (the quotation from the Land Reclamation Head Office is on pp. 362–3). An example of a village that started as a spontaneous settlement by one family is described in Peter Ho, 'China's Rangelands under Stress: A Comparative Study of Pasture Commons in the Ningxia Hui Autonomous Region', *Development and Change*, Vol. 31, No. 2 (March 2000), pp. 385–412, at p. 402. See also Flemming Christiansen, 'New Land in China, 1900–1937: State Intervention and Land Reclamation', *Leeds East Asia Papers*, No. 10 (1992), pp. 61–5.

[14] As Van den Bergh notes: 'Ownership is the supreme right, there can be no rights which would not be contained in ownership. Ownership is abstract: its content cannot be described by enumerating single powers, and none of these powers needs to be legitimized specifically, or related to an acceptable social purpose. Ownership is absolute: apart from what the law expressly forbids the owner may do whatever he likes, he can exclude everybody else from influencing the goods, everybody else is obliged to abstain from breaching his ownership rights, the owner is the supreme ruler over his goods.' Govaert C. J. J. Van den Bergh, 'Property versus Ownership: Some Cursory Notes', in Spiertz and Wiber (eds.), *The Role of Law in Natural Resource Management*, p. 172.

[15] Hann cites Hoebel for a textbook anthropological definition: 'Property, in other words, is not a thing, but a network of social relations that governs the conduct of people with respect to the use and disposition of things.' C. M. Hann, 'The Embeddedness of Property', in C. M. Hann (ed.), *Property Relations: Renewing the Anthropological Tradition* (Cambridge: Cambridge University Press, 1998), p. 4. Rowton Simpson gives an exhaustive listing of the distinctive features of customary tenure. See Rowton Simpson, *Land Law and Registration*, pp. 223–5.

and wasteland ownership created by the 1954 Constitution. Most of China's forest, grassland, and wasteland is located in the frontier zones and inhabited by ethnic minorities that use these natural resources in common under unwritten, customary arrangements. In addition, settler communities have moved into these areas under the instigation of Republican and Communist governments that wanted to colonize the frontier. Under the 1954 Constitution forest, grassland, and wasteland were formally nationalized. Village communities of ethnic minorities and Han settlers now found themselves in national territory without recognition of their common property. The addition of the 1982 Constitution that these natural resources can also be owned by the collective if so stipulated in law did not clarify the issue because it is precisely the formal title to land that these communities lack.[16]

A second strand of thought that runs through this chapter is the argument that the historical legacy captured in the aforementioned three reasons for the villages' lack of control over land plagues China's land administration today. We will see that this legacy becomes obvious in land ownership disputes that are brought to court. Over the years, an increasing number of legal documents have been published, of which Anthony Dicks has remarked that 'few are more interesting than the growing body of reported decisions by courts'.[17] This is exactly the reason why this chapter has opted for a rather unusual methodology in the social sciences basing the analysis mainly on a review of translated legal cases. Detailed court cases might be tedious to read, in particular for the non-legal specialist. Yet I chose to translate these court cases from Chinese into English because they are unique. To date, there are no English translations of court cases that record Chinese land disputes.

China's legal culture is far from what Western jurists value. It is characterized by the fragmentation of law, the dependency of the courts on local government, and the subordination of law to policy: in other words, the distinction between the judicial and administrative powers is blurred.[18]

[16] These problems are noted in 'Remarks on the "Land Administration Law (Revised Draft)" by Relevant Departments, Several Experts and Grassroots Units of Heilongjiang Province', in Renda Fazhi Gongzuo Weiyuanhui (RFGW) (ed.), *Zhonghua Renmin Gongheguo Tudi Guanlifa Shiyi* [An Interpretation of the Land Administration Law of the People's Republic of China] (Beijing: Falü Chubanshe, 1998), p. 352. See also Peter Ho, 'The Clash over State and Collective Property: The Making of the Rangeland Law', *The China Quarterly*, Vol. 161 (March 2000), pp. 245–6.

[17] Anthony R. Dicks, 'Compartmentalized Law and Judicial Restraint: An Inductive View of Some Jurisdictional Barriers to Reform', in Stanley B. Lubman (ed.), *China's Legal Reforms* (Oxford: Oxford University Press, 1996), p. 82.

[18] Dicks (*ibid.*, p. 84) noted that '[o]ne of the results of the diversity of law-making and law-finding authority within the same legal system is excessive fragmentation, not merely of legislative, judicial and administrative jurisdiction, but ultimately of the law itself, with the potential further risk of conflicts of law and jurisdiction'. Clarke remarked that '[i]t is not simply some vague notion of respect for local leaders that makes courts reluctant to go against their wishes. There is a very specific institutional basis: the dependence of local court personnel upon local government at the same level for their jobs and finances.' Donald C. Clarke, 'The Execution of Civil Judgments in China', in Lubman (ed.), *China's Legal Reforms*, p. 71. And Albert Chen observed a violation against Montesquieu's principle on the separation of legislative, executive, and judicial powers: '[T]he principle of the supremacy of state law as against the edicts, policy documents and exhortations of the

It is in this context that the Chinese courts have to perform a complex juggling act with conflicting and often unverifiable claims, intervention by the local government, and a faint hope of rectifying past wrongs. In dealing with land disputes, Chinese judges have to administer justice while working with laws that are intentionally shrouded in institutional ambiguity. Villages and individual farmers have become victims of land theft by higher administrative levels. But dispensing justice is not easy, as considerable investments have been made in the stolen land over time, while new customary land claims have emerged, making it all the more difficult to 'simply' return the land to the original owner. All this we learn from the court cases covered in this chapter.

The cases have been grouped in such a way that each section (although with some overlap) illustrates one of the three reasons why the natural village lacked control over land: the incoherent legal framework and the absence of the rule of law; the lack of land registration; and the problems related to customary tenure. The case descriptions are revised translations drawn from the two-volume *Encyclopedia of the New Land Administration Law* edited by Liu Xinhua, and the compilation of administrative cases released by the Supreme People's Court in 1997.[19] A translator should not revise, but is professionally obliged to render in another language the intended meaning of the source text. However, at this point I was confronted with texts that not only teem with details that are completely irrelevant for those interested in land issues, but also contain a great number of mistakes and inconsistencies. I was therefore obliged to render the original sources in a strongly revised version.

The cases recorded here date from the early 1990s. Since then, two prominent developments have taken place in the legislation on land: (*a*) the proclamation of the 1998 Revised Land Administration Law and (*b*) the replacement of the 1989 State Land Administration's Suggestions on the Assessment of Land Titles (hereafter 'the 1989 Suggestions') with the 1995 Regulations on the Assessment of Land Ownership and Use Rights (hereafter 'the 1995 Regulations').[20] Where necessary, the legal

Chinese Communist Party and the orders, directions and instructions of senior officials has not yet been firmly established in constitutional theory . . . The effect of these factors has been to blur the distinction between law and policy.' Albert Hung-yee Chen, *An Introduction to the Legal System of the People's Republic of China* (Hong Kong: Butterworths, 1992), p. 77.

[19] Xinhua Liu (ed.), *Xin Tudi Guanlifa Quanshu* [Encyclopedia of the New Land Administration Law], Vols I and II (Beijing: Zhongguo Wujia Chubanshe, 1998); Zuigao Renmin Fayuan (ed.), *Renmin Fayuan Anli Xuan—Xingzheng Juan: 1992–1996* [A Selection of Cases from the People's Courts—Volume for Administrative Cases: 1992–1996] (Beijing: Renmin Fayuan Chubanshe, 1997). Legal terms have been translated according to Shutong Yu and Jia Wen (eds.), *Xin Han-Ying Faxue Cidian* [A New Chinese–English Law Dictionary] (Beijing: Falü Chubanshe, 1998). Material covered in the original cases that were irrelevant to the verdict of the court has been omitted or included in footnotes.

[20] See the State Land Administration's 1995 Regulations on the Assessment of Land Ownership and Use Rights, in Jianhong Sun (ed.), *Tudi Quanshu Shiwu Zhinan* [Practical Compass on Land Title] (Beijing: Zhongguo Dadi Chubanshe, 1998), pp. 282–93, and the State Land Administration's 1989 Suggestions on the Assessment of Land Titles in Zhongguo Tudi Guanli Zonglan Bianji Weiyuanhui (ZTGZBW) (ed.), *Zhongguo Tudi Guanli Zonglan* [An Overview of Land Management in China] (Beijing: Falü Chubanshe,

implications of these new rules on the specific case under review will be discussed.[21] Note that the State Land Administration in this chapter refers to the Ministry of Land Resources, which it became in 1998. Despite the legal and socio-economic developments since the early 1990s, it may be assumed that the six cases are typical of land disputes in China, many of which have only recently been brought into the open through petition and lawsuit.[22]

Economic Development Needs No Land Requisition

The law cases in this section[23] illustrate two points. First, under collectivism the 'theft of land' was possible because the legal framework was incomplete and inconsistent. In the first lawsuit this even leads the local government to attempt to deny the possibility of land ownership by the natural village altogether. In the next case, the ambiguity in the legal framework causes the court to resort to regulations of uncertain legal status, which stipulate issues not yet resolved at the national level. Second, land requisition from the village during the collective period was effected by administrative rather than legal measures. For purposes of economic development, land from the natural village could be easily expropriated by the commune and higher administrative levels. In addition, appropriate compensation for economic loss was seldom given.

To meet the need for water, Shiqiao Commune in Hubei Province built a small water reservoir in 1959, which was expanded one year later. In 1963, the party branch of the Provincial Bureau of Water Conservancy issued a directive ordering the transfer of the reservoir's ownership and capital assets to the county. De facto, the reservoir and its land became state property. In 1965, the Bureau of Water Conservancy planned another expansion of the reservoir and requested land from the county. Through oral communication the head of Xiangyang County determined that 210mu of land of the Third Villagers' Group of Hongdao Administrative Village should be requisitioned. To date, none of the formalities for land requisition has been fulfilled.

The requisition resulted in a series of conflicts between the villagers' group and the state water reservoir. In March 1993 the county government

1992), pp. 68–71. The terms 'tudi quanshu' and 'tudi suoyouquan' have been respectively translated as 'land title' and 'land ownership'. Note that 'title' refers to the formal document with which, within a given legal system, certain rights can be proven to a tract of land. The title is not necessarily issued by the state; for example, there are also customary titles issued by native peoples. Yet the general problem for native peoples is that they claim rights to land without title.

[21] References in the Chinese sources to the 1989 Administrative Litigation Law have been omitted out. These pertain to the procedures of litigation and are irrelevant for our analysis that focuses on land administrative laws and regulations.

[22] According to Li and O'Brien, formal petitions from the rural populace have increased dramatically over the past ten years. See Lianjiang J. Li and Kevin J. O'Brien, 'Villager and Popular Resistance in Contemporary China', *Modern China*, Vol. 22, No. 1 (1996), pp. 28–61.

[23] Cases drawn from Zuigao Renmin Fayuan (ed.), Cases from the People's Courts, pp. 334–40 (second case) and 341–7 (first case).

issued a document which marked the land as a 'disputed area'. This strengthened the villagers' group in its conviction that the land was indeed its property, and it started to petition the authorities. A month later the county bluntly ruled that the land was state-owned according to the 1989 Suggestions. In a lawsuit the villagers' group claimed that the county ruling was illegal and should be annulled. The county requested that the plaintiff's claim be dismissed 'to safeguard the correct enforcement of the state's laws'.[24] Of specific interest is the county's claims that the villagers' group *by law* could not enjoy collective ownership and thus was not entitled to act as a legal person, and that such a role belonged to the administrative village under which jurisdiction the villagers' group falls.

The court, however, decided that the villagers' group *could* own land. This decision was based on the State Land Administration's interpretation of article 8 of the 1986 Land Administration Law: 'The land originally owned by the team belongs to the farmers' collective of the agricultural collective economic organization of the corresponding villagers' group.' The court read this interpretation as meaning that 'there are two kinds of collective land ownership: ownership by the villagers' committee *and* ownership by the villagers' group' (emphasis added).[25] The court nullified the county's ruling that the disputed land was state-owned, because the 1989 Suggestions had not been appropriately used. Article 8 of the 1989 Suggestions stipulates that the collective's land is state-owned if it had been used by state institutions before the proclamation of the 1962 Sixty Articles and not so far returned. But as the disputed plot was appropriated in 1963, this rule did not apply. Article 8 also stipulates that the collective's land is state-owned if it was used between 1962 and 1982 and a land transfer agreement signed or formal approval obtained by the county government.[26] However, the county head had given only an oral commitment, while no requisition procedures had been followed. Therefore, the court decided that the land should be returned to the villagers' group.

A second case, related to the first, concerns a dispute between a commune and three brigades. In 1975 Shifo Commune in Shandong expropriated a

[24] Cases drawn from Zuigao Renmin Fayuan (ed.), Cases from the People's Courts, p. 343.
[25] *Ibid.*, p. 344.
[26] The original text of article 8 reads: 'If before the proclamation of the Work Regulations for the Rural People's Communes in September 1962 (hereafter: Sixty Articles), state institutions, urban collective institutions, and collective farms of overseas Chinese, used land originally owned by the farmers' collective (including individual land prior to cooperativization), which has not been returned to the farmers' collective in the period after the proclamation of the Sixty Articles until the present, it is state-owned. If after the proclamation of the Sixty Articles in September 1962 until the proclamation of the Regulations for the Requisitioning of Land for State Construction in May 1982, state institutions and urban collective institutions used land originally owned by the farmers' collective, it is state-owned under one of the following conditions: 1) after an agreement or any other relevant document has been signed for the transfer of land; 2) if it has been used after approval from the county people's government; 3) if compensation or settlement of labour force has taken place; 4) if it has been donated by the farmers' collective; 5) if the farmers' collective enterprise has become state-owned. In all other cases, the farmers' collective land . . . must be returned to the farmers' collective or the then current procedures for the compensation of land requisition must be followed.' See article 8, Suggestions on the Assessment of Land Titles, in ZTGZBW (ed.), Overview of Land Management in China, p. 69.

total of 170mu from Xulou, Weihai, and Qianchenhai Brigades to set up a pig farm. Typically, no land requisition procedures had been followed. Since 1978 the three brigades had petitioned the commune authorities to return the land and compensate them for financial losses. An agreement was signed between the commune and the brigades in 1980. The agreement stipulated how much land had been requisitioned and at what price. It also determined that the land ownership belonged to the pig farm, but would be sold back to the brigades at the purchase price if the farm were to be closed down. The brigades were paid partly in cash and partly in kind. With the demise of Shifo Commune and subsequent change to a township in 1983, the pig farm was also closed. From then on, the land was used for forestry. In 1990 the trees were felled and one-third of the land was leased for agriculture to farmers from Hanzhuang village for a period of thirty-five years. Immediately, disputes erupted between the township and the three administrative villages. The county government intervened on several occasions. In 1988 and 1991 directives had been issued stating that the land was owned by the township (*gui xiang suoyou*). In the end, the villages filed a case against the township and county governments.

The villages claimed that the land was theirs because the commune had requisitioned the land without their consent and the land use had been changed, whereas the 1980 agreement stipulated that the ownership was to be sold back if the farm was closed down. The county invoked the 1989 Suggestions to prove that the land belonged to the township. According to these regulations, a change in the level of collective land ownership is possible for the establishment of enterprises (however, at the national level there is no agreement over this issue). For land in use between 1962 and 1982 this is effected if an agreement has been signed (excluding land lease); approval from the county, township, and village authorities has been obtained; or the ownership structure of the user has changed (article 14).[27] As an agreement had been signed and compensation paid, the land ownership should belong to the township, the county claimed. The township authorities added that land use had not changed at all: its former forestry activities were geared to animal husbandry, while the farm had not been dissolved: the director, the buildings, and the pigsties were still there.

[27] The original text of article 14 reads: 'If before the proclamation of the Sixty Articles, land is in use by entrepreneurial units of the township (town) or village, it is owned by the farmers' collective of the respective township (town) or village. If it is used after the proclamation of the Sixty Articles in September 1962 until the proclamation of the State Council's Administrative Regulations on Town and Village Construction Land in September 1982, it is owned by the farmers' collective of the respective township (town) or village under one of the following conditions: 1) after an agreement has been signed for the use of land (not including lease); 2) if it has been approved by the county, township (commune) and village (brigade), and an appropriate land adjustment or compensation has been given; 3) if the nature of the entrepreneurial unit of the township (town) and village has been lawfully altered. If entrepreneurial units of the township (town) and village have occupied land with other than aforementioned means, or used the aforementioned means but presently use the land irrationally, for example, leaving land idle, transferring land, and so forth, it must be entirely or partly returned to the original farmers' collective of the village or township, or be handled according to relevant regulations.' See Suggestions on the Question of the Assessment of Land Titles, in ZTGZBW (ed.), Overview of Land Management in China, pp. 69–70.

Also, the lease for agriculture was permitted, the township stated, as it owned the land.

The county court yielded to pressure from the local government and ruled that the disputed land belonged to the township. The villages appealed to the intermediate court of Liucheng Prefecture. The intermediate court annulled the verdict of the lower court and decided that the ownership of the disputed land should be allocated to the three villages. This decision was taken on three grounds: (*a*) the three villages' land had been appropriated without formal approval and the correct procedures being followed; (*b*) land use had been changed with the demise of the farm and the lease for agriculture; and (*c*) the law had been inappropriately applied to sustain the 1988 and 1991 county directives that vested land ownership in the township.

The legal twilight zone of the past has created the courts' present dilemmas. A major problem is the nature of collective ownership. As explained in Chapter 1, collective ownership is intentionally left undefined in law because of the central government's fear of widespread social conflict: 'intentional institutional ambiguity'. The land ownership of the team (natural village) has therefore been in limbo since the start of the economic reforms. In particular, in the urbanized, coastal regions, legal indeterminacy is used to deny land ownership by the natural village. For example, during the revision process of the 1998 Land Administration Law, Zhejiang Province suggested altering the land tenure structure stipulated in the Sixty Articles and abolishing the natural village's land ownership.[28]

It is the old debate over the level of collective land ownership that also divided the central leadership during the early 1960s: should land ownership be granted to the lowest collective level or to the next highest level? Zhejiang Province reasoned that collective ownership by a higher level would facilitate urban and spatial planning. However, the village would then be completely denied the possibility of contesting forced land requisitions. With the current boom in land prices and frenzy of real estate development, there is a significant danger that the legal rights of the natural village and its inhabitants will be violated if the natural village is not vested with the authority to represent collective ownership. For these reasons, the central government has called for the creation of new institutions, among them a rural land registry.

Against this backdrop, the first case is nothing less than a landmark. We see that Xiangyang County uses the ambiguity in the law to delegitimize the Third Villagers' Group's claim to be the legal owner of land. For this reason, it is important that the court interprets the law as meaning that the villagers' group *can* enjoy ownership to land, not merely the right to its use and management. If Xiangyang County had eventually brought the case to the Supreme People's Court, it would have become a crucial test of the legal and political limits of China's land tenure. Yet, in the light of the legislative restraint exercised by the central government on this

[28] 'Remarks on the "Land Administration Law (Revised Draft)" by Relevant Units and Personnel of Zhejiang Province', in RFGW (ed.), An Interpretation of the Land Administration Law, p. 366.

issue, one wonders whether the present land rights system is ready for such a test.

Legal rules are lacking also in areas other than ownership. As a result, courts have no option but to rely on administrative measures of unclear legal status. This problem arises in the second case. The main question here is whether the land appropriation from the three villages by Shifo Commune can count as an act of land requisition. According to Chinese law, land is requisitioned for purposes of *state* construction whereby collective land ownership is turned into state ownership. In fact, under the past *and* current legal framework this is also the sole condition under which the nature of collective ownership can be changed. In other words, there are no legal rules under which the various collective levels can transfer ownership of land.[29] For this reason, the 'land requisition' by the commune was illegal. Furthermore, the 1980 agreement whereby land ownership would be sold back to the original owners in case the enterprise was dissolved was also unlawful, as it envisaged *a sale of encumbered land ownership*.[30] Since its 1988 revision, the Constitution allows only the non-commercial transfer of the use right to rural land, although Chinese jurists and politicians expect that the free sale (and mortgage) of rural *use rights* will at some stage also be incorporated in law. Although this issue is still hotly debated, the latest amendment to the Land Administration Law is silent about it. This is problematic given that the appropriation of land for township and village enterprises is widespread in rural China. The court cannot but resort to interpreting administrative regulations issued by the executive branch of the state—the 1989 Suggestions. However, as these have not been reviewed, debated, or enacted as law by the NPC, or issued by the State Council as binding rules for implementation (*shishi tiaoli*), nobody knows their exact legal implications.[31] In fact, the rules applied here do not even have the status of an administrative regulation (*guizhang*) but are merely 'suggestions'.

No Cadastre, a Disaster!

The cases in this section[32] illustrate the issues related to China's lack of a land registry, or 'cadastre'. The attentive reader will note that the cases discussed also concern customary tenure. The customary rights problem,

[29] See '1958 Measures on Land Requisition for State Construction'; '1982 Administrative Regulations for Land used for Building Construction in Villages and Towns'; and the '1982 Regulations on Land Requisition for State Construction', in Xiang (ed.), Manual for the Assessment of Land Title, pp. 108–28.

[30] About this, a Chinese jurist remarked that, at the time of the transfer, the Sixty Articles were still valid, which stipulated: 'The land owned by the production team . . . can by no means be rented or sold' (article 21). See Liu (ed.), Encyclopedia of the New Land Administration Law, Vol. I, p. 900 (in which this case is also described).

[31] According to Dicks, the administrative regulations or guizhang are 'falling short of the status of "law" '. Dicks, 'Compartmentalized Law and Judicial Restraint', in Lubman (ed.), *China's Legal Reforms*, p. 106.

[32] Case drawn from Liu (ed.), Encyclopedia of the New Land Administration Law, Vol. I, pp. 909–13 (second case) and 990–2 (first case). In the first case, the names of the villages and county have not been given in the original Chinese source. For this reason, they are referred to as X and Y Villages, and Z County.

however, is most apparent in the clash between state and collective property. The two cases here relate to disputes between rural collectives. For this reason, this section limits the discussion to the registration of land titles. An effective and efficient land policy needs ownership to be clarified and collective land registered. As Rowton Simpson remarked:

> Land records . . . are of great concern to all governments. The framing of land policy, and its execution, may in large measure depend on the effectiveness of 'land registration', as we can conveniently call the making and keeping of these records.[33]

Yet land registration should not be an end in itself. It is an instrument that is an integral part of sound land administration, but it cannot automatically produce rational land use and development. For land registration to be effective it should be placed in the wider context of the strengthening of state institutions, legal and political reform, and the establishment of a well-functioning land market. However, land registration in China has never been completed because of the intentional actions by the central state to uphold 'institutional ambiguity', as shown in Chapter 1. The lack of land title registration poses great problems for the judiciary when it has to adjudicate in land disputes, as the two cases recorded below demonstrate.

In 1992, X Village filed a lawsuit against Y Village in a dispute over 257mu of land located on the Daozhai Mountains between the two villages. In Republican times, this land was used as a military depot by the Nationalist army. Before collectivization X Village used this land for marginal activities, but it became the common property of both villages during the 1950s. In 1966 the prefecture wished to construct a silk farm on the common land. A requisition certificate was signed between Y Village and the silk farm, but none with X Village because no agreement could be reached. Some time later, X Village consented to the expropriation, for which it received a financial compensation of 1,000 RMB. In 1980 the county government planned a new county capital and requisitioned land, including that of the silk farm. The county informed the two villages of the forthcoming expropriation, which they understood as renewed requisition—in other words, the villagers believed they were still the owners of the tract. The villages appealed to the county to recognize their ownership and grant them appropriate compensation. The county ignored the requests and proceeded with the construction, whereupon a group of thirty farmers from Y Village demolished the new buildings. After two years of conflict, the county appointed an investigation team, which concluded that the land had been requisitioned in 1966 with the agreement of both villages. Therefore, they were not entitled to dispute the ownership of the area or to demand compensation.

But Y Village was not that easily put off, and it kept appealing to the authorities. In 1985 the county issued a notice stating that the land rights of the disputed plot had always been unclear. Therefore, the land should be divided equally between the two villages and once more requisitioned against compensation. The conflict between the villages and the county

[33] Rowton Simpson, *Land Law and Registration*, p. 3.

then turned into a boundary dispute between the two villages. In court, X Village claimed ownership to the land on the basis of the texts of two stone stelae (one from the Kangxi period and another engraved in 1922). Y Village argued that even before liberation it had used the land for animal husbandry, agriculture, and brick production. The court adopted the county's 1985 notice and ruled that the land was commonly owned by X and Y Villages because written land titles were lacking, meaning that the land had to be equally divided among the two villages and re-requisitioned. X Village appealed to the prefectural court, which ruled that, by recognizing the villages' dual ownership to the disputed land, the county had illegally returned the land to the original owners, when in fact it was state-owned. According to the 1986 Land Administration Law the 'collective land that is requisitioned by the state for construction is owned by the state; the unit that uses the land [in this case the silk farm] only enjoys the right to use'.[34] Therefore, the county's land appropriation of the land from the silk farm was a matter of changing use rights, not ownership (an issue we encountered in the previous section). The villages' claims to ownership and compensation were declared unfounded.

The following case is a fascinating account of the struggle over rights to newly formed land. The case is so interesting because, to my knowledge, it is the first documented case on riparian rights in China. What are riparian rights? Suppose a tract of land borders a river or lake and the title mentions the body of water as part of the boundary. The owner may then claim so-called riparian rights. These usually include the use of the water for boating, docking, fishing, and swimming. As Frank Emerson Clark wrote in his authoritative 1939 *Fundamentals of Law for Surveyors*: 'Once a tract of land acquires riparian rights, any land that is added to the shore line becomes a part of the tract.'[35] However, when the land is not registered, as is the case in China, then 'water bodies [can] make especially troublesome boundaries' because they 'shift as streams meander, lake levels fluctuate, and coasts erode'.[36]

Bolin and Xiaqu are two villages located on the northern bank of the Weihe River and south to the Shanghai-Lanzhou railroad in Gansu Province. Along the river there used to be a stretch of common land that was jointly cultivated by farmers from the two villages. After a big flood in 1954[37] this land was submerged. During the Four Fixes Movement in 1962 Bolin and Xiaqu exchanged two plots of land of equal size situated north of the railway track. The boundary between the plots was the 305 landmark east of the Jiashigou Canal. As the land south of the rail had been washed away by the flood, nothing was agreed on its boundaries. In 1972 Xiaqu built a dam upstream. The dam diverted the course of the Weihe River

[34] Article 24 of the 1986 Land Administration Law in Nongyebu Zhengce Tigai Faguisi (ed.), *Nongyefa Quanshu* [Encyclopedia of Agricultural Laws] (Beijing: Zhongguo Nongye Chubanshe, 1994), p. 557.

[35] Frank Emerson Clark cited in Mark Monmonnier, *Drawing the Line: Tales of Maps and Cartocontroversy* (New York: Henry Holt and Company, 1996), p. 123.

[36] *Ibid.*, p. 126.

[37] The original text states 1984, but the text is corrupt as it later talks about 1954. From the context it is also clear that the year 1954 is meant here.

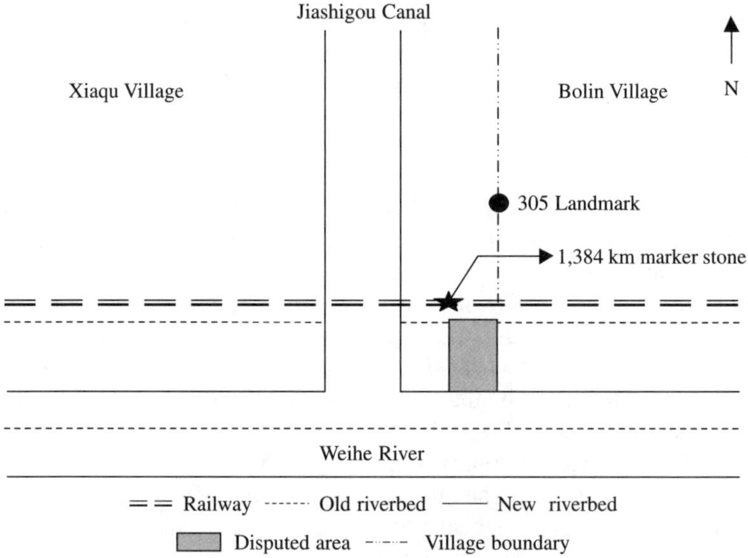

Figure 3: **Schematic map of a dispute over riparian rights.**
Source: Drawn by Zhao Heng.

southwards and a stretch of wasteland surfaced on its northern bank. Xiaqu claimed that the boundary of this land should follow the boundary north of the railroad: the 305 landmark east of the Jiashigou Canal. Bolin maintained that the boundary should be the 1,384km marker stone of the railroad. Neither of the two villages could furnish any written evidence to support its claims (see Fig. 3).

In 1990 Xiaqu Village filed an administrative litigation with the Beidao County government. A year later, the county pronounced: 'Through examination of maps of land requisition for the Shanghai-Lanzhou railroad before the founding of the People's Republic and through on-site investigation, it is confirmed that the boundary between the two villages at the time of the Four Fixes Movement ran from Jiashigou to the north of the railroad . . .'[38] For this reason, the county decided that the boundary north of the railway would also apply to the new land south of the railway. The land east of the 305 landmark would be allocated to Bolin, the land west of it to Xiaqu.

Bolin did not submit and took the case to the county court. Bolin claimed that the boundary laid down in documents from the Republican period was not a fair standard for demarcation:

> The Weihe River is not a stream that can be fixed to its river bed. Some years it flows southwards, some years northwards, flooding and damaging arable land. As early as during Land Reform, cooperativization and collectivization, this tract was foreland, yet river bed during floods. . . . [U]sing maps . . . that date from before the founding of the PRC cannot explain the natural changes of thirty years.[39]

[38] Liu (ed.), Encyclopedia of the New Land Administration Law, Vol. I, p. 910.
[39] *Ibid.*, p. 911.

The court confirmed the evidence put forward by Bolin Village that 'before 1954 there was land south to the railroad and east of the 1,384 kilometer marker stone of the Shanghai-Lanzhou railroad, which was commonly tilled by Xiaqu and Bolin Villages'. But the court also stated that 'the title to this disputed land has never been determined since Land Reform or the Four Fixes Movement in 1962'.[40] The verdict of the Beidao government, which determined that both villages held title to the land, was annulled and the county was ordered to pay the legal costs.

In both cases, the local government attempted to find a fair solution to land disputes arising from long-term use without clear ownership. In the first case, the county proposed to reverse the unclear past requisition through renewed requisition with equal financial compensation for each village. However, this action only led to a new dispute over the boundaries between the villages. Several issues were at stake. First, as the prefectural court also noted, the silk farm was by law not entitled to act as a legal person because it enjoyed only the use right to land and not ownership. The requisition should have been handled by the prefecture as the representative of the state. Second, after requisition the change in land titles from collective to state ownership should have been registered with the county, as the then current regulations also determined.[41] Third, it goes without saying that this conflict could have been avoided if land titles had existed from the start. In a case where the plaintiff's evidence consisted of only stone stelae without detailed boundary descriptions and maps, while the defendant merely resorted to oral history, the county's ruling was probably the best option.

In the second case too the local government was attempting a Solomon's judgement. Yet this conflict was far more complex than the first: the disputed land alternately was submerged and resurfaced; and it was commonly tilled by two villages, neither of which could prove title. As Monmonnier rightly remarks: 'Riparian principles sometimes seem grossly unfair, especially when a river's arbitrary wandering creates big winners and big losers.'[42] In this sense, the current case was also a legal test case; its complexity brutally exposed the legal shortcomings over newly formed land that must be addressed to safeguard the interests of the state, the collective, and the individual.

The first question in this case is: who holds the ownership to land that accrues from shifting river flows? Some Chinese jurists argue that it should be the state, not the collective.[43] They invoke two legal rules. According to the 1950 Land Reform Law, 'the land for protective water storage and dykes on both sides of rivers . . . may not be allocated' (article 26). In the same vein, the 1988 Administrative Regulations on Rivers stipulate for flood control that 'the land added for the realignment and consolidation of

[40] Liu (ed.), Encyclopedia of the New Land Administration Law, Vol. I, p. 912.
[41] Article 14 of the 1958 Regulations on Land Requisition for State Construction, in Xiang (ed.), Manual for the Assessment of Land Title, p. 111.
[42] Monmonnier, *Drawing the Line*, p. 124.
[43] Liu (ed.), Encyclopedia of the New Land Administration Law, Vol. I, p. 913.

rivers is state-owned' (article 18).[44] On closer inspection, these legal rules do not apply, as they concern land that has been specifically designated or added for water conservancy. The tract disputed by Bolin and Xiaqu was land that was naturally formed through a change in the river's course. And this is a typical case of riparian rights: a void in China's present legal system.[45] One of the solutions adopted by courts in the United States is to label such radical shifts 'avulsion'. Thus, property and political boundaries can be left intact wherever possible.[46]

The second fundamental problem here is the lack of written evidence that could be used as a standard in adjudication. For its judgement, Beidao County could rely only on maps from the Republican era. And here we chance upon a critical issue in China's land registration, because the use of historical documents to prove title is not uncontested. As the commentary on this case stated: 'The Beidao government used land material of the old system [society] as evidence to arbitrate in a land dispute forty years after liberation. We feel that a verdict on such a basis is wrong.'[47] According to law, the legal basis for the assessment of land titles is Land Reform and the Four Fixes Movement, as 'all land deeds before Land Reform are invalid'.[48] In addition, the 1989 Suggestions stipulate that 'urban land and land that has not been allocated to farmers during Land Reform through the issue of a land deed, including arable land, forest, waters, waste mountains and sandy beaches, and so forth, are state-owned'.[49] This regulation has remained unchanged in the successor of the 1989 Suggestions, namely, the State Land Administration's 1995 Regulations on the Assessment of Land Ownership and Use Rights.[50]

There are great difficulties in taking land deeds issued during Land Reform and the Four Fixes Movement as the norm for collective ownership today. The registration of land titles during Land Reform was fragmentary, whereas many such titles were lost over time. Moreover, during Land Reform the land was generally distributed to individual farm

[44] See article 26, 1950 Land Reform Law, in Sun (ed.), Practical Compass on Land Titles, p. 110; and article 18, 1988 Administrative Regulations on Rivers of the PRC, in Xiang (ed.), Manual for the Assessment of Land Title, p. 136.

[45] In Qing times this was more clearly stipulated, as the government stipulated time and again that newly emerged land along rivers, creeks, and the coast was state property. See also Liu Jinzao, *Qingchao Xuwenxian Tongkao* [A Continued Encyclopedia of Documents of the Qing dynasty] (Shanghai: Shanghai Commercial Press, 1936 reprint of 1921 edition), p. 1904. With thanks to Eduard Vermeer.

[46] A typical dispute over riparian rights occurs when a river forms the boundary between two plots. The centre line or the line of the fastest current is then regarded as the theoretical boundary. But as long as the river does not change its course there is little incentive to determine the exact dividing line, and when it does disputes have already erupted. In our case, the situation is different as the land emerged between two villages on the same side of the river. Monmonnier, *Drawing the Line*, p. 128.

[47] Liu (ed.), Encyclopedia of the New Land Administration Law, Vol. I, p. 913.

[48] See article 30, 1950 Land Reform Law, in Sun (ed.), Practical Compass on Land Titles, p. 111.

[49] Article 1, Suggestions on the Question of the Assessment of Land Titles, in ZTGZBW (ed.), Overview of Land Management in China, p. 69.

[50] See article 4 of the State Land Administration's 1995 Regulations on the Assessment of Land Ownership and Use Rights, in Sun (ed.), Practical Compass on Land Titles, p. 282.

households and not the village as a whole. All privately owned rural land was transferred—on a 'voluntary' basis—to the collective when the Higher Agricultural Production Cooperatives were set up in 1956.[51] The Four Fixes Movement should have led to the registration of the production team as the basic owner of land as the Sixty Articles stipulated.

However, as the recorded cases demonstrate, systematic land registration was the exception rather than the rule. The illegal requisition of village land by higher administrative levels led to further ambiguity over the rightful ownership to collective land. For these reasons, the state called for the first nationwide registration of collective land in 1984 which, due to the minefield it uncovered, halted at the level that mattered most: the natural village. It is certain that, during the establishment of a national cadastre, China cannot avoid taking into account the historical claims that predate Land Reform and the Four Fixes Movement. Claims by customary tenure, discussed in the following section, are even more complicated.

Customary Rights, Silent Rights?

The terms 'customary rights'[52] or 'traditional land tenure' invoke a dim and distant past—something that has existed for so long that 'the memory of man runneth not to the contrary'.[53] Yet the two cases reviewed here show that entitlements do not necessarily have to date back centuries ago to be called 'customary', but might equally have evolved over only a few decades. Moreover, customary entitlements are—in the Chinese context—often associated with the rights of ethnic minorities, such as the forest rights of mountain tribes in Yunnan or the traditional grazing arrangements of Mongols and Kazakhs—but again, not necessarily so. The cases demonstrate that customary rights may be defined as the rights that have evolved at the grass roots in the absence of or alongside state law. In the near future, China will encounter great difficulties in assessing customary land titles because of their unwritten nature. The challenge to the Chinese state is to grant a fair recognition of such claims that can satisfy both state and collective interests rather than simply to suppress them.

The following case was not decided in court but arbitrated by the Shaanxi Provincial Bureau of Land Administration. In 1984, Beiying Village occupied 361mu of steppe from a farm of the Air Force Telecommunication College. The village claimed this land was ancestral steppe (*zuyi tandi*).[54] According to the village authorities, farmers had tilled and afforested the land in the past, as recognized in a land permit issued during Land Reform. In addition, the village furnished land tax statistics and a clarifying map drafted by the Goutai Administrative Region in 1951

[51] Article 13, Exemplary Regulations on the Higher Agricultural Production Cooperatives, in *ibid.*, p. 131.

[52] First case drawn from Liu (ed.), Encyclopedia of the New Land Administration Law, Vol. I, pp. 1039–41. Second case drawn from Zuigao Renmin Fayuan (ed.), Cases from the People's Courts, pp. 450–4.

[53] A. W. Motion, cited in Rowton Simpson, *Land Law and Registration*, p. 220.

[54] Literally 'sandy land inherited from the ancestors'. The term *tandi* literally means 'sandy land' but is best translated as 'steppe' or 'sandy waste'.

(by which Beiying Village was administered at the time). The material demonstrated that Beiying Village paid tax for over 500mu of steppe, which included the disputed land. Lastly, the village referred to a map of the Yellow River Water Conservancy Committee that showed the disputed plot falling within the jurisdiction of Xianyang and not Xi'an City, to which the Air Force's farm belonged. The farm, on the other hand, claimed that the disputed tract had always been public land (*gongdi*) and was commonly used by the Shaanxi Province financial, forestry, and educational departments. In 1951 the land was transferred to the farm for use, with the consent of the Shaanxi Provincial Bureau of Agriculture. The transfer of the use right was formally approved by the Shaanxi and Xi'an Party Committees in 1965. In addition, the farm's archives produced a series of land use maps dating from 1954, 1960, 1963, and 1964 which assessed the boundaries of the farm. The maps were drafted by the Agricultural Surveyor Team of the Shaanxi Bureau of Agriculture.

The Shaanxi Bureau of Land Administration ruled that the disputed land was state-owned, while the Air Force's farm held the use right. Beiying Village had to be penalized for the illegal occupation of land. But, in view of the village's considerable investments in afforestation, no redress was imposed. Instead, the Air Force's farm had to pay 20,000 RMB for the fruit trees, which it would then own. The verdict was based on the following considerations: (*a*) the land permit issued during Land Reform, which the Beiying village authorities mentioned, was not found in the archives; (*b*) the land tax statistics and accompanying map did not indicate whether the disputed tract was part of the land for which tax was due; nor was it clear whether the village paid taxes for land owned or leased; (*c*) since the map of the Yellow River Water Conservancy Committee was drafted for the construction of the Sanmen Gorges Reservoir and not for the assessment of administrative boundaries, it could not be admitted as evidence; and (*d*) the farm's claim that the use rights were formally transferred in 1965 could be corroborated.

The second case, too, concerns a land dispute between a village and a state institution. On the western side of Mount Zechongqiao in Liuzhou City (Guangxi Province) lies a forest of around 550mu that is contested by the Sanmenjiang State Forest Farm and Niucheping Village of Liudong Township. No title of the land has been assessed since Land Reform. Under the instigation of the township head and team leader, villagers sowed pine seeds on the mountain hill in 1953 and planted tree saplings the following year. In 1955 a part of the land was used by the villagers for shifting cultivation. In that same year, workers of the state forest farm planted fir trees on the land. The trees were carefully maintained and protected by villagers and foresters. In 1960, the East-is-Red Commune (later Liudong Township) carried out a general survey of the afforested land and had it registered as property of Niucheping Brigade.[55] Three years

[55] The original text speaks of Liudong Brigade and Niucheping Team. However, the text later mentions Niucheping as a brigade that administers the fourth, sixth, and seventh production teams. It is likely that after the Great Leap Forward the East-is-Red Commune was decreased in size. That is the reason why Liudong Brigade became a commune and

later, after the proclamation of the Sixty Articles, Niucheping Brigade granted ownership of the forest to the fourth, sixth, and seventh production teams (*huafen gei xiaodui suoyou*).[56] During the same period the state forest farm strengthened its claims to the land. In response to regulations of the provincial forest bureau, the disputed plot was included in the farm's regional planning of 1954 and 1963. In addition, the Forest Mapping and Survey Institute drew maps of the area in 1973 and 1984.

Towards the late 1970s, the trees had matured and conflicts erupted over the mountain forest. For years the conflict lingered on despite repeated mediation by the Liuzhou City Government. In 1991 the city authorities issued a verdict that assigned half of the tract to Niucheping Village and the other half to the state, while the use rights were granted to the state forest farm. The Sanmenjiang State Forest Farm did not accept the verdict and filed a suit against the city government. The farm claimed that peasants from Niucheping had illegally felled trees on the land since the end of the 1970s. Not only was the plot included in the farm's regional planning, but the farm was still formally responsible for forest protection on Mount Zechongqiao. On these grounds, the Sanmenjiang Forest Farm contested the 1991 verdict of Liuzhou City that attempted to appease both the village and the forest farm by dividing the land equally between them. The defendant, the Liuzhou City government, retorted that the title to the forest had never been assessed, although the land was used and managed by both claimants. Because the claimants could not furnish any evidence to prove title, the city government requested the court to sustain its verdict to 'prevent a continuation and worsening of the conflict'.[57]

The court judged that both the 1960 land title registration of Niucheping and the forest farm's 1954 and 1963 regional planning were illegal because they had not been approved by the county government and relevant departments. For this reason, the Liuzhou City verdict was sustained by the court and deemed 'factually clear, and [supported by] a correct use of the laws and legal procedures'.[58] A later appeal to the higher court by the village and the state forest farm was dismissed.

The typical land resources claimed by customary right include forest, grassland, and wasteland—which is not say that there are no customary claims on agricultural land.[59] The greater part of these resources are located in the frontier zones and inhabited by ethnic minorities that use the resources in common under customary regulations. Moreover, in those areas traditionally occupied or colonized over time by Han peasants, forest, grassland, and wasteland are generally common property, owned and used by the village community.[60] With the proclamation of the 1954

Niucheping became a brigade under its jurisdiction. See Zuigao Renmin Fayuan (ed.), Cases from the People's Courts, p. 452.

[56] *Ibid.*, p. 452. [57] *Ibid.*, p. 452. [58] *Ibid.*, p. 454.

[59] For examples of customary rights on agricultural land in Kenya and Indonesia, see H. W. J. Sonius, *Introduction to Aspects of Customary Land Law in Africa: As Compared with Some Indonesian Aspects* (Leiden: Universitaire Pers, 1963), pp. 14, 32; M. de Muinck, 'Onteigening in de Nederlandsche Koloniën' ['Requisition in the Dutch Colonies'] (Groningen: PhD Dissertation, 1911), p. 5.

[60] One needs to think only of the colonization of state forest reserves in former Manchuria by rural collectives. An instance of a recently developed common property of

Constitution, forest, grassland, and wasteland were formally nationalized, unless collective ownership could be proven, which implied that the burden of proof lay with the collective. The opposite applies to rural land, which is considered collective unless state ownership can be proven. This principle forms the legal basis for state and collective ownership and has been enshrined in the 1954 Constitution and its amendments to date.[61]

The administrative measures proclaimed by the State Land Administration take the Constitution's basic principle of legal proof for state and collective ownership one step further. The 1989 Suggestions and the 1995 Regulations stipulate that land that has not been *legally* (that is, according to the 1950 Land Reform Law and the Sixty Articles) allocated to farmers during Land Reform and the Four Fixes Movement is state-owned.[62] The problem is that the common property aspect of customary entitlements is frequently regarded by the state as 'nobody's property'. Therefore, during Land Reform and the Four Fixes Movement titles to forest, grassland and wasteland were only rarely issued to farmers and collectives, especially as the (local) state considered these natural resources national property since 1954. In other words, from the viewpoint of the state, forest, grassland, and wasteland are regarded as state-owned unless otherwise proven. From the viewpoint of Chinese villages, this land is owned by the community, which faces the impossible task of proving that decades of land use is sufficient to establish a 'customary right'. The two cases in this section present the issue in all its starkness.

Both Beiying and Niucheping Villages claim wasteland on the basis of land use before Land Reform. The steppe and forest farms—as state representatives responsible for the management and development of national resources—challenge the villages' claim and maintain that the disputed area is state-owned. Exactly how this land has become state-owned is unclear, because no official land requisition has been carried out. It is certain, however, that state institutions have often invested considerable human and financial resources in land development. So simply reinstating the village's ownership of land that is claimed by oral history is not an option. But again, a glance at the 1989 Suggestions and 1995 Regulations shows how potentially explosive the situation is. The stipulation that land is state-owned unless registered as collective during Land Reform and the Four Fixes Movement provides the state with a powerful instrument to dismiss all customary land claims. If this rule were to be rigorously applied it would become a seed-bed for ongoing social conflict. It is no surprise that the newly Revised Land Administration Law has

forest is described by Emily T. Yeh, 'Forest Claims, Conflicts and Commodification: The Political Ecology of Tibetan Mushroom-Harvesting Villages in Yunnan Province', *The China Quarterly*, Vol. 161 (March 2000), pp. 264–78.

[61] A chronological listing of the Constitution's stipulations on natural resources is given in Wenzheng Shi, *Caoyuan yu Caoye de Fazhi Jianshe Yanjiu* [Research of the Construction of a Judicial System for Rangeland and Pastoralism] (Hohhot: Neimenggu Daxue Chubanshe, 1996), pp. 37–8.

[62] Article 1 of the State Land Administration's 1989 Suggestions on the Assessment of Land Titles and the State Land Administration's 1995 Regulations on the Assessment of Land Ownership and Use Rights. Xiang (ed.), Manual for the Assessment of Land Title, pp. 312, 351.

shrouded this issue in vagueness rather than adopting the stipulations of the 1995 Regulations.

In dealing with customary entitlements, the judiciary and the executive walk a fine line between social justice and safeguarding the state's interests. The solutions adopted by the courts and local governments in the two cases described above surely refrain from using the extreme measures available under the 1989 Suggestions and 1995 Regulations. Instead, the formal verdicts are a veiled recognition of villages' customary claims. In the first case, the local government attempts to effect some sort of retroactive land requisition by demanding financial compensation from the state farm. However, it is doubtful whether this compensation comes anywhere near the real value of the requisitioned land. In the second case, the local government and the court steer a middle course through an equal division of the disputed land between the village and the state farm.

Caught between Historical Heritage and Social Justice

This chapter sought to answer the question why collective land ownership has become unclear even though formal ownership was vested by Party regulations in the production team. It was argued that the natural village, in its capacity as the team, possessed no real power over land. Actual control was exercised by the commune and higher administrative levels. Through the review of lawsuits, three main reasons for this situation were identified: the inconsistency of the legal framework and the absence of a rule of law during the collective period; the lack of a cadastre; and the state's difficulties in recognizing customary tenure. These three reasons represent a historical legacy that affects China's land administration and jurisdiction even today.

How can the (local) government and courts strike the right balance between unclear historical land claims and social justice? It requires steering carefully through a minefield of irreconcilable interests: villages' land has been 'stolen' because of a weak legal culture, while those that profited have invested considerable resources in the 'stolen goods'. Yet this is an overly simplified picture, as for decades land has been used and developed by governments *and* villages, precisely because ownership is unclear. From this perspective, both state and collective are victim and culprit. For the People's Republic there will be no easy answer to this complex matter and, in this respect, it finds itself in the same boat as those governments that struggle with indigenous and pre-colonial land claims.

The Chinese government needs to consider several critical issues if it wishes to establish institutions that can sufficiently protect the rural weak while at the same time ensuring stable economic growth. As we saw in Chapter 1, the ambiguous legal framework around property rights has allowed the cropland tenure system to function as a social security system. On the other hand, this institutional ambiguity—particularly in the wealthier and increasingly urbanizing areas—has also tempted local governments to deny land ownership to the natural village altogether. This is a matter of serious concern and threatens the long-term credibility of land property rights. In locations where land prices are booming and land ownership cannot be verified beyond doubt or dealt with in a fair manner, the central state must primarily choose to safeguard the legal interests of the weakest: the villages and farmers. The first case discussed shows how the courts can play a crucial role in establishing jurisprudence that confirms the natural village as the basic legal owner of land—as included in the Sixty Articles. To date, however, procedures for the establishment and the status of case law are still weak. This remains an area for further strengthening.

A second problem that spawns from unclear land laws and regulations is related to the level of collective ownership and changes therein. Under the past and present legal framework, the level of collective ownership cannot be changed. But during the collective period it was not uncommon for the team's land to be requisitioned for the establishment of collective enterprises of the commune or brigade. Many current township and village enterprises were established in this way. Over time it became increasingly unclear which collective level could claim ownership to the land on which the enterprises were built. The 1998 Land Administration Law provides no decisive answer to this question, which is why the State Land Administration proclaimed rules of its own: the 1989 Suggestions on the Assessment of Land Titles.[63]

The legal cases reviewed in this chapter show that the 1989 Suggestions are frequently used by the judicial and the executive authorities in the arbitration of land disputes. However, the use of these administrative regulations is problematic. They fall short of the status of law as they have not been reviewed or passed by the NPC. Moreover, they are also not 'rules for implementation' as issued by the State Council to provide binding rules for legal interpretation by the courts (as is common also in other civil law countries).[64] The 'suggestions' also do not belong to the regular set of administrative documents issued by ministries and state departments.[65] Probably for these reasons, the Suggestions were upgraded in 1995 to Regulations on the Assessment of Land Ownership and Use Rights. The use of administrative regulations of unclear legal status for the adjudication of fundamental issues that should have been stipulated in law is bound to create problems. It is evident that the National People's Congress during a future revision of the Land Administration Law can no longer avoid a debate on a new institutional design of collective ownership.

Although the government halted—with reason—the registration of rural land in the mid-1990s, land titling cannot and should not be avoided in the long run. As processes of urbanization and commercialization sweep through the Chinese countryside, the recording of property rights becomes inevitable in the industrialized society. On the establishment of a national

[63] The State Land Administration has also released a large collection of administrative questions and answers on land title issues as a sort of prejudicial procedure. Those included in Xiang (ed.), Manual for the Assessment of Land Title, pp. 398–459, date from 1989 to 1996.

[64] For example, in the Netherlands such 'rules for implementation' are issued by the law-making authority, and are called *Memorie van Toelichting* [Memoire of Explanation].

[65] See also Chen, *Introduction to the Legal System of China*, pp. 88–90.

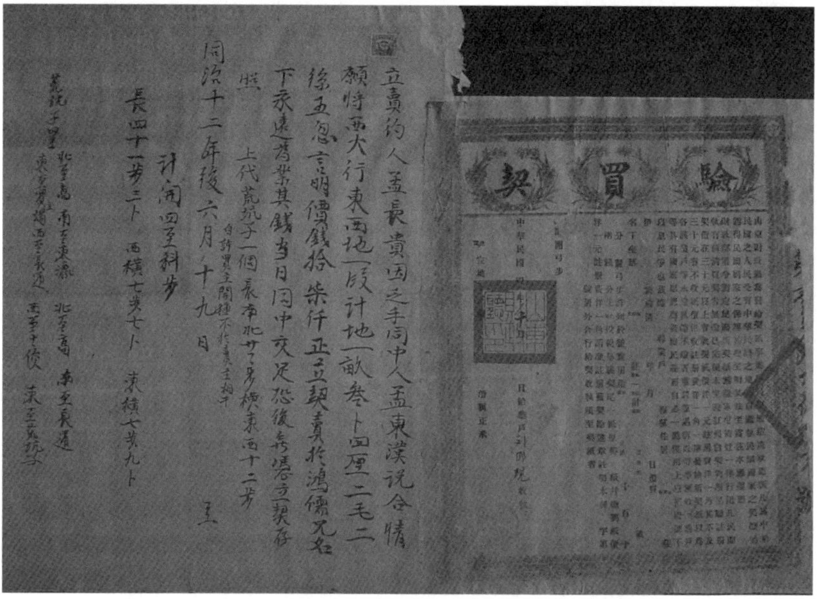

Plate II: **A Qing dynasty land ownership certificate from Qingyun County, Shandong Province.**

On the left-hand side is the handwritten original dating from 19 June of the twelfth year of the reign of the Tongzhi emperor (1873). On the right-hand side is the renewed version of the certificate issued in October of the fourth year of the Chinese Republic (1915) when local authorities engaged in land titling. The small stamp on top of the document is proof that administrative fees have been paid.

land cadastre, a solution must be found for the assessment of title on the basis of historical claims. Under current law, the validity of claims is limited to land deeds issued after Land Reform and the Four Fixes Movement. The Chinese government has chosen this path in order to avoid the social conflict over past ownership that has broken out in other transitional economies in eastern and central Europe. On the one hand, China's strategy of privatizing land property rights through lease rather than by reinstating former owners has successfully avoided raking up disputes over pre-socialist property similar to those in Hungary, Albania, and the former German Democratic Republic.[66] On the other hand, the

[66] In dealing with the legacy of the former German Democratic Republic (DDR), the German authorities proclaimed the Agricultural Adjustment Law during the early 1990s. The law explicitly addresses issues of previous ownership in two ways. First, the law stipulates the return of land and capital shares to the original owners or their successors from whom property has been seized after 1949. Even landowners who had left East Germany were entitled to land holdings. Second, members of the cooperatives—also known as LPGs (*Landwirtschaftliche Produktionsgemeinschaften*)—have a valid claim to the collective property of the farm on condition that it has a positive value after debt clearance. In the final days of the DDR, Prime Minister Hans Modrow ordained that full ownership be granted to the LPG farmers and their heirs. The Kohl administration, however, reversed this measure in 1992. In reaction, around 70,000 former LPG members and their descendants filed a case at the European Court for Human Rights in Strasbourg, which in January 2004 ruled that the decision by the Kohl administration was unlawful. In addition, the German government was ordered to provide suitable financial redress to the expropriated victims. At the time of

critical question is whether the state can maintain its disregard of historical claims in the long run. A national cadastre needs to be established sooner or later, even though the regions that are still dominated by traditional agriculture, strong customary rights systems, and subsistence farming might need to be (temporarily) exempted. Yet, when titling is to proceed, claims to historical rights cannot be completely brushed aside. In many village communities people are still aware of pre-socialist boundaries. As we saw earlier in this chapter, in a dispute between two villages over land in the Daozhai Mountains one village furnished text material dating from the Qing dynasty and Republican era as evidence of its claim. As we can see from Plate II, this is no isolated case. Many more pre-socialist land claims could be revived when land registration is carried out in China's countryside.

The recognition of historical claims is intertwined with the extent to which the state takes seriously villages' territorial claims under customary tenure. The present legal principle that forest, grassland, and wasteland are state-owned unless proven collective property might prove untenable in the process of title recognition and registration. The common ownership of these natural resources—not necessarily limited to a single village community—and the unwritten character of customary rights make them difficult to authenticate. Laying the burden of proof with the collective can lead to the abuse of state power, as it is a strong legal instrument with which customary claims can be brushed aside. The attempts by the State Land Administration (and present Ministry of Land Resources) at a further codification of the principle of 'state-owned unless proven collective' have created a potentially explosive situation. The local government and the courts walk a fine line between the protection of the state's interests and meeting the collectives' demands for social justice. Yet the cases reviewed here show that the local government and the courts were capable of making independent judgements. Their verdicts could be regarded as veiled recognitions of customary claims without sacrificing economic interests.

On these issues, the central government presently had adopted a rather passive stance by intentionally leaving them undefined in law. By upholding such 'intentional institutional ambiguity' it hopes to provide sufficient leeway for local experimentation with new property arrangements, while simultaneously avoiding widespread social conflict. If local practices have proven feasible they can subsequently be institutionalized. As the economic reforms progress and agrarian China undergoes an inevitable commercialization, the number of land claims will rise disproportionally. These will prove a veritable test for the Chinese judiciary and executive authorities.

writing, the German government is still studying the possibility of a higher appeal. See Michel Kerres, 'Hof voor Mensenrechten: Onteigening in ex-DDR onrechtmatig' ['Court for Human Rights: Expropriation in former DDR unlawful'], *NRC Handelsblad* (23 January 2004), p. 5.

3
Governing China's Grasslands: The Creation of Empty Institutions

Though there are numerous attempts, we know of no case in which a government agency ... has successfully persuaded pastoral households, or a pastoral group to voluntarily reduce livestock numbers on rangeland to satisfy an estimated carrying capacity.

(Gerrit B. Bartels, Brien E. Norton, and Gregory K. Perrier, 'An Examination of the Carrying Capacity Concept'[1])

China's Grasslands and Grassland Policy

'Do you have some material about grassland laws and regulations in the West? It does not matter from which country, we urgently need some material to give us new ideas about grassland management', said Li Shoude, the highest ranking official responsible for grassland policy formulation in China.[2] His request illustrates three points. First, it shows that, on the way to becoming a market economy, after more than two decades China is still very much in the process of designing and redesigning a viable institutional system for grassland management. Second, it is indicative of the growing awareness within the Chinese Ministry of Agriculture that grassland policy[3] as it emerged after the demise of the people's communes in the 1980s is ripe for revision. Finally, it suggests an interest in examining and learning from the experience of other countries, particularly Western ones.

This chapter charts the Chinese state's attempts to effect institutional change in the pastoral sector, with particular reference to the privatization of property rights. We will learn that these efforts generally proved ineffective and resulted in the creation of an 'empty institution' or 'symbol law': the Grassland Law. Different from agricultural land, grassland in the arid pastoral regions manifests a highly variable productivity. For this reason, grassland resources benefit more from communal than from privatized management regimes. Here we will not delve into the question of why grassland is more efficiently and effectively managed under common property arrangements, an issue taken up in Chapter 6. This chapter, however,

[1] In Roy H. Behnke, Ian Scoones, and Carol Kerven (eds.), *Range Ecology at Disequilibrium: New Models of Natural Variability and Pastoral Adaptation in African Savannas* (London: Overseas Development Institute, 1993), p. 99.

[2] Section Head of the Grassland Section of the Department of Animal Husbandry and Veterinary Science (oral communication, 1996).

[3] By 'policy' is meant the body of aims and means, of which laws are a part. I talk about 'grassland policy' when referring to the entire body of grassland policy measures, laws, and regulations. However, in the Chinese setting the distinction between policy and law is often blurred. For example, the Grassland Law (*caoyuanfa*) is frequently equated with grassland policy (*caoyuan zhengce*).

explores the main institutional variables that led to the failure of the Grassland Law and finds that the culprit is the political stalemate over state and collective property.

Of the total surface of the People's Republic (9.6 million square kilometres), it was estimated that around 400 million ha (41.7 per cent) was grassland. This natural resource exhibits great geographical and ecological diversity, varying from the alpine meadows on the Tibet-Qinghai Plateau at an altitude of over 4,000m above sea level, to the steppe and desert in arid regions such as Xinjiang (with less than 150mm of annual precipitation), the hilly grassland in the sub-tropical zone of Yunnan Province and the semi-arid Loess Plateau. The diversity is no less when seen from the socio-economic and ethnic perspectives. The people dependent on grassland include (semi)nomadic Mongols, Tibetans and Kazakhs, as well as sedentary livestock farmers like Hui Muslims, or Han Chinese. Over 50 per cent of China's grasslands is located in the north, which is regarded as the traditional pastoral region. The northern grasslands are strategically important, being located in the frontier zones and inhabited by ethnic minorities with possible separatist agendas.

Table 1 shows that the pastoral region's contribution to the national agricultural output is relatively small, varying from 0.2 per cent (Tibet and Qinghai) to 2.1 per cent (Inner Mongolia). The provinces that rank highest nationwide—Shandong, Henan, and Jiangsu—respectively contribute 9.2, 8.0 and 7.3 per cent. The per capita rural net income of the pastoral region lies on the lower rungs of the national ladder: Inner Mongolia ranked twenty-first, while Tibet, Gansu, and Shaanxi occupied the bottom positions (twenty-ninth to thirty-first). Nevertheless, the pastoral region represents vast grazing areas for a livestock sector with relatively promising prospects. China is one of the largest meat producers in the world and could become a major exporter of pork. Since the economic reforms started in 1978 and the world's largest remaining socialist economy embarked on an arduous transition to a market economy, meat production (including pork, beef and mutton) has undergone tremendous development, from 9 kg per capita in 1978 to 51.3 kg in 2002. Exports of live animals and animal products were worth $US4,730 million in 2002. In the same year, the total output of animal husbandry was worth more than 30 per cent of the total agricultural output.[4] It is said that the rapid increase of grazing animals in the pastoral areas (from approximately 29 million ruminants in 1949 to 90 million in the early 1990s), as well as the decline in the area of grassland due to reclamation (an estimated loss of 6.5 million ha over 1949–92), has led to serious grassland degradation and desertification. In 1994, over one-third of usable grassland had been reported to have suffered some degradation, while total biomass production per ha had declined by

[4] National Bureau of Statistics (ed.), *Zhongguo Tongji Nianjian 2003* [China Statistical Yearbook 2003] (Beijing: Zhongguo Tongji Chubanshe, 2003), pp. 97, 416, 436, 655. For more information on China's rangelands and the livestock sector, see also Committee on Scholarly Communication with the PRC (ed.), *Grasslands and Grassland Sciences in Northern China* (Washington, DC: National Academy Press, 1992); J. R. Simpson, Xu Cheng, and Akira Miyazaki, *China's Livestock and Related Agriculture: Projections to 2025* (Wallingford: CAB International, 1994).

Table 1: **Total agricultural output value and rural net income per capita by region in 2002**

Region	*Total agricultural output (million RMB)*	*% of national figure*
	2,739,080	100.0
Shandong	252,600	9.2
Henan	219,480	8.0
Jiangsu	201,150	7.3
Inner Mongolia	58,700	2.1
Shaanxi	50,910	1.9
Xinjiang	52,500	1.9
Gansu	35,940	1.3
Ningxia	9,250	0.3
Qinghai	6,550	0.2
Tibet	5,590	0.2
Region	*Rural net income (million RMB)*	*National position*
Shanghai	6,223.55	1
Beijing	5,398.48	2
Zhejiang	4,940.36	3
Inner Mongolia	2,086.02	21
Ningxia	1,917.36	25
Xinjiang	1,863.26	26
Qinghai	1,668.94	27
Shaanxi	1,596.25	29
Gansu	1,590.30	30
Tibet	1,462.27	31

Source: National Bureau of Statistics, *Zhongguo Tongji Nianjian 2003* [China Statistical Yearbook 2003] (Beijing: Zhongguo Tongji Chubanshe, 2003), pp. 368, 416.

30–50 per cent since the 1950s.[5] In the arid and semi-arid steppes of north and north-west China, most grassland has been reported affected by desertification. Nationwide, estimates of desertification vary from 84 million to 166 million ha (8–27 per cent of total land surface).[6]

For a long time, China had no comprehensive long-term grassland policy . In the past, policy-makers saw no need for one since the communes seemed to provide at least some sort of institutional structure for the use and protection of pasture. However, when the communes were dismantled it became apparent that collectivist structures had in many cases been the very basis of a 'tragedy of the commons' in pastoral and semi-pastoral areas, particularly in Inner Mongolia, Gansu, and Ningxia.[7] It was also

[5] Yutang Li, *Caoye: Fuguo Qiangmin de Xinxing Chanye* [Pastoralism: The Newly Established Industry to Strengthen the People and Enrich the Country] (Yinchuan: Ningxia Renmin Chubanshe, 1994), p. 29.

[6] CERES Consultants, *The Social and Economic Impact of Desertification in Several Asian Countries: Inventory Study for the Interim Secretariat of the Convention to Combat Desertification* (Amsterdam: CERES, 1998), p. 25.

[7] The situation, however, is not that unequivocal. For other regions, such as Tibet and Xinjiang, a 'tragedy of the commons' did not seem to have taken place. Instead a substantial

clear to many that pastoral areas had been disregarded by reformist policy-makers and that grassland would become seriously degraded unless the institutional vacuum left by the communes was not dealt with. This background prompted the proclamation of the Grassland Law in 1985.

The Grassland Law is the official expression of a grassland policy that attempts to devolve use rights and liability from the state and collectives to the individual. In this respect, it is the prime embodiment of the state's efforts to privatize grassland property rights. Under the principle that grassland is owned by either the state or the collective, households and collectives are allowed to lease the use of grassland for the 'long term' in a similar vein to the agricultural lease system. Currently, the lease term for grassland is from thirty to fifty years.[8] In order to effect the privatization of grassland through the pasture contract responsibility system (further referred to as the pasture contract system), the Chinese Ministry of Agriculture envisaged a four-stage policy. First, animals would be distributed to individual households (essentially completed by the end of the 1980s). Second, grassland boundaries between collectives would be assessed or, in some cases, reassessed, and grassland use rights subsequently allocated to collectives and households (allegedly completed by the end of the 1980s). Third, pastures would be appraised in terms of stocking rates (completed by the end of the 1980s). Finally, a system of incentives and penalties would be implemented to ensure that producers abided by the carrying capacities of the plots of land assigned to them (allegedly completed during the 1990s). In theory, the greater part of grasslands in China has already been contracted out.[9] The time has thus arrived to assess the carrying capacities of the various plots of contracted pasture and to enforce them.

The Failure of the Grassland Law

Currently, some policy-makers believe that the rationale of the grassland policy of the 1980s reforms—privatization through lease—is outdated, or at least insufficient to deal with the new socio-economic environment of the early twenty-first century. This idea has prompted policy-makers at the central and the provincial levels to rethink and reshape the Grassland Law and the grassland policy it represents. However, policy- and law-making in China is a rather opaque area in which too many questions remain unanswered. For example, why is the Grassland Law so difficult to implement? Who or which department(s) took the initiative to formulate the Grassland Law and grassland policy? Is there any underlying rationale

continuity in customary grassland allocation has been observed. See, for example, Tony Banks, 'State, Community and Common Property in Xinjiang: Synergy or Strife?', *Development Policy Review*, Vol. 17, No. 3 (1999), pp. 293–313.

[8] The Grassland Law does not specify as such the period of contracting. However, the thirty to fifty years lease term for grassland is stipulated in the 2002 Rural Land Contracting Law.

[9] The following percentages of contracted grassland in China have been mentioned: 90% for Gansu, 80% for Sichuan, 70% for Inner-Mongolia, 79% for Qinghai, 69% for Ningxia, 26% for Heilongjiang, 30% for Xinjiang, 37% for Jilin, and 30% for Liaoning. See Li, Pastoralism: The Newly Established Industry, p. 101.

for the Grassland Law at all, or is it no more than a symbolic political compromise between contending factions?

We have already learned that the central government intentionally maintains a certain degree of institutional ambiguity in order to avoid widespread social conflict over land resources. But the situation pertaining to grassland property rights is dominated by more than state-supported institutional ambiguity, because—as I will show—the Grassland Law is a classic example of what Aubert and Aalders termed a 'symbol law', and elsewhere has been described as an 'empty institution'.[10] The 'empty institution' embodies certain rules not yet widely accepted in society, but in such a manner that the newly created institution is generally ineffective. Empty institutions often emerge as compromises over sensitive political issues. The interests opposed to them ensure that they are established in such a way that they cannot achieve their aims, whereas the interests supporting them win a pyrrhic victory as their rules, as represented by the new institution, have no practical impact on social actors' behaviour.[11]

The symbolic character of the Grassland Law negatively affects the management and use of grassland resources. It embodies a political compromise over an issue that lies at the heart of grassland tenure: the distinction between state and collective property. In contrast to agricultural land, grassland, like forest and wasteland, is state-owned unless collective title can be proven. However, as the Grassland Law is intentionally unclear about the legal basis for collective property, rural communities have few means to substantiate ownership claims to grassland. As discussed in detail in Chapter 2 and Chapter 6, this is particularly problematic for the (semi)nomadic peoples in traditional pastoral areas. Their mobile use of grassland resources over great distances makes collective title difficult to prove. In addition, the rural collectives established since the second half of the 1950s also lay ownership claims to state-owned grassland reserves. It is therefore no wonder that the implementation of grassland policy has been greatly hampered. In this respect, Longworth and Williamson have observed the following:

> At central government level certain policies are in place and provincial, prefectural, county and even township officials will describe . . . how the policy is working. However, at the village and household level, the policy does not exist. Situations illustrating this policy failure problem were observed in relation to the policing of pasture stocking rate limits . . .[12]

[10] See the introduction in Peter Ho (ed.), *Developmental Dilemmas: Land Reform and Institutional Change in China* (Routledge: London and New York, 2005).

[11] With his research on the Norwegian 1948 Housemaid Law, Vilhelm Aubert opened up a new area of research on 'symbol laws' in the sociology of law. See also Vilhelm Aubert, 'Some Social Functions of Legislation', *Acta Sociologica,* Vol. 10, Nos. 1–2 (1966), pp. 98–121; and Marius Aalders, 'Industrie, Milieu en Wetgeving: De Hinderwet tussen Symboliek en Effectiviteit' ['Industry, Environment and Legislation: The Nuisance Act between Symbolism and Effectivity'], Ph.D. thesis (Amsterdam: Kobra, 1984), p. 13.

[12] John W. Longworth, and Gregory J. Williamson, *China's Pastoral Region: Sheep and Wool, Minority Nationalities, Grassland Degradation and Sustainable Development* (Wallingford: CAB International, 1993), p. 322. In this context Albert Chen writes: 'the question of legal efficacy, or the gap between the law as stated in the statute book and actual behaviour on the part of officials and citizens, presents probably the most serious

In addition, official claims that the pasture contract system is firmly in place are questionable.[13] In the words of the former Deputy Head of a provincial Department of Animal Husbandry (*xumuju*), 'The figures of contracted grassland have no importance at all. They are administrative figures, which the central government has required us to report, and exist on paper only.'[14]

The unclear property rights structure, along with the low economic value of grassland, in particular in the semi-arid and arid areas, has generally led to overgrazing, desertification and soil degradation due to the exploitation of medicinal herbs. (A poignant example of the struggle over scarce natural resources—the 'liquorice wars' in the arid steppe area—is given in Chapter 6.) This is not to say that the failure of grassland policy can be attributed solely to an unclear property rights structure. Many other factors are at play, such as rural poverty, weak and understaffed state institutions, and the lack of alternative employment.

To answer the questions posed above, I will review the central government's efforts to change the institutions that govern the pastoral sector. As defined in the introduction of this book, institutions are here conceived as 'institutional arrangements embodied in promulgated policies, formal laws and customary rules, and the state administration'.[15] Following this review, I will provide a historical perspective of the main pastoral institutions around the ownership and use of grassland, as well as the rules of its protection and improvement, from the latter half of the 1940s to the present.

obstacle . . . of the Chinese legal system.' He cites the example of a study in Heilongjiang Province, where only 10% of all existing laws were being effectively implemented or enforced. See Albert Hung-yee Chen, *An Introduction to the Legal System of the People's Republic of China* (Hong Kong: Butterworths Asia, 1992), p. 92.

[13] See also Peter Ho, 'Ownership and Control in Chinese Grassland Management: A Case Study of the Free-rider Problem in Pastoral Areas in Ningxia, China', in Eduard B. Vermeer, Frank Pieke, and Woei Lien Chong (eds.), *Cooperative and Collective in China's Rural Development: Between State and Private Interests* (New York: M. E. Sharpe, 1998); Robin Mearns, 'Community, Collective Action and Common Grazing: The Case of Post-Socialist Mongolia', *Journal of Development Studies*, Vol. 32, No. 3 (1996), pp. 304–5; Caoyuanchu and Caoyuan Jianli Zhan (ed.), ' "Caoyuanfa" Zhishi Jiangzuo' ['Intellectual Discussion about the Grassland Law'], *Xinjiang Xumuye: Zengkan* [Animal Husbandry in Xinjiang: Special Issue] (1995), p. 40; and Dee Mack Williams, 'The Barbed Walls of China: A Contemporary Grassland Drama', *Journal of Asian Studies*, Vol. 55, No. 3 (1996), pp. 665–91. In their extensive study of animal husbandry in Inner-Mongolia, Gansu and Xinjiang, John Longworth and Gregory Williamson note the following: 'Another serious source of uncertainty surrounding pasture use contracts in some areas is that while the contract specifies the area assigned to the household, it does not designate the precise location of this pasture land. These 'partial' contracts obviously encourage grazing-in-common practices and discourage investments in pasture conservation and improvement by individual households.' See Longworth and Williamson, *China's Pastoral Region*, p. 321.

[14] Statement by Guo Sijia, former Deputy Head of the Ningxia Autonomous Region Department of Animal Husbandry and professor in grassland management (oral communication, 1996).

[15] In this chapter, I have used fixed designations for departments and offices at a given administrative level. I have used the term 'department' (*si/ju/ting*) for any government body at the state and provincial level; 'section' (*chu*) corresponds to a state organ at the county level; and 'bureau' (*ke*) is reserved for the township level.

Making the National Grassland Law

Setting the agenda. A few years before the official drafting of the Grassland Law began, the idea of drafting so-called National Grassland Regulations was taken up.[16] However, as soon as the project got under way it acquired a momentum of its own and gradually evolved into what would eventually become the first national Grassland Law. The inclusion of the Grassland Law on the agenda confirms Tanner's observations that China's agenda-setting is 'characterized by a good deal of "competitive persuasion" by the senior policy advisers to top leaders' and that 'top leaders appear to depend heavily upon their key advisers and their advisers' subordinates to generate and screen policy options for them'.[17] The route the Grassland Law took in order to end up on the agenda of the National People's Congress was similar to that of some other major laws, which were formulated only after top leaders had publicly stressed the need to draft them.[18]

The most active proponent of the Grassland Law was Li Yutang, the former section head of the Grassland Section (*caoyuanchu*) within the Department for Animal Husbandry and Veterinary Science (*xumu shouyisi*, hereafter Department for Animal Husbandry) of the Ministry of Agriculture. In order to get the Grassland Law included in the legislative agenda of the NPC, Li lobbied many high-ranking officials and influential scientists. In the end, he managed to secure the support of Qian Xuesen, a famous aeronautical scientist and the former executive chairman of the Chinese Academy of Sciences, who was concurrent Deputy Chairman of the People's Political Consultative Conference. With the help of Qian, Li Yutang was able to bring the idea of the Grassland Law to the attention of China's paramount leader, Deng Xiaoping. In his speech at the Central Working Conference of the Party on 13 December 1978, Deng Xiaoping stated:

> We must concentrate on enacting criminal and civil codes, procedural laws and other necessary laws, like the factory law, the people's communes law, the forest law, the grassland law . . .[19]

[16] Murray Scot Tanner has given a detailed description of the five different phases in the Chinese national procedure for law formulation: (*a*) agenda-setting: which consists of getting a particular draft law on the agenda of major state legislative agencies; (*b*) inter-agency review: referring to the period of consensus-building about the draft law among major state agencies; (*c*) top leadership approval of a draft 'in principle'; (*d*) review, debate, and passage by the National People's Congress; and (*e*) implementation of the law. Murray Scot Tanner, 'How a Bill becomes a Law in China: Stages and Processes in Lawmaking', in Stanley B. Lubman (ed.), *China's Legal Reforms* (Oxford: Oxford University Press, 1996), p. 45.

[17] Tanner, 'How a Bill becomes a Law', p. 48.

[18] Also, at present, securing support of top leaders is essential for the survival of a bill. Until the Fifteenth Party Congress, one of the main political patrons for legislative initiatives of the Department for Animal Husbandry was Shandong-born Jiang Chunyun—Vice Prime Minister and concurrent member of the Politburo responsible for agriculture. A powerful ally for the Department for Animal Husbandry yet a rather distant personality, he was once characterized as a 'modern Chinese mandarin' by the Dutch Minister of Agriculture, Jozias van Aartsen (oral communication, 1997).

[19] Deng Xiaoping, 'Emancipate the mind, seek truth from facts and unite as one in looking to the future', in Editorial Committee for Party Literature (ed.), *Selected Works of Deng Xiaoping (1975–1982)* (Beijing: Foreign Languages Press, 1984), p. 158. The translation in

Thus the green light was given to the Grassland Law and the work could begin.

The clash of interests over grassland. The initiative for the formulation of the Grassland Law was taken in 1978 by the Department for Animal Husbandry of the Ministry of Agriculture. Yet it would be another seven years before the Grassland Law was formally promulgated. What were the reasons for this protracted formulation process? An official formerly involved in the drafting of the Grassland Law remarked:

> There are basically two reasons why it took so long to draft this law. First of all, because of the lengthy and complicated legislative procedures that require us to solicit the opinions of concerned departments several times, organize meetings, and send investigation teams into the field, before the bill can be passed by the NPC. Secondly, because of contradictions between departments over certain issues.[20]

The latter point relates in particular to the struggle over responsibilities between the Ministry of Agriculture, the former Ministry of Forestry (downgraded to the State Bureau of Forestry), the former State Land Administration Department (*tudi guanliju*, currently the Ministry of Land Resources) under the State Council, and the State Environmental Protection Agency (*huanbao zongju*): a struggle that culminated in the debate over ownership rights.

The unclear lines of authority between the State Land Administration, the Ministry of Agriculture (including the Department for Animal Husbandry) and the Ministry of Forestry have their origin in article 5 and article 9 of the 1986 Land Management Law. Article 5 states that 'the state institution for land administration under the State Council is the main responsible unit for the unified management of land of the entire nation', while article 9 stipulates that the 'use and ownership rights of specified forest, and grassland . . . are to be dealt with according to the relevant provisions of the Forest Law and Grassland Law'.[21] Article 11 of the Forest Law states that the forestry departments at all levels are responsible for the management and supervision of forest resources, while article 3 of the Grassland Law stipulates that the agricultural and veterinary departments of the State Council are responsible for national grassland management.[22]

The vague task definition between the Ministry of Agriculture, the State Land Administration, and the Ministry of Forestry has given rise to frequent haggling over policy issues. Recent policies that touch on land tenure problems, such as the Four Wastelands Auction Policy (see Chapter 5), have only sharpened the contradictions between these three state organs at

the edition of the Foreign Languages Press is corrupt in the last sentence, as it speaks of 'laws concerning . . . grasslands', while the original text refers to 'a grassland law'. It has been corrected here.

[20] Ni Dongça (oral communication, 1997). Ni Dongça is a present member of the Amendment and Drafting Group for the revised Grassland Law.

[21] See Nongyebu Zhengce Tigai Faguisi (NZTF) (ed.), *Nongyefa Quanshu* [A Complete Edition of Agricultural Laws] (Beijing: Zhongguo Nongye Chubanshe, 1994), pp. 555–6. This stipulation has remained unchanged in the 1998 Revised Land Administration Law (included in article 11).

[22] *Ibid.*, pp. 594, 686.

every administrative level. Says one official of the Provincial State Land Administration:

> We are entitled to hand out land use permits. Any other department, like the Department of Animal Husbandry or the Department of Forestry, that hands out land use permits for grassland or forest must ask our prior approval. For us the division of responsibilities is clear: the Department of Animal Husbandry and the Department of Forestry only have authority over the soil surface, while we control the subsurface as well. However, these departments wrongly assume that they have subsurface authority, which has created conflicts.[23]

The friction between the Ministry of Forestry (including the Provincial Departments of Forestry, *linyeting*) and the Department for Animal Husbandry concerns the definitions of forest and grassland. In particular the steppe in semi-arid and arid areas poses a problem as it is an ecological mixture, consisting of sparse tree vegetation on grassland. For example, how should grazing that takes place on forest land be dealt with? In addition, the term 'wasteland' is notoriously ambiguous in this context. For example, in one county the Department of Animal Husbandry can claim to be in charge of the management of wasteland, while in a neighbouring county the Department of Forestry does so. Recently, talks have been held about a redefinition of the term 'grassland'. For example, Heilongjiang Province has proposed the following definition:

> Grassland used for, or planned for the use of grass collection or pasturing, with a predominant grassy vegetation (trees or shrubs with a canopy density below 30 per cent).[24]

At least there seems to be more consensus between the forestry and animal husbandry institutions about this definition. Whether this will also positively affect the working relation between these two departments remains to be seen.

Finally, there is discussion over the division of responsibilities between the Ministry of Agriculture (and Department for Animal Husbandry) and the State Environmental Protection Agency. Although at present the State Environmental Protection Agency is mainly concerned with pollution problems in urban areas, it also has legal responsibilities for forests, grasslands, and nature reserves.[25] Due to the perceived problem of increasing grassland degradation caused by overgrazing, the Environmental Protection Agency has gradually come to interfere with grassland matters as well. However, the friction between this state institution and the Department for Animal Husbandry seems less than in the other two preceding cases.

[23] Section Head of the Land Pricing Section, Ningxia Land Administration (oral communication, 1996).

[24] See Wang Kuilong, Shang Lisheng, and Zhang Xiuzhi (eds.), *Heilongjiangsheng Shishi 'Zhonghua Renmin Gongheguo Caoyuanfa' Tiaoli Yiyi* [An Interpretation of the Grassland Regulations of Heilongjiang according to the 'National Grassland Law'] (Harbin: Heilongjiang Renda Nonglin Bangongshi, internal publication, 1994), p. 14.

[25] For a description of tasks and mission of the Environmental Protection Commission and Agency, see B. J. Sinkule and Leonard Ortolano, *Implementing Environmental Policy in China* (Westport, CT: Praeger Publications, 1995), pp. 1–23.

One of the issues that sparked the hottest debate between the various parties involved in the formulation of the Grassland Law concerned state and collective ownership. In March 1982 the Secretariat of the State Council issued a notice soliciting the opinions of all provinces in China on grassland ownership. It attracted a variety of reactions. Some provinces were in favour of retaining ownership of grassland in state hands, as had always been the case since land reform, because collective property had not been defined by law. Others advocated a distinction between state and collective property of grassland. For example, Hebei, Inner Mongolia, and Heilongjiang proposed that grassland in long-term use by the collectives should be formally declared collective property, either automatically or through the issue of land use permits. This is a critical proposal as it recognizes and formalizes the customary rights of communities of users.

Because of the controversy over unresolved grassland tenure, the draft version of the Grassland Law presented to the NPC for passage was based on the principle of dual coexisting ownership of grassland: state *and* collective. This simultaneously implied that, sooner or later, a legal definition of collective property would have to be sought. At the time, the Ministry of Agriculture felt confident that the bill would pass, since formal approval by the Legislative Affairs Department as well as the State Council had already been obtained. However, during the last meeting of the Standing Committee of the NPC, in which the bill actually had to be passed, things turned out quite differently. Speaking for many others, the Deputy Director of the Legislative Affairs Work Committee, Song Rufen, argued against it on two grounds. First, the Grassland Law could not possibly deviate from article 9 of the 1982 Constitution, which states only the basic principle of state and collective grassland without defining the two ownership forms. Second, as grassland had always been state property since it was nationalized in the early 1950s, it was not necessary to grant ownership rights to collectives: use rights would suffice.

Through the intervention of Song Rufen, the earlier draft version was rejected after long debate. On 18 June 1985 the Standing Committee of the NPC finally adopted the version that literally copied article 9 of the 1982 Constitution on the issue of ownership rights. It is important to realize that article 9 is in itself a political compromise, as it states that grassland is in principle state-owned *unless otherwise defined* by national law as collective property. As no such law exists to date, the Grassland Law simply maintains the status quo in which the enigmatic nature of collective property persists. Eight years later, when the drafting of the revised Grassland Law began, a group of reformers would launch a renewed attack on the faction represented by Song Rufen.[26]

Revising the Grassland Law

At the time when the Grassland Law was formulated, the philosophy behind it was based on two premises: (*a*) the possibility of delineating and

[26] Wen Jianguo (oral communication, 1997). Shi Wenzheng is a present member of the Advisory Group for the revised Grassland Law.

classifying grassland by means of objective criteria of productivity and sustainability (stocking rates or carrying capacity); and (*b*) an interventionist and active state to ensure that pastoralists complied with stocking rates. The Department for Animal Husbandry had envisaged grassland policy developing in several stages. In the first stage, stocking rates of grassland had to be assessed. For this purpose, the subordinate organs of the Department for Animal Husbandry were charged with classifying grassland in terms of typical vegetation and productivity (in kilograms per mu of pasture) divided over warm and cold seasons. The pasture categories included plain grassland, steppe, sandy pastures, desert pastures, and grassy desert pastures. Stocking rates are expressed in sheep equivalents, which is a weighted total of all the various kinds of ruminants.[27] During the ensuing phase, grassland was to be delineated (if necessary by means of fencing) and allocated to collectives and individual users. Livestock holders could then contract pasture use rights for a period of thirty to fifty years, while the ownership of grassland remained in the hands of the state. In this manner liability for grassland utilization would be effectively decentralized, thus relieving the government of the burden of control, and leaving it with the sole task of ensuring that grassland users abided by the prescribed stocking rates.

However, as noted in the introduction of this chapter, the enforcement of stocking rates has proved to be extremely difficult, and in the majority of pastoral regions the pasture contract system for grassland has not been implemented at all. In the process of rural reform, livestock farmers and pastoralists have gained more managerial freedom and countervailing power. As a result, the enforcement of stocking rates by means of purely administrative measures in a command-like fashion, as during the era of the people's communes has become increasingly ineffective, leading to free-riding and overgrazing. On top of this, the retrenchment of the Chinese state is incompatible with the high transaction costs for the enforcement of stocking rates.

A few years ago, officials in the Ministry of Agriculture claimed that the Grassland Law is becoming outdated as a result of rapid socio-economic change kindled by the economic reforms. Although the problems with the implementation of the contract system for grassland have not been officially acknowledged,[28] a red alert has been raised for the pastoral areas in reaction to perceived problems of grassland degradation and lawlessness among the rural population.

In 1993 the NPC Standing Committee officially approved an Amendment and Drafting Group, responsible for formulating the revised version of the Grassland Law. The bill was then included in the annual legislative plan of the Standing Committee of the NPC without any time specification

27 See Wenzheng Shi, *Caoyuan yu Caoye de Fazhi Jianshe Yanjiu* [Research for the Construction of a Judicial System for Grassland and Pastoralism] (Hohhot: Neimenggu Daxue Chubanshe, 1996), pp. 220–1. For the Chinese standard sheep equivalent conversion, see Longworth and Williamson, *China's Pastoral Region*, p. 112.

28 Neither officials responsible for grassland policy nor literature about grasslands in China mention anything about the gap between the official statistics of contracted grassland and the actual rate of implementation of the HCRS for grassland.

for its review and debate. After many rounds of 'opinion solicitation', during which the various ministries and provincial and national departments had to be brought in line, consensus was finally reached at the Taiyuan conference in May 1997. Six draft versions had already been formulated when the bill was sent for approval to the State Council in August of the same year. The bill was scheduled for presentation to the NPC in 1998. According to one member of the Advisory Group of the revised Grassland Law, the changes in leadership during the Fifteenth Party Congress in September 1997 caused a major setback in the revision process and impaired the formulation and revision of less important laws such as the Grassland Law. Moreover, due to the institutional restructuring of major ministries and departments proclaimed during the Ninth NPC in March 1998, the review of the revised Grassland Law by the NPC Special Committees was stalled at the time of this writing in 2004. The issue on the agenda for amendment accorded the highest political priority by the Department for Animal Husbandry concerns grassland ownership and use.

Clearing up the Rights of Ownership and Use

In the drive of the Department for Animal Husbandry of the Ministry of Agriculture to establish a coherent tenure system for the pastoral sector, the first thing that needs to be cleared up is the confusion surrounding the 'collective' as an institution. For grassland tenure this issue is linked to the wider political debate on the level of collective land ownership. As this question was not resolved during the revision process of the 1998 Land Management Law (see Chapter 1), the Grassland Law can only follow the present legal framework. This means that the following step—the establishment of grassland ownership rights for the collective—likewise cannot be effected yet. As discussed above, local People's Congresses have generally found four different solutions to assess collective ownership of grassland: (*a*) copying the Constitution and the Grassland Law, thus not specifying what grassland is owned by the collective and what by the state; (*b*) formalizing customary law by establishing collective property for all grassland that has been in permanent use or in long-term use by the collective; (*c*) granting collective title only if a 'land use permit' has been granted by the county or a higher-level government; and (*d*) automatically granting collective title for all flatland and mountain meadows located *in the neighbourhood* of collective economic organizations or collective agricultural fields.

If the central government follows the solutions incorporated in provincial regulations, two questions need to be addressed. First, if grassland in long-term use by the collective were declared collective property, should that apply to all or only some of it? In other words, should all grassland that is claimed to be in use by the collective be declared collective property, or should some stretches of grassland be left in the hands of the state? In particular, grassland located further away from the collective is often considered state property—and thus nobody's property—yet in use by farmers from different villages. If only certain parts are declared collective property, what are then the standards by which the area of collective pasture will be assessed? This question touches on the authority of the legislative bodies that establish (or have established) the legal basis of collective property. In other words, should national law directly stipulate the conditions under which grassland can be owned by the collective, or should this be left to the People's Congresses of provinces and autonomous regions to legislate? And what should be the legal status of the land use permits that have already been issued in some areas by the government at the county level or above?[29]

In the area of user rights, the discussion focuses on the legal basis of the pasture household contract system. As noted earlier, a small group of scholars and officials, some of whom participate in the Amendment and Drafting Group of the revised Grassland Law, argue that the present tenure system for grassland does not offer enough legal security to pastoralists. According to them, agricultural land and pasture contracts in China belong to the realm of personal rights, or *droits de suits* (in Chinese, *zhaiquan*). For example, in the case of contract transfer prior approval has to be obtained from the party that issued the contract, namely, the collective. This has given rise to many conflicts between the contractor and the collective, as the collective can, in principle, block any transaction of which it does not approve. Moreover, transfer of agricultural land or pasture is restricted to the rural population.[30] One author writes that this situation is 'harmful for safeguarding farmers' production and management incentives . . . for the economic exchange and flow of agricultural land . . . and for the stability of the agricultural land tenure system'.[31] Instead, it is claimed, the contract right would best be turned into a real right (or *wuquan*), which would allow for more legal protection of the contractor as well as a free transfer of contract rights. In this way, the Department for Animal Husbandry hopes that the revised Grassland Law can lay the foundation for a more stable and secure pasture contract system.

Clearing up the confusion around the term 'collective', vesting formal ownership rights in the collective, and establishing real rights for the pasture contract system: it all sounds very plausible. But the fight over these issues has been waged before, and it does not seem that the struggle has come to an end. The advocates of these changes are pessimistic that their proposals will be accepted by the contending factions. A Chinese jurist remarked: 'The Grassland Law cannot be a legal forerunner. As long as the issue of ownership and user rights to land has not been dealt with in the General Principles of Civil Law [China has no Civil Code, P.H.], we cannot hope that the Grassland Law will bring this up on its own.'[32] At present, the Advisory Group on the revised Grassland Law has proposed that 'the three-level ownership and management rights of collectively

[29] For details on the debate on land tenure of grassland see Wenzheng Shi, Research for a Judicial System for Grassland pp. 45–7, 49.

[30] See Albert Chen, *Introduction to Legal System of China*, and Wang Cunxue *et al.*, 'Nongye Falü Tixi Jianshe Jiben Wenti' ['Fundamental Problems in the Establishment of an Agricultural Legal System'], *Faxue Yanjiu*, 18/6 (1996), pp. 66–77.

[31] Albert Chen, *Introduction to Legal System of China*, p. 89.

[32] Ni Dongfa (oral communication, 1996).

owned grassland should refer to land laws that have already made clear stipulations and have solved the problem who manages [the land]'.[33] A Chinese legal expert, however, said that the grassland ownership issue is still fiercely debated within the NPC; and at the time of writing an eventual proclamation of the revised Grassland Law seems far away.[34]

In order to provide a full grasp of the historical roots of the political controversies over grassland policies, I will review the various regulations and institutions of grassland ownership, use, and protection over time.

Land Reform: Grassland to the Herdsman?

After the Land Reform, individual ownership was abolished, but it was not until 1956 that grassland was officially nationalized. At present, there are two forms of ownership for grassland: state and collective ownership.[35]

The above quotation is the response of a senior official of the Department of Animal Husbandry in Ningxia when I asked him *when* grassland was nationalized and which forms of grassland ownership exist in China. A team leader, a township head, or any other official will most likely give a reply that is a variation of this theme. The year given for nationalization can vary a little, but all will agree in principle on state and collective ownership of grassland. Yet requests to point out which grassland is state-owned and which is collectively owned elicit a dazzling diversity of answers. Moreover, the detailed observer is struck by the apparent contradiction between village and official accounts of grassland ownership. How does the confusion about the rights of ownership and use arise?

To answer this question it is first necessary to examine more closely the 1985 Grassland Law. One of the crucial stipulations in the Grassland Law, article 4, clearly states:

Grassland is state-owned, apart from grassland that is collectively owned as stipulated by the law. Collectives are entitled to the long-term use of state-owned grassland. State-owned grassland, collectively owned grassland and state-owned grassland, which is in long-term use by the collective, can be contracted by the collective or the individual for animal husbandry production.[36]

However—and this is the catch—the Grassland Law does not *define* state-owned and collectively owned grassland, for a range of historical reasons.

Before Land Reform, grassland in China was owned by princes, lamaseries, landlords or clans, yet it was commonly used by herders and livestock farmers.[37] Land Reform heralded the end of the traditional property

[33] 'Zhonghua Renmin Gongheguo Caoyuanfa Xiuding Cao'an: Songshengao de Jidian Shuoming' [Some Explanation on the Revised Draft for the Grassland Law of the People's Republic of China: Draft for Approval and Revision] (15 July 1999), p. 1.

[34] Shi Wenzheng (oral communication, 2001).

[35] Oral communication (1996).

[36] In the translation, 'owned by the people' has been consistently rendered as 'state-owned', while 'fixed' for '*guding*' has been left out. See NZTF, A Complete Edition of Agricultural Laws, p. 685.

[37] For a detailed discussion of the history of grassland tenure in the Qing and Republican period, see also Peter Ho, 'The Myth of Desertification at China's Northwestern Frontier (1929–1960)', *Modern China*, Vol. 26, No. 3 (2000), pp. 348–95.

rights system in China. The timing of Land Reform for grazing lands differed among the various pastoral regions. In Inner Mongolia it was executed simultaneously with agricultural Land Reform, from 1947 until 1952. In Xinjiang it took place over the period 1953–4, in Qinghai it was conducted from 1952 until 1958, in Sichuan it lasted from 1955 until 1960, while Tibet was the latest (1959–61). In addition, the extent to which grazing lands were expropriated from landlords and rich peasants differed over time and place.[38] The early Land Reform in the 'old revolutionary base areas' (Shaan-Gan-Ning border region) adopted a more radical stance against landlords, most of whose land (including grazing land) was confiscated and redistributed. However, in the later period a more moderate line was followed and rich and middle peasants were allowed to keep part of their landholdings.[39] By the time Land Reform had come to an end, grassland had been declared public property with the policy line 'grasslands are public, grazing is free' (*muchang gongyou, fangmu ziyou*), although small portions had remained in private hands.[40]

In his excellent work on the Grassland Law, the Chinese jurist Shi Wenzheng gives a detailed account of the history of grassland institutions. He is the first to note that grassland in China was declared public property without any legal expression; it was incorporated neither in the Constitution nor in any other law. This might be symptomatic of the highly politicized and revolutionized atmosphere in which land-to-the-tiller movements generally tend to take place, but it is best understood in relation to the low priority the Chinese government accorded to grassland as compared with forests and other natural resources. The Constitution of 1954 stipulates only that 'Mineral resources, water, forest, wasteland and other resources specified by law as state property, are all owned by the whole people'. Neither the Constitution of 1975 nor that of 1978 mentions grasslands. It was not until the 1982 Constitution that grassland was formally designated as state property.[41]

What about collective property? At the time of Land Reform in China there were no collectives and as a result no collective property. Yet herder communities in the traditional pastoral areas continued to make customary claims to the right to use grassland resources. When the higher agricultural production cooperatives were established in 1956 and ownership rights of

[38] See Tu Ba and Lin Tai, *Zhongguo Caoyuan Xumuye Jingji Fazhan Gailun* [General Discussion of China's Economic Development of Animal Husbandry and Pastoralism] (Beijing: Minzu Chubanshe, 1993), p. 45.

[39] Richard Madsen, 'The Countryside under Communism', in Roderick MacFarquhar and John K. Fairbank (eds.), *Cambridge History of China. The People's Republic, Part 2: Revolutions within the Chinese Revolution 1966–1982* (Cambridge: Cambridge University Press, 1991), p. 624; and Ningxia Nongye Hezuo Jingji Shiliao Bianxiezu (ed.), *Ningxia Hezuo Jingji Shiliao* [Historical Material of the Cooperative Economy of Ningxia], Vol. I (Yinchuan: Ningxia Renmin Chubanshe, 1988), pp. 50, 98–101.

[40] In 1948 the provincial governor of Inner-Mongolia, Wu Lanfu, had declared that in all banners and leagues the herders had free grazing rights. This became the official policy for the pastoral regions in China. See Tu Ba and Lin Tai, General Discussion of Animal Husbandry, p. 48.

[41] See Wenzheng Shi, Research for a Judicial System for Grassland, pp. 37–8.

all land, including grassland, were vested in the collective,[42] collective property was still not defined. As in the case of state property, not until 1982 did article 9 of the Constitution finally specify what had already become customary practice:

> Mineral resources, waters, forests, mountains, grassland, wasteland, sandy waste and other natural resources are owned by the state, that is, by the whole people, with the exception of the forests, mountains, grassland, wasteland and sandy waste that are owned by collectives in accordance with the law.[43]

For the first time the Constitution stipulates that grassland can be owned by the collective, only simultaneously to create a problem by providing no clue whatsoever to the meaning of the term 'collective grassland'. This question pertains to grassland that has been in long-term, customary use by the collective after Land Reform. In order to clarify ownership and use rights of grassland, and to provide a sound legal basis for the pasture contract system, the Chinese government faces the following problem: must collective grassland claimed through customary rights be formally declared state property, since de jure collective grassland does not exist? Or would it be better to formalize that which was or has already become customary practice, namely, ownership of grassland by the collective?

It is striking that the provincial governments, in attempting to deal with the definitional problem of collective property, responded in diverse ways to the 1982 Constitution. Four categories of responses can be identified:

1. Adherence to the Constitution, with no further specification of the nature of collective property. The grassland regulations of Ningxia, Gansu, Qinghai, Guizhou, Sichuan, and Liaoning belong to this category. Most importantly, the Grassland Law falls within this group as well.
2. A formalization of customary practice, that is, the stipulation that all grassland that has been in permanent or long-term use by the collective is automatically collective property. The grassland regulations of Hebei and Inner Mongolia adopt this solution.
3. The stipulation that grassland is collective property only when a 'land use permit' has been issued by the county or a higher level government. An example of this settlement is the grassland regulations of Heilongjiang.

[42] Ningxia Nongye Hezuo Jingji Shiliao Bianxiezu (ed.), *Ningxia Nongye Hezuo Jingji Shiliao* [Historical Material of the Agricultural Collective Economy of Ningxia], Vol. I (Yinchuan: Ningxia Renmin Chubanshe, 1988), p. 205.

[43] In my translation I have chosen to render *huangdi* as 'wasteland' and *huangtan* as 'sandy waste' instead of 'unreclaimed land' and 'beaches' as in the official translation by the Institute of Chinese Law. The term 'unreclaimed land' does not account for the fact that much wasteland is actually illegally under cultivation, or has been reclaimed in the past and left fallow again. The term 'beach' has connotations with the seaside, whereas *huangtan* in Chinese refers to pockets of desert in steppe or grassland. For the official English translation, see Institute of Chinese Law (ed.), *Statutes and Regulations of the People's Republic of China*, Vol. IV (Hong Kong: Institute of Chinese Law Publishers, 1989), p. 2. For the original Chinese text, see article 9 of the 1982 Constitution, NZTF (ed.), Complete Edition of Agricultural Laws, p. 3.

4. The solution of Jilin and Xinjiang, such that 'all scattered grassland, hill and mountain meadows that are located in the neighbourhood of collective economic organizations or agricultural fields, is collective property'.[44] In a veiled manner, this solution, too, is a recognition of customary rights in a similar vein to the second proposition.

It should be remarked that only the first category has a basis in national law. In fact, the institutional solutions proposed by provinces such as Jilin, Heilongjiang, and Hebei are far ahead of the national debate on state and collective ownership of grassland.

At a time when Inner Mongolia (1984), Ningxia (1983) and Heilongjiang (1984) had already promulgated local grassland regulations, the central government followed suit with the Grassland Law in 1985, which ideally had to provide the legal basis for the local regulations. However, the Grassland Law failed to do so in this respect and, as we will see in a later section, increasingly in many others as well as the rural reforms progressed.[45] In any case, the central government has resolved to deal with the differences in provincial grassland regulations over state and collective property in the future Grassland Law.

In attempts to solve the issue on state and collective ownership, one further problem remains: the conceptualization of the 'collective' as an institution. As I pointed out in Chapter 1, there is wide disagreement in China over the exact definition of the collective. It is therefore difficult to specify which administrative unit has de jure (and, for that matter, de facto) use rights, let alone ownership rights. In the rural setting alone, the institution of the 'collective' refers simultaneously to several administrative levels and units: the township, the administrative village, the natural village, and any collective township or village enterprise. This ambiguity becomes apparent at the grass-roots level, as the township, the administrative village and the natural village frequently disagree over the unit in which use and ownership rights of grassland are to be vested.

Yet the discussion about the level of (grass)land ownership is not new. Before the layout of the people's communes was finally consolidated in the early 1960s by the grace of the 'Work Regulations for the Rural People's Communes', the central government wavered between land ownership by the production brigade (roughly equivalent to its successor, the administrative village) and the production team (the present natural village). When the Great Leap Forward was launched in China, the higher agricultural production cooperatives were overnight organized into huge organizational units: the people's communes. These massive units, which owned all the means of production in their territory, sometimes encompassed ten to twenty villages and had a total average population of 25,000 people. Soon enough, the communes proved to be too large and ineffective. In response to the initial problems encountered during the Great Leap, the communes'

[44] See Wenzheng Shi, Research for a Judicial System for Grassland, p. 45.

[45] See Difangxing Fagui Xuanbian Bianxiezu (ed.), *Difangxing Fagui Xuanbian* [A Compilation of Local Laws and Regulations] (Beijing: Zhongguo Jingji Chubanshe, 1991), pp. 493–8, 702–4, 877–81, 1019–22, 3578–82, 3699–702, 3892–8; and NZTF (ed.), Complete Edition of Agricultural Laws, p. 685.

ownership of the means of production, including agricultural fields, farm animals, implements and so forth, was broken up into 'three-level ownership'. Below the commune level of administration were the levels of the production brigade and the production team.[46] At the work conference in Zhengzhou in February 1959, central leaders decided that 'three-level ownership, with the brigade as primary accounting unit' would be the basic structure for the communes.

In the following year the complete failure of the Great Leap became apparent. As grain production plummeted and a nationwide famine engulfed the countryside, the government proclaimed the 'Urgent Notice concerning the Political Problems facing the People's Communes', also known as the Twelve Articles. The new notice did not change the situation of the brigade as the basic accounting unit. In March 1961, the draft version of the 'Work Regulations for the Rural People's Communes' (popularly known as the Sixty Articles) was adopted at the work conference of the Chinese Communist Party in Guangzhou. Article 17 of the Sixty Articles determined that 'all land . . . within the territory of the production brigade is owned by the production brigade . . . '; article 18 continued, 'the production brigade must register and give land . . . in permanent use to the production team'.[47]

However, in September 1962 the Eighth National Party Congress (NPC) adopted the revised draft of the Sixty Articles, in which the basic accounting unit was changed from the brigade to the team, which from then on would also hold ownership rights to the land. Article 22 of the Sixty Articles stipulated the following:

> Collective forest, water resources, and grassland are all owned by the production team . . . The management and ownership rights to land, animals, agricultural implements, forest, water resources, and grassland as described above, remain unaltered for a long term, after they have been fixed through negotiation and agreement of the Commune Members Committee or the Commune Members Representatives Committee.

This tenure system would remain essentially unchanged until the start of the demise of the communes in 1983.[48]

In the course of time, the production teams—which included traditional herder communities and the rural collectives established since

[46] See Madsen, 'Countryside under Communism,' pp. 640–4.

[47] Zhongguo Renmin Jiefangjun Guofang Daxue Dangshi Yanjiushi (ZRJGDDY) (ed.), *Zhonggong Dangshi Jiaoxue Cankao Ziliao* [Reference and Teaching Material for the History of the CCP], Vol. 23 (Beijing: Guofang Daxue Chubanshe, 1986), p. 454. Note that the version of the Work Regulations published by the Chinese Nationalist Government is incorrect both as regards the date (March 1961 instead of June), and the title (the draft not the revised draft). See Kung-fei 'Nung-ts'un Jen-min Kung-she Kung-tsuo T'iao-li' Hsiu-cheng Ts'ao-an ['Revised Draft of "The Work Regulations for the Rural People's Communes" by the Communist Bandits'] (Taipei: unpublished, 1965), article 17.

[48] See ZRJGDDY, Reference and Teaching Material for History of the CCP, Vol. 24, pp. 137–8, 141–2; Jiyuan Chen (ed.), *Zhongguo Nongcun Shehui Jingji Bianqian: 1949–1989* [Socio-economic Change in China's Countryside: 1949–1989] (Taiyuan: Shanxi Jingji Chubanshe, 1993), pp. 333–7; Qibin Ma and Wenbin Chen (eds.), *Zhongguo Gongchandang Zhizheng Sishi Nian* [Forty Years of Chinese Communist Party Rule] (Beijing: Zhonggong Dangshi Chubanshe, 1989), pp. 190, 197, 220.

1956—came to regard the grassland they used as their own. The property rights system of the collectivist period, however, was formally incorporated in Party regulations but never in law. At the time when the communes were dismantled and the commune replaced with the township, the brigade with the administrative village, and the team with the natural village, grassland ownership became ambiguous, particularly as the ownership rights stipulated in the Sixty Articles were not followed up in national law. As a result, no one knew which unit held ownership rights of grassland: was it the former production team, which held de facto ownership rights of land? Or was it the brigade, the present administrative village? Collective and state ownership of grassland was officially included in the Constitution only on the eve of decollectivization. But the level of collective ownership remained an enigma, as did the legal procedures to establish it. Legally, all grassland is therefore still state-owned, whereas the practice of the pasture contract system is gradually forcing the Chinese government to clarify the uncertainty over state versus collective ownership of grassland and, where collective, the level of ownership.

The discrepancy between higher and lower administrative levels in their understanding of ownership is clearly captured in two statements by officials in Ningxia. When asked about the difference between state and collective grassland, the Deputy Head of the Ningxia Department of Animal Husbandry answered that 'all grassland is state-owned, but we have given use rights of grassland to collectives or individuals under the pasture contract system'.[49] But a township head in the pastoral region in Ningxia surprisingly stated that 'most of the grassland in our township is collective property of administrative villages, while only a minor part, maybe a half per cent of all pasture, is state-owned, namely by state cattle farms'.[50] Below I will discuss the practical consequences of the unclear institutional structure for the pasture contract system.

Continued Confusion over Definitions: Who May and Who May Not Use and Contract Pasture

The first reference to use rights of grassland in contemporary Chinese legal texts appeared in the 'Grassland Regulations' enacted by the Inner Mongolian government in 1965. They were amended in 1973, and two years later the Ministry of Forestry and Agriculture provisionally approved their extension to eleven provinces and autonomous regions. The 1975 regulations stated that each county and banner (administrative unit equal to county) could allocate use rights (*a*) to state-owned profit and non-profit enterprises and (*b*) to production teams of the people's communes. In addition, they stressed the need for clear boundaries for grassland, and called for well-defined use rights to be vested in the commune or the team.[51]

The use rights of grassland were not defined in national law until 1985, three years later than those for ownership rights. Article 4 of the Grassland

[49] Oral communication (1996). [50] Oral communication (1996).
[51] See Wenzheng Shi, Research for a Judicial System for Grassland, p. 48.

Law provides that long-term use rights to state-owned grassland can be allocated to the collective. Furthermore, under the same article state- and collectively owned grassland, as well as state-owned grassland in long-term use by the collective, may be contracted to collectives or individuals for purposes of animal husbandry. The level of government immediately above the county (prefecture) is responsible for the registration and issue of user permits for the lease of state-owned grassland, while the county government can assume those responsibilities for collectively owned and used grassland.[52]

In order to be able to exercise stricter control over grassland use and management, some policy-makers propose that use rights be vested in the township (*sumu* in Inner Mongolia)[53] or any other collective economic organization at the township level. The township would then be charged with coordinating grassland use by the individual herders. Others argue against this on the grounds that pastoralists' incentives for sustainable livestock production can be enhanced only if use rights are vested in the lowest possible unit, the administrative village (*gacha*), or even the natural village. Among the proponents of the latter view are those who plead for the politically sensitive option of recollectivizing livestock production, or a land tenure system based on more traditional social ties. Under this proposal pasture contracts would be issued to traditional groupings such as the *khot ail* in Mongolia. These are herders' groups of between two and over a dozen families, depending on the region. The *khot ail* is responsible for the socialization of children, for the performance of familial rites, and for economic activities such as the herding of collective flocks. However, much of this discussion is still going on, and a resolution does not seem to be imminent.

Little is still known about the actual implementation process of the pasture contract system in China. However, it seems that in Gansu and Inner Mongolia the administrative village is generally seen as the owner of grassland and therefore responsible for the issue of contracts, while the township acts as a monitoring unit.[54] Ningxia, on the other hand, presents a much more amalgamated picture. In the pastoral region, user contracts have been issued directly by the county government to the natural villages. After use rights had thus been fixed, the township issued pasture contracts to the individual households (implying that the township is the owner of grassland), with the administrative village as a monitoring unit. In the semi-pastoral regions, no pasture contracts have been issued either to natural villages or to farm households. The pasture is used in common by the administrative or natural village on the basis of boundary agreements issued by the township or drawn up by administrative villages themselves.

[52] See NZTF (ed.), Complete Edition of Agricultural Laws, p. 685.

[53] In Inner Mongolia the equivalents of the prefecture, county, township, and administrative village are, respectively, *meng* (league), *qi* (banner), *sumu* (township), and *gacha* (administrative village).

[54] In Balinyou and Alukeerqin County, Inner Mongolia, the administrative village is the owner while the township supervises. The same goes for Sunan County, Gansu. See Longworth and Williamson, *China's Pastoral Region*, pp. 183, 231, 259–61.

In general, natural villages do regard grassland in their vicinity as their own and, in spite of overlapped grazing and frequent grazing disputes, boundaries are quite clear to all.

Another aspect on which the Grassland Law is imprecise is the transfer of grassland use rights. Article 80 of the General Principles of Civil Law, based on article 10 of the Constitution, states that 'land may not be sold, leased, mortgaged or illegally transferred by any other means'. This situation was altered by article 2 of the constitutional amendment adopted by the first session of the seventh NPC in April 1988. The constitutional amendment stipulates that 'the use right of land may be transferred according to the regulations of the law'. In the same year, the amendment to the 1986 Land Management Law was adopted, which provided that land use rights may be granted to others in return for payment.[55] Moreover, article 4 of the Land Management Regulations of 1991 prescribes that ownership and use rights of grassland must be regulated according to the Grassland Law.[56] Article 4 of the Grassland Law provides for contracting state and collective pasture to collectives and individuals. But the Grassland Law does not state whether pasture contracts may be transferred or sold, in contrast to another basic law, the Agriculture Law, article 13 of which stipulates that 'The contractor may transfer the contracted land, mountain, grassland, wasteland, sandy waste and waters . . . if permission from the party that issued the contract has been obtained'.[57] Several Chinese jurists have remarked that the fact that basic national laws such as the Land Management Law and the Agriculture Law allow the transfer of land contracts while the Grassland Law does not has created a legal twilight zone.

The fuzziness around the transfer of the right of use and contract created by the Grassland Law translated into legal chaos at the provincial level, as a brief review of provincial legislation makes clear. The grassland regulations proclaimed by the governments of Inner Mongolia (1984), Jilin (1987) and Heilongjiang (1984), and the former provisional grassland regulations of Ningxia (1983), permit no transfer of grassland. These regulations also make no distinction between transfers of use rights and of contract rights. On the other hand, the regulations of Liaoning (1988) and Xinjiang (1989) allow only the transfer of the use right (whatever that may imply, as neither province has legal procedures to formalize grassland use rights) while no mention is made of the transfer of use rights under the pasture contract system. The regulations issued by Gansu do not even mention the transfer of grassland.[58] It is clear that the Grassland Law must be more specific on the transfer of use and contract rights, in particular on the distinction between the two, and on the conditions under which the

[55] Albert Chen, *Introduction to Legal System of China*, p. 198.
[56] NZTF (ed.), Complete Edition of Agricultural Laws, p. 562. [57] *Ibid.*, p. 7.
[58] Inner Mongolia Grassland Regulations, article 9; Ningxia Provisional Grassland Regulations, article 3; Liaoning Grassland Regulations, article 5; Jilin Grassland Regulations, article 9; Gansu Detailed Rules on the Implementation of the Grassland Law; Heilongjiang Grassland Regulations, article 6; Xinjiang Grassland Regulations, article 12. See Difangxing Fagui Xuanbian Bianxiezu (ed.), A Compilation of Local Laws and Regulations, pp. 494, 703, 877, 1020, 3578, 3742, 3893.

transfer of land use and contract rights is allowed. In fact, the revised draft of the Grassland Law that was sent in July 1999 to the NPC for review and discussion includes the stipulation that 'the contract and management right to grassland can be transferred according to the law'.[59] But the revised provincial grassland regulations of Inner Mongolia (1991) and Ningxia (1994) already provide for the transfer of pasture contracts.[60]

According to a small group of Chinese scholars and officials, the present laws and regulations on the transfer of land lease contracts do not offer sufficient legal protection for the contractor. For example, any transfer of land lease rights has to be approved beforehand by the party that issued the contract, namely, the collective. Arguably, such an arrangement allows the collective to misuse land through administrative measures, as it always has the final say in any land transaction. A Chinese scholar at the Chinese Academy of Social Sciences comments:

> The use of such administrative means in order to effect land management and the best allocation of land neglects farmers' right of independence, and is principally harmful to the stability of rural production. The fact that the transfer of lease rights to land has to be approved by the party which issued the contract actually restricts the free transfer of land use rights.[61]

A case that illustrates some of the current problems involved in the transfer of pasture contracts is that of a certain farmer Wang, living in Zhengyi Village, Hongri Township, Inner Mongolia. In the spring of 1991, he contracted 5,000 mu of pasture from the villagers' committee for a period of five years, for which he paid a contract fee of a half RMB per mu. One year later, Wang sold the land use rights for one RMB per mu to another farmer without the consent of the villagers' committee. The county grassland management station charged him with an 'illegal contract transfer' and imposed a 500 RMB fine. Wang appealed, but the court ruled that he had violated the Agriculture Law. However, in the meantime the grassland station had dropped the charges and annulled its former verdict. The case was then left to the villagers' committee to resolve.[62]

Apart from the fact that one might wonder why the villagers' committee would oppose the transfer of pasture contracts, the first question that comes to mind in this case is: why was the Agriculture Law used as the legal basis on which Wang was found guilty? Wang had surely breached the Inner

[59] Article 15, 'Zhonghua Renmin Gongheguo Caoyuanfa Xiuding Cao'an: Songshengao' [Revised Draft for the Grassland Law of the People's Republic of China: Draft for Approval and Revision] (15 July 1999), p. 4.

[60] See 'Ningxia Huizu Zizhiqu Caoyuan Guanli Tiaoli' ['Grassland Management Regulations of the Ningxia Hui Autonomous Region'], article 10, *Ningxia Ribao* [Ningxia Daily] (29 December 1994), p. 3; and '1991 Regulations for Grassland Administration in the Inner Mongolia Autonomous Region', article 7, in Inner Mongolia Law Institute of Social Academy of Sciences (ed.), *A Collection of Selected Translations of the Inner Mongolia Autonomous Region Local Legal Regulations* (Hohhot: Neimenggu Renmin Chubanshe, 2000), p. 256.

[61] Su Chen, 'Tudi Chengbao Jingying Wuquanhua yu Nongdi Shiyongquan Zhidu de Queli' ['Changing the Contract Right to Land into a Real Right and the Establishment of a System for Agricultural Land Use Rights'], *Zhongguo Faxue* [Chinese Law], Vol. 3 (1996), p. 89.

[62] Wenzheng Shi, Research for a Judicial System for Grassland, pp. 190–1.

Mongolia Grassland Regulations, which prohibit any transfer of grassland. However, national law always has precedence over provincial law. The national law most closely related to this case is the Grassland Law, which unfortunately contains no clause on the transfer of land use rights. The verdict was therefore based on the Agriculture Law. As we saw earlier, this law states that '...the contractor may transfer the contracted grassland...if permission from the party that issued the contract has been obtained'. Wang allegedly had not asked for permission from the villagers' committee; thus, he had committed an offence. Also intriguing is the sudden change of attitude from the grassland station: the charges were suddenly dropped, although it was clear that Wang had violated the law by selling the right of use without permission from the villagers' committee. The end of the episode is typical for a society dominated by the 'rule by men' instead of the 'rule of law': it is left to the villagers' committee to mediate and resolve the conflict.[63]

Protect the Grassland, Prohibit Reclamation

The third category of rules reviewed in this chapter pertains to the protection and improvement of grassland. One of the most important aspects of grassland protection is the prohibition of reclamation for agricultural purposes. The official and academic view in China holds that reclamation directly leads to land degradation and soil erosion. However, reclaimed pasture unsuitable for agriculture is often abandoned after a certain length of time, after which the original vegetation can recover. For example, in Qitai County in Xinjiang over 1.0 million mu of grassland were reclaimed in the period of the early People's Republic. At present not even one-fifth of it is under cultivation. The same applies for Qinghai Province, where 5.7 million mu have been reported reclaimed in the 1950s, whereas in 1963 only 3.2 million mu were still under cultivation.[64] The long term effects and the extent of irreversibility of degradation and erosion caused by reclamation are issues that grassland scientists need to study in more detail.[65]

[63] Albert Chen notes 'the system of mediation of disputes by people's mediation committees has always been stressed as an important feature of the Chinese legal system'. People's mediation committees are established under villagers' committees or resident committees (urban areas). Also the judicial assistants at the county and township people's governments and county courts may help in the settlement of disputes through mediation. Chen gives figures for 1989, stating that there were more than 1 million mediation committees that successfully handled over 7.34 million civil cases. Albert Chen, *Introduction to Legal System of China*, pp. 150–1.

[64] Wenzheng Shi, Research for a Judicial System for Grassland, p. 94.

[65] Roy Behnke, Ian Scoones, and other scientists have written extensively on the misconceptions of grassland ecology and grassland degradation. See Roy H. Behnke, Ian Scoones, and Carol Kerven (eds.), *Range Ecology at Disequilibrium: New Models of Natural Variability and Pastoral Adaptation in African Savannas* (London: Overseas Development Institute, 1993). In another article I have used the theoretical underpinnings proposed by Behnke and Scoones to examine the allegation of grassland degradation by Chinese officials and scholars. See Peter Ho, 'Rangeland Degradation in North China Revisited? A Preliminary Statistical Analysis to Validate Non-Equilibrium Range Ecology', *Journal of Development Studies*, Vol. 37, No. 3 (2001), pp. 99–132.

Reclamation of grassland does incite, however, ongoing conflicts between pastoralists as opposed to sedentary farmers, whose origins can be traced back a long time.[66] Encroachment of pastoral areas has become commonplace because of rising population pressure and the search for short-term economic gains unleashed by the reforms. Livestock farmers and pastoralists urgently need stricter control on reclamation.

The earliest legal codes on grassland use and conservation are the Great Law promulgated by Genghis Khan, the Tsaaziing Bichig Code (1230), and the Laws of Khubilai Tsetsen Khan (1321). Naturally, the articles on environmental protection included in these codes have completely different meaning from those developed in the twentieth century. In general, these regulations restricted hunting and prohibited fire on pastures. This is true also of the Mongol codes of the eighteenth century, such as the Khalkh Jirum (1709) and the code of Woqilai (1728/9).[67] For example, the fifth code of Woqilai Tuxietuhan[68] provides that anyone who accidentally sets fire to pasture will be fined one horse and five head of cattle, and must also compensate for pasture losses. The witness will be rewarded with one head of cattle of the five aforementioned, while the one who extinguishes the fire will acquire the remaining four. If the offender puts down the fire himself he may be exempted from prosecution. On the eve of the proclamation of the People's Republic, a policy that explicitly prohibited grassland reclamation was proclaimed by the government of Inner Mongolia. In 1947, the newly established Inner Mongolia Autonomous Region adopted the policy to 'protect the grassland, prohibit reclamation' (*baohu muchang, jinzhi kaihuang*). Elaborating on the same theme, the central government proclaimed the 'Fundamental Summary of Animal Husbandry in Pastoral Regions such as Inner Mongolia, Suiyuan, Qinghai and Xinjiang' in 1953. The Fundamental Summary provided for the practice of rotational grazing, and pasture protection and improvement. Other pastoral regions adopted local norms of grassland protection along the lines of the 1953 Fundamental Summary.[69]

The first national law in Chinese history that deals explicitly with the protection and improvement of grassland is the 1985 Grassland Law.

[66] For a historical description of the shifting frontier between Mongols and Han Chinese, see for example Eduard B. Vermeer, 'Checks without Balances: Manchu State Building and Chinese Agricultural Expansion on the Inner-Mongolian Frontier', in James Reardon-Anderson (ed.), *Continuities and Changes on the Mongolian Steppe: Implications for Land Use* (forthcoming); Thomas J. Barfield, *The Perilous Frontier: Nomadic Empires and China* (Cambridge, MA: Basil Blackwell, 1989).

[67] See Pieter W. Germeraad, *The Mongolian Landscape Tradition: A Key to Progress–Nomadic Traditions and their Contemporary Role in Landscape Planning and Management in Mongolia* (Rhoon: Pieter Germeraad and Zandangin Enebisch, 1996), pp. 51–4.

[68] The name Tuxietuhan Woqilai (the clan name comes first in Mongol, as in Chinese) would in modern Mongol transcription most likely be 'Tüsiyetü Ochir'. The term 'Tüsiyetü' (literally, 'providing support to the ruler') is an honorific title, in former times equal to a counsellor of a monarch. However, in the eighteenth century this term could also have been the clan name of the person or even the name of a place. 'Ochir' comes closest to the Chinese transcription, but leaves the ending '-ai' unsolved, which could be a genitive case here. Nugteren (oral communication, 1997).

[69] Su Chen, 'Changing the Contract Right to Land', p. 17; and Tu Ba and Lin Tai, General Discussion of Animal Husbandry, pp. 48–9.

In contrast to the regulations concerning ownership and use rights, those dealing with grassland protection are quite comprehensive and complete, ranging from illegal reclamation to the exploitation of medicinal plants. In addition, many provincial regulations provide a detailed system of fines and punishment for the various offences.

Moreover, unlike in the regulations on ownership and use there is no apparent contradiction between central and provincial regulations concerning protection and improvement.[70] Many of these rules exist on paper only and have barely any direct influence on the people at the grass-roots level to whom they are directed. The failure to implement them arises from the weakness of the state institutions that have to enforce them rather than from inconsistencies between the rules themselves.

The Catch-22 Situation of Chinese Grassland Policy

An attempt to chart grassland policy in China from the centre to the locality has often been greeted with the reaction: why bother? Chinese bureaucrats justify their reaction by saying, 'oh, the cultural level of the peasants is too low' (*wenhua suzhi tai di*), or 'our legal system is incomplete' (*fazhi bu jianquan*), and would leave it at that. However, it is important to consider the formulation process of the Grassland Law, for two basic reasons.

First, if we want to understand the institutional changes in property rights we need to consider the history of the Grassland Law and grassland policy. Their history is a chronicle of the arduous struggle by the Chinese government to build up a coherent and effective body of laws and regulations to provide the basis for the 'rule of law' in the pastoral sector. In fact, after the establishment of the People's Republic in China there was no such body of rules. Only when China gradually started to dismantle its collectivist institutions in the late 1970s did new possibilities open up in grassland management. The study of the formulation processes of the Grassland Law and grassland policy is thus also the study of a trial-and-error policy-making process of a government attempting to bring about social change by means of new institutional arrangements. Every amendment in this process signifies a new stage, a new awareness of changed circumstances in the economy, as well as a political will to respond to these different circumstances.

Second, I maintain that the problems in grassland management that we encounter at the grass roots level in China can be fully understood only if we also study the content of grassland laws and policies and how they came into being. The content of laws and policies is intricately linked to

[70] The Chinese Constitution stipulates that national laws should not conflict with the Constitution, administrative regulations (promulgated by the State Council) should not conflict with the Constitution and laws, and local regulations (proclaimed by the People's governments of provinces and autonomous regions) should not conflict with the Constitution, laws, and administrative regulations. A legal system has been established for invalidating norms at lower echelons that are inconsistent with norms at higher levels. However, Albert Chen notes that up to 1992 the system has not become operational. See Albert Chen, *Introduction to Legal System of China*, pp. 90, 92.

inter-ministerial and inter-departmental struggles, and this is nothing new. The Grassland Law, however, is a classical example of an empty institution or symbol law. This becomes clear, in particular, from article 4, which defines the framework of the pasture contract system based on the principle of state and collective grassland. This article falls short of defining the nature of state and collective ownership, thus undermining the entire legal basis of the pasture contract system. At this point the main feature of an empty institution becomes clear: article 4 is the result of a political compromise between a faction striving to have the issue of state and collective grassland included in law, and a faction that has succeeded in postponing an effective solution for this politically sensitive issue through an *intentionally* ambiguous formulation, rendering the law virtually impossible to enforce. I have shown that the core of this problem is partly historical.

Over forty years have elapsed since grassland was nationalized during Land Reform in the 1950s. However, state ownership of grassland was not inscribed in law until much later. When the people's communes were established shortly after, certain portions of grassland were included in their land holdings. Yet these were still state property, thus producing a murky area of ownership and management. The layout of the communes was finally consolidated in 1962 and ownership of land was vested in the production team by the grace of the so-called Sixty Articles. But this left critical issues of the level of ownership unresolved. The Constitution of 1982 finally mentioned the existence of state and collective ownership of grassland, but failed to clarify the meaning of collective property. This touches on the critical issue of customary rights. Was grassland in long-term, customary use by the collective also its property? And, if so, how were customary, collective ownership rights to be legally established: automatically or through the issue of land property permits? Moreover, since the term 'collective' comprised the commune, the brigade, as well as the team, the level of ownership was also ambiguous.

In this legal vacuum, the 1985 Grassland Law defined the pasture contract system under which individuals and collectives could lease collective or state grassland. But as long as state and collective ownership of grassland and the level of collective ownership are not clarified, the consistency of the entire pasture contract system will be in jeopardy. A small group of officials and scholars within the Ministry of Agriculture is quite determined to solve the implementation problems of the Grassland Law by resolving the issue of grassland ownership. However, it seems that the current political tide is flowing against them, and the chances that the revised Grassland Law will provide a final and clear-cut decision on this matter are slim.

In this chapter, I have also paid some attention to the relationship between central and provincial regulations on grassland management and use. The first thing that strikes the observer is the inadequate demarcation of responsibilities between the legislative bodies at different administrative levels. In some cases provincial regulations have run ahead of national law. This is not a problem as long as provincial regulations have been formulated within the legal framework of the Grassland Law. However, in the case of a delicate issue such as the definition of state and collective ownership, provinces have gone far beyond the boundaries of this framework and have taken political decisions over matters that have not even been resolved at the national level. This has happened because provincial governments are under pressure to stretch the limits of a national legal framework that no longer deals with the problems they encounter at the grass roots. Their legislative actions are attempts to innovate in areas where the centre is politically hamstrung by power struggles between departments and ministries.

Guiding the pastoral sector safely through the reform period is a complex and difficult task for the Ministry of Agriculture. The establishment of a coherent grassland policy and a sound system of laws, regulations, and institutions for grassland management and use is hampered by many contradictions, both in the content of laws and policies and between the various policy-makers. Sometimes the solution to one problem merely prompts the emergence of another. The present Grassland Law reflects the political compromises that have been struck over sensitive issues, thereby allowing certain contradictory situations to persist. Although we cannot hope that the revised Grassland Law—at the time of writing this chapter still without a fixed schedule for being voted on by the NPC—will be able to deal with all these conflicting issues, there is no reason for pessimism. Within the Ministry of Agriculture and within research institutes scattered over the country, a small but growing group of officials and scholars are continuously testing the limits of the politically possible. It has always struck me how knowledgeable and critical they are of the problems of grassland policy formulation and implementation.[71] It is time that will chart the way out of the catch-22 situation of grassland policy.

[71] However ironical it may seem, a good thing about the Cultural Revolution is that it brought into being this group of critical officials and scholars. At the time, many intellectuals were sent to the pastoral areas to labour or herd sheep and goats. Several of those working in research institutes that presently advise the Ministry of Agriculture on grassland policy were once sent to the countryside.

4
Contested Spaces: Forest Rights, Registration, and Social Conflict

As forest policies of China are unstable, the ownership rights of mountain forests—in particular the common forests (*gongyoulin*) of townships and villages—have not been formally determined. . . . Because of ownership shifts during the socialist transformation, the restructuring of the commune system, and ambiguously drawn and redrawn boundaries, the limits and titles of some forests are unclear, which has resulted in disputes over forest rights.

(State Forestry Bureau[1])

Forest under Pressure

Although the epigraph of this chapter dates from the late 1980s, it is still valid today. The clarification of forest ownership and subsequent registration of forest land are among the Chinese government's major unaccomplished tasks. Yet forest registration is particularly complicated because it involves the handling of claims by the collectives and customary titles for which the present legal framework offers no formal status. In addition—and this fact is frequently brushed aside in present-day China because of its sensitivity—poor and landless farmers were once lured into the communist revolution with the promise of land. During Land Reform, they did obtain private land titles. However, the Machiavellian policies of the CCP, under which new elites were continuously created and old elites destroyed, also caused land holdings to be frequently reshuffled. How this land theft affects forest administration today is uncertain, but that it does so is beyond doubt. For this and other reasons, the forest tenure system is plagued by conflict.

At present China has approximately 133 million ha of forest covering 14 per cent of its surface. The largest forest areas can be found in the north-eastern tip (Inner Mongolia and former Manchuria), in the eight southern provinces (Guangdong, Guangxi, Fujian, Jiangxi, Hubei, Hunan, Sichuan, and Yunnan), and in mid-China (Shaanxi Province). Together they make up around 80 per cent of the total forestry area.[2] The majority of forests in the north are mixed coniferous, whereas the southern ones are lowland rain and monsoon forests. The native woody vegetation of the evergreen broad-leaved forest in the south is unique. China boasts about 2,500 species of forest trees—many of which are indigenous—ranging from oak (*Quercus*), elm (*Ulmus*), and lime (*Tilia*) to trees yielding important by-products such

[1] State Forestry Bureau (ed.), *China Forestry Yearbook 1949–1986* (Beijing: Zhongguo Linye Chubanshe, 1992, reprint of 1987), p. 476.

[2] Each of these provinces has over 8 million ha of forestry area. See State Forestry Bureau (ed.), *China Forestry Yearbook 1998* (Beijing: Zhongguo Linye Chubanshe, 1999), p. 105.

as the tung-oil trees (*Paulownia*), lacquer trees (*Rhus vernicifera*), and star anise (*Ilicium verum*).[3]

The People's Republic belongs to the world's five largest wood-producing countries, with 7 per cent of total production used as fuel. In recent times, the central government has invested heavily in expanding the wood-processing facilities and upgrading the outdated small mills of the past. In 1999 a total of 48.5 million cubic metres of raw wood, 7.3 million of plywood, and 3.9 million of fibreboard was produced. But as the domestic demand for forest products outweighs the domestic supply, China has become a significant importer of wood products (including raw wood, plywood, veneer, pulp, and paper) as well as some non-wood forest products since the 1980s.[4] There is increasing evidence that the domestic shortages in wood products are forcing Chinese logging companies abroad. Like their Indonesian, Korean, and Japanese counterparts, Chinese logging companies are seeking—if necessary by illegal means—to expand their activities in other countries, in particular in South and Latin America.[5]

In addition to lagging production, rapid urbanization and economic development have put mounting pressure on China's forest resources. The relatively low economic value attached to forests has led to the reclamation of forests for non-agricultural purposes and a sharp decline in the total area of forestry land. Between the national forest inventories of 1984–8 and 1989–93, the area of forestry land dropped by 4.54 million ha,[6] while since the fifth forest inventory of 1994–8 another 1.23 million ha of forestry land was lost due to illegal reclamation.[7] Here it should be noted that the Chinese statistics make a distinction between forest area (*senlin mianji*) and forestry land (*linye yongdi mianji* or, for short, *lindi mianji*). The former term refers to land covered with trees and a canopy or foliage exceeding 20 per cent, whereas forestry land is all the land with a present or potential future forest cover or land allocated for forestry purposes.[8]

[3] Food and Agriculture Organization (FAO) (ed.), *China Forestry Report* (Rome: FAO, 1998), p. 1.

[4] State Forestry Bureau (ed.), *China Forestry Statistical Yearbook 1999* (Beijing: Zhongguo Linye Chubanshe, 2000), p. 156. In 1998, China's net imports of paper and cellulose pulp and waste paper were worth $US3.7 billion; net imports of wood and wooden products were worth $149 million. See National Bureau of Statistics (ed.), *China Statistical Yearbook 1999* (Beijing: Zhongguo Tongji Chubanshe, 1999), p. 581. A good description of China's forest industry and economy is provided in Yaoqi Zhang, Guangcui Dai, Heyu Huang, Fanwen Kong, Zhiwei Tian, Xuan Wang, and Lei Zhang, 'The Forest Sector in China: Towards a Market Economy', in Matti Palo and Jussi Uusivuori (eds.), *World Forests, Society and Environment* (London: Kluwer Academic Publishers, 1999), pp. 379–82.

[5] See also Nigel Sizer and Dominiek Plouvier, *Increased Investment and Trade by Transnational Logging Companies in Africa, the Caribbean and the Pacific* (Brussels: World Wide Fund for Nature, 2000); Linda van der Valk en Peter Ho, 'Van Kaalslag naar Duurzaam Bosbeheer? Het Surinaamse Bosbeleid in Beweging' [From Deforestation to Sustainable Forestry? Surinam Forest Policy in Motion], in Arthur P. J. Mol en Bas van Vliet (eds.), *Suriname, Schoon Genoeg?*, Van Arkel, Utrecht, 2004.

[6] Changjian Li and Jipang Yang (eds.), *Zhongguo Linye Wushinian: 1949–1999* [Fifty Years of Forestry in China] (Beijing: Zhongguo Linye Chubanshe, 1999), p. 874 (table on forestry land).

[7] State Forestry Bureau (ed.), *China Forestry Yearbook 1999–2000* (Beijing: Zhongguo Linye Chubanshe, 2000), p. 110.

[8] For an explanation of the statistical definitions, see State Forestry Bureau (ed.), *Zhongguo Linye Tongji Zhibiao Jieshi* [Explanation on the Indicators of China's Forest Statistics] (Beijing: Zhongguo Linye Chubanshe, 2000), pp. 34–5.

According to the Forest Law revised in 1998, there are five types of forest: (*a*) productive timber forest (*yongcailin*), which includes the forests for bamboo production; (*b*) economic forest (*jingjilin*) meant for providing food and non-wood forest products, such as tung oil, resins, mushroom, and medicinal plants; (*c*) protection forest (*fanghulin*) for soil and water conservation; (*d*) fuel-wood forest (*xintanlin*) for the sole purpose of fuel production; and (*e*) special purpose forest (*tezhong yongtulin*), which includes nature reserves and forests meant for national defence, biodiversity conservation, and scientific research.[9]

The destruction of forest resources has serious environmental drawbacks. In 1998 the nation was confronted with large-scale flooding which left 4,150 people dead and caused material damages of $US 32 billion. Deforestation at the upper and lower reaches of the Yangzi River was identified as one of the main causes.[10] Also, the scale and intensity of desertification have been increasing in recent years. Deserts are expanding at an estimated 156,000 ha per year, causing annual economic losses of $2 billion to $3 billion. The decreasing forest area has per substantial impact on biodiversity. China possesses a wealth of flora and fauna; an estimated 2,400 species of vertebrates—including 301 endangered ones—account for 10 per cent of the world's vertebrates' species. In terms of richness in plant species, the country ranks third in the world (after Brazil and Indonesia). It contains 32,800 species of plant (only Brazil and Indonesia have more); over 10,000 of these are indigenous and 288 are threatened with extinction. The World Bank reported in 1994 that 200 species of plants have already become extinct in China.[11] The central authorities have put environmental protection high on the political agenda. In line with the United Nations Conference on Environment and Development (UNCED) in 1992, the Chinese government produced China's Agenda 21 as a means to promote sustainable development. Within this framework a Biodiversity Conservation Action Plan, a National Action Plan to Combat Desertification,[12] and a National Forestry Action Plan were developed. Along with the Forestry Action Plan, a logging ban was introduced in 1998 whereby commercial logging in natural forests was prohibited.

What Is Specific about Forest Tenure?

The various problems in the Chinese forestry sector reflect an ineffective and poorly functioning forest tenure system. In fact, deforestation, desertification, and biodiversity loss are likely to worsen with progressive urbanization and commercialization. Are the dynamics of the forest tenure

[9] Article 4 of the 1998 Revised Forest Law, NPC, *Zhonghua Renmin Gongheguo Senlinfa* [Forest Law of the People's Republic of China] (Beijing: Fazhi Chubanshe, 1999), p. 8.

[10] State Forestry Bureau (ed.), *'98 Hongshui Jujiao Senlin* [The 1998 Floods: Focusing on Forests] (Beijing: Zhongguo Linye Chubanshe, 1999), pp. 1–2.

[11] Zhang, 'The Forest Sector in China', pp. 375–7. An interesting study of the socio-economic background of diversity loss is by Changjin Sun, 'The Socio-Economic Root Causes of Biodiversity Loss: A Case Study in Deqin and Pingwu Counties of China' (Beijing: unpublished, December 1998).

[12] This has already led to the proclamation of the Law of Desertification Prevention and Control in August 2001, effective since January 2002.

system markedly different from the agricultural land tenure system? In this chapter I argue that they are. In fact, the forest tenure system in China enjoys much less credibility with state and society than the tenure system for cropland. In this sense, China's forest tenure displays marked similarities with grassland tenure. I will demonstrate that the malfunctioning of forest tenure is apparent from the loss of forest—in particular that due to illegal reclamation—and the high incidence of social conflict over forest rights. This is not to say that changes in socio-economic factors (population pressure, the possibility of alternative income-generating activities, the price levels of wood products, and so forth) could not affect the forest tenure system's credibility. But forest tenure differs from agricultural land tenure, in several ways.

The first stems from the nature of the resource itself. At the very beginning of forestry studies, a forester is taught that forest land differs from agricultural land in being inseparably linked to the trees. And as Louise Fortmann rightly remarked:

> Rights over trees are often distinct from rights over land. Tree tenure consists of a bundle of rights over trees and their produce which may be held by different people at different times. These rights include the right to own or inherit trees, the right to plant trees, the right to use trees and tree products, the right to dispose of trees and the right to exclude others from the use of trees and tree products.[13]

In addition, a forest is a complex ecosystem containing a broad diversity of flora and fauna. Apart from wood products, the forest generally yields many non-wood products, such as medicinal herbs, fruit, and game. Forest management is characterized by long-term investments and revenues; high transaction costs (information, contracting, and enforcement costs); substantial non-monetary costs and benefits (in terms of scenic beauty and biodiversity); and potential irreversible environmental effects (climatic change, soil degradation, and desertification).[14]

The second way in which forest tenure differs from agricultural land tenure is that forest serves a different socio-economic function from agricultural land. In 2002 over 368 million people were registered as employed in the agricultural realm. This figure hides a high level of unemployment. Due to frequent land reallocations, the agricultural lease system can function as a means of basic social security for the vast numbers of surplus rural labourers. The majority of the rural populace depends on subsistence agriculture for a living. Forestry, on the other hand, is generally a sideline activity, which is also reflected in the statistics. Of the rural net income per capita of 2,475 RMB, 35 per cent was derived from farming, while only 1 per cent came from forestry.[15] This does not

[13] Louise Fortmann, 'The Tree Tenure Factor in Agroforestry with Particular Reference to Agrica', in Louise Fortmann and John W. Bruce (eds.), *Whose Trees? Proprietary Dimensions of Forestry* (Boulder, CO: Westview Press, 1988), p. 16.

[14] There is even evidence of a relation between desertification and climate change. See, for example, Mike Hulme and Mick Kelly, 'Exploring the Links between Desertification and Climate Change', in Lewis Owen and Tim Unwin (eds.), *Environmental Management: Readings and Case Studies* (Oxford: Blackwell, 1997), pp. 213–30.

[15] National Bureau of Statistics (ed.), *China Statistical Yearbook 2003* (Beijing: Zhongguo Tongji Chubanshe, 2003), pp. 124, 367.

imply that in some regions forestry might not constitute a very significant sideline in people's livelihood.

Finally, the legal basis of forest ownership is different from that of agricultural land. Agricultural land is owned by the collective unless the law stipulates it is state-owned. Forest, grassland, and wasteland, however, are state-owned unless collective ownership can be legally proven. This is a crucial difference, because the burden of proof for forest, grassland, and wasteland rests with the collective. There are four critical issues at stake here.

First, legal evidence of land ownership is hard to obtain in present-day China, where land was never systematically registered and there is no cadastre. The collective is more likely to lose out in this 'battle for evidence' as collective ownership is intentionally left undefined in law and the collective lacks countervailing power against the (local) government (see also Chapters 1 and 2). Moreover, the future struggle over forest ownership will probably culminate in a clash between the state and the collective rather than in a collective versus collective or state versus state conflict;

Second, under present legal arrangements, ownership by customary right will be difficult, not to say impossible, to validate, because customary rights are generally unwritten and predate Land Reform. Article 30 of the 1950 Land Reform Law—still in force today—unequivocally stipulates that 'all land titles from before Land Reform are invalid'.[16] This regulation was reiterated in the important 'Measures for the Handling of Forest Disputes' issued by the former Ministry of Forestry in 1996.[17] One may be certain that, when forest registration progresses, article 30 will need to be seriously reconsidered if widespread social conflict is to be avoided. The fact that China's forest laws leave little space for local management and customary rights is not an exception to the forest laws of other developing nations. As the Food and Agriculture Organization (FAO) writes:

> Historically, forest laws in many countries have tended to be inhospitable to local forest management. Although older laws have often given recognition to limited usage rights, they have provided little scope for local people to play a meaningful part in the planning and management of forest resources on which they may have depended for generations. In many cases, the State has arrogated this role to itself through the creation of State forests. In other contexts, national law may have left tenurial status of forest areas unclear, giving weak or no legal protection to existing community-based tenure systems.[18]

Third, and related to the second issue, is the problem of agricultural reclamation in state-owned forest. Reclamation in China's frontier areas is certainly not new. Both the Imperial Qing and Nationalist governments promoted the reclamation of wasteland for agriculture and reasons of

[16] Article 30, 1950 Land Reform Law, in Jianhong Sun (ed.), *Tudi Quanshu Shiwu Zhinan* [Practical Compass on Land Titles] (Beijing, Zhongguo Dadi Chubanshe: 1998), p. 111.

[17] Article 9: 'The forest permits from before Land Reform cannot be admitted as evidence nor reference material in the handling of forest disputes.' See Lei Zhang and Hongxiang Wang (eds.), *Zhongguo Linye Falü Shiyong Shouce* [A Practical Manual for China's Forestry Laws] (Beijing: Zhongguo Linye Chubanshe, 2000), p. 382.

[18] FAO (ed.), *State of the World's Forests: 1999* (Rome: FAO, 1999), pp. 67–8.

national defence. The reclamation continued under the People's Republic, as state farms were established in the forests of former Manchuria, Inner Mongolia, and Chinese Turkestan. At the same time, farmers had historically been encouraged to open up new land in the border zones, yet suddenly found themselves enclosed in state property when forests were nationalized during Land Reform. The recognition problem of reclaimed wasteland in state-owned forests features prominently in Heilongjiang Province. As the official reaction of Heilongjiang Province to the NPC's debate on the 1998 Revised Land Administration Law stated:

> The problem of village land enclosed in forest (*cun tudi chahua*) is widespread in Heilongjiang. It leads to an overlap between agriculture and forestry, and has resulted in the nation's most serious land disputes.... After the establishment of the PRC, a stream of an estimated 10 million migrants from within the Great Wall (*guannei*) settled in Heilongjiang. Many of them reclaimed and colonized wasteland in state forests and formed settler villages... According to the policies of that time, this reclaimed land is considered collectively owned and is currently leased and cultivated by farmers. In some cases, land permits have been issued. In other cases, settler villages existed before and were enclosed into [state] forest area after the establishment of the PRC.[19]

Fourth, an issue that is barely researched because of its sensitivity and lack of information concerns private land ownership and its relation to forest disputes. Under Nationalist rule, most forest was privately owned. And although the communists gradually worked towards the abolition of private ownership after they had gained power, private forest holdings continued to exist until the collectivization of the countryside. At the time of Land Reform, common and private forests were allocated to the poor and landless. As the 1950 Land Reform Law stipulates: 'All the confiscated land... apart from that which is owned by the state as stipulated in this law, is uniformly, fairly and rationally allocated and given in ownership to... poor farmers (*pinkun nongmin suoyou*).'[20] When the Higher Agricultural Production Cooperatives were established in 1956 it was decreed: 'The privately owned land... of farmers entering the cooperative, must become the collective ownership of the cooperative.'[21] The political campaigns in later years, such as the Four Cleanups and the Cultural Revolution, were

[19] 'Remarks on the "Land Administration Law (Revised Draft)" by Relevant Departments, Several Experts and Grassroots Units of Heilongjiang Province', in Renda Fazhi Gongzuo Weiyuanhui (ed.), *Zhonghua Renmin Gongheguo Tudi Guanlifa Shiyi* [An Interpretation of the Land Administration Law of the People's Republic of China] (Beijing: Falü Chubanshe, 1998), p. 352.

[20] Article 10, 1950 Land Reform Law. See Jianhong Sun (ed.), *Tudi Quanshu Shiwu Zhinan* [Practical Compass on Land Title] (Beijing: Zhongguo Dadi Chubanshe, 1998), p. 107.

[21] Article 13, Exemplary Regulations on the Higher Agricultural Production Cooperatives. See Sun (ed.), Practical Compass on Land Titles, p. 131. Private land must not be confused with the land for individual use (*ziliudi*); the latter is also owned by the collective (*shengchandui suoyou de tudi, baokuo... ziliudi*). See article 21, Sixty Articles. See 'Nongcun Renmin Gongshe Gongzuo Tiaoli Xiuzheng Cao'an' [Revised Draft of the Work Regulations of the Rural People's Communes], 27/9/1962, in Zhongguo Renmin Jiefangjun Guofang Daxue Dangshi Yanjiushi (ed.), *Zhonggong Dangshi Jiaoxue Cankao Ziliao* [Reference and Educational Material on the History of the Chinese Communist Party], Vol. 24 (Beijing: Guofang Daxue Chubanshe, 1986), p. 141.

frequently used to reshuffle land from departing elites to incoming ones.[22] How this reshuffling affected land tenure in the village communities and provided the seedbed for future land disputes is a topic that is still wide open to research. In the case of forest holdings, the matter is even more complicated, as forest is in principle state-owned and the collective is laden with the burden of proving title. When titles within the village (if they were issued in the first place) have been destroyed because of struggles within the community, that task is especially arduous. One of the two cases of forest disputes dealt with in this chapter is testimony to this.

As stated earlier, the forest tenure system's lack of credibility is most clearly reflected in the relatively high incidence of social conflict—particularly between the state and the collective—and in the problems of forest loss and illegal reclamation. Before substantiating these issues with some statistics, concrete case studies, and forest disputes, I will give an overview of the major issues in national forest policy and administration so that we can better appreciate the institutional changes that underlie the forest tenure system. The Forest Law is among the earliest administrative laws that were proclaimed in the People's Republic. A trial Forest Law was already passed by the NPC in February 1979. It was revised in September 1984, and again in April 1998. This latest revision of the Forest Law revolved around three crucial questions—which have interesting parallels with national land policy and administration (see Chapter 1): (*a*) the stabilization of the forest tenure system with particular reference to forest registration; (*b*) the downgrading of the Ministry of Forestry; and (*c*) the establishment of a market for forest lease.

Critical Issues in National Forest Policy

Mission impossible: registering the forest. Already in the early 1980s great importance was attached to forest registration as the authorities feared the mining of forests if titles were left unclear. As we saw in Chapter 1, the registration of agricultural land halted at the level that mattered most: the villagers' group or original land owner. It thus created sufficient institutional ambiguity to allow the tenure system to function. By contrast, the forest administration seems determined to proceed with registration down to the lowest collective level. It is therefore no wonder that forest registration has incited some of the fiercest conflicts in rural society.

The official legal interpretation of the 1998 Revised Forest Law mentioned that 'although the original Forest Law had no clear regulations about forest land, the area of regulation of the Forest Law does include forest land', touching on stipulations such as 'the issue of forest land titles,

[22] As Madsen writes: 'Most poor peasants took part in Land Reform out of the hope of getting property. After the landlords (and during radical phases of policy, the rich peasants) had been expropriated, a large proportion of their land, together with all land owned corporately by such traditional organizations as clans and temples, was redistributed to the poor, usually after heated discussions about who really was poor.' Richard Madsen, 'The Countryside under Communism', in: Roderick MacFarquhar and John K. Fairbank, *Cambridge History of China. The People's Republic, Part 2: Revolutions within the Chinese Revolution 1966–1982* (Cambridge: Cambridge University Press, 1991, p. 628).

the expropriation of forest, the lease of wasteland and mountains suitable for forestry... The reason why the Forest Law is revised this time is to clearly include forest land as an area of regulation.'[23] And indeed, due to rapid commercialization and economic development forest tenure has become one of the most pressing issues in forestry.

In the early Republican period only a minor proportion (11 per cent) of the (registered) forests was in the hands of the state; 55 per cent was privately owned and 34 per cent held in common.[24] Under the Forest Laws of 1914 and 1945, private as well as common forest property had a legal status which, however, did not mean that this status was secure or significant. The 1914 Forest Law, for example, stated that 'if the Ministry of Agriculture and Trade deems that certain common and private forests have important links with the management of state-owned forest, it can be nationalized at a suitable price', whereas the 1945 Forest Law stipulated that 'there is state forest, common forest and private forest. Forest is in principle state-owned.'[25]

As early as 1947, when the Communist Party proclaimed the Outline of the Land Law of China, it was clear that forest would from then on come under direct government administration. To be sure, when the communists took power in China in 1949 the forests were nationalized.[26] Land reform in the early 1950s and the following collectivization had a profound impact on forest ownership and customary forest titles.[27] Private ownership and customary common ownership were delegitimized and replaced by state and collective ownership.[28] It is difficult to obtain accurate data on the

[23] Fuqing Wu and Kangtai Cao (eds.), *Zhonghua Renmin Gongheguo Senlinfa Shiyi* [An Interpretation of the Forest Law of the People's Republic of China] (Beijing: Falü Chubanshe, 1998), p. 6.

[24] In 1914, 332,350 ha was state-owned forest; 1.1 million ha common property forest; and 1.7 million ha private forest. In fact, this is only a fraction of the total area of forest land. See Xiang Yuan (ed.), *Zhongguo Nianjian Di Yi Hui* [China Yearbook No. 1] (Shanghai: Commercial Press Ltd., 1924), p. 1207. The greater part was unregistered forest and must have amounted to between 48 million and 125 million ha, depending on whether we use the estimated figures of 5% forest coverage or 13% forest coverage before 1949. See Yaoqi Zhang, 'Institutions in Forest Management: Special Reference to China', in M. Palo, J. Uusivuori, and G. Mary (eds.), *World Forests, Market and Policy* (London: Kluwer Academic Publishers, 2001), p. 423.

[25] Datong Xiong (ed.), *Zhongguo Jindai Linyeshi* [A History of Forestry in Modern China] (Beijing: Zhongguo Linye Chubanshe, 1989), pp. 603, 609–10.

[26] See article 9, 1947 Outline of the Land Law of China, and article 18 of the 1950 Land Reform Law, 'Large forests... wastelands and waste mountains... are all owned by the state', in Sun (ed.), Practical Compass on Land Titles, pp. 99, 109.

[27] Xueying Zhuang provides a brief description of the so-called Fung shui woods in Hong Kong villages before 1945. Xueying Zhuang, 'Rehabilitation and Development of Forest on Degraded Hills of Hong Kong', *Forest Ecology and Management*, No. 99 (1997), pp. 197–201. Other good descriptions of customary forest rights are provided in Nicholas K. Menzies, *Forest and Land Management in Imperial China* (London: St Martin's Press, 1994), and Ulrich Apel, 'Der Dorfwald von Moxie: Traditionelle Dorfwaldbewirtschaftung in Xishuangbanna, Südwest-China', Ph.D. thesis (Göttingen: Georg-August University of Göttingen, 1996).

[28] A surprisingly detailed yet not always accurate account of Land Reform and the impact on common forests in a village in Anhui is provided in Can Liu (ed.), *Shequ Linye Fazhan yu Xiaochu Pinkun de Zhidu ji Anli Yanjiu* [Case Studies in Community Forestry Development and Poverty Alleviation] (Beijing: Zhongguo Nongye Keji Chubanshe, 2000), pp. 66–81.

Table 2: **National forest registration in 1997 (in 10,000ha)**

Region	*Forestry area*	*Registered area*				*Unregistered area*			
		State forestry area	*% of total state forestry area*	*Collective forestry area*	*% total collective forestry area*	*State forestry area*	*% of total state forestry area*	*Collective forestry area*	*% total collective forestry area*
National	26,610.9	9,402.6	82.4	12,787.9	78.9	2,000.7	17.6	3,418.5	21.1
Beijing	92.0	5.2	82.5	0.0	0.0	1.1	17.5	85.7	100.0
Tianjin	7.3	1.9	99.0	4.1	75.9	0.02	1.0	1.3	24.1
Hebei	563.0	69.8	98.4	419.7	85.3	1.1	1.6	72.4	14.7
Shanxi	355.9	123.6	90.2	131.5	60.1	13.4	9.8	87.4	39.9
Inner Mongolia	3,314.1	1,264.9	49.5	644.1	84.7	1,288.5	50.5	116.6	15.3
Liaoning	566.9	68.7	97.4	446.8	90.0	1.8	2.6	49.6	10.0
Jilin	983.0	605.7	90.1	246.6	79.4	66.7	9.9	64.0	20.6
Heilongjiang	979.2	617.9	79.3	66.2	33.1	161.0	20.7	134.1	66.9
Shanghai	1.6	0.3	100.0	1.3	100.0	—	—	—	—
Jiangsu	59.2	9.3	96.9	31.6	63.7	0.3	3.1	18.0	36.3
Zhejiang	593.5	28.3	99.9	551.9	97.6	0.02	0.1	13.3	2.4
Anhui	413.3	32.7	98.2	340.0	89.5	0.6	1.8	40.0	10.5
Fujian	2,109.5	156.5	97.0	1,834.5	94.2	4.9	3.0	113.6	5.8
Jiangxi	1,051.8	136.2	93.5	895.6	98.8	9.5	6.5	10.5	1.2
Shandong	238.4	12.6	72.8	63.9	28.9	4.7	27.2	157.2	71.1

Henan	419.3	36.0	91.6	266.7	70.2	3.3	8.4	113.3	29.8
Hubei	835.4	56.3	97.7	395.5	50.8	1.3	2.3	382.3	49.2
Hunan	1,216.5	80.7	100.0	1,063.1	93.6	0.0	0.0	72.7	6.4
Guangdong	1,083.4	70.3	89.1	740.3	73.7	8.6	10.9	264.2	26.3
Guangxi	1,340.4	146.2	96.4	875.8	73.7	5.5	3.6	312.9	26.3
Hainan	182.1	61.4	62.5	10.8	12.9	36.8	37.5	73.1	87.1
Chongqing	300.8	34.1	92.4	62.1	23.5	2.8	7.6	201.8	76.5
Sichuan	1,997.2	953.5	83.1	583.8	68.7	194.4	16.9	265.5	31.3
Guizhou	740.8	36.7	93.1	507.1	72.3	2.7	6.9	194.3	27.7
Yunnan	2,793.2	615.3	86.7	1,880.5	83.1	94.7	13.3	382.7	16.9
Tibet	—	—	—	—	—	—	—	—	—
Shaanxi	1,197.5								
Gansu	—	997.1	—	8.4	—	—	—	—	—
Qinghai	121.5	111.4	98.8	6.1	69.3	1.3	1.2	2.7	30.7
Ningxia	102.7	35.8	100.0	66.9	100.0	—	—	—	—
Xinjiang	—	—	—	—	—	—	—	—	—
Longjiang Forest Corp.	1,006.0	974.1	96.3	—	—	31.9	3.2	—	—
Jilin Forest Corp.	n.a.	n.a.	n.a.	n.a.	n.a.	n.a.	n.a.	n.a.	n.a.
Neimenggu Forest Corp.	935.9	899.5	96.1	—	—	36.4	3.9	—	—
Daxing' an Ling Forestry Co.	829.5	829.5	100.0	—	—	—	—	—	—

Source: State Forestry Bureau, *China Forestry Yearbook 1998* (Beijing: Zhongguo Linye Chubanshe, 1999), p. 105.

current area of state and collective forestry land. According to Table 2, over 114 million ha is state-owned and 162 million ha is collectively owned forestry land, which gives a total forestry area approximately 10 million ha more than the official figure! However, most sources indicate that 60 per cent of forestry land is collective and 40 per cent state, and this is also the ratio that can be calculated from Table 2.[29]

Most of the collective forests are located in south and central China. In the provinces of Anhui, Fujian, Guangdong, Guangxi, Guizhou, Hainan, Hubei, Hunan, Jiangxi, and Zhejiang, the proportion of collective forestry area is around 90 per cent, and in Yunnan and Sichuan combined it is 65 per cent. The state forestry area is concentrated in north-east China (Liaoning, Jilin and Heilongjiang) and north-central China (Inner Mongolia). Table 2 also lists several state forest companies. These represent the 84 State Forestry Bureaux of Jilin, Heilongjiang, and Inner Mongolia, which were merged into four large forestry corporations in the early 1990s in order to enhance the competitiveness, vertical integration, and economies of scale of the forestry operations of state institutions.[30]

The reforms in the forestry sector began in March 1981 when the central authorities issued the 'Decision on Some Issues concerning Forest Protection and Forestry Development', popularly known as the Three Fixes. This term stood for (*a*) the assessment and registration of forest titles which provided the basis for (*b*) the distribution of 'family land' (*ziliushan*)—tiny patches of wasteland or degraded forest meant to supply the farm household's need for firewood. At the end of 1984, a total of 31 million ha of forest was distributed as family land to over 57 million households (an average of approximately 0.5 ha per household); and (*c*) the establishment of the forestry contract responsibility system under which so-called responsibility hills (*zerenshan* or non-timber plantations, fuel-wood forests, and small-scale timber forests unsuitable for collective management) were leased to individual farm households. The responsibility hills developed in three separate directions in later years. Some were included in the family land, such as happened in 1984 in Anhui Province. Others were returned to the collective after a national ban on the new allocation of responsibility hills was issued in 1987 in response to reports about deforestation by farmers. In most cases, however, the responsibility hills simply remained under individual lease.[31]

The forest registration of 1981 was trumpeted in overly confident tones.

The 'Three Fixes' in forestry is the Party and government's policy that shows their love for the people. Wherever the leadership attaches importance to it,

[29] See Dachang Liu, 'Tenure and Management of Non-State Forests in China since 1950: A Historical Review', *Environmental History*, Vol. 6, No. 2 (2001), p. 240. If one uses the figures given by Changjian Li and Jipang Yang, the ratio becomes 39.9% state and 60.1% collective forestry land. See Li and Yang (eds.), Fifty Years of Forestry in China, p. 86.

[30] See also Yaoqi Zhang, 'Costs of Plans vs Costs of Markets: Reforms in China's State-Owned Forest Management', *Development Policy Review*, Vol. 18 (2000), p. 291.

[31] A detailed account of the forestry reforms is provided by Liu, 'Tenure and Management of Non-State Forests', pp. 247–9.

policies are correct and the work is solid, the 'Three Fixes' in forestry will be done right.[32]

Yet eighteen years later the optimism had swung to alarmism:

It happened that permits were sometimes issued twice or not at all. In addition, due to the need for economic construction and the changes in management since 1981, there have been great changes in forest titles. . . . The many changes in forest titles have not been assessed in time, as a result of which many places 'have permits but no forest, or have forests but no permits'. Even worse, the content recorded by some forest permits does not match the actual site, which has resulted in numerous forest disputes. And lastly, to date there is no national standardized model for the forest permits.[33]

The conflicts stirred up by forest registration were not limited to the grass roots. During the first few years of registration, provincial-level disputes were particularly intense and became a matter of national interest. In 1984 the State Council circulated a report by the former Ministry of Forestry and the Ministry of Civil Affairs, which stated: 'Many provincial mountain forest disputes have not been solved yet. To date there are still 1,360 unsolved cases concerning a contested area of more than 1.4 million mu. Disputes are most frequent in the southern provinces.'[34]

Forest registration remains an unresolved issue. Current registration problems are evident from the data in Table 2. Of the twenty-six provinces and municipalities directly under the State Council, sixteen provinces had more than 20 per cent of the total area of forestry land still unregistered, whereas in four localities—Heilongjiang, Shandong, Hainan, and Chongqing—more than 60 per cent was unregistered. In addition, the vast territory and remote location of China's forests cast serious doubt on the reliability of these data. As we saw in Chapter 3, grassland was allegedly registered and contracted out. But in reality most of the data consisted merely of 'paper figures'. In response to the problems, in 1999 the State Forestry Bureau replaced the old permits with a national model of forest permits, to be used whenever forest is newly registered or changes in registration occur. In 2000, renewed forest registration was attempted in a few pilot areas, including Liaoning and Sichuan Provinces.[35]

The Revised Forest Law included a specific clause to facilitate the registration of forest under the jurisdiction of the state forest corporations: 'The State Council can entrust the responsible forest department of the State Council to register and issue permits for forest and trees of the state-owned key forest areas, as well as to notify the relevant local governments.'[36]

[32] State Forestry Bureau (ed.), *China Forestry Yearbook 1949–1986* (Beijing: Zhongguo Linye Chubanshe, 1986), p. 480.

[33] State Forestry Bureau (ed.), *China Forestry Yearbook 1999/2000* (Beijing: Zhongguo Linye Chubanshe, 1999/2000), p. 113.

[34] State Council (ed.), *Guowuyuan Pizhuan Linyebu, Minzhengbu deng Bumen guanyu Tiaochu Shengji Shanlinquan Jiufen Wenti de Baogao de Tongzhi* [Notice approved and circulated by the State Council on the Report of the Ministry of Forestry, Ministry of Civil Affairs, and other Ministries regarding the Arbitration of Provincial Mountain and Forest Rights Disputes], Document No. 95 (17 July 1984), p. 1.

[35] *Ibid.*, p. 113; and Lei Zhang (oral communication, 2001).

[36] Article 3, NPC, Forest Law of the People's Republic of China, p. 8.

From Table 2 it can be seen that the forest holdings of the state corporations have mostly been registered. However, the official legal interpretation of the Forest Law states that 'the operational terrain of these state forest companies exceeds provincial boundaries, while some of the boundaries are unclear, as a result of which registration is difficult for provincial governments to handle'.[37] The state forestry area encompassed by these corporations is substantial: the territory of the Longjiang, Inner Mongolia, and Daxing'an Ling corporations represents approximately a quarter of the total state forestry area (27 million ha). In addition, the central government is concerned with recent reports of illegal logging in these areas.

A second critical issue in forestry policy is unified land administration. In China today, land administration is fragmented and its authority divided among several ministries (see Chapter 1). According to the Land Administration Law, the Ministry of Land Resources is entrusted with the administration and supervision of the nation's land. But law also stipulates that the assessment and registration of forest and grassland are the responsibility of the State Forestry Bureau and the Ministry of Agriculture.[38] It is a typical case of state-supported institutional ambiguity: on the one hand, the central government aims to (re)centralize and unify land administration; on the other hand it has to deal with the reality of the historically scattered nature of land administration. In the following subsection, we will see how this affects the dynamics of forest tenure.

Stripping the ministry of its powers: fragmentation in land administration. The issue of unified land administration—or, better, the lack of it—is most clearly evident from a communication to the NPC by experts and institutions of Heilongjiang Province. They wrote: 'Forest permits are issued by the forestry departments, while land permits are issued by the land administration. The fact that the issue of these permits is not coordinated is one of the roots of land title disputes.'[39]

The origins of the problem can be traced to 1950, when the leaders of the young People's Republic put an end to the unified land administration that existed in the Republican era. From then on, land administration was divided between urban and rural land, as well as between different land resources—forest, grassland, and wasteland. A Ministry of Forest Reclamation was established (*Linkenbu*), which was changed into the Ministry of Forestry (*Linyebu*) in 1951. Its tasks comprised the 'overall protection of forest, the afforestation in key areas, and the rational use and exploitation of forest'. In order to meet the growing demand for lumber and wood products, a separate Ministry of Forest Industry was set up in 1956. But only two years later, the two ministries were merged into what

[37] Wu and Cao (eds.), An Interpretation of the Forest Law, p. 9.

[38] Articles 5 and 11, Revised Land Administration Law, in Weilian Fang (ed.), *'Zhonghua Renmin Gongheguo Tudi Guanlifa' Shiyong Jianghua* [A Practical Discussion of the 'Land Administration Law of the People's Republic of China'] (Beijing: Zhongguo Minzhu Fazhi Chubanshe, 1998), pp. 207–8.

[39] ''Remarks on the ''Land Administration Law (Revised Draft)'' by Relevant Departments, Several Experts and Grassroots Units of Heilongjiang Province' in RFGW (ed.), An Interpretation of the Land Administration Law, p. 352.

would later become the Ministry of Agriculture and Forestry (*Nonglinbu*). The Cultural Revolution brought nothing less than an institutional shake-up of forest administration when the authority of the forestry departments of Heilongjiang, Inner Mongolia, and Jilin was transferred to provincial revolutionary committees, and 83 per cent of the state forest farms were decentralized to counties and communes.[40] To undo the damage, a new State Forestry Bureau (*Guojia Linyeju*) was set up under the Ministry of Agriculture in May 1978. Exactly one year later, this ministry was split into a Ministry of Agriculture and a Ministry of Forestry.[41]

During the organizational reforms of 1998 a total of fifteen state commissions and ministries were axed, including the ministries of Power, Coal, Metallurgy, Chemistry, and Internal Trade. The Ministry of Forestry was also axed, downgraded after almost two decades once more to a bureau-level organ. At the same time, the State Land Administration was elevated to ministerial level and became the new Ministry of Land Resources by merging with the Ministry of Geology and Mineral Resources, the State Bureau of Marine Resources and the State Topography Bureau. Some voices within the central government maintain that the downgrading of the Ministry of Forestry and the simultaneous elevation of the State Land Administration is related to a wider strategy of concentrating power over land in a single ministry. The developments around the revision of the Land Administration Law lend support to this notion.

During the NPC debates on the Revised Land Administration Law in the summer of 1998, some delegates proposed that the 'scope of the [Land Administration] Law be expanded . . . by abolishing the regulation that the Forest Law controls the forest and trees, and the Grassland Law controls the grassland . . . and including this scope of control into the Land Administration Law. In this way permits can be uniformly issued, and [land] managed in a unified manner.'[42] However, the Vice Chairman of the NPC Legal Committee, Li Boyong, stated that the current circumstances did not permit such radical reform. He argued that the law should be left as it was, on the common understanding that unified land administration was the ultimate goal of the central government. Specifically for this purpose, the Revised Forest Law left some space for legal and institutional manoeuvring. As the official legal interpretation reads: 'As we considered the possible changes in . . . the current administrative set-up due to changes in economic conditions and organizational reforms, the Forest Law does not directly mention the term "State Forestry Bureau".'[43]

Officials within the forestry administration feel little enthusiasm for the idea of unified land administration, let alone their downgrading to bureau level. When I asked Zhang Lei, a senior official within the State Forestry

[40] Li and Yang (eds.), Fifty Years of Forestry in China, pp. 221–2. [41] *Ibid.*

[42] Boyong Li, Quanguo Renda Falü Weiyuanhui guanyu 'Zhonghua Renmin Gongheguo Tudi Guanlifa (Xiuding Cao'an)' chubu Shenyi Qingkuang de Huibao ['Report on the Preliminary Review of the Situation on the "Land Administration Law of the People's Republic (Revised Draft)" by the Law Committee of the National People's Congress'], Speech at the Third Session of the Standing Committee of the Ninth National People's Congress (24 June 1998), p. 3. [43] Wu and Cao (eds.), An Interpretation of the Forest Law, p. 27.

Bureau, why the ministry was downgraded, she answered:

Ask Premier Zhu Rongji, we don't know why we were downgraded! Our authority has declined; our director-general is now only as high as a vice-governor and that has made our work more difficult. Unified land management certainly does not mean that each department and ministry can act on its own accord. As the State Forestry Bureau we must observe the Land Administration Law, and we have no jurisdiction over land that has not been designated as forest by the Ministry of Land Resources. However, we are also responsible for protecting forest and increasing the forest reserves. If we were to be abolished and our tasks transferred to the Ministry of Land Resources, I assure you it would not have the ability or the resources to protect the forest.[44]

A striking illustration of the problems created by the fragmentation of land administration is the case of the Fengchanlin Pulpwood Base Sino-Singaporean Cooperative Company Limited in Qingyuan City in Guangdong Province. In June 1995 the Qingyuan Forestry Company signed an agreement with the Singapore Asia Pulp Limited Company to set up a joint venture for pulpwood production. The establishment of the joint venture took place in two steps. First, the Qingyuan Forestry Company signed use right certificates for fifty years with agricultural economic collective organizations and farmers holding forest permits to collective land. Thus, they become shareholders in the joint venture in return for which they provided the land use right. The certificates were examined and approved by the county forestry department and government. Second, after the use rights were obtained an agreement was signed between the Qingyuan Forestry Company and the Singaporean company. Under this contract, the former would bring in 580,000 mu of land for a lease period of seventy years, while the latter would invest 420 RMB per mu of land, bringing the total investments to 243.6 million RMB.

Probably because of the difference in lease period between the joint venture contract and the use right certificates signed with the collectives and the farmers, the Singaporean company started to have second thoughts. It seriously doubted whether the forestry department was in fact entitled to handle the entire affair. In addition, the company questioned the validity of the forest permit as legal proof of land ownership. Fearing for the security of its investments, the company requested that the State Land Administration validate the land titles, issue land ownership certificates to the rural collectives and farm households, and provide a new land use permit for the joint venture. The Qingyuan City Government and forestry department retorted that the State Land Administration had nothing to do with it and referred to the official legal interpretation of the Forest Law: 'the forest permit is the ownership and use certificate for land, it is the legal evidence for the title to forests and trees.'[45] The negotiations reached a stalemate and the forestry operations were temporarily aborted.[46]

[44] Lei Zhang (oral communication, 2001). She is the deputy director of the Forestry Economics Institute of the State Forestry Bureau.

[45] Wu and Cao (eds.), An Interpretation of the Forest Law, p. 8. Also stated in article 6 of the 1996 Measures for the Handling of Forest Disputes issued by the Ministry of Forestry. See Zhang and Wang (eds.), A Practical Manual for China's Forestry Laws, p. 381.

[46] Case described by the Law Implementation Inspection Group (ed.), *Zhongwai Hezuo Jinqingyuan Fengchanlin (Zhicai) Jidi Youxian Gongsi de Youguan Qingkuang* [Situation

The commercialization of forestry: an imperfect market? One aspect of the case covered in the previous subsection is rather interesting: how can the term of lease in the contract for the joint venture be shorter than the term of lease stipulated in the agreements with the rural collectives and farmers? The Singapore Asia Pulp Company Limited had actually asked the Qingyuan City Government to change the lease term for these agreements to seventy years from the original fifty, as the county forestry department had also approved the joint venture. However, the Qingyuan government—one administrative level higher than the county—replied that this was not possible because local regulations stipulated that the maximum lease term was thirty years, but could be extended to fifty if the provincial government was notified and approval obtained from the state institution that had examined and approved the lease. This lack of clarity of the term of lease is typical of the chaotic situation in what in Chinese is termed the 'valued use' of land (*youchang shiyong*) or, in other words, the commercialization of land use.

Nowhere is the tension between socio-economic rapid change and the central government's need to regulate such change through new institutions (be they policies, laws, or organizations) more pronounced than in the realm of the 'rural land market'. One could rightly remark that China has no rural land market in the true sense of the term. Yet what the central government has not forbidden and, therefore, does increasingly occur as the reforms progress is the sale of rural land lease rights and, worse, ownership rights. The trade in land use rights was not permitted until the 1988 revision of the Constitution. However, it is officially restricted to the urban (state-owned) sector. The Revised Land Administration Law stipulates only that 'the State exercises according to the law, a system of valued use for state-owned land'.[47] Whether this also applies to collective (and, thus, to the greater part of rural land) is intentionally left undefined. In Chapter 1, we saw that this intentional institutional ambiguity allows for regional experimentation in the commercialization of agricultural lease rights—sometimes with success, as experience in Hubei and Zhejiang Provinces has shown.[48]

However, agricultural land is quite a different natural resource from forest. Forest operations are characterized by long-term investments, high transactions costs, uncertain future prospects, and possible externalities with irreversible ecological effects. In this respect, one can seriously doubt whether forest management should be left to the market. As Daniel Bromley has warned, 'it would be a mistake to assume that leaving things to the

of the Sino-Foreign Cooperative Fengchanlin (Paper) Base Company Ltd. of Jinqingyuan], presented at the 28th Session of the Standing Committee of the Eighth National People's Congress (31 October 1997), pp. 3–4. The case description is unclear about the Chinese partner in the joint venture. The text sometimes says that the contract with the Singaporean company was signed by the Qingyuan City Government, and sometimes by the Qingyuan City Forestry Company. It was most likely signed by the latter, as many forest companies are owned by the (local) state.

[47] Article 2, Revised Land Administration Law in Fang (ed.), A Practical Discussion of the 'Land Administration Law', p. 207.

[48] Guangming Huang, 'Xin Tudi Geming' ['The New Land Revolution'], *Nanfang Zhoumo* (14 June 2001), pp. 1–2.

market will offer a solution to environmental conflicts' with the features described above.[49] Many international donors and scholars have argued—in particular for village forests in developing nations—for the establishment of community forestry as opposed to leaving the forest to the state or the market. Although the concept of community management is more widely known among professionals in forestry circles[50] than among their colleagues in the pastoral sector—the Chinese Academy of Forestry even publishes its own journal in this area, *Forestry and Society*—mainstream policies are still geared towards the commercialization of forestry. There is a substantial risk that in the process of fast socio-economic change, in particular when institutions are not well-equipped to handle such change, forests might be expropriated from local communities and reclaimed for non-forestry purposes. The free transfer of forest rights through sale, mortgage, lease, and auction might have a significant impact on farmers' livelihoods, even when forestry is a sideline activity. One positive sign in the commercialization of forestry is that the so-called wasteland auctions did not lead to widespread open auctions in which villagers, rich and poor alike, would have to compete with village and foreign investors, as that would have given rise to a sharp increase in social tension (see also Chapter 5).

However, what did happen—and not only in the case of wasteland auctions—is that forest was illegally requisitioned and subsequently converted into non-forestry land. Revision of the Forest Law was therefore urgently required. As the legal interpretation explains, 'The crux is that we lack comprehensive and unified standards for the valued use of forest resources. . . . The standardization of the valued use of forest resources is inevitable under the circumstances, it is also one of the focal points for revising the [Forest] Law this time.'[51] For this reason, the Revised Forest Law now stipulates that

> the use right for the following forests, trees and woodlands can be transferred according to the law. It can also, according to law, be priced and converted into shares or used as conditions for equity or cooperative joint ventures for forestation and operation of trees. However, forestry land shall not be converted into non-forestry land: (*a*) timber stands, economic forests and firewood forests; (*b*) the forestry use right for timber stands, economic forests and firewood forests; (*c*) the forestry use right for cleared and burned land of timber stands, economic forests and firewood forests; and (*d*) the use right for other forests, trees and other forestry land stipulated by the State Council.[52]

[49] Daniel W. Bromley, *Environment and Economy: Property Rights and Public Policy* (Oxford: Blackwell, 1991), p. 20.

[50] See also, for example, Hongqian Tang and Shougu Du (eds.), *Lindi, Linmu Quanshu yu Shehui Linye* [Property Rights of Forestland and Trees and Social Forestry] (Chengdu: Chengdu Keji Daxue Chubanshe, 1995); and Ting Zuo, 'Shehui Linye Shijian zhong Zhidu Fangmian de Ruogan Wenti' ['Some Issues Regarding the System of the Practice of Social Forestry'], *Zhongguo Nongcun Jingji*, Vol. 179, No. 11 (1999), pp. 19–24.

[51] Wu and Cao (eds.), An Interpretation of the Forest Law, p. 39.

[52] Article 15, NPC, Forest Law of the People's Republic of China, p. 10. The official English translation of the Forest Law available on internet (www.lawinfochina.com) renders *lindi* as 'woodland'. This term, however, conveys the wrong meaning as *lindi* also refers

The three above subsections provided a review of the main issues in national forestry policy: forest registration, the unification of land administration, and the commercialization of forestry. Together these are part of the underlying institutional framework that influences the dynamics of forest tenure. As I argued, the current forest tenure system enjoys little credibility in Chinese rural society, as can be inferred from the relatively high incidence of social conflict and the unsustainable management and use of forest resources.

Deforestation and Illegal Reclamation

The problems of deforestation and soil erosion have a long history in China. According to an excellent study by Kenneth Pomeranz, forest had come under considerable pressure in the 1700s, yet 'at least with respect to trees and soil, the rate of decay in China was probably slower than that seen in eighteenth-century western Europe'.[53] By the turn of the nineteenth century, deforestation had reached a serious level. Norman Shaw wrote in 1914: 'It is noticeable that wherever there is a waterway suitable for floating timber, the forest has already receded and there is no large timber left. There has been no reafforestation, and the timber-cutting has been conducted in a very wasteful way.'[54] Deforestation was not only a matter of wasteful forestry practices, but was also linked to the socio-economic upheaval of the era. As Shaw noted: 'The area between Tungjên and Chenyüan was formerly covered with a dense growth of trees, but here, as on the hills north of the capital, the woods were demolished during the Miao revolt on account of the shelter they afforded to the rebels.'[55]

Scholars and officials generally agree that the black pages in China's forestry history were written under communist rule, and it is not difficult to find accounts that support this view. Some scientists noted that 'deforestation problems have plagued China for hundreds of years, but accelerated more in the late 1950s when Great Leap Forward planners authorized the clear cutting of massive forest areas to fire China's backyard steel furnaces'.[56] And the period of the Cultural Revolution is virtually without exception described in overly negative terms: 'Everywhere in the countryside the policy of "Take Grain as the Key Link" was implemented... Because of large-scale reclamation for agriculture, great tracts of woods were destroyed. In order to level the land, the shelter belts and economic forests between the fields were even destroyed in some places.'[57] It is beyond doubt that the collectivist period led to environmental pressure, yet in-depth historical research is still needed to assess the extent of the

to land with a potential forest cover or designated as forest land. As elsewhere in the text, I have translated '*lindi*' as 'forestry land'.

[53] Kenneth Pomeranz, *The Great Divergence: Europe, China and the Making of the Modern World Economy* (Princeton, NJ: Princeton University Press, 2000)

[54] Norman Shaw, *Chinese Forest Trees and Timber Supply* (London: T. Fisher Unwin, 1914), p. 120.

[55] *Ibid.*, p. 99.

[56] Scott Rozelle, Jikun Huang, and Linxiu Zhang, 'Poverty, Population and Environmental Degradation in China', *Food Policy*, Vol. 22, No. 3 (1997), pp. 229–51.

[57] Zhiyong Dong (ed.), *Dangdai Zhongguo de Linye* [Forestry in Contemporary China] (Beijing: Zhongguo Shehui Kexue Chubanshe, 1985), p. 114.

damage inflicted on the environment by China's political campaigns.[58] In fact, recent research has provided some evidence that the official, Communist reading of environmental history during the socialist era might be ready for a revisionist view.[59]

In contrast, the period of reform and its impact on the forests is a much more thoroughly researched topic. In an article in *Science* it was noted:

> A half century of forest exploitation and monoculture in China has led to disastrous consequences, including degradation of forests and landscapes, loss of biodiversity, unacceptable levels of soil erosion, and catastrophic flooding.... Although a large-scale increase of plantation-style forests in non-forested areas increased total forest coverage in China from 5.2% in 1950 to 13.9% in 1995, natural forests declined to 30% of the total forest area in China and unit-area stocking of natural forests decreased by 32%.[60]

Scholarly attention focuses in particular on the impact of the privatization of forest tenure on forest use. It is said that the introduction of the contract responsibility system for forest has led to widespread felling of trees by individual households eager for short-term profit, in particular in the early years of reform. Rozelle et al. remarked that

> the optimism born from the 8 per cent increase in forest cover during the 1980s may need to be carefully reevaluated in light of the steep drop in forest volume. Most of the volume decline has been caused by the rapid harvesting of China's old-growth forests—up to 27 percent in some regions during a period of only about 10 years.[61]

However, later research has proved that a negative relation between the privatization of forest tenure and forest coverage is actually not that easy to demonstrate. In another study by Rozelle et al., it was noted that 'afforestation effort is greatest on Forest Household Responsibility System and private plots.... Descriptive statistics show that within the non-state sector.... increases in forest area happen most frequently when individuals have more control and income rights.'[62] And an exhaustive study

[58] This is not to deny that there are some excellent studies of forest policies during the collectivist period. See, for example, S. D. Richardson, *Forestry in Communist China* (Baltimore, MD: Johns Hopkins University Press, 1966); S. D. Richardson, *Forests and Forestry in China: Changing Patterns of Resource Development* (Washington, DC: Island Press, 1990); and Lester Stuart Ross, 'Forestry Policy in China', Ph.D. dissertation (Ann Arbor: The University of Michigan Microfilms International, 1980). However, detailed studies of Chinese forest history—with particular reference to the environmental effects of mass campaigns—are still scarce, not least because of the difficulty in obtaining reliable time-series data.

[59] For a revisionist view on China's environmental history during the socialist period, see also Peter Ho, 'Mao's War Against Nature? The Environmental Impact of the Grain-first Campaign in China', *The China Journal*, No. 50 (July 2003), pp. 37–59; Jiang Hong, 'Cooperation, Land Use, and the Environment in Uxin Ju: A Changing Landscape of a Mongolian-Chinese Borderland in China', *Annals of Association of American Geographers*, Vol. 94, No. 1 (2004), pp. 117–39.

[60] Peichang Zhang, Guofan Shao, Guang Zhao, Dennis C. Le Master, George R. Parker, John B. Dunning Jr, and Qinglin Li, 'China's Forest Policy for the 21st Century', *Science*, Vol. 288 (23 June 2000), pp. 2135–6.

[61] Scott Rozelle, Heidi Albers, Guo Li, and Vincent Benziger, 'Forest Resources under Economic Reform in China', *China Information*, Vol. 13, No. 1 (Summer 1998), pp. 106–30.

[62] Scott Rozelle, Jikun Huang, Syed Arif Husain, and Aaran Zazueta, *China: From Afforestation to Poverty Alleviation and Natural Forest Management* (Washington, DC: World Bank Operations Evaluation Department, 2000), p. 44.

by Zhang et al., using statistical data from Fujian, Jiangxi, Anhui, and Henan over the period 1978–95, reached the conclusion that 'land tenure reform in general has had a positive effect on forest land expansion, but the absolute size of the effects varies from province to province. The positive impact of the reform on timber harvesting has not taken place at the cost of forest land cover.'[63] This does not imply that there is reason for optimism. In the foreseeable future, pressure on China's forests will remain strong.[64]

Furthermore, the loss of forest through illegal conversion to non-forestry land remains a source of serious concern for the central leadership. Surveys by the State Forestry Bureau found that, of the forest area requisitioned for (local) government development projects in the years 1993, 1994, and 1996, over 60 per cent had not been approved by the forestry administration.[65] Illegal reclamation frequently leads to the destruction of forest resources. For example, over the period 1989–93 a total of 2 million ha of forestry land was converted into non-forestry land, whereas an estimated 7.6 million ha of forest was cleared or degraded by illegal felling, forest fires, or bad management practices.[66] The central authorities commissioned a major investigation in 1997, covering 830 forest development and requisition projects in ninety-eight counties across the nation. This survey yielded a bleak picture of the forestry sector: only 53 per cent of all development projects had been approved through the Forestry Bureaux, in only 46 per cent of the cases had an official forest use permit been issued, felling permits had been obtained in 53 per cent of the cases, while fees for reafforestation were paid in only 23 per cent of the cases.[67] Shocked by these findings, the government ordered an immediate standstill on all forest requisition for land development.[68]

Since it imposed its 'freeze', the state has closely monitored developments in forestry. The results of its investigations are shown in Table 3. These figures, too, present a rather grim picture. Several provinces have a bad record in forest management. In Jiangxi Province only 17.7 per cent of the land development projects had been approved by the forestry administration, 1.3 per cent of the permits that should have been issued were given, while a meagre 2.4 per cent of the total reafforestation fees had actually been collected. Other notorious 'record-holders' are Henan,

[63] See Yaoqi Zhang, Jussi Uusivuori, and Jari Kuuluvainen, 'Impacts of Economic Reforms on Rural Forestry in China', *Forest Policy and Economics*, No. 1 (2000), p. 27.

[64] Yin Runsheng concludes, 'it is very likely that China will remain short of wood. This conjecture is strengthened by the observation that bold assumptions were made with regard to panel and other substitutes. Likewise, the imbalance of fuelwood supply and demand was neglected in forecasts. Recall that designated fuelwood forests account for only 0.7% of the closed forest volume, whereas annual fuelwood consumption amounts to over 30% of total resource use.' See Yin Runsheng, 'Forestry and the Environment in China: The Current Situation and Strategic Choices', *World Development*, Vol. 26, No. 12 (1998), p. 2159.

[65] Wu and Cao (eds.), An Interpretation of the Forest Law, p. 196.

[66] *Ibid*., p. 195.

[67] State Forestry Bureau (ed.), *China Forestry Yearbook 1998*, p. 103 (see table).

[68] Two subsequent state documents were issued: the State Council's notice on 'The Protection of Forest Resources and Halting the Destruction, Reclamation and Indiscriminate Occupation of Forest' of 5 August 1998 and the notice on 'The Continuation of Freezing All Forest Requisition for Construction Projects' of 30 July 1999. See State Forestry Bureau (ed.), *China Forestry Yearbook 1999/2000*, pp. 110–11.

Table 3: **Requisition of forest 1998–1999**

Region	*No. of projects*	*No. of projects examined and approved by forest dept.*	*Requisitioned area (in ha)*	*Situation on forest exploitation and felling*		*Situation on reforestation fee (in 10,000 RMB)*		*No. of illegal projects after 1998 freezing*
				Area for which permit required	*Area for which permit obtained*	*Fee required*	*Fees collected*	
National	1,527	953	7,929.3	5,311.0	2,986.3	10,548.3	1,987.4	211
Beijing	1	1	1.0	0.1	0.1	0.5	0.5	0
Tianjin	2	2	3.6	3.6	3.6	34.7	34.7	0
Hebei	15	3	373.1	358.2	235.7	352.1	0.0	3
Shanxi	8	7	54.8	52.5	49.2	106.1	8.5	0
Inner Mongolia	21	14	45.8	41.6	37.1	80.5	39.9	1
Liaoning	16	15	1,629.4	1,393.9	1,393.9	408.1	408.1	2
Jilin	6	6	106.9	77.1	77.1	105.6	105.6	0
Heilongjiang	11	9	56.0	29.6	28.9	27.5	27.5	1
Shanghai	0	0	0.0	0.0	0.0	0.0	0.0	0
Jiangsu	8	4	10.7	3.8	3.8	23.6	7.8	1
Zhejiang	250	191	410.2	264.6	184.9	646.1	329.7	53
Anhui	118	80	118.7	57.8	25.3	267.4	177.5	9
Fujian	363	360	194.9	99.2	95.8	375.2	365.8	0

Jiangxi	181	32	434.0	45.6	0.6	308.0	7.5	39
Shandong	17	2	29.2	12.8	12.0	41.9	39.0	4
Henan	27	0	230.5	6.0	0.0	2,601.1	0.4	5
Hubei	35	11	221.5	176.6	75.2	747.6	21.3	9
Hunan	55	14	460.9	395.6	117.5	918.8	99.6	18
Guangdong	38	31	452.3	370.6	133.4	219.5	94.4	3
Guangxi	40	24	114.1	36.8	77.6	33.4	18.0	0
Hainan	27	13	192.3	168.7	90.2	123.0	16.7	7
Chongqing	63	53	54.3	773.1	1.6	71.9	27.0	5
Sichuan	94	11	810.3	38.9	2.2	1,724.0	34.2	27
Guizhou	16	6	226.1	137.6	133.9	13.4	10.5	3
Yunnan	34	21	569.9	412.9	131.4	600.1	10.4	1
Shaanxi	39	26	384.8	21.4	3.4	136.6	62.1	8
Gansu	19	0	88.3	20.2	4.5	231.4	0.0	9
Qinghai	0	0	0.0	0.0	0.0	0.0	0.0	0
Ningxia	1	1	46.4	26.8	0.0	139.3	34.8	0
Xinjiang	2	0	121.4	65.5	11.8	87.4	0.0	1
Longjiang Forest Corp.	2	0	5.0	1.7	0.0	0.0	0.0	2
Jilin Forest Corp.	13	13	163.5	55.6	55.6	6.1	6.1	0
Neimenggu Forest Corp.	1	0	86.2	26.8	0.0	8.5	0.0	0
Daxing Anling Forestry Co.	4	3	233.2	85.6	0.0	8.9	0.0	0

Source: State Forestry Bureau, *China Forestry Yearbook 1999–2000* (Beijing: Zhongguo Linye Chubanshe, 2000), pp. 112–13.

Hubei, Hunan, and Sichuan.[69] Nor has there been much improvement: in some provinces (Jiangxi, Hunan, and Sichuan) the number of illegal development projects after the freeze is considerably higher than the legally approved number before 1998! It is worth noting that illegal forest reclamation (at least to judge from the available figures) seems to be particularly a problem in the collective forest zones. One of the possible reasons for this is the poor legal protection of collective forest ownership; other explanatory factors include the rate of urbanization, price levels of timber and land, and alternative employment opportunities. As forest is by law state-owned unless proven collective property, it might be easier for the (local) state to expropriate forest for land development purposes.

Forest Fights: What to do with Customary and Private Ownership?

The shift of rural society into the market economy has led to stronger economic interests in land. And that has brought about a sharp rise in the number of forest conflicts as well, in particular as the ambiguity in current forest tenure impedes a proper balance of economic interests. The need to clarify boundaries for forest registration has brought into the open disputes that simmered for years in legal fuzziness. In the first three years of forest registration, a total of 1.4 million disputes were recorded—an annual average of 350,000—of which 91 per cent had been resolved. Provincial-level disputes posed a particular problem; the forestry administration noted that 'some *lao danan* [''great old troubles'', as the provincial-level disputes are termed] from the past still had not been resolved'.[70] In 1999, a special mission for dispute resolution and the reassessment of provincial administrative boundaries was organized by the State Forestry Bureau and the Ministries of Land Resources and Civil Affairs (responsible for drawing administrative boundaries).[71] From Table 4 we can see that during 1993–6 inter-provincial disputes gradually decreased, from 719 unsolved cases to 430, with a dramatic drop in contested area, from 114,357 ha to 49,439. Initially, the tenure disputes within the province gradually decreased, but a sharp rise (50 per cent) in the number of unresolved conflicts occurred during 1995–6. The scale of intra-provincial tenure conflicts, however, has decreased.

The legal set-up of forest ownership—state ownership unless proven collective—is an invitation for social conflict, in particular between the state and the rural collectives. Two cases could illustrate the relevant issues in such disputes. In Baolin Township in Heilongjiang Province a plot of forest is disputed by the township and the Gangfeng State Forest Farm.[72]

[69] These figures are respectively, 0% approved, 0% issued, and 0.02% collected (Henan); 31.4%, 42.6%, and 2.8% (Hubei); 25.5%, 29.7%, and 10.8% (Hunan); and 11.7%, 5.7%, and 2.0% (Sichuan). It is interesting that in the wealthy, coastal regions such as Zhejiang, Fujian, and Guangdong, where the drive for urban construction is strong, the problem of illegal forest reclamation is not prominent.

[70] State Forestry Bureau (ed.), *China Forestry Yearbook 1949–1986*, pp. 55, 480.

[71] *Ibid.*, p. 480; State Forestry Bureau (ed.), China Forestry Yearbook 1999/2000, p. 110.

[72] Case drawn from Xinhua Liu (ed.), *Xin Tudi Guanlifa Quanshu* [Encyclopedia of the New Land Administration Law], Vol. I (Beijing: Zhongguo Wujia Chubanshe, 1998, pp. 1023–4.

Table 4: **Record of forest tenure disputes, 1993–1996**

Year	*Status*	*Forest tenure disputes*			
		Inter-provincial		*Intra-provincial*	
		No.	*Area (ha)*	*No.*	*Area (ha)*
1993	Settled	56	837.0	12,921	126,285.4
	Unsettled	719	114,357.2	26,709	527,562.1
1994	Settled	47	3,070.4	11,365	106,376.3
	Unsettled	584	310,110.3	21,247	578,347.3
1995	Settled	23	27,792.6	9,556	183,691.6
	Unsettled	409	254,827.9	16,554	491,263.7
1996	Settled	107	4,669.0	12,413	43,332.0
	Unsettled	430	49,439.0	24,921	363,225.0

Source: State Bureau of Forestry.

Neither the township nor the forest farm has a forest or land permit to prove title to the land. After the approval of the township and village authorities in October 1985, a certain farmer Yang went into the disputed area to fell trees. He was arrested by a forester of the forest farm, who charged him with 'destroying the forest for agricultural reclamation'[73] and seized his tractor. The police fined him 1,600 RMB for the illegal reclamation of 264 mu of land, threatening to confiscate his tractor if he refused to pay.

Yang stood his ground and managed to persuade the police to return his tractor. But during his detention his tractor had been wrecked beyond use. From that day on Yang continuously appealed to the authorities, but to no avail. Instead, in July 1992 the Baolin police imposed an administrative penalty: the reclaimed land was confiscated, while Yang also had to pay 390 RMB for incurred losses. The verdict made no mention of his tractor. Angry about this injustice, Yang filed a suit at the local court. The court quashed the confiscation of reclaimed land, but maintained the claim for damages of 390 RMB and on top of that awarded additional compensation to the farm of three times the amount of timber cut. Still defiant, Yang appealed to the intermediate court. His defence revolved around two arguments: (*a*) the reclamation had taken place *after* approval of the township and village authorities, and within the area included in their regional planning; and (*b*) the Baolin police exceeded their jurisdiction by imposing a forestry administrative penalty on him. The police retorted that Yang had obviously destroyed forest by reclamation. The subsequent penalty imposed on him had not exceeded the police's jurisdiction, as provincial regulations stipulated that police had jurisdiction over forestry matters. The police denied any responsibility for the loss of the tractor.

The intermediate court referred the case back to the lower court. The lower court left the penalties unchanged, but ordered the police to pay financial compensation for Yang's tractor and travel expenses (2,070 RMB).

[73] Liu (ed.), Encyclopedia of the New Land Administration Law, Vol. I, pp. 1023.

Yang appealed once again to the intermediate court, which now ruled that the Baolin police had indeed exceeded their jurisdiction as national law did not stipulate that regular police forces had powers in forest administration (in fact, such powers are reserved to the Forestry Police).

This case typifies problems in border regions such as Inner Mongolia, Xinjiang, and former Manchuria. Upon the nationalization of forest in 1950, pre-existing settler communities suddenly found themselves included in state-owned territory without their ownership having been acknowledged. Rural collectives thus face a great challenge to protect their legal interests in forest. Although the case recorded here seemingly concerns the illegal reclamation by one individual, it is clear that it actually pertains to a state–collective dispute. The township and village wilfully provoked a conflict with the forest farm by sending farmer Yang into the forest area to fell trees. In his higher appeal, Yang claimed that his action was justified because he had obtained approval from the township and village authorities and because it was by no means clear that the land he had reclaimed was owned by the state forest farm. However, the respective court rulings ignored these arguments and focused on a different issue: the transgression of jurisdiction by the Baolin police. Indeed, the police went beyond their authority because forest administration is the exclusive domain of the State Forestry Bureau and its subordinate Forest Police. Regular police do not have the right to confiscate land, which is—albeit contested by the State Forestry Bureau—the exclusive domain of the Ministry of Land Resources.

In the second case[74] too an individual is victimized for what is in fact a state–collective dispute. During Land Reform, Qu Daming, a native of Yongxin Village (Sichuan Province), was granted *private ownership* and issued a title for some bamboo forest.[75] The forest was located on the border of the tea garden of the Zhao family. However, during the Four Cleanups campaign[76] in 1965 the Qu family fell into disgrace, and their forest was expropriated and returned to the village collective. Following the lease of forest to individual farmers and households in 1981, the county government reallocated 0.4 mu of this forest to Qu. He also obtained a county forest permit with the number 024619. Trouble began in the following year, with the implementation of the Household Contract Responsibility System, when the village leased the same tract of forest to a farmer, Jiang Zongming.

The conflicts between the Qu and Jiang families reached a peak in December 1989, when Qu Daming's mother cut bamboo in the disputed area. The Jieshi Town Government was asked to mediate. Qu produced his forest permit, which recorded the plot's location and area, but

[74] Case drawn from Zuigao Renmin Fayuan (ed.), *Renmin Fayuan Anli Xuan–Xingzheng Juan: 1992–1996* [A Selection of Cases from the People's Courts–Volume for Administrative [Cases]: 1992–1996] (Beijing: Renmin Fayuan Chubanshe, 1997), pp. 443–5.

[75] According to article 10, 1950 Land Reform Law. See Sun (ed.), Practical Compass on Land Titles, p. 107.

[76] For more details on the impact of this campaign on rural society, see Anita Chan, Richard Madsen, and Jonathan Unger, *Chen Village under Mao and Deng* (Berkeley: University of California Press, 1992), pp. 70–2.

characteristically lacked the date of issue, a boundary description, and the signature and seal of the issuing agency. In October 1991, the town government ruled that Qu's forest permit was invalid and Jiang had the right to manage the forest. Qu Daming lodged an appeal with the county court on the grounds that the town government overstepped its authority in invalidating a document issued by a higher-level government. But the town government claimed that Qu's permit was a forgery by his father. The evidence for this was clear: the permit neither had a date of issue and boundary description nor had it been authenticated by designated authorities. However, this is not an unusual practice in rural China (see, for instance, also Appendix C).

The county court acknowledged that Qu Daming's permit was incomplete, but did not conclude that it was a forgery. The court's ruling read: 'Although forest permit 0246191 issued by the county government to Qu Daming is not entirely perfect, the town government could only have appealed to the county government that had issued the permit to handle the case. By declaring of its own accord the forest permit invalid, the town government exceeded its jurisdiction.'[77] The town government's verdict was quashed. None of the parties appealed to a higher court.

Whereas the previous case was a state–collective conflict between a state forest farm and the local government, the present case is more complicated. First of all, it is a dispute between the township and village collective governments on the one hand and the county state government on the other. As forest is in principle state-owned, the county, regarding itself as the official representative of state ownership (which in fact it is not)[78] deemed it legal to allocate forest land as it saw fit. But the law does recognize collective ownership of forest if title can be proven. Unfortunately, collective ownership has never been registered because to date it is still unclear what collective ownership represents. Second, and this is where the case becomes extremely murky and sensitive, it is also a collective–private dispute. During Land Reform, Qu Daming, being from a poor peasant background, had obtained *ownership* to the bamboo forest for which he had been issued a title.

The CCP employed political campaigns to create loyal constituencies for new policy lines. This was effected through the continuous swing of a Machiavellian pendulum allowing new cadres to be recruited and old, disloyal ones to be disposed of. As Madsen notes: 'Many cadres who had come from poor peasant backgrounds . . . had used their positions during Land Reform to prosper and thus to become "new middle peasants." So the CCP had to ease them aside if it were to carry out its programs.'[79] The Four Cleanups campaign in 1965 was no exception to this.[80] During the

[77] Zuigao Renmin Fayuan (ed.), Cases from the People's Courts, p. 444.

[78] The 1998 Land Administration Law aims to put an end to such practices by defining the State Council as the sole legal representative of state land ownership. Article 2, Revised Land Administration Law in Fang (ed.), A Practical Discussion of the Land Administration Law, p. 207.

[79] Madsen, 'The Countryside under Communism', p. 655.

[80] 'The CCP launched a "Four Cleanups Campaign" to cleanse rural cadres of economic, political, ideological, and managerial errors. The main problem to be cleaned up, though, was economic.' *Ibid.*, pp. 656–7.

cleansing of class ranks, property was frequently stolen. The case of Qu Daming illustrates this. Being one of the 'new middle peasants', Qu was criticized and struggled against (*pidou*) during the Four Cleanups. His land was taken from him and returned to the collective. Legally, he had no leg to stand on, as statutory law stipulated that since 1956 all private rural land had become collective property.[81] For this reason, the village authorities of Yongxin felt they were justified in leasing the bamboo forest to another family. The fact that the county returned his former forest holding to him is an indication that the legacy of private ownership from pre-socialist times is not forgotten. And that remains a minefield for the Chinese judiciary.

Forest Institutions in Transition

Considering the dynamics of Chinese forest tenure, the outside observer is struck by two features: bad management leading to the degradation and illegal reclamation of forest, and a relatively high incidence of social conflict. The widespread illegal conversion of forest into non-forestry land has received high political priority. In 1998 it prompted the central authorities to freeze all forest reclamation projects. Yet the demand for cheap land to accommodate rapid urbanization remains strong. Recent data show that, in the areas where indiscriminate reclamation was rampant before 1998, the number of illegal forest reclamation projects has not diminished. In addition, the multitudinous forest disputes, even at the provincial level, are a source of serious concern for the national government, especially because they severely impede the registration of forest.

Compared with agricultural tenure, the forest tenure system seems to lack social acceptability and credibility. At the beginning of this chapter, several underlying reasons for this difference were identified. First, the nature of the resource itself: forest needs long-term investments, it is difficult to exclude others from it or to divide its use without forcing up transaction costs, and it is a complex biotope prone to irreversible degradation. Second, in contrast to agricultural land that serves as a basic means of social security for the overall majority of the rural populace, forest is exploited more as a sideline. And this affects the valuation and use of forest land as compared with agricultural land. Finally, the legal framework for forest ownership is different from that for agricultural land. Whereas agricultural land is in principle collectively owned, forest is state-owned unless legal evidence to the contrary can be furnished.

The latter point is of great importance, as legal proof of land ownership is scarce in a country like China, where no land registry exists. It also implies that the collective, or the rural community for that matter, is at a disadvantage when it comes to defending its interests over land, especially when customary rights are involved. Customary rights are generally neglected and violated because of their fluid and unwritten character; moreover, the People's Republic has conferred no legal status on customary rights.

[81] Article 13, Exemplary Regulations on the Higher Agricultural Production Cooperatives. See Sun (ed.), Practical Compass on Land Titles, p. 131.

In addition, widely ignored—because of its sensitivity in a formerly socialist economy—is the question of the expropriation of private forest holdings. This issue is not to be underestimated because it might be the seedbed of many current forest disputes. During China's erratic and turbulent history in the twentieth century, the right to forest—whether use or ownership—has been extremely insecure. The forest that was not nationalized during Land Reform remained in the ownership of the village community or was redistributed from landlords and rich peasants to the poor and landless. The waves of political campaigns over the following decades caused frequent disruption of the rural social structure. Those who were considered the backbone of the CCP at one time could lose this status with a shift in policy line. Losing one's status and becoming a class enemy also implied fundamental reshuffles of forest land. Naturally, this problem does not pertain only to forest, but involves land holdings in general. Yet the issue is more complicated than for agricultural land, as forest is in principle state-owned and the collective is laden with the burden of proving title. The destruction of private forest titles during political campaigns—if issued at all during Land Reform—might prove a major impediment to the validation of forest ownership by the collective.

National forestry policy has great influence on the dynamics of forest tenure. For this reason, the chapter provided a review of the three most important issues, as well as the central government's stance and intentions in these issues: (*a*) the registration of forest holdings; (*b*) the unification of land administration; and (*c*) the commercialization of forest lease. Land registration as a basis for the forest contract responsibility system (see Appendix G) began in the early 1980s, and led directly to great social tensions. Because of registration, fuzzy boundaries had to be reassessed, which reignited old conflicts. The widespread social conflict and weakness of (local) state institutions led to double permitting, ambiguity, and a lack of uniformity in forest titles. To date, much forest remains unregistered, especially in the collective forest area. The fragmentation in land administration in itself was a decisive factor in the failure of forest registration. The State Forestry Bureau clashed with the Ministry of Land Resources over the final authority in land registration, while provincial-level forest disputes were extremely difficult to resolve because of the poor coordination between the state institutions involved. The final issue that influences forest tenure is the commercialization of forest lease. On this matter, the central government continuously wavers between policies of intervention and laissez-faire. The free transfer of forest rights through sale, mortgage, lease, and auction can have a major impact on farmers' livelihoods. Moreover, there is a danger that, in the process of rapid socio-economic change, in particular when existing institutions are ill-prepared to meet such changes, farmers will lose forest holdings to the expanding cities. At such critical moments, commercialization must make way for state intervention in order to safeguard social stability. It is the essence of a balanced transition of institutions.

5
Going, Going, Gone! The Four Wastelands Auction Policy

The policy is there and all relevant documents and regulations have been promulgated, but the implementation is our biggest problem. We are under pressure from higher levels to execute a policy that might not be executable, and when it fails we get all the blame. We cannot disagree, as we are the representatives of the government at the grass roots level. I have my own opinion about the Four Wastelands Auction Policy, but it might be better if you also interview others to avoid getting a one-sided view.

(Local Party Secretary, 1996)

Wasteland: A Potential Source of Wealth?

According to the statistics, China had a total of 108 million ha of undeveloped land or wasteland in 2002. Of this figure, 35.4 million ha is suitable for agriculture and 53.9 million ha is suited for forestry purposes.[1] Wasteland includes a wide variety of land resources scattered over the whole country. It varies from forested hills and mountains in the subtropical region of Yunnan Province to the dry steppe and pockets of desert in the Inner Mongolia Autonomous Region. According to the definitions of the Chinese Ministry of Agriculture, this undeveloped land can be divided into wasteland, waste mountains, sandy waste, and waste gullies (*huangdi*, *huangshan*, *huangtan*, and *huanggou*). The term 'wasteland', however, is misleading as a great portion of this land is used by peasants for animal grazing, small-scale forestry, and the exploitation of forest by-products, such as Matsutake mushrooms, medicinal herbs, and animals. The direct use of wasteland generally yields low economic returns, while its ecology is often fragile. For this reason, the Chinese state has long sought means to develop wasteland for purposes of rural poverty alleviation, soil and water conservation, and even defence.

The property rights structure of wasteland comes under the same legal arrangements as grassland and forest: it is state-owned unless collective ownership can be proven. This implies that the problems that afflict grassland and forest tenure also affect wasteland rights. An additional problem is that wasteland is not legally defined as a separate natural resource (except in the Constitution). As a result, its administration can fall under either the Ministry of Agriculture or the State Bureau of Forestry depending on whether it is 'forested grassland' or 'grassy forest'. In this chapter, we will see that the ambiguous definition of wasteland as a natural resource creates serious problems for the implementation of a nation-wide wasteland policy.

[1] National Bureau of Statistics (ed.), *Zhongguo Tongji Nianjian 2003* [China Statistical Yearbook 2003] (Beijing: Zhongguo Tongji Chubanshe, 2003), p. 5.

The revised Land Administration Law allows for the 'valued use' (*youchang shiyong*, see also Chapter 1) of urban but not of rural land. In other words, there are no regulations governing the free transfer, sale, and mortgage of rural land. However, there is nothing unusual about that. As a Chinese expert on land rights remarked: 'If it is not forbidden, it is allowed (*wu jinzhi, ji xuke*). It provides space for local experimentation.'[2] Like experiments with the commercialization of agricultural land in the wealthy, coastal regions such as Zhejiang Province, the development of wasteland has also gradually entered the marketplace. Due to its low economic value and importance in soil and water conservation, the central government has been most lenient with experiments in a 'wasteland market'. Yet, as with most new socio-economic developments in China, such as the household contract responsibility system, a more commercial use of wasteland originated in the grass roots.

In the late 1980s, Lüliang Prefecture in Shanxi Province embarked on a new path to tackle soil erosion on the barren mountains of the Loess Plateau. Instead of being allocated to farmers on the basis of household size, wasteland use rights were put up to auction. It was thought that the bidding process would stimulate free competition and give farmers more incentive to develop marginal lands. In addition, the sale of wasteland would allow for greater economies of scale because land would no longer be allocated in an egalitarian manner. It would thus also be a means to alleviate rural poverty. The use of the auctioned wasteland was strictly regulated. Economic forestry (fruit and nut growing) and animal husbandry could be practised but agricultural activities were prohibited. By 1992, the Luliang auctions had gained widespread fame and subsequently formed the basis of a national model under the name of the 'Four Wastelands Auction Policy' (*Sihuang Paimai Zhengce*; hereafter the Wastelands Policy). It soon spread to other provinces and autonomous regions. By 2000, the use rights to 6.4 per cent of the total wasteland resources designated for auction had been sold.[3]

The Wastelands Policy entails great institutional changes in property rights and land tenure, not only because wasteland rights are commercialized on a much greater scale than was ever possible for agricultural land but also because the policy closes the so-called rural–urban divide. The policy permits 'open auction' in which not only farmers but also cadres, urban entrepreneurs, and legal persons such as mass organizations and companies are allowed to participate and, more importantly, gain access to rural land. The main instrument that institutionalizes the rural–urban divide is the household registration system (*hukou*). In the past, rural–urban migration was strictly controlled through the *hukou* system. Those with a rural *hukou* were excluded from the urban job market, social welfare system, and education. Over the years, government control on migration

[2] Weiguo Wang (oral communication, 2001).

[3] See Shouhu Du, 'Wo Guo Tudi Zhidu you yici Da Geming' ['Another Revolution in the Land System of China'], in Shouhu Du and Xiaomin Guo, *'Sihuang' Ziyuan Liuzhuan: Lilun, Zhengce, Shijian* [The Circulation of 'the Four Wastelands' Resources: Theory, Policy and Practice] (Beijing: Dabaike Quanshu Chubanshe, 2000), p. 6.

has been relaxed.[4] The rural–urban divide also ensures that the right to lease agricultural land is reserved to members of rural collectives. Some policy-makers believe that wasteland can be adequately developed only through free market competition, which requires closing the divide in order to bring out the most capable and financially strong. Others argue that free competition and sale in land rights, especially wasteland rights, will only result in making the poor poorer and the rich richer, possibly leading eventually to the rise of a new class of impoverished, landless peasants.

The Importance of Institutions . . . and Socio-Economic Parameters

In this chapter, I analyse the impact of the Wastelands Policy on rural society and assess its importance in the overall reform of the Chinese land property rights system. For this purpose, I draw on one case study, the implementation of the Wastelands Policy in the Ningxia Hui Autonomous Region (or Ningxia). In Ningxia the Wastelands Policy was hailed as a breakthrough in land management which would open up undeveloped natural resources, improve the ecological environment, and increase farmers' incomes. Two years after the first wasteland contracts were sold to the highest bidding party, the auctions were suddenly halted because of widespread soil erosion induced by agricultural reclamation. Although the Wastelands Policy is still implemented elsewhere in China, it has come to a complete standstill in Ningxia. The regional authorities are reluctant to give an adequate explanation.

At this point two questions arise. Why was the Wastelands Policy halted in Ningxia? More importantly, did the policy fulfill its intended role in the reform and commercialization of land tenure? I will demonstrate that it did not. I will do this by examining the case-study material in the light of one of this monograph's central premises as set out in the Introduction: institutions are both the *driving force* of, and *subjected* to, the evolutionary process of socio-economic change. In other words, if neither the institutions nor the socio-economic parameters are conducive to socio-economic change, reform in property rights is likely to fail. The Wastelands Policy will be analysed in terms of the origins of the policy, its institutional (legal, political, and administrative) framework, the problems encountered during implementation, and the manner in which these were dealt with by the responsible authorities.

Why choose Ningxia as a case study? There are two main reasons. First, like Lüliang Prefecture, where the Wastelands Policy originated, the southern part of Ningxia belongs to the Loess Plateau. This plateau covers seven provinces and autonomous regions: Shanxi, Inner Mongolia, Henan, Shaanxi, Ningxia, Gansu, and Qinghai. The Loess Plateau is notorious for

[4] See also Tiejun Cheng and Mark Selden, 'The Origins and Social Consequences of China's Hukou System', *The China Quarterly*, No. 139 (September 1994), pp. 644–69; Mark Selden, 'Household, Cooperative, and State in the Remaking of China's Countryside', in Eduard B. Vermeer, Frank N. Pieke, and Woei Lien Chong (eds.), *Cooperative and Collective in China's Rural Development: Between State and Private Interests* (New York: M. E. Sharpe, 1998); Sulamith Heins Potter, 'The Position of Peasants in Modern China's Social Order', *Modern China*, Vol. 9, No. 4 (October 1983), pp. 465–99.

its soil erosion; as a popular adage goes: 'The Loess Plateau is the reason why the Yellow River is yellow: it's all soil.' The total area of the Loess Plateau is 626,800 square kilometres, of which 530,000 has been reported affected (430,000 seriously) by erosion.[5] The second reason for selecting Ningxia is that it is one of the officially designated poverty regions of China. As we will see in Chapter 6, poverty dictates to a great extent the use of grassland and the effectiveness of policies. The region was ranked first among all provinces and regions with a provincial poverty rate of 28.47; Gansu was second at a rate of 25.95, Yunnan third at 23.67, and Guizhou fourth at 21.89.[6] In terms of rural net income per capita, Ningxia ranked second lowest in 1996 with 998.75 RMB; Shaanxi was lowest with 962.89 RMB.[7] Poverty is concentrated mainly in the rural area in the south termed the 'Southern Mountains Region' (*Nanbu Shanqu*), which comprises eight counties: Yanchi, Tongxin, Guyuan, Haiyuan, Xiji, Longde, Jingyuan, and Pengyang. Ningxia receives the highest political priority for poverty alleviation from the central government. State subsidies accounted for approximately two-thirds of total regional expenses in the 1980s.

Ningxia borders Shaanxi Province on the east, Inner Mongolia on the north and west, and Gansu Province on the south (see Figure 4). Instead of being administered as a province, it was carved out as an Autonomous Region for the Hui Muslim minority in 1958. The region is situated in the central Asian steppe and desert region with a continental, temperate climate increasing in aridity from the south (sub-humid) to the north (arid). In the north, it is enclosed by the Tengger (north-west) and Mu'us deserts (north-east). The total land surface is 51,800 square kilometres and the total population is 5.7 million, of which approximately 33 per cent are Hui.[8] The Hui are a religious and ethnic minority that lags behind the Han Chinese majority in socio-economic terms. This becomes clear from the statistics: 64 per cent of the Hui live in the seven poorest counties[9] in the Autonomous Region, in contrast to only 29 per cent of the Han Chinese. Furthermore, 60 per cent of the Hui, including 78 per cent of females, are defined as illiterate, against 36 per cent of the Han, including 49 per cent of females.[10] The survey counties (Guyuan and Pengyang) are located in the Loess Plateau in the south of Ningxia, with a mixed farming operation

[5] See Wenzhi Yang and Cunzu Yu (eds.), *Huangtu Gaoyuan Quyu Zhili yu Pingjia* [Evaluation and Control of the Loess Plateau Region] (Beijing: Kexue Chubanshe, 1992), p. 1.

[6] Fengqi Zhu, cited in Shaoguang Wang and Angang Hu, *The Political Economy of Inequality in China* (Armonk, NY: M. E. Sharpe, 1999). The provincial poverty rate is a weighted total including indicators such as income, education, consumption, and housing.

[7] State Statistical Bureau (ed.), *Zhongguo Tongji Nianjian 1997* [China Statistical Yearbook 1997] (Beijing: Zhongguo Tongji Chubanshe, 1997), p. 302.

[8] The official statistics give a total surface of 66,400km^2. But recent surveys have shown that the actual surface is much smaller. The Hui are the predominant ethnic minority in Ningxia; other minorities like the Mongols and Uyghur account for only a minor proportion of the population. National Bureau of Statistics (ed.), China Statistical Yearbook 2003, p. 98.

[9] Tongxin, Guyuan, Haiyuan, Xiji, Longde, Jingyuan, and Pengyang. The rural net annual income per capita has been taken as a poverty indicator for the counties.

[10] See Ningxia Tongjiju (ed.), *Ningxia Tongji Nianjian 1994* [Ningxia Statistical Yearbook] (Yinchuan: Ningxia Renmin Chubanshe, 1994), p. 65; Guiying Gao, 'Yisilanjiao yu Ningxia Funü Wenti' ['The Issue of Women in Ningxia and Islam'], *Huizu Yanjiu* [Research on the Hui], No. 2 (1995), p. 57.

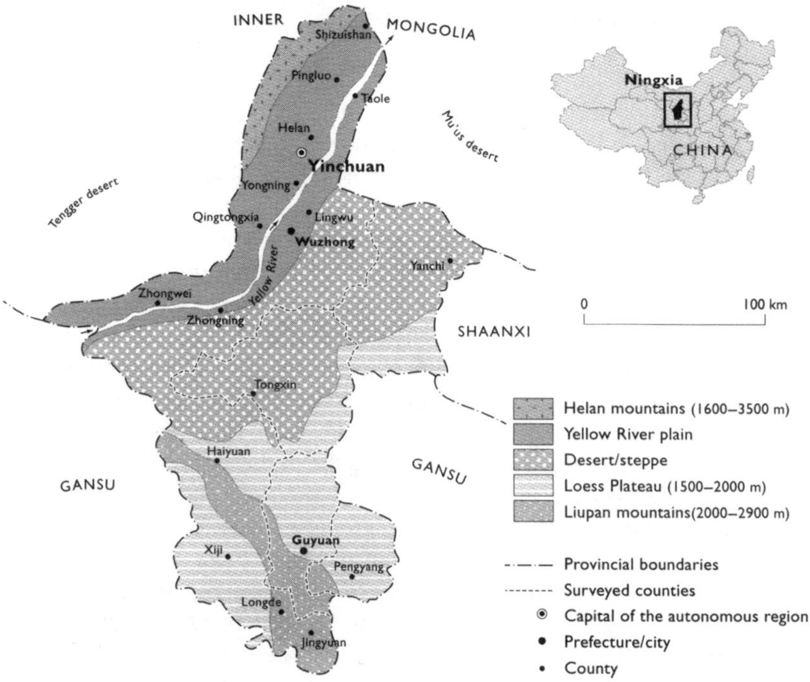

Figure 4: **Map of the Ningxia Hui Autonomous Region.**
Source: Author.

of agriculture and animal husbandry. Guyuan is the poorer of the two counties and has been declared a poverty region by the Ministry of Agriculture. The county has inadequate access to drinking water and a poorly developed infrastructure.[11] Compared with Guyuan, Pengyang is relatively wealthy.[12] Farmers earn considerable incomes through tobacco cultivation, which can yield an annual gross income of 1,500–2,000 RMB per mu. The cultivated area of tobacco in Pengyang is 11,000 mu.[13]

This chapter begins by exploring the historical background of the Wastelands Policy. In the following sections, I describe the auction procedures, the policy content, and context (the institutions and administrative layers involved in the drafting and implementation process).[14] The

[11] Guojia Tongjiju (ed.), *Zhongguo Tongji Nianjian 1994* [China Statistical Yearbook 1994] (Beijing: Zhongguo Tongji Chubanshe, 1994); Jeanne Frances and Runyu Su, *Baseline Study Report: Improving the Status of Rural Women through Income-generating Activities*, CPR/89/P03 (New York: UNDP, 1990).

[12] Pengyang County was administered by Guyuan before 1988.

[13] Figures provided by the Pengyang County Section of Forestry for the year 1996.

[14] My analysis of state organs at the county and township level is based on the Institution Building Model designed by Milton Esman and further adapted to rural development studies by Jan-Michiel Otto. I have made particular use of Esman's 'institution variables': leadership, doctrine (the inherent mission and duties of an institution), programme (the policy that has to be implemented), resources (financial and personnel), and internal structure (management divisions and their interrelations). See Milton J. Esman, 'The Elements of

implementation process will be illustrated with two village case studies: the village 'where it all began' (Changcheng village in Pengyang County) and a village to which it spread in a later stage (Guanting village in Guyuan County).

The Foolish Old Man who Removed the Mountains: Origins of the Policy

During the first years of the People's Republic, the Chinese government was already concerned about soil degradation and rural poverty on the mountainous, eroded Loess plateau. A great effort was made constructing dykes and terraces to reduce the soil run-off. After the Communist take-over, the new leaders viewed the 'development of the mountainous regions' with optimism and enthusiasm: China had ample labour resources, and by deploying the masses, the barren and eroded mountains could be turned into lush, fertile fields and rural poverty overcome. In the old revolutionary base areas (the Shaan-Gan-Ning border region and Jiangxi Soviet) the need to harness nature and build a new rural society was strongly felt, as development of these regions was also a tribute to the Communist revolution. In line with Mao's speech at the Seventh National Congress of the Chinese Communist Party, the local authorities exhorted farmers to work in the spirit of Yugong, the foolish old man who, according to legend, attempted to remove the mountains.[15] In the struggle against the vicissitudes of nature, will-power was more important than anything else. It was believed that with science man could and should dominate nature. In Mao's words: 'If people living in nature want to be free, they will have to use natural sciences to understand nature, to overcome nature and to change nature; only then will they obtain freedom from nature.'[16]

Chen Yonggui, the leader of Dazhai Production Brigade in Shanxi Province, took great pains to propagate the transformation of nature through labour-intensive mass movements. During the Cultural Revolution (1966–76), the achievements in soil and water conservation in Chen's brigade would evolve into a nationwide campaign and spiritual model for all collectives in China: 'Learn from Dazhai' (*xuexi Dazhai*). Not only the land management measures were widely copied but so were the remuneration system (the so-called work-point system) based on labouring ability and the intangible criterion of 'political attitude'. The reasons for the failure of the Dazhai model lie in the extreme moral and social exhortation with which collectives were forced to adopt it. Since the model was officially

Institution Building', in Joseph W. Eaton (ed.), *Institution Building and Development: From Concepts to Application* (London: Sage Publications, 1972); Milton J. Esman, *Management Dimensions of Development: Perspectives and Strategies* (Bloomfield, CT: Kumarian Press, 1991); and Jan-Michiel Otto, *Aan de Voet van de Piramide: Overheidsinstellingen en Plattelandsontwikkeling in Egypte* [At the Foot of the Pyramid: Government Organs and Rural Development in Egypt] (Leiden: DSWO Press, 1987).

[15] Zedong Mao, 'The Foolish Old Man who Removed the Mountains', 11 June 1945, reprinted in: *Selected Works of Mao Tse-Tung*, Vol. 3 (Beijing: Foreign Languages Press, 1977).

[16] Zedong Mao, *Nongken* [Agricultural Reclamation], No. 6 (1966), p. 44.

deemed 'good', regional variations were easily overlooked.[17] Although the Dazhai work-point system was a fiasco and the model with its false claims about land improvement was exposed in later years, the overall effect of mass movements on agriculture remains uncertain.[18] At the end of the Cultural Revolution, the government changed its view on the value of mass movements for natural resource management. The Dazhai model, with its emphasis on collective action and responsibility, was replaced by the principles of the Household Contract Responsibility System (hereafter: Household Contract System). The initial successes of the economic reforms after 1978 (increased grain production and a bumper harvest of over 400 million tons in 1984) legitimized the trend in rural policies towards a privatization of agriculture through land leases.

The Household Contract System was also applied to the management of wasteland. Long before the Wastelands Policy became official policy in the early 1990s, the idea of individual management of wasteland had already firmly taken root. In line with national policy, the provincial governments stipulated that use rights of wasteland could be vested in the natural village, the joint household, or the individual farmer. The term of the lease was initially fifteen years, corresponding to the stipulations in the 1984 Rural Work Document No. 1 of the Chinese Communist Party. In the early 1990s, the Party determined that the period of land leases (including wasteland) in the original contracts could be extended by up to thirty years. In contrast to the Grassland Law (but not the Forest Law), the transfer of wasteland use contracts was allowed, which conformed to the trend of national land policies during 1984–7 promoting the 'mobility of land'.[19]

General Procedures of the Auctions

Local people's congresses were originally responsible for initiating the formulation and implementation of the Wastelands Policy. In response to a rapid proliferation of local wasteland auctions, the central government

[17] See Roderick MacFarquhar and John K. Fairbank (eds.), *Cambridge History of China. The People's Republic, Part 2: Revolutions within the Chinese Revolution 1966–1982* (Cambridge: Cambridge University Press, 1991), pp. 140, 524, 652–3.

[18] *Ibid.*, p. 517. For more details on the 'Learn-from-Dazhai' movement in Ningxia, see for example Jianmin Kang, 'Shenru Kaizhan Nongye Xue Dazhai Qunzhong Yundong' '[Deepen the Launching of the Learn-from-Dazhai Mass Movement'], reprint Party Archive 1973, Vol. 587, in Ningxia Nongye Hezuo Jingji Shiliao Bianxiezu (ed.), *Ningxia Nongye Hezuo Jingji Shiliao* [Historical Material of the Collective Agricultural Economy of Ningxia], Vol. 1 (Yinchuan: Ningxia Renmin Chubanshe, 1988), p. 589.

[19] See Yuk-shing Cheng and Shu-ki Tsang, 'Agricultural Land Reform in a Mixed System: The Chinese Experience of 1984–1994', *China Information*, Vol. 10, Nos. 3–4 (Winter 1995/Spring 1996), pp. 53–4; Zizhiqu Dangwei, 'Guanqie Zhixing Zhonggong Zhongyang (1985) 1 Hao Wenjian de Shixiang Zhengce Guiding' ['Ten Policy Regulations concerning the Implementation of Document No. 1 (1985) of the Communist Party and Central Government'], reprint, *Ningxia Daily* (5 April 1985), in Ningxia Nongye Hezuo Jingji Shiliao Bianxiezu (ed.), *Historical Material of the Collective Agricultural Economy of Ningxia*, Vol. 2 (1988), p. 819; Xiyu Wang, 'Huangshan Kaifa Zhili Zhong de Zhidu, Zhengce he Nonghu Xingwei—Shanxi Sheng Lüliang Diqu Paimai "Sihuangdi" Ge'an Yanjiu' ['System, Policy and Behaviour of Rural Households within the Control and Development of Barren Mountains—A Case Study of the Auction of "Four Wastelands" in Lüliang Prefecture in Shanxi Province'], *Zhongguo Nongcun Jingji* [Rural Economy of China], No. 11 (1994), pp. 4–5.

issued the Notice on the Control and Development of the Rural 'Four Wastelands' in 1996, stating the general principles and purposes of the policy.[20] Up to the start of the twenty-first century, it was the first and only guideline proclaimed by the central state. Within the Ministry of Agriculture, the Bureau of Law and Policy System Reform is charged with the coordination, monitoring, and evaluation of the Wastelands Policy. In spite of some regional differences in the periods of the lease or the terms of the contract, the basic format of the Wastelands Policy is similar throughout China. In principle, auction methods follow the model of Lüliang Prefecture. In this section I describe the procedures adopted in Lüliang and indicate where they deviate from those in Ningxia.

In policy documents and writings on auctions, it is repeatedly stressed that the use rights are sold but *not* the ownership rights. The use rights are surface rights and do not extend to subsoil use rights (such as mining rights). Wasteland is divided into four kinds: waste slopes, waste mountains, waste gullies, and waste river beds, together called the Four Wastelands. The term 'wasteland' is not defined ecologically and includes different land types, such as forested land, steppe, and mountain pastures. As a result, the responsibility for wasteland management falls under different ministries and bureaux. The use rights are sold in three ways: (*a*) the open auction, in which people from outside the village can participate; (*b*) the closed auction, held when farmers in the village show sufficient interest in buying wasteland leases and there is no need to invite outsiders; and (*c*) negotiated sales, if wasteland is of inferior quality or the plot has already been contracted for afforestation purposes and the tenant wants to extend the contract.

The preparatory work for the auction starts with the establishment of a Four Wastelands Leading Team consisting of leaders from relevant county sections. The leading team is responsible for the formation and training of a Four Wastelands Work Team, in which township cadres and village representatives chosen by the farmers participate. The Four Wastelands Work Team carries out the actual auction and preparations, such as a wasteland survey, a list of the plots up for auction, determination of land categories (soil fertility, relief, vegetation, and so forth), and the opening bidding price. The work team also decides on the method of payment. Payment can take place through lump sum payments, installments, and mortgage with land use rights as collateral. In reality, payment methods other than lump sum are rarely used. In Ningxia, it is stipulated that the revenues of the auctions belong to the administrative village, but are administered by the Township Financial Office as a special afforestation fund. The administrative village can apply for afforestation and revegetation subsidies from the fund.[21] Approximately one month prior to the

[20] Secretariat of the State Council, 'Zhili Kaifa Nongcun "Sihuang" Ziyuan Jin Yi Bu Jiaqiang Shuitu Baochi Gongzuo de Tongzhi' ['Notice on the Control and Development of the Rural "Four Wastelands" Resources and the Intensified Strengthening of Soil and Water Conservation'], in Zhongguo Falü Nianjian Bianji Weiyuanhui (ed.), *Zhongguo Falü Nianjian 1997* [China Legal Yearbook 1997] (Beijing: Zhongguo Falü Nianjianshe, 1997).

[21] Article 19 of the prefectural regulations. Zhonggong Guyuan Diwei, *Guyuan Xingzheng Gongshu Guanyu Paimai 'Sihuangdi' Shiyongquan Ruogan Zhengce Guiding* [Some Policy Regulations concerning the Auction of Use Rights to the 'Four Wastelands'—the

auction the work team provides information to the villagers about the auction and the wasteland plots.

To avoid a clash of interests, the 1997 Auction Law makes distinctions between the auctioning party, the commissioning party (selling party), and the buying party,[22] such that the auctioning and commissioning parties are forbidden to buy under penalty of revocation of the right to auction, or confiscation of acquired goods and property.[23] The structure of the Four Wastelands Work Team, however, does not conform to the stipulations of the Auction Law. The commissioning party (the villagers' committee) is simultaneously the auctioning party[24] and, worse, sometimes the buying party. This can and, as we will see below, does give rise to monopolization and the abuse of power by village cadres.

The wasteland contract is signed between the tenant and the administrative village. The contract is issued in triplicate and notarized at the Township Rural Economic Station. Copies of the contract are held by the tenant, the administrative village, and the Rural Economic Station.[25] According to the prefectural stipulations, the contract should state:

- term of the lease (50–100 years);[26]
- rights of the tenant, including: usufruct, transfer, mortgage, inheritance, and right to construction, such as fences, houses (forbidden in Ningxia), corrals, or other structures for wasteland development;
- duties of the tenant and lessor, in terms of afforestation and revegetation (in Lüliang 30 per cent of wasteland must be developed in three years). The lessor must supervise wasteland development and provide seeds, saplings, and technical support;
- restrictions on use: wasteland can be used only for forestry and animal husbandry, whereas agriculture is allowed only on slopes with a gradient of less than 25°;
- reward and penalty rules (in case of serious mismanagement, authorities can revoke the contract and re-auction the plot); and
- description of the physical boundaries of the lease.

The fact that the Lüliang regulations—in line with article 14 of the Soil and Water Conservation Law—prohibit agricultural reclamation on slopes

Guyuan Communist Party Committee and the Administrative Office], Party Document No. 1994/20 (1994).

[22] The buying party is in fact further divided into the competing party and the buying party or the (legal) person who buys the good against the highest bidding price.

[23] See 1997 Auction Law in Zhongguo Falü Nianjian Bianji Weiyuanhui (ed.), China Legal Yearbook 1997, pp. 285–8.

[24] It should also be noted that the Four Wastelands Work Team seldom meets the requirements of the auctioneer or auctioneering firm stipulated in articles 10–17 of the 1997 Auction Law. According to law, the auctioneer must have had special training and two years of relevant experience. In addition, he needs to be registered with a national or local auction association. See Auction Law, in Zhongguo Falü Nianjian Bianji Weiyuanhui (ed.), China Legal Yearbook 1997, pp. 285–6.

[25] See also Tim Hanstad and Ping Li, 'Land Reform in the People's Republic of China: Auctioning Rights to Wasteland', *Loyola of Los Angeles: International and Comparative Law Journal*, Vol. 19, No. 3 (1997), p. 558.

[26] Fieldwork findings in Lüliang Prefecture indicate that the actual period of the leases varies between thirty and sixty years. *Ibid.*, p. 557.

steeper than 25° does not imply that the cultivation of all land beneath this gradient is encouraged.[27] More detailed regulations for wasteland use can be drafted by local authorities. To conserve the ecological benefits of certain lands, the following categories of wasteland cannot be auctioned in Ningxia: (*a*) wasteland located in arid areas with an annual precipitation less than 200mm; (*b*) forests or afforested area; and (*c*) state and collective forests, livestock farms, and nature reserves.[28] In addition to the wasteland contract, the County Land Management Section is required to issue a land use permit. The daily supervision of the tenants' fulfilment of their obligations, the handling of matters relating to the lease (transfer, inheritance, extension, revocation, and so forth) and the mediation of land disputes arising from the auctions rest with the villagers' committee. Overall supervision and serious conflicts are dealt by the Township Rural Economic Station, the Township Forestry Management Station, and the County Land Management Section.[29]

Evolution of the Wastelands Policy

Lüliang Prefecture in Shanxi Province is the region where in the early 1980s the first wasteland auctions were organized. The initial results were not encouraging as the majority (a report mentioned 60–80 per cent) of the contracted wasteland was managed poorly or not at all. Problems encountered arose from the lack of security in the contract period, the right of transfer and inheritance of contracts, and the legal basis for capital investments in wasteland development.[30]

In addition, conservative forces in the Prefectural Party Committee opposed the 'open auction', which allows the rural and non-rural populace to participate and thus gain access to rural land. The green light to the auctions in Lüliang was given after Deng Xiaoping's 'southern tour' in 1992 prompted a renewed emphasis on the need for reform.[31] In the same

[27] The 25° gradient is defined as a guideline. The Soil and Water Conservation Law stipulates that the norms for the gradient of land on which agricultural reclamation is prohibited should be determined by the County People's Congresses. In Ningxia reclamation is forbidden on all wasteland. Guojia Jihua Weiyuanhui Guotudiqusi (ed.), *Zhonghua Renmin Gongheguo Guotu Fagui Huibian: 1988–1996* [Compilation of Regulations on State Land of the People's Republic of China: 1988–1996] (Beijing: Zhongguo Jihua Chubanshe, 1996), p. 156.

[28] Zhonggong Guyuan Diwei, Some Policy Regulations concerning the Auction, article 8, pp. 2–3.

[29] For a discussion of the auction procedures in Lüliang Prefecture, see Hanstad and Li, 'Land Reform in the People's Republic of China', pp. 548–54; Yunhang Ai, 'Jiakuai "Sihuang" Ziyuan Kaifa de Zhongyao Tujing' ['Speed up the Important Means to Develop "Four Wastelands" Resources'], *Zhongguo Nongcun Jingji* [Rural Economy of China], No. 11 (1995), pp. 42–7; Yongmin Li, Zhiquan Bai, and Shiling Li, 'Lüliang Diqu Paimai "Sihuang" de Zuofa yu Xiaoguo' ['Methods and Results of the "Four Wastelands" Auctions in Lüliang Prefecture'], *Zhongguo Nongcun Wenti* [Rural Economy of China], No. 5 (1994), pp. 27–9.

[30] Wang, 'System, Policy and Behaviour of Rural Households', p. 5.

[31] Wenxue Wang, 'Paimai "Sihuang" Zhishan Zhifu–Shanxi Sheng Pinkun Shanqu Paimai "Sihuang" Shiyongquan de Shijian yu Sikao' ['Auctioning "Four Wastelands": Harness the Mountains, Extend Wealth—Reflections and Practice on the Auction of Use Rights to the "Four Wastelands" in the Poor Mountainous Area of Shanxi Province'], *Nongye Jingji Wenti* [Problems of Agricultural Economy], No. 8 (1994), p. 21.

year, the Four Wastelands Auction Policy was formalized and auctions were organized throughout the prefecture. The Wastelands Policy gained national fame after the auctions of Lüliang were promoted through the media as a breakthrough in land policy. The auctions gradually evolved into a new model for rural development and soil conservation. The Wastelands Policy is not restricted to Shanxi Province. Similar policies for the management of wasteland are implemented in widely different ecological locations such as Chifeng (Inner Mongolia), Huaihua (Hunan), Hechi (Guangxi), and Yao'an (Yunnan).[32] Over time the national government attempted to standardize the amalgam of variations in wasteland auctions. In 1996 the Secretariat under the State Council promulgated a notice on the control and development of wasteland resources.[33]

The Notice is important on several accounts. First, it offers legitimacy to the use of auctions to develop wasteland resources. There is a legal problem of definition involved in the term 'auction'. According to the 1997 Auction Law, 'an auction is the manner of buying and selling whereby the rights to specific goods or property are transferred to the bidder of the highest price by means of open competition' (article 3). However, in most localities the use rights are not auctioned but bought by farmers through negotiated sales, while farmers have also been forced to buy land leases: practices not very different from the allocation of land leases in the Household Contract System. Li Sheng[34]—one of the most fervent advocates of the Wastelands Policy and simultaneously also its strongest critic—commented: 'The "Four Wastelands" auction is actually not an auction, but a lease of the "Four Wastelands" . . . To call this lease an auction falls short of reality and causes confusion in the use of fundamental concepts, although it may appeal to the psychological needs of buyers.'[35]

Second, the Notice stresses that 'entrepreneurial work units, social and other organizations, or individuals may use various methods to manage and develop "Four Wastelands"' on condition that 'villagers of the village itself enjoy priority'.[36] This stipulation is most contested. Its

[32] For a short discussion of the Wasteland Policies in Inner Mongolia and Guangxi, see Shuchen Zhang, 'Guanyu "Sihuang" Paimai de Diaocha yu Sikao' ['Research and Reflections about the Auction of the "Four Wastelands"'], *Jingji, Shehui* [Economy, Society], No. 2 (1997), pp. 49–52; and Xiangmou Huang, 'Shenhua Shanqu Nongcun Gaige de yige xin Luzi: Hechi Diqu Paimai "Wuhuang" Shiyongquan de Diaocha' ['A New Road for the Deepening of the Rural Reforms: Research of the Auction of the "Five Wastelands" in Hechi Prefecture'], *Guangxi Minzu Yanjiu* [Guangxi Ethnic Studies], No. 1 (1996), pp. 23–6. The procedures of the auctions in Yao'an County, Yunnan, are described in Baohua Zheng, 'Security of Use Rights for Forest Land: A Case Study of the Compensated Transfer of Use Rights over Collective Wasteland in Yao'an County, Yunnan Province', unpublished report prepared for project of Ford Foundation, Beijing.

[33] Secretariat of the State Council, 'Notice on the Control and Development of the Rural "Four Wastelands" Resources', pp. 425–6.

[34] Li Sheng is a Director General within the Bureau of Law and Policy System Reform of the Ministry of Agriculture, which is responsible for the national coordination of the Wastelands Policy.

[35] Sheng Li, '"Sihuang" Shiyongquan Paimai zhong de Falü Wenti' ['Legal Issues of the Auction of Use Rights of the "Four Wastelands"'], *Nongye Jingji Wenti* [Problems of Agricultural Economy], No. 4 (1995), p. 30.

[36] In practice this probably means that outside buyers can acquire use rights to wasteland only if there are no interested parties within the village. Secretariat of the

advocates assert that the best way to develop wasteland is to encourage competition among the most capable and financially equipped. Others argue that competition will lead to further impoverishment of the rural poor. Third, the Notice determines that wasteland can be used for 'agriculture if suited to agriculture, forestry if suited to forestry, fruit cultivation if suited to fruit cultivation . . . and animal husbandry if suited to animal husbandry'. At the same time, it stipulates that agricultural reclamation is prohibited on slopes or hills steeper than 25°. Fourth, guidelines are given for the wasteland contracts in terms of (*a*) the contract period (not longer than fifty years—in Lüliang 100 years); (*b*) the right to inherit, transfer, and mortgage the contract; (*c*) the right to set up shareholding cooperatives supervised by the township government and with the permission of the county government. The contract procedures (number of copies, notarization, need for land use permit, and so forth) are less clearly spelled out. Lastly, the legal definition of wasteland is addressed. At this point, there are two issues at stake: the difference between state and collective ownership of land and the ecological definition of wasteland, notably the distinction between forest and grassland. In Ningxia, wasteland comprises desert-steppe and dry grassland, seldom forested. But in provinces such as Guangxi and Yunnan, wasteland might well refer to (communal) forests. The Notice does not clarify what 'wasteland' denotes ecologically, but briefly stipulates that it is 'strictly forbidden to auction forest land as "Four Wastelands"'.[37]

Concerning state and collective wasteland, both the 1984 Forest Law and the 1985 Grassland Law define forest and grassland as state-owned unless owned by the collective. Before decollectivization, collective land ownership rights were laid down in Party documents ('Sixty Articles'), but not in law. When the former collectives (commune, brigade, and team) were dismantled and replaced by the township, administrative village, and natural village, collective ownership rights to grassland and forest were formalized in the 1982 Constitution, yet the nature of the 'collective' was not specified. Over time, the commune, brigade, and team came to regard the forest and grassland in their vicinity as their own, which led to ambiguity and controversy over state and collective property, both between state institutions and the collectives and among collectives themselves.[38] In order to avoid problems over state and collective property rights, the Notice states that wasteland should not be leased if the defining lines between state and collective wasteland are unclear or disputed. It adds that 'it is strictly forbidden to change state-owned land into collectively owned land'.[39] Yet, as property rights to grassland and forest are unclear, in some

State Council, in Zhongguo Falü Nianjian Bianji Weiyuanhui (ed.), *China Legal Yearbook 1997*, pp. 425–6.

[37] *Ibid.*

[38] For a discussion of this problem, see also Peter Ho, 'The Clash over State and Collective Property: The Making of the Grassland Law', *The China Quarterly*, Vol. 161 (March 2000), pp. 227–50.

[39] Secretariat of the State Council, in Zhongguo Falü Nianjian Bianji Weiyuanhui (ed.), China Legal Yearbook 1997, pp. 425–6.

cases collectives will unavoidably auction use rights to land not legally their own, in defiance of article 6 of the Auction Law:

> The commissioning party must own or be able to take legal disciplinary action against the good or property for which a bid is made at the auction.[40]

The confusion about the legal definition of wasteland (forest versus grassland, and collective versus state-owned land) translates into dual confusion about the duties of land tenure and management. On the one hand, the duties are confounded between the State Forestry Bureau (former Ministry of Forestry), the Ministry of Agriculture (and the subordinate Bureau of Animal Husbandry), and the Ministry for Land and Natural Resources (former State Land Administration). On the other hand, the responsibilities are unclear between the aforementioned state institutions versus the rural collectives (township, administrative village, natural village) that lay ownership claims to forest, grassland, or wasteland. The case studies will demonstrate the effects of this confusion on the implementation of the Wastelands Policy.

Convincing the Leaders: Changcheng Village

Village description. Changcheng village ('Great Wall' village) owes its name to some of the most ancient stretches of the Great Wall in its neighbourhood. These sections of the wall were constructed during the reign of Qin Shi Huangdi, China's first emperor (221–207 BC). Today, not much more remains of them than some man-sized heaps of mud scattered in the fields.[41] But they do bestow on the village a halo of historical romanticism of which the farmers are proud. The surrounding landscape of the village is typical for the Loess Plateau: high hills interspersed with gullies and chasms formed by erosion. The landscape has changed little since Andrew Findlay described it in the 1930s: 'Water erosion has carved out of a surface once level, strange gullies and ravines, weird pillars, great arches and tunnels, which make a journey into this area a memorable experience for the present-day traveller.'[42]

Changcheng Administrative Village[43] is located about 5km away from Chengyang Township by which it is administered. Changcheng counts fourteen natural villages within its jurisdiction, with 611 households and a total population of 3,080. The population in the village is fully Han. The total area of agricultural land within the boundaries of the administrative village is 20,896mu. The main agricultural crops are wheat, linseed, corn, millet, and potato. Parts of the fields are irrigated for the cultivation of tobacco. Tobacco makes all the difference for Pengyang: farmers can earn

[40] See Auction Law, *ibid.*, p. 285.

[41] In addition to the Qin Great Wall, parts from other dynasties can be found, including the Tang, Song, and Ming. See Renyong Lu, Zhongli Wu, and Zhuang Xu, *Ningxia Lishi Dilikao* [A Historical Geography of Ningxia] (Yinchuan: Ningxia Renmin Chubanshe, 1993), pp. 14–16.

[42] Andrew G. Findlay, 'Men and Matters in the Land of the Yellow Earth', *Journal of the North China Branch of the Royal Asiatic Society*, Vol. 68 (1937), p. 57.

[43] All the data for Changcheng village and Chengyang Township apply to 1996 unless otherwise indicated.

up to 2,000 RMB per month during harvest time.[44] The major natural constraints are a lack of level land and a harsh climate. Annual precipitation is 450–500mm. Frequent droughts, hail, storms, frost, and occasional earthquakes ravage rural life.[45]

Forestry has good development prospects in this region and the local authorities have promoted it. Tree species mostly planted are Xinjiang poplar (*Populus alba var. pyramidalis*) and almond (*Prunus armeniaca*). The Xinjiang poplar is a fast-growing, drought-resistant tree, suitable for paper pulp, building material, and furniture. It has been planted with relative success in Pengyang since the early 1950s, though it is vulnerable to pests. The almond, too, is suited to semi-arid conditions and provides farmers with a welcome extra source of income. The tree bears fruit after five years (it can be eaten fresh or dried) and the nuts can be processed into valuable almond oil or Chinese medicine.[46] Guided by the County Section of Forestry, the villagers have planted alfalfa (*Medicago sativa*), Siberian pea tree (*Caragana korshinskii*), and milkvetch (*Astralagus adsurgens*) as forage for livestock. Virtually every open space, shoulder, or gully has been planted.[47] Although sheep and goats are held as a sideline and flocks are small (between fifteen and twenty ruminants), the grazing of animals poses a serious threat to forestry. The farmers say that the custom of overlapped grazing (*chuanmu*) makes tree planting a precarious undertaking, while fencing leads to land disputes.

The village is relatively well-developed, with good infrastructure and a daily bus service to the county seat. Marketing of agricultural produce is undertaken in Pengyang, although the township market is also popular. Changcheng has its own market every three days, attracting farmers from far and wide. There are about ten shops, a small infirmary, and a primary school. The village school is better equipped than other schools nearby, where pupils are forced to write characters on the ground for lack of paper. An important centre for social gatherings is the temple, which hosts festivals to which the village *qinqiang* opera group adds lustre. That Changcheng is no ordinary village becomes obvious from the many state awards and prizes proudly suspended next to Mao's portrait in the village meeting hall. The most prominent and active figure in the village is the young Party Secretary, Li Yurong. Under his leadership, the villagers' committee developed into a relatively efficient and effective institution, and recently moved to newly built offices.

A tale of village assertiveness. The Wastelands Policy is confined to Guyuan Prefecture (six counties in total: Pengyang, Guyuan, Haiyuan, Xiji, Longde, and Jingyuan).[48] The policy was initiated by neither the

44 Average net annual per capita income in 1995 was 786 RMB.

45 Zhongguo Ziran Ziyuan Congshu Bianyi Weiyuanhui (ed.), *Zhongguo Ziran Ziyuan Congshu: Ningxia Juan* [Encyclopaedia of China's Natural Resources: Ningxia Volume] (Beijing: Zhongguo Huanjing Kexue Chubanshe, 1995).

46 In 1996, the price for 1kg of apricots was 1–2 RMB, while the almonds went for 12 RMB.

47 In Chengyang there is 12,000 mu of forage base area.

48 In 1996, a few experimental auctions were also launched in Yinnan Prefecture, but at the time of writing this chapter there has been no follow-up to them.

provincial nor the prefectural authorities, but originated in Changcheng Administrative Village. In 1992, a small trial auction was held without the township being informed. As the auction seemed successful, Li Yurong, the village Party Secretary, decided to put the entire wasteland area under the hammer and sought permission from the Chengyang Township authorities. The township government feared getting its fingers burned over an issue that directly pushed at the limits of the 'socialist market economy', and passed the plan to the County Forestry Section, which assisted Changcheng village in organizing and preparing for the auctions. The delicacy of the Wastelands Policy became obvious in a speech about it by the Deputy Prefect, in which he stressed the need to eliminate 'leftist' thinking to develop the rural economy of Guyuan.[49]

The first fully-fledged 'Four Wastelands Auction' of Changcheng village was held in the spring of 1993. The auction corresponded to those of Lüliang. In a few months, the use rights to over 1,000mu of wasteland had been sold. The County Section of Forestry planned to bring the auctions to the attention of Rui Cunzhang, the Prefectural Party Secretary, through the *Guyuan Daily*, the most widely read newspaper in the prefecture.[50] At the time, a more liberalized atmosphere in China as a result of Deng's southern tour was already being felt. Moreover, the Four Wastelands Auction Policy of Lüliang had by then gained full political approval. Rui ordered the powerful Agricultural Work Department of the Secretariat of the Prefectural Party Committee to develop a policy framework for the auctions.[51] At the end of the year, the Changcheng villagers' committee had earned 6,885 RMB by selling use rights to 4,950mu wasteland. A total of 473 households (77 per cent of all households in the administrative village) had participated in the auction. The smallest area leased per household was 5mu, whereas one farmer broke the village record with 120mu. The minimum bid price per mu had been set at 1 RMB, although some farmers claimed to have paid only 0.5 RMB per mu. There was no maximum price level. The highest price was 50 RMB.[52] The auctions were deemed a success and a political victory for the village authorities.[53]

[49] Zhonggong Guyuan Diwei Nonggongbu, *Nanbu Fangkai Wenjian Xuanbian* [A Selection of Documents on the Opening Up of the South] (restricted, 1994), p. 196.

[50] For the central policy level, Murray Scott Tanner notes the same 'adept use of publications and other mass media' in order to push a new policy proposal through the bureaucracy. See Murray Scott Tanner, 'How a Bill becomes a Law in China: Stages and Processes in Lawmaking', in Stanley B. Lubman (ed.), *China's Legal Reforms* (Oxford: Oxford University Press, 1996), p. 50.

[51] This department is responsible for agricultural policy. It drafts local regulations, recommends and initiates changes in policies, and is in charge of policy monitoring and evaluation. It is accountable to the Policy Research Office of the Autonomous Region Party Committee.

[52] Changcheng Cunmin Weiyuanhui (ed.), *Changchengcun Yilin 'Sihuangdi' Paimai Zhili Qingkuang Jianjie* [A Short Introduction to the Control and Auction of 'Four Wastelands' suitable to Forestry of Changcheng Village] (28 September 1994); Pengyang Xian Linyeju (ed.), *Changcheng Cun Paimai Yilin 'Sihuangdi' Shiyongquan de Zuofa* [The Methods of the Auction of Use Rights to 'Four Wastelands' suitable for Forestry by Changcheng Village] (28 January 1994).

[53] This is the story as it has been narrated by the Village Party Secretary and the village leader of Zhaoling. The story has been confirmed by officials of the Township Forestry Management Station and the County Section of Forestry.

On 18 March 1994, Rui Cunzhang talked at a demonstration wasteland auction in Changcheng[54] which marked the beginning of the campaign 'Learn from the "Four Wastelands" Auctions of Pengyang County' (*xuexi Pengyang Xian 'Sihuang' Paimai*). Despite the suspicions aroused by the movement's name, the tone of his speech was pragmatic and in no way reminiscent of past Communist rhetoric of the 'learn-from-Dazhai' or any other 'learn-from' campaign. Rui stressed several rules that were incorporated in regulations proclaimed a few days later. It should be noted that he emphasized the necessity of trial auctions before the formal implementation of the Wastelands Policy. Important were his 'four no's', some of which—through an ironic twist of fate—were disregarded and led to the failure of the auctions. The 'four no's' were: (*a*) no egalitarian sales (dividing the wasteland into equal plots and selling the use rights to farmers at uniform prices); (*b*) no monopolization by clan heads; (*c*) no abuse of power by the cadres; and (*d*) no grain cultivation on wasteland. In order to allay the suspicion of the rural populace that the auctions were just another excuse by the government to extract money from the farmers, Rui stated explicitly that 'the reason why we auction "the Four Wastelands" is to step up the afforestation of waste mountains and not to earn a few more pennies'.[55] Two days after Rui's speech, the 'Four Wastelands Auction Policy' was officially proclaimed in the prefecture.[56]

The executive agency: the County Section of Forestry. The Agricultural Work Department charged the County Section of Forestry with coordinating the auctions in Pengyang County. Therefore, the majority of the members in the Four Wastelands Leading Team were ex officio from the Section of Forestry. As stated earlier, this team established a Four Wastelands Work Team for surveying and mapping the wasteland, providing free nursery stock, and supervising afforestation and planting activities. In practice, these tasks were carried out by subordinate units of the Section of Forestry.

The Section of Forestry seems an obvious choice for running the wasteland auctions. First, in Guyuan the Section of Animal Husbandry assumes a great share of the duties in soil and water conservation. In Pengyang, by contrast, due to ecological differences the Section of Forestry is responsible for this. The area of forested wasteland in Pengyang is larger because of higher precipitation (450–550mm against 350–450mm in

[54] Before the speech in March, Rui had already approved of the auctions at the Rural Work Meeting in January 1994. In his words: '[We] have to step up the integral management of the gullies . . . and boldly auction wasteland, waste mountains, waste gullies and waste riverbeds.' Zhonggong Guyuan Diqu Weiyuanhui Bangongshi (ed.), *Guyuan Diqu Nongcun Gongzuo Huiyi Cailiao Huibian* [Proceedings of the Rural Work Meeting of Guyuan Prefecture] (January 1994), p. 6.

[55] Zhonggong Guyuan Diwei, *Guanyu Yinfa Diwei Shuji Rui Cunzhang, Xingshu Fuzhuanyuan Tai Weimin Zai Paimai 'Sihuangdi' Xianchang Huiyi Shang Jianghua de Tongzhi* [Notice of the Speech delivered at the Occasion of the Auction of the 'Four Wastelands' by Prefectural Party Secretary Rui Cunzhang and Deputy Prefect Tai Weimin], Party Document No. 1994/28, p. 3.

[56] Zhonggong Guyuan Diwei, Some Policy Regulations concerning the Auction of Use Rights, pp. 2, 6.

Guyuan).[57] For this reason, Pengyang is an important link in the 'Green Great Wall'—the shelterbelt covering China's northern provinces. A considerable portion of the prefectural funds is channelled to the Section of Forestry for afforestation. Another reason why preference was given to the Section of Forestry instead of the Section of Animal Husbandry is its extensive network of township-based Forestry Management Stations. The staff of the Forestry Stations are backed up by a Forestry Police Force with similar rights to the regular police force (the rights to arrest, detain, and carry weapons). The stations are the instruments that allow the Section of Forestry to reach well into rural society and maintain close relationships with farmers. In contrast, the Section of Animal Husbandry has to operate from the county and has only an economic police force with insufficient powers.

The main activities of the Township Forestry Station are:

- afforestation, management, and improvement of forest (including disease prevention and control, and pruning);
- support to farmers in fruit cultivation;
- supervision of grazing in forest and conflict resolution; and
- promotion of income-generating activities and organization of rural credits (for corn and tobacco cultivation).

The station is staffed by four people, all graduates of the forestry department of the middle agricultural school in Guyuan. The office is a shabby house in the township government compounds and provides simultaneously the living quarters for one staff member and his young wife. The relatively low salary (300 RMB per month)[58] is regarded as 'just enough', but the people at the Forestry Station seem well-motivated. When asked what the office still needs, one staff member replied: 'We most certainly lack a motorcycle.' The villages are visited on foot. Every staff member visits twenty to thirty households a day, while covering a distance varying from 5km to 10km. The members of the Forestry Station frequently visit Changcheng village to remain updated on calls for assistance, land disputes, or other relevant news.

Hearing the Farmer: Results of the Auctions

The auctions in Changcheng were considered successful by the local authorities. But how were the auctions experienced by the farmers themselves? To obtain a view from below, a small survey of ninety households (forty-seven in Guyuan and forty-three in Pengyang, including buyers and non-buyers) was carried.[59] The survey was not representative

[57] See also Ningxia Nongye Kancha Shejiyuan (ed.), 'Ningxia Zhibei Quhuatu' ['Regional Planning Map of Vegetation in Ningxia'], in *Ningxia Zhibei* [The Vegetation of Ningxia] (Yinchuan: Ningxia Renmin Chubanshe, 1988).

[58] The salary figures in this chapter all pertain to 1996.

[59] Among both samples the percentage of cadres is approximately the same: 11–12%. The sample from Pengyang contains more and higher educated farmers (only 9% with no education, as against 19% in Guyuan; and 32% with a senior middle school degree—*gaozhong*—as against 12% in Guyuan).

and was implemented to give a general idea of farmers' opinions on the Wastelands Policy. The experiences of farmers in Changcheng village are grouped around four items: (*a*) the procedures and practice of the auctions; (*b*) the awareness of the policy aims and regulations; (*c*) the use of wasteland before and after the auctions; and (*d*) the appraisal of the policy.

Auction procedures and practice. The majority of respondents (81 per cent) indicated that they had bought wasteland. About one-third of the farmers had bought less than 4mu of land, while around 40 per cent had bought plots between 5mu and 10mu. Only one farmer had felt confident to buy a tract of wasteland larger than 20mu. The chief limitation to wasteland development is the lack of labour capacity. Of the sample, 63 per cent indicated they wanted to buy more land, but lacked the labour to work the land. Approximately 12 per cent stated that their financial situation did not allow them to buy more land, and another 12 per cent mentioned that the villagers' committee had imposed a limit on the land bought per household. The wasteland plots sold in Pengyang were not small and dispersed but consisted of larger, consolidated plots in order to facilitate land management. In some cases, land consolidation occurred by the reselling of wasteland that had been previously auctioned. In Pengyang there is a rather even distribution among the various methods of price determination. Around 30 per cent of the farmers obtained wasteland in open sales with fixed prices posted prior to the selling. Another 30 per cent had negotiated with the villagers' committee and bought land outside the auctions. The remaining 40 per cent acquired land through real auctions at which land was sold to the highest bidder (two respondents said they did not know how they had bought land). There was no variation in the payment method. Despite the prefectural regulations, only lump-sum payments were accepted by the villagers' committee.

Awareness of the policy. The farmers in the region around Changcheng were well-informed about the auctions. The Township Forestry Station and the villagers' committee had made every effort to inform the farmers. Village meetings had been held, information about the wasteland plots had been posted, and forestry personnel had paid regular visits to prepare the auctions. The majority of farmers (93 per cent) heard about the auctions through the villagers' committee. In addition, a body of county regulations had been proclaimed, which provided the local interpretation of prefectural rules.[60] Interesting is also the proclamation of the 'Changcheng Village Forest Management Regulations', similar to the county notices and posted in a conspicuous place to serve as a reminder to the farmers.

[60] See Pengyang Xian Renmin Zhengfu, *Guanyu Yinfa 'Yilin "Sihuang" de Paimai, Chengbao, Lühua Shixing Yijian' de Tongzhi* [Concerning the Distributed Notice 'Remarks on the Implementation of the Auction, Contracting and Afforestation of the "Four Wastelands"'], Government Document No. 1994/8 (1 March 1994); Pengyang Xian Renmin Zhengfu, *Guanyu Yifa Jiaqiang Linmu Guanli, Zhizhi Daofa Huangshan de Tonggao* [Proclamation Concerning the Strengthening of Forest Management according to the Law and the Prevention of Illegal Felling at Waste Mountains], 1 August 1994.

Table 5: **What rights are included in the wasteland contract? Pengyang sample (n = 43)**

Type of right	*Yes (%)*	*No (%)*	*Total (%)*
Use right	88.4	11.6	100
Transfer of use right within village	14.0	86.0	100
Transfer of use right outside village	4.7	95.3	100
Inheritance right	30.2	69.8	100
Ownership right within village	11.6	88.4	100
Ownership right outside village	0.0	100.0	100
Usufruct	55.8	44.2	100
Mortgage right	2.3	97.7	100

Source: Author's survey.

The aims of the Wastelands Policy are soil and water conservation, and poverty alleviation, while the authorities gave explicit assurances that the auctions were *not* meant to generate revenues for the government. The farmers in Changcheng were aware of the first policy aim (70 per cent of the total sample), but the second aim was less known (44 per cent). When farmers were asked what rights they enjoyed, most knew that the contract granted use rights but not ownership. It is striking that the farmers were unaware of the rights to transfer, inherit, usufruct, and mortgage of wasteland (see Table 5). The rights to transfer and inheritance of agricultural and wasteland are laid down in the 1993 Agriculture Law.[61] The only exception is the mortgage of land. However, according to the 1996 Notice on the Wastelands Policy 'those who buy use rights, have the right to inherit, transfer, mortgage and shareholding management' (article 6).[62]

Farmers knew the restrictions imposed on the use of wasteland (prohibition of reclamation, road and house construction). But again, the rights they enjoyed—land development and improvement by fencing and constructing corrals and rainwater reservoirs—were less known (see Table 6). If we look at the contract (standardized in the township), some things become clear: it does not mention the rights of transfer and inheritance, or the extension of the contract when expired. Reflecting the spirit of county rules, the contract specifies the duties and penalty rules rather than the rights of the tenant (see Appendix H).

Wasteland use. Seventy per cent of the respondents indicated that, prior to the auctions, wasteland was mainly used as pasture. After the auctions, wasteland was used for economic forestry purposes (81 per cent of whom

[61] Agriculture Law, articles 12–15. See Nongye Zhengce Tigai Faguisi (ed.), *Nongyefa Quanshu* [A Complete Edition of Agricultural Laws] (Beijing: Zhongguo Nongye Chubanshe, 1994), pp. 6–12.

[62] Secretariat of the State Council, in Zhongguo Falü Nianjian Bianji Weiyuanhui (ed.), China Legal Yearbook 1997, pp. 425–6. In the 'Suggestions Concerning the "Reform of the South" and the Speeding Up of Economic Development' issued by the Prefectural Party Committee in August 1994, the right to mortgage land was explicitly put forward as a privilege for the poor regions. See Zhonggong Guyuan Diwei Nonggongbu, A Selection of Documents on the Opening Up of the South, p. 13.

Table 6: **What are the prohibitions on the use of wasteland? Pengyang sample (n = 43)**

Type of prohibition	*Yes (%)*	*No (%)*	*Total (%)*
Agricultural reclamation	81.4	18.6	100
Cultivation of sorghum	69.8	30.2	100
Cultivation of millet	65.1	34.9	100
Cultivation of alfalfa	7.0	93.0	100
Afforestation	4.7	95.3	100
Fencing	37.2	62.8	100
Construction of corral	51.2	48.8	100
Construction of house	67.4	32.6	100
Construction of road	55.8	44.2	100
Construction of rainwater reservoir	25.6	74.4	100

Source: Author's survey.

90 per cent planted almond) and sometimes forage cultivation; sixteen farm households managed one common almond orchard and paid 2 RMB each to hire someone to guard an area of 40mu against sheep and goats.

Policy appraisal. The villagers of Changcheng were positive about the auctions. Of the sample, 67 per cent regarded the Wastelands Policy as 'quite successful' and 23 per cent as 'very successful'. The most common reason cited for the success was the increase in income (70 per cent). However, it is unclear how the planting of almond, which takes five years to bear fruit, could yield returns within three years after the auctions had taken place. There were also some disgruntled voices about the benefits of afforestation. One farmer said that 'the Wastelands Policy succeeded, but we have seen no economic benefits yet. The trees grow slowly and there is the risk of them freezing to death.' Another remarked that 'there really has not been much guidance on how we had to plant trees. Well, once a year someone of the Forestry Station came by to check on us.' The possibility of income-generation by the Wastelands Policy remains a topic of future research.

There have also been complaints about the Party Secretary. A farmer described the secretary's behaviour with the adage by the Song dynasty scholar Yu Wenbao: 'I really resent that Li Yurong arranged the best land for himself. Well, that is clearly "the tower closest to the water gets the moon" (*jin shui loutai xian de yue*).'[63] Regardless of whether the Party Secretary did buy the best tracts, he violated the law when, as a member of the village authorities, he participated in the auction. Article 22 of the Auction Law states that 'the auctioning party and its employees are not allowed to participate in the capacity of a competing party in auctioning activities organized by itself, nor to entrust others to compete on its

[63] On the other hand, some villagers defended the criticism by saying that the ones in office are always easy to blame. 'Isn't it true that the birds that stretch out their neck are the first ones to be shot?' remarked an elder farmer (*qiang da chu tou niao*).

behalf'.[64] The 1996 Notice on the Wastelands Policy does not exclude state officials from the auctions. But a senior official within the Ministry of Agriculture warned against the participation of cadres: 'It may seem rational that state and Party organs participate in the management of the "Four Wastelands", but it can easily foster unhealthy tendencies . . . We should prohibit the lease of the "Four Wastelands" by cadres of state organs.'[65]

According to the Pengyang Section of Forestry, agricultural reclamation of wasteland did take place, notably in the poorer regions. Despite this, the prefectural authorities were satisfied with the results. The auctions were extended to other counties in the prefecture. However, less than two years after its promulgation, the Wastelands Policy was suddenly halted. According to the Agricultural Work Department, over 50 per cent of wasteland in the prefecture was reclaimed for agriculture, causing widespread soil erosion. In the following sections, the background of the policy failure is provided through a case study of Guyuan County.

Imposing Implementation: Guanting Village

Village description. Nested in mountains whose terraced fields make them look like huge birthday cakes, Guanting village is conveniently located at the main road to Guyuan. It is an hour's bumpy ride from Guanting to the county seat (20km north-east from Guyuan). Guanting Administrative Village[66] is concurrent seat of the Guanting Township Government. Contrary to what one might expect, the name 'Guanting' has nothing to do with a Qing dynasty (1644–1911) sub-prefecture.[67] At the time when Mao's First Front Army marched into Guyuan in October 1935, Guanting had already developed into a walled market town, housing the public office of the township (hence its name, meaning 'public office').

Guanting administers eleven natural villages, a total of 398 farm households, and 2,046 people. The population is predominantly Hui, with a few Han Chinese (in Guanting are only four Han Chinese). There is no significant ethnic tension, but the Han—condescendingly called 'the old Han' (*lao Hanren*) by the Hu—are aware of their minority status. The agricultural crops grown are the same as in Chengyang. The main difference is the lack of irrigation, which makes tobacco cultivation impossible and the population much poorer.[68] The total cultivated area in Guanting village is 11,105mu. Annual precipitation is lower than in Chengyang (around 450mm), which seems to make a critical difference for forestry. Afforestation has been attempted through repeated planting campaigns since the founding of the People's Republic. But the farmers say that the saplings die a certain death due to the frequent droughts. Trees grow only in the vicinity of fields or close to cave dwellings (or *yaodong*), where small-scale irrigation is possible. The barren hills of Guyuan contrast

[64] See Auction Law, Zhongguo Falü Nianjian Bianji Weiyuanhui (ed.), China Legal Yearbook 1997, p. 286.
[65] Li, 'Legal Issues of the Auction of Use Rights', p. 30.
[66] All the data for Guanting (village and township) apply to 1996 unless otherwise indicated.
[67] Lu et al., A Historical Geography of Ningxia, pp. 1–2, 312.
[68] In 1995 net average annual income was 312 RMB.

strongly with the green, forested mountains of Pengyang. Sheep and goat raising is more important in Guanting than in Changcheng, but farmers say that animal husbandry has been declining over the last ten years, mainly because of increased reclamation of village pastures as a result of population pressure.[69] Hills once in use as pastures have been turned into terraced—or, worse, non-terraced—fields.

As Guanting is also the township seat, many state institutions are located in the village. The village hosts the granary, the Supply and Marketing Cooperative, a credit cooperative, a veterinary station, and a forestry management station. In addition, there is a market, a primary school, an infirmary, a few groceries, and an antique shop that purchases jade seals, bronze buckles, Han-dynasty mirrors, and other objets d'art robbed from graves in the neighbourhood. Important, too, is the mosque, which forms one congregation (or *fang*) of believers from the eleven natural villages.

Guanting has frequently been the site of poverty alleviation projects. Poverty is aggravated by poor infrastructure. Although Guanting itself is relatively easy to reach, the other natural villages are remote and dispersed. In some cases, only ten to fifteen isolated cave dwellings, scattered over a distance of several kilometres, constitute one 'natural village'. This fragmented structure of villages in Guyuan inhibits contact with the farmers, a complaint often heard from the township cadres. Landslides cause major damage to the rural infrastructure. In contrast to the air of dynamism in Changcheng, Guanting seems sunk in apathy and indifference. The officials at the township are difficult to contact. Cadres have been temporarily laid off and encouraged to become independent entrepreneurs.[70] Even the township head left the township for three years to set up a business. At the forestry station, the staff, unpaid for months, frequently while away the time playing chess and mahjong. Cynical laughter was their response when asked what their main tasks were. 'It does not matter what we do', said an official, 'the trees we plant are eaten by the sheep and we have no money to carry out our tasks anyway.'

The executive agency: who is responsible?

> The prefectural Agricultural Work Department is responsible for the Wastelands Policy. In each county a section is charged with policy implementation. For Pengyang this is the Section of Forestry. And in Guyuan . . . I'm not sure which section would be responsible.
>
> (Official at Guyuan Section of Animal Husbandry)

On paper the Section of Animal Husbandry is charged with the auctions. But talks with officials in this institution and at the grass roots reveal there is no consensus on which state organ is responsible. Before turning to the

69 There are 1,115 sheep and 290 cashmere goats (1996) in Guanting.

70 Under the *fenliu* system, cadres may apply to be discharged from office to engage in entrepreneurial activities. In return for two months of salary per year, the original position as well as the terms of employment of the cadre remain unchanged for a period of two years in order to allow him to set up his own enterprise. This is different from the *xiagang* system under which cadres are released from office permanently. See Zhonggong Guyuan Diwei Nonggongbu, A Selection of Documents on the Opening Up of the South, p. 19.

details of the implementation or non-implementation of the Wastelands Policy, I will summarize this government body's tasks, mission, resources, and internal structure.

The prime responsibility of the Section of Animal Husbandry is the management and development of grassland. In contrast to Pengyang, where most wasteland is forest, wasteland in Guyuan is generally grassland. Therefore, the Section of Animal Husbandry is the obvious institution to implement the Wastelands Policy. The institutional structure of the Section of Animal Husbandry is less extensive than that of the Section of Forestry. In the 1980s there were veterinary stations at the township level for livestock disease prevention and veterinary care. But in recent years township personnel have been laid off and stations contracted out to 'individual entrepreneurs' (in fact, former state personnel). For effective grassland management, the Section of Animal Husbandry is in dire need of extension into the grass roots. At present, however, this agency operates from the county level.

There are thirty-two people at the county level, including sixteen grassland (economic) police officers, responsible for twenty-six townships (compare this with the Section of Forestry, which employs thirty-six people at the county level, not to speak of the staff at the township). Despite provincial salary norms for state organs, the monthly income of personnel at the Section of Animal Husbandry is far lower (210–20 RMB) than that of their colleagues in the Section of Forestry (300 RMB). The salary difference is just one of many that separate these two institutions, stimulating envy and competition. The regular duties of the Section of Animal Husbandry comprise:

- the development and management of wasteland (revegetation and construction of forage bases);
- grassland protection and increase in grassland production (rodents and pest control, fire management, weeding of unpalatable plants, and aerial sowing—halted for budgetary reasons);
- technical/veterinary extension and services;
- the development and introduction of new forage varieties; and
- law enforcement and conflict mediation (patrolling, control of illegal reclamation and grazing).

One is least likely to encounter people in the county office between April and July, when the staff 'go down to the countryside' (*xia xiang*) to patrol and investigate legal cases. These activities are impeded by the poor financial situation. The grassland police officers travel to the township by bus or, when there is money to buy petrol, by car. The office has a 13-year-old rusty Beijing Jeep. To reach farmers, grassland police often walk from the township to the villages.

The Section of Animal Husbandry had to carry out a comprehensive survey of wasteland resources in the county. For unknown reasons county funds were not committed to the Wastelands Policy, as a result of which no survey was done, nor support given to villages in setting up the auctions. It appears that the poorly equipped townships were fully saddled with the survey of wasteland and the organization of the auctions. Moreover, the implementation was hampered by a disagreement over the division of duties between the Section of Animal Husbandry and the Section of Forestry. These two institutions have clashed many times over policies deemed the responsibility of both. As noted earlier, the legal status of wasteland is unclear, which leads to confusion over the tasks.

According to article 13 of the 1991 Executive Regulations of the Land Management Law, the development of state-owned wasteland must be approved by the (former) State Land Administration if the area is between 10,000 and 20,000mu, and by the State Council if it exceeds 20,000mu.[71] On this basis, a bureaucrat within the Ningxia State Land Administration asserted that the Wastelands Policy was illegal. He said: 'The State Land Administration alone has the authority to issue land use permits. The Pengyang Section of Forestry should not have approved of the auctions without our prior consent. The sections of forestry and animal husbandry believed they have authority, which created chaos.'[72]

What interest did the Section of Animal Husbandry and the Section of Forestry have in quarrelling over responsibilities? One reason, of course, is their perception of their own mission. As remarked earlier, the greater part of wasteland in Guyuan is grassland rather than forested pasture. Therefore, the Section of Animal Husbandry felt it should be the agency to execute the Wastelands Policy. But this does not explain why the Section of Animal Husbandry was willing to implement a policy for which no funds had been committed.

Several other factors do provide an adequate explanation. First, the auctions relieved the duties of the Section of Animal Husbandry. Each year the prefecture imposes a revegetation quota for the construction of artificial grassland and forage bases. The Wastelands Policy shifted responsibility for wasteland development from the local state to individual farm households. In 1996, the Section of Animal Husbandry revegetated 2,000mu of wasteland and planned to revegetate an additional 20,000mu. However, one-third of this area had already been auctioned to farmers. Contrary to the policy guidelines, the Section of Animal Husbandry did not provide the farmers with free grass seed. This institution, therefore, has effectively allocated a substantial portion of its tasks to farmers without having to pay a penny. Another reason for the involvement of the Section of Animal Husbandry in the Wastelands Policy was the high political priority attached to it. In complete contrast to the pragmatism of the Party Secretary, who called for trial auctions and control over reclamation and abuse by cadres, the Deputy Prefect proclaimed in a speech:

> We demand that every county move quickly, and with great strides. One cannot deliberate first, try, and then execute . . . Of course, one will meet with problems

[71] Executive Regulations of the Land Management Law (*tudi guanlifa shishi tiaoli*), in Guojia Jihua Weiyuanhui Guotudiqusi (ed.), Compilation of Regulations on State Land, pp. 93–4.

[72] In Yao'an County (Yunnan Province), where experimental wasteland auctions have been held, strife over the eventual division of responsibilities between state organs also led to the obstruction of the Wastelands Policy. Jim Harkness (oral communication, 1998).

during implementation, but we firmly believe that under the correct leadership of the prefecture and counties . . . a new breakthrough of the 'Four Wastelands' auctions can be realized.[73]

Failure of the auctions. Reactions to the Wastelands Policy differed widely in Guanting. Like the Section of Animal Husbandry, the township authorities wanted to distinguish themselves with the auctions. In addition, there was a financially attractive aspect: revenues from the auctions would go into the township accounts. The lure of money provided a strong incentive, in particular for the poor townships.

Opposition arose from the village leaders. The auctions were contested on two grounds: (*a*) privatization of wasteland would exclude herders from grazing grounds, because most of it was used as common pasture; and (*b*) the area of wasteland was insufficient to auction to the farmers: either some would obtain large plots or everyone would obtain too little land for efficient management, a problem of which the Prefectural Party Secretary had already warned. There was no fear of unfair competition from cadres and legal persons from outside the village. The prefecture had allowed open auctions, but the county restricted the auctions to the population of each village to avoid social unrest.[74] Despite the opposition, the policy was forced through under pressure from the county and township authorities. It rapidly gained momentum and in a year, over 40,000mu of wasteland (one-third of the area planned for auction) had been sold. To evaluate the policy results, I will, as in the previous section on Pengyang, discuss four factors: (*a*) the auction procedures and practice; (*b*) the awareness of the policy; (*c*) the use of wasteland before and after the auctions; and (*d*) the appraisal of the policy.

Auction procedures and practice. A majority (87 per cent) of the households in the sample (n = 47) stated they had bought wasteland. Many farmers (70 per cent) wanted to buy more, but decided not to because of insufficient funds (39 per cent), a lack of labour capacity (27 per cent), intervention by the villagers' committee (21 per cent), or a lack of suitable wasteland (13 per cent). For Guanting, the word 'auction' is misleading as the price was fixed by the township prior to the sale. In a few cases, the price was determined by negotiation. The average price was 4 RMB per mu, with a maximum price of 6 RMB. A land ceiling of 5 mu per household was imposed. As a result, wasteland was distributed evenly but in fragmented lots. An attempt was made to set up communal wasteland management, but village leaders said 'the undertaking failed as there was not enough non-disputed wasteland to sell'. Of the total sample, almost 50 per cent did not secure a consolidated tract, but obtained small and dispersed pieces of land.

[73] In Yunnan the Wastelands Policy was executed overnight, uniformly, and with scant regard for local variations after the provincial governor had spurred authorities to organize auctions. He commented afterwards that his call had been meant as a suggestion and not an order because experiments still had to be carried out. Jim Harkness (oral communication, 1998).

[74] Zhonggong Guyuan Diwei, Some Policy Regulations concerning the Auction of Use Rights, p. 3.

Awareness of the policy. As in Changcheng village, the overall majority (96 per cent) of respondents heard about the auctions through the villagers' committee. The policy objectives were not well understood. Of the sample, one-quarter did not respond. Of the remaining three-quarters who did respond, 34 per cent said the auctions were intended to protect the environment, 27 per cent said they were intended to increase farmers' incomes. On the other hand, 15 per cent said the auctions helped the government to obtain revenues and 12 per cent, ironically, thought wasteland was sold to increase the acreage of agricultural land. Respondents were less aware of the rights and prohibitions than the Changcheng farmers. Remarkable is the high proportion (21 per cent) of farmers that did not answer (see Tables 7 and 8).

Wasteland use. Before the auctions, wasteland in Guyuan was virtually without exception used for herding, more than in Pengyang, where forestry is another option. After the auctions, the wasteland was used for several

Table 7: **What rights are included in the wasteland contract? Guyuan sample (n = 47)**

Type of right	*Yes (%)*	*No (%)*	*Don't know (%)*	*Total (%)*
Use right	66.0	12.7	21.3	100
Transfer of use right within village	17.0	61.7	21.3	100
Transfer of use right outside village	6.4	72.3	21.3	100
Inheritance right	23.4	55.3	21.3	100
Ownership right within village	4.2	74.5	21.3	100
Ownership right outside village	2.1	76.6	21.3	100
Usufruct	29.8	48.9	21.3	100
Mortgage right	2.1	76.6	21.3	100

Source: Author's survey.

Table 8: **What are the prohibitions on the use of wasteland? Guyuan sample (n = 47)**

Type of prohibition	*Yes (%)*	*No (%)*	*Don't know (%)*	*Total (%)*
Agricultural reclamation	74.5	21.2	4.3	100
Cultivation of sorghum	55.3	40.4	4.3	100
Cultivation of millet	53.1	42.6	4.3	100
Cultivation of alfalfa	0.0	95.7	4.3	100
Afforestation	4.2	91.5	4.3	100
Fencing	8.5	87.2	4.3	100
Construction of corral	34.0	61.7	4.3	100
Construction of house	57.4	38.3	4.3	100
Construction of road	46.8	48.9	4.3	100
Construction of rainwater reservoir	19.1	76.6	4.3	100

Source: Author's survey.

purposes, such as afforestation, pasturing, the cultivation of forage and grass, and, unfortunately, grain cultivation. Large tracts of wasteland were reclaimed, even though the majority (74.5 per cent) of the farmers were aware that agricultural reclamation was forbidden (see Table 8). How can this be explained? The Wastelands Policy stipulates that wasteland can be used for planting trees or grass (*zhong shu, zhong cao*). The government used the word 'grass' to refer to 'forage': alfalfa, milkvetch, and Siberian pea tree. Of the respondents in Guanting, 46 per cent said they used wasteland for planting grass (as opposed to 25 per cent in Changcheng). The crux is *what* was planted. Of the respondents in Guyuan who planted 'grass', most of them (81 per cent) had in fact planted sorghum and millet. In Changcheng, by contrast, the majority (82 per cent) of those who planted grass indicated they planted alfalfa. The blatant difference between the Guanting and Changcheng villagers' notions of 'grass' seems ludicrous. The following dialogue with a Guanting farmer might clarify this misunderstanding:

> 'Is it allowed to plant grain on wasteland?'
> 'No', the farmer said.
> 'What do you plant at present?'
> 'Sorghum, millet and corn.'
> 'But isn't that grain?'
> 'No, it's grass, because we use the stalks as forage for our sheep and oxen.'

Other farmers answered in a similar fashion and claimed the government never clarified the meaning of 'planting grass'. As demonstrated above, the farmers of Guanting were badly informed about the auctions. The contract, which ideally should have stipulated the rights and duties of the contractor and the administrative village, is no more than a farce.

Unlike with the 1996 Notice, no farmer signed or saw a contract. Moreover, the prefectural regulations stipulate that the contracts must be notarized and issued in triplicate (for the tenant, the lessor—the administrative village—and the Township Rural Economic Station). In practice, the contracts were held by the village leaders and the township. Although *individual* farmers bought use rights, there were *common* copies for every five to ten households, labelled 'joint households' without their knowledge. In one case, a village of twenty-five households had only four contracts for all the farmers. The contract—a one-page, handwritten sheet of paper full of grammatical mistakes and unreadable characters—states not more than the price, the names of the farmers of the 'joint household', the lease term, and the wasteland boundaries. The duties, explained in such detail in the Changcheng contracts, are merely described as 'planting trees and grass', not to mention the rights of the tenant (see Appendix I).

The policy failed for an additional reason. Half of the respondents were aware that the cultivation of millet and sorghum was prohibited (see Table 8). Why did farmers decide to reclaim wasteland when they knew it was prohibited? The probable answer is provided by the deputy director of the Agricultural Work Department: 'The timing of the auctions in Guyuan County was most unfortunate. It coincided with a prolonged drought.

Of course farmers illegally reclaimed the land they had gained. If we had not auctioned the land, they might not have had enough to eat.'

Appraisal of the policy. In Guyuan, the effects of illegal reclamation were not limited to soil erosion. Herding families complained that reclamation had destroyed the watering tracks for animals. Herders also witnessed a rapid decline in grazing grounds, forcing them to move to more remote pastures. In recent years, land disputes between pastoralists and farmers have intensified. Moreover, according to the township, the number of ruminants in Guanting fell by more than half after the auctions. The destruction of the watering tracks has also made villages and individual farm households more isolated. As villages are often no more than a few isolated cave dwellings, watering tracks are a crucial part of the rural infrastructure. The overall experience of the wasteland auctions is negative. Of the total sample, only 6 per cent believed their income had increased, while 15 per cent said that forage availability had improved. Many (49 per cent) said that finding suitable pasture was more difficult. When asked what they thought of the auction policy, 55 per cent said it had 'mostly failed', while 40 per cent felt it had 'completely failed'.

The prefectural authorities reacted to the news of large-scale illegal reclamation with an immediate halt to the auctions. The townships in Guyuan, where the situation had got most out of hand, were called upon to check illegal reclamation with heavy penalties. Special teams were established, consisting of township and village cadres, charged with surveying the wasteland, reporting the reclaimed area, and imposing fines on the culprits. The fines varied from 50 to 200 RMB per mu of reclaimed land.[75] The revenues from the fines were supposed to go to an afforestation fund (as were the profits from auctions) administered by the township. However, the fund was never established, which gave rise to suspicions of rent-seeking. The government's aggressive response stirred up ill-feeling among the rural populace. Farmers felt the authorities had once more imposed their will upon them. One farmer commented: 'The Wastelands Policy failed for us, because we are fined, again and again. But it was a success for the government, because they get our money again and again. And I don't even know why we are fined.' And another said: 'The government tells us to plant grass, but if we plant millet and sorghum we are fined! Can you understand that? From now on I won't plant anything, no grain, no trees, no grass.'

The End of the Rural–Urban Divide?

To put things mildly, the implementation of the Four Wastelands Auction Policy in Ningxia has proved to be a major failure: despite its explicit goal of conserving soil and water, the policy has resulted in widespread

[75] See Guanting Xiang Renmin Zhengfu, *Guanyu Zhizhi, Zhili luan kai Shanhuang Gongzuo de Anpai Yijian* [Suggestions for the Arrangement of Work concerning the Prevention and Control of the indiscriminate Reclamation of Barren Mountains], Government Document No. 1996/24.

agricultural reclamation. Eduard Vermeer once remarked that '. . . politics in China is still conducted in an overall campaign-style manner, rather than being geared to the specific needs of each separate economic sector . . . further decentralization and functional specialization of political and administrative powers are called for.'[76] But although the commandist mode of implementation is an important reason for the failure of the auction policy, it is not the only one. If we analyse the issue at a more abstract level, we will see that it is linked to the evolutionary relation between institutions—understood as policies, laws, state administration, and property rights—and socio-economic parameters. The Wastelands Policy in Ningxia did not fulfill its proclaimed role in the reform and commercialization of land tenure. I argue that the Wastelands Policy might fail in China as a whole because neither the current institutions nor the socio-economic parameters are conducive to changes in the property rights system.

The Wastelands Policy entails great possible socio-economic changes because it closes the rural–urban divide by allowing open auctions. Under the current Household Contract Responsibility System, the lease right to agricultural land is restricted to rural residents, although this is stipulated neither in the 1993 Agriculture Law nor in the 1998 Land Management Law.[77] By contrast, the open auction implies the end of the rural–urban divide as it allows urban cadres, entrepreneurs, and legal persons to participate in the auctions, and thus gain access to rural land. The idea of the open auction incited fierce debate among policy-makers and scholars. Its proponents believe that, in a Darwinian process of 'survival of the fittest', open competition will force the less educated and 'culturally backward' to innovate or leave the agricultural realm. The Deputy Head of the Ningxia Provincial Bureau of Animal Husbandry thinks the auctions are an excellent opportunity to encourage the most active and capable of the rural and urban population to develop marginal lands. Yet many others—not least some high officials within the Ministry of Agriculture—argue that auctions may increase rural poverty. As Du Shouhu remarked:

> During the auction of the 'Four Wastelands' resources, frequent conflict over property rights arises because of the buyers' demand for large-scale exploitation and the interests and compensation of the local households . . . The poor households that 'cannot afford to buy or do not have the means to manage the mountains' not only lose the opportunity to buy wasteland, but are also deprived of the rights to graze, hunt and collect fodder, firewood and medicinal herbs. It decreases their chances to raise their income and even adds to their poverty.[78]

[76] Eduard B. Vermeer, 'Decollectivization and Functional Change in Irrigation Management in China', in Vermeer et al., *Cooperative and Collective in China's Rural Development*, p. 165. Murray Scott Tanner notes the use of orthodox models in policy implementation in present-day China. See Tanner, 'How a Bill becomes a Law in China', p. 56.

[77] The revised 1998 Land Management Law is the first law that distinguishes between land lease by work units and people *within* and *outside* the collective economic organization (article 15). However, there are no specifications regarding the household registration of the lessee. See Yuan Li (ed.), *Zhonghua Renmin Gongheguo Tudi Guanlifa Shiyi* [An Interpretation of the Land Management Law of the People's Republic of China] (Beijing, Falü Chubanshe, 1998), p. 79.

[78] See Du, 'Another Revolution in China's Land System', p. 8.

Although the regulations of the State Council permit the use of open auctions for wasteland, the need to protect the rural poor often outweighs the argument for improved soil and water conservation by attracting village-external investments and expertise. This was also the rationale of the ban on open auctions in Ningxia and the adoption of negotiated sales instead. It is an instance of the socio-economic parameters affecting the possibility of institutional change.

However, in the course of socio-economic development, a further erosion of the rural–urban divide might be expected. That divide is less pronounced in suburban areas and more developed coastal regions, where ample employment opportunities outside the agricultural realm have made farmers less dependent on the land. Under these conditions, the rural collectives are more inclined to grant leases to marginal lands to companies or urban entrepreneurs, as they command greater financial and material resources and can operate on a larger scale. In Hubei Province, for example, farmers who have left agriculture generally return their contract land to the village collective, which in turn leases the land to fewer farmers or a company. In Jianli County a total of 35,000ha was reallocated in this way, taking up one-third of the county's total arable land.[79] A clear illustration of the greater economies of scale and opportunities for commercial agriculture allowed by off-farm employment is given in Appendix J, which shows a handwritten contract (the first of a series of three) under which the farmers of Qingtian Village agree to lease all their land to the Longquan Vegetables Limited Company. And in Fujian Province there is even an instance of a foreign investor obtaining use rights to wasteland.[80] However, for poverty areas such as Ningxia, with almost no rural industrialization and few alternative income sources, open auctions will surely prove socially disruptive. The counties' preference for closed auctions and negotiated sales can therefore only be welcomed.

At which point in this case study do the institutions affect socio-economic change? Not a few instances can be mentioned. First of all, the government organizations responsible for implementation were poorly equipped with material, financial, and human resources, which is mainly why the policy, despite intentions, was executed in a campaign-like manner reminiscent of the mass movements of the past. Although the Party Secretary of Guyuan Prefecture warned against rigid implementation that left little room for local variation, and stressed the necessity of trial auctions, the policy became another model turned orthodox. Once it had been proclaimed, every state institution, county, and township strove to be the first to implement the policy, even when responsibilities were unclear, farmers

[79] See Guangming Huang, 'Xin Tudi Geming' [The New Land Revolution], *Nanfang Zhoumo* (14 July 2001), p. 1. Also at www.southcn.com.

[80] See Hongkui Yang, 'Contract Dispute of Taiwanese Hou Ren Shou accusing Liu Yi of transferring Contract Management Rights over Hilly Lands owned by the Countryside Collective Economic Organization', *China Law*, Vol. 18, No. 1 (March 1999), pp. 89–90. Note that in the English translation of page 90 of this article the term 'use right' has been wrongly translated as 'ownership right'. In the course of recent fieldwork in Zhejiang and Inner Mongolia, I encountered several cases in which private companies or individuals with an urban registration obtained leases to wasteland.

had not been well informed, and no funds had been committed to finance basic operations such as wasteland surveys and guidance for the auctions. From the case studies it is clear that the information given to the rural populace was deficient. Many interviewed farmers were aware neither of the policy goals nor of their specific rights and duties. The widespread illegal agricultural reclamation after the auctions is partly a result of this.

Quite apart from the manner of implementation, the Wastelands Policy could be improved in many ways by strengthening legal and regulatory institutions relating to the method of payment, the control on monopolization by cadres and village elites, and effective legal protection of the lessees. Particularly in poor regions, lump sum payments pose a problem to farmers. The possibility of payment by installments, mortgage, and rural credit are essential instruments to enable the rural poor to compete on a more equal footing with the financially strong. The danger of monopolization by village elites and cadres can be averted through better supervision of the auction practices—virtually absent in Guyuan Prefecture as no budget had been committed to the policy and responsibilities for the implementation were unclear. In fact, if the wastelands auctions are executed as auctions in the strictest sense, they should also conform to the Auction Law, which prohibits overlap between the buying, commissioning, and auctioning parties. The village authorities would then be automatically excluded from executing and participating in the auction. In addition, the use of land ceilings per bidder can prove an effective means to prevent the concentration of land in the hands of a few. The eventual future success of the Wastelands Policy also turns on effective legal protection of the lessees' economic interests. In Ningxia, the practice of issuing contracts that are common to five or ten households labelled 'joint households' without their knowledge, the lack of standardized contracts with clearly spelt-out rights and duties for lessor and lessee, and the absence of notarization are evidence of cadres' lack of legal awareness.

Let me return to a point raised two paragraphs earlier: why were responsibilities over policy implementation unclear? First, the distribution of responsibilities for wasteland management between the rural collectives and state institutions is unclear. This relates to a problem of a more general order that we also encountered for forest and grassland: as there are no clear standards to establish collective ownership, wasteland is by law state property because collective property cannot be proven. If wasteland is state property, it should be registered and managed by the land, the grassland, or the forest department. However, as wasteland is not properly defined as a natural resource, it is uncertain which one of the three state institutions is responsible for its registration, management, and administration. Moreover, as we saw in the Guyuan case, under the Wastelands Policy no funds were committed to state institutions, as a result of which no wasteland survey was executed. Second, if wasteland is collective property, the village groups and administrative villages should have had primary responsibility during the auctions, which they did not. Even worse, the village collectives had no say whatsoever over the implementation of the Wastelands Policy, while their concerns about the loss of common pastures and the fragmentation of land were ignored. For these reasons, it is no surprise that government authorities had no clue about what land had been put up for auction. In this sense, the auctions might have acted as a means to legalize 'black land' that had been illegally reclaimed and cultivated. As an official at the Agricultural Work Department of the Prefectural Party Committee claimed:

> There has been no supervision over the auctioned land, which is due to the lack of control by the townships and the county forestry authorities. Ningxia is poor . . . Township cadres easily become corrupt while the farmers face a harsh environment. If there is drought they have no other alternative than to reclaim wasteland. It is certain that land which should not have been auctioned, was auctioned. Even more so, because we have no solution for land that has been illegally reclaimed prior to the Wastelands Policy. Such land should have been requisitioned, taken out of use, and only then put up for official auction.[81]

A final point is whether the privatization of land use through auctions was a wise option for the development of wasteland. Several issues are at stake here. Wasteland is a marginal natural resource with low and long-term economic returns. If the economic interests of the lessees are not adequately safeguarded, they will be unwilling to incur the cost of the long-term investments necessary for developing marginal land. In the event that developed wasteland is expropriated, the lessee is concerned about an appropriate valuation of investments. The 1986 Land Management Law did not provide for an adequate valuation of wasteland to cover investments in development.[82] This problem has been partly overcome in the revised Land Management Law, which came into effect on 1 January 1999. It stipulates higher levels of compensation of expropriated agricultural land. However, the rule that 'expropriated land will be compensated according to the original use of the expropriated land' (article 47) is problematic. If this implies 'that what is originally waste mountain and wasteland without economic profit, will in principle not receive compensation', as the legal interpretation by the Deputy Minister of Land Resources reads, the raising of the compensation standards will have been in vain.[83] As the revised Land Management Law was proclaimed only very recently, it is too early to assess its effects on the expropriation of wasteland.

Privatization of wasteland also leads to a decrease in the economies of scale. In particular for marginal land resources, community management or common property arrangements are more economically viable and socially acceptable. The results of the village surveys support this argument. The privatized wasteland plots had few income-generating effects for the rural populace; only 6 per cent of the Guyuan sample stated

[81] Jingzhen Li (oral communication, 1996).

[82] See Li, 'Legal Issues of the Auction of Use Rights', pp. 30–1; Hanstad and Li, 'Land Reform in the People's Republic of China', pp. 571–2.

[83] The revised Land Management Law stipulates that the expropriated tenant receives a compensation based on six to ten times (formerly three to six times) the average production value of the land calculated over the last three years (article 47). See Fang, A Discussion on the Use of the Land Management Law of the People's Republic of China, pp. 216–17; and Li (ed.), An Interpretation of the Land Management Law, pp. 144–5.

that their income had increased. And the fragmentation of wasteland had a negative impact on animal husbandry as many valuable common pastures were lost (in Guyuan 49 per cent of the respondents faced increasing difficulties in finding pasture). It is therefore crucial for the Wastelands Policy to promote collective action in wasteland management, such as through joint households, share-holding cooperatives, or voluntary peasant associations. Cooperation can pool the financial and labour resources of several farming families, while greater economies of scale will allow for more efficient investments. This point will be taken up in Chapter 6.

6
Between Nationalization and Privatization: Common Property as the Third Way?

That which is common to the greatest number has the least care bestowed upon it.
(Aristotle, *The Politics*)

China's Dust Bowl

The Chinese government has long been concerned with problems of environmental degradation and rural poverty in the west. However, two events truly made the central leadership face the fact that poverty and the destruction of the natural environment are inextricably linked. The floods in 1998, which caused serious economic losses, were one of the direct causes of the 'Great Development Scheme of the West' (*Xibei da kaifa*), also known as the 'Go West Programme'. Harnessing the Yellow River through improved soil and water conservation became the government's top priority. At the beginning of the programme, Prime Minister Zhu Rongji announced:

> All provinces and regions along the upper and lower streams of the Yellow River must free their thinking and adopt measures such as taking fields out of production in favour of forest and grassland, afforestation . . . and the improvement of the ecological environment, in order to lay a foundation for the permanent control of the Yellow River.[1]

Three years later, the national authorities were once more confronted with the dire necessity to link socio-economic development with environmental protection. In April 2001 Beijing was plagued by dust storms that were a direct result of large-scale desertification in the poverty-stricken regions of western China. The Chinese desertification problem soon took on an international dimension as the National Oceanic and Atmospheric Administration (NOAA) brought the shocking news that a vast area from Canada to Arizona had been covered with a thin layer of dust blown over from the deserts of China. Moreover, scientists also warned about the possible health and ecological hazards (specifically for coral reefs) from germs carried along with the desert sand.[2] These new developments led to the promulgation of the Law of Desertification Prevention and Control (effective since January 2002), which was drafted in line with the International Convention for the Combat against Desertification.

Grassland degradation and desertification occur mainly in the ar
west of China (Xinjiang, Qinghai, Inner Mongolia, Gansu, and N

[1] Rongji Zhu, cited in Qiangzhi Lu (ed.), *Xibu Da Kaifa Zhinan* [Compass o
Development of the West] (Beijing: Zhongguo Shehui Chubanshe, 2000) p. 9.

[2] Henk Donkers, 'Stofstorm over China' ['Duststorm over China'], *NRC H*
(2 June 2001), p. 43. Eugene Shinn wrote about this new issue in *Geophysica*
Letters. See Peter Vermeij, 'Out of Africa', *Intermediair*, Vol. 24 (14 June 2001), pp

To date, the Chinese state has attempted to halt the decline of grassland resources mainly by means of technical measures, such as aerial sowing (by plane), the construction of man-made ranges, and the sinking of wells. However, due to the difficulties encountered in the implementation of grassland policies, officials have gradually become aware that technical measures are only part of the picture, and that grassland management can be successful only if technical, legal, and institutional problems are addressed at the same time. As we saw in Chapter 3, one of the pressing issues that await a political solution is the unclear tenure system for grasslands: the heritage of a collectivist past. During the reign of Mao Zedong, customary rights structures for grassland were delegitimized and supplanted by the institutional system of the people's communes. Although ownership rights were formally vested in the production teams (an administrative unit below the commune), the pastures were open to all. This practice of uncontrolled grazing persisted after the demise of the communes in the 1980s, as free-riding becomes the most natural grazing strategy.

In Chinese political and academic circles it is felt that a mix of population pressure, overgrazing, and pastoralists' lack of responsibility towards grassland has led to a 'tragedy of the commons'. In the process of solving this free-rider problem, or 'eating from the common rice-pot' (*chi da guo fan*) as the Chinese say, a heated debate has emerged about the proper land tenure structure. The discussion about property rights in China flares up now and then in political and academic circles, influenced by experiences from other ex-socialist countries and renowned economists such as Douglass North, who argues that clear property rights are a necessary precondition for a well-functioning market economy. Three schools of thought are engaged in the debate on land tenure: (*a*) the proponents of rigorous land tenure reform through privatization of grassland; (*b*) those who call for complete nationalization; and (*c*) those who demand that the current property rights system be improved so that individual or joint households could lease user rights of state and collective grassland for a period of thirty years.[3]

Within the latter school, some have proposed that collectives or associations of pastoralists should be granted ownership and user rights, while the first and second schools argue that common use and ownership will only lead to free-riding by the users and eventually to a complete destruction of the natural resource. In their view, only privatization or the establishment of strong supervisory organs (generally, state institutions)

[3] See Erwin Reisch, 'Land Reform Policy in China: Political Guidelines and Tendencies', in Eduard B. Vermeer (ed.), *From Peasant to Entrepreneur: Growth and Change in Rural China* (Wageningen: Pudoc, 1992) pp. 15–20; Yuk-shing Cheng and Shu-ki Tsang, 'Agricultural Land Reform in a Mixed System: The Chinese experience of 1984–1994', *China Information*, Vol. 10, Nos. 3/4 (Winter 1995/Spring 1996), pp. 44–74; Linxiu Zhang, Jikun Huang, and Scott Rozelle, *Land Management, Tenure and Ownership Policies: Land Policy and Land Use in China*, Workshop on Agricultural Policies in China (OECD Headquarters, 12–13 December 1996, restricted); Ronald C. Keith, *China's Struggle for the Rule of Law* (New York: St Martin's Press, 1994) pp. 121–42; and Qiren Zhou, *Zhongguo he Suoyouquan Guanxi de Bianhua* [Changes of the Relationship between the State and Ownership] Nos. 1 and 2, Rural Institutions Research Group of the State Council (Beijing: Rural Development Research Centre, 1993).

can offer a solution to free-riding. However, in the present stage of a 'socialist market economy with Chinese characteristics' it seems unlikely that the government will opt for any solution other than sustaining the current land tenure arrangement. Seen in this light, experimentation with land tenure forms other than nationalization or semi-privatization through lease is essential. This experimentation is particularly important in view of the sheer impossibility of nationalization, and the implementation problems of the grassland lease system, the so-called Household Pasture Contract Responsibility System (hereafter the pasture contract system).

In fact, the importance of alternative land tenure arrangements is not limited to grasslands. In Chapter 5 I argued that for marginal natural resources with slow and long-term economic returns, such as forest, wasteland, and grassland, community-based management is to be preferred to privatization and nationalization, even more so when the demand for the resource is high. In Chinese forestry circles, the concept of community forestry has been known and propagated for a long time, to which international donors have made a substantial contribution.[4] However, the general tendency of property rights reform is still geared towards privatization rather than community-based arrangements, particularly at the local state level. In the current chapter, I discuss the political implications, possibilities, and constraints of community-based natural resource management for grassland. For this purpose, two village case studies from the Ningxia Hui Autonomous Region will be reviewed. Before that I will provide a brief overview of the theories of common property and collective action that will be employed in the analysis. This is followed by a discussion of customary grassland tenure and the current practice of the pasture contract system in Ningxia, as well as an explanation of the research methods and sites.

The Academic Debate on Common Property

In academic circles there is considerable debate about the way in which natural resources can be managed without squandering them. The debate touches on questions such as sustainability, the means to call forth and guide collective action, and the land tenure of the resource. In the past, some scholars maintained that supervision and coercion external to the direct group of users of a natural resource was inevitable if it was not to be destroyed. A name that is closely associated with this belief is that of Garrett Hardin. The title of his article—'The Tragedy of the Commons'—has become shorthand for the idea that people who make use of a natural resource without external guidance will tend to free-ride. As he put it: 'Freedom in a commons brings ruin to all.'[5] Following his argument, some

[4] The Ford Foundation has been most active in propagating social and community forestry in China. It led—among other things—to the establishment of the Chinese journal 'Forestry and Society' (*Linye yu Shehui*) run by the Chinese Academy of Forestry.

[5] See Garrett Hardin, 'The Tragedy of the Commons', *Science*, Vol. 162, 1968, pp. 1243–8, reprinted in Garrett Hardin and John Baden (eds.), *Managing the Commons* (Washington, DC: Freeman and Co., 1977), p. 20.

have inferred that there are only two possible solutions for the management of a natural resource: (*a*) privatization of the resource by allocating property rights to individuals through a free market;[6] and (*b*) nationalization or the establishment of an external agency with full authority for the regulation of the resource.[7] Since the 1980s, however, a rapidly increasing number of scholars have argued for a third option, namely, (spontaneous or guided) collective action from within the community of resource users. This approach, which has become known by such terms as 'common property regime' or 'common pool resource management', evolved into a widely held opinion on natural resource management in the 1990s. The literature on common property disputes the claim that the only viable options are privatization and nationalization, on several grounds.

First of all, a natural resource regulated by a so-called common property regime is frequently confounded with a situation of 'nobody's land' or 'open access', which would automatically lead to the destruction of the resource. At this point, we should note that Hardin was actually not writing about 'common property', as he termed it, but about 'open access'. To distinguish clearly between the two notions, it is necessary to define the term 'property'. I will adhere to Daniel Bromley's definition: 'Property is not an object such as land, but rather is a right to a benefit stream that is only as secure as the duty of all others to respect the conditions that protect that stream.'[8] In effect, common property can be regarded as private property for a group—as opposed to those who are excluded from the resource in use and decision-making—while all group members have rights as well as duties regarding the resource. Therefore, a common property *regime* is a body of rules that governs the use and management of a resource as a property by a group of users. Second, Hardin's road to ruin rests on the proposition that individuals make choices independently of the expectations of others: it does not deal in any way with the concept of uncertainty about each others' choices. In a common property setting, it is quite impossible for one individual to act completely independently of the others.[9] Moreover, both privatized and state-controlled regimes are very expensive to make effective, as they involve high transaction costs (costs, other than production costs, incurred by acquiring information, contracting, and enforcement). In the grazing context, one just needs to think of the formidable expenses for fencing pasture, the administration of a cadastre, and the sheer impossibility of patrolling the vast grasslands. And lastly, leaving the resource to the regulation of the market through privatization is not always preferable in view of the issues of externalities and wealth

[6] Douglass North and R. Thomas, 'The First Economic Revolution', *Economic History Review*, Vol. 30 (1977), pp. 229–41; and A. Picardi and W. Siefert, 'A Tragedy of the Commons in the Sahel', *Technology Review*, Vol. 78 (1976), pp. 42–51.

[7] W. Ophuls, 'Oblivion or Leviathan', in H. Daley (ed.), *Toward a Steady State Economy* (San Francisco: W. H. Freeman, 1973); and D. Ehrenfeld, *Conserving Life on Earth* (New York: Oxford University Press, 1972).

[8] Daniel W. Bromley (ed.), *Making the Commons Work: Theory, Practice and* Policy (San Francisco: ICS Press, 1992), p. 2.

[9] Uncertainty, it has been treated in game theory as the 'assurance problem'. The game starts from the principle of cooperation, not conflict. The participants of this game correlate their expectations, which assures that cooperation will be the final outcome.

effects, which will differ considerably according to who buys out whose right in order to use the common property.[10]

Denying the possibility of the sustainable use of, for example, grasslands through common property arrangements disregards the viability and strength of traditional customary rights systems and newly established community-based management systems. Robert Wade and many others have documented instances in which local communities have developed successful systems for managing natural resources.[11] Unfortunately, the current view of Chinese policy-makers on natural resource management leans heavily towards privatization or nationalization. However, we should not forget that the failure of collectivism in the Maoist era plays an important role in this respect.

The critical question that research on common property attempts to answer is: what are the conditions under which successful management of a resource as a common property becomes feasible? Various answers to this question have come from many a scholar. An important analytical tool for the study of common property is institutional analysis.[12] For example, Ronald Oakerson has developed a conceptual framework along these lines that is designed specifically for research on common property.[13] A number of studies have been conducted with the use of this research instrument.[14] In this chapter, I will analyse the village case studies by means of Oakerson's framework. However, I will mainly employ his notion of 'decision-making arrangements' between the users of the resource. The decision-making arrangements, or rules, consist of 'operational rules' and 'rules about rules'. The former set of rules regulates the relations between the users of the resource. These rules can be divided into boundary, allocation, membership, input, and penalty rules. The 'rules about rules', or meta-rules, prescribe the procedures to be followed when any changes in the operational rules are required, and generally pertain to the relations between the users and the appointed leaders of the management system.

Ningxia's Grasslands: From Customary Grazing to the Pasture Contract System

In Chapter 3, I discussed the shortcomings of the present pasture contract system and showed how these are caused by historical factors and political

[10] Daniel W. Bromley, *Environment and Economy: Property Rights and Public Policy* (Oxford: Blackwell, 1991), p. 19.

[11] Robert Wade, 'The Management of Common Property Resources: Collective Action as an Alternative to Privatisation or State Regulation', *Cambridge Journal of Economics*, Vol. 11 (1987), p. 102.

[12] Larry L. Kiser and Elinor Ostrom, 'The Three Worlds of Action: A Metatheoretical Synthesis of Institutional Approaches', in Elinor Ostrom (ed.), *Strategies of Political Inquiry* (London: Sage Publications, 1982) and Norman Nicholson, 'The State of the Art', in Vincent Ostrom, David Feeny, and Hartmut Picht (eds), *Rethinking Institutional Analysis and Development: Issues, Alternatives and Choices* (San Francisco: ICS Press, 1988).

[13] See Ronald J. Oakerson, 'Analyzing the Commons: A Framework', in Daniel Bromley (ed.), *Making the Commons Work: Theory, Practice and Policy* (San Francisco: ICS Press, 1992).

[14] Panel on Common Property Resource Management, *Proceedings of a Conference prepared by the Panel on Common Property Resource Management* (Washington, DC: National Academy Press, 1986); and Bromley, *Making the Commons Work*.

choices at the national level. Detailed information about the actual implementation of the pasture contract system is scarce and there is wide regional variation within China. For example, in Xinjiang customary grassland tenure has persisted under a veneer of collectivism and continues to this day. As Tony Banks writes in an illuminating article:

> Although the grassland use contracts have usually been issued to individual households and contain the area of grassland supposedly contracted to them, neither contracts nor pastoralists have demarcated individual household boundaries and small-group common property arrangements persist. Thus the overstretched nature of state administration has created sufficient political space for the realities and informal tenure practices of the pastoralists to influence policy implementation . . . [15]

However, in many other regions such as Inner Mongolia, Tibet, Gansu, and Ningxia customary land tenure was delegitimized through the imposition of collective structures. In theory, these have been replaced by the pasture contract system since the mid-1980s, yet in reality a situation of open access and overgrazing prevails.[16] As in other regions, the implementation of the contract system in Ningxia is characterized by a wide discrepancy between political intention and actual practice. The pasture contract system should have been implemented in three phases:

1. the assessment of township and village boundaries of grassland, through official (sometimes hand-written) agreements (see Appendix K);
2. the issuance of pasture use contracts to the natural village by the county government (note that no carrying capacities were specified in the contracts, see Appendix L);
3. the issuance of pasture contracts to joint (two or more) and individual farm households by the administrative village (see Appendix M).

In practice, however, the agreements between townships were not always signed, certainly when boundaries were disputed. Generally, these agreements date back to boundary agreements that had been made between communes in the late 1970s. On the basis of the village contracts, individual pasture contracts were issued to the farm households. These pasture contracts were issued in triplicate: one copy to be kept by the Township Rural Economic Station, one by the administrative village, and one by the contractor himself.

Awareness of the pasture contract system is low among the Ningxia farmers. In my survey of 284 households in four counties (Tongxin, Yanchi, Guyuan, and Pengyang), only 7 per cent of the respondents indicated they

[15] See Tony Banks, 'State, Community and Common Property in Xinjiang: Synergy or Strife?', *Development Policy Review*, Vol. 17, No. 3 (September 1999), p. 304.

[16] See Camille Richard, 'Rangeland Policies in the Eastern Tibetan Plateau: Impact of China's Grassland Law on Pastoralism and the Landscape', *Issues in Mountain Development*, Vol. 4 (September 2000), pp. 1–3; Dee Mack Williams, 'The Barbed Walls of China: A Contemporary Grassland Drama', *Journal of Asian Studies*, Vol. 55, No. 3 (August 1996), pp. 665–91; John W. Longworth and Gregory J. Williamson, *China's Pastoral Region: Sheep and Wool, Minority Nationalities, Grassland Degradation and Sustainable Development* (Wallingford: CAB International, 1993) p. 321.

had contracted grassland, while 62 per cent stated that they had never heard of pasture contracts at all![17] There are two reasons for this. In some counties, the third phase of the pasture contract system (issue of contracts to the farm households) was never implemented. In other counties, such as Yanchi, the contracts were allegedly issued to the contractors, but in reality farmers never saw a contract as it was kept by the villagers' committee or the village leader of the natural village. Here we also touch on the legal notion of a contract. In the Western legal tradition, a contract is a voluntary agreement between two parties, but the pasture contract seems a far cry from this as it is a duty imposed by the state on the village and the farmers.

In all villages where the survey was conducted (ten natural villages) the pattern of resource use was, with a few exceptions, the same: open access. Regardless of whether pasture had de jure been contracted to villages, individual farmers, or joint households (sometimes grassland was contracted to a group of households without their knowledge), grassland was viewed as a resource that should be open to everybody and for which nobody within the village was responsible in terms of management. This is not to say that natural villages did not lay any ownership claims to grassland. In most cases it was quite clear to the herders which tracts of grassland belonged to which natural village. But the exclusion of people outside the village from pasture use has never been considered as an option for herders. As a result of the above-mentioned situation, bureaucrats and farmers view the pasture contract system in a generally negative light. In the words of one village leader in Yanchi:

> The pasture contract system was not invented by us. All these problems and boundary conflicts, because it is just another whim of the Communist Party. The Kuomintang [KMT or Nationalist Party] would never have done such a thing. In fact, during the KMT we managed our range in such a way that no conflicts could arise. Times were much better when the land had not been allocated to the individual users, when there was overlapped grazing and the boundaries were still vague.[18]

The original underlying cause of the present situation of open access, or 'eating from the common rice pot', in Ningxia is actually the establishment of collectivist institutions (the people's communes) that delegitimized customary rights structures over the regulation of grassland usage. During the nineteenth and early twentieth centuries, the majority of the Ningxia population consisted of migrants that had fled from war and natural disasters and were settled through government-induced reclamation schemes. The immigration of Han and Muslim Hui farmers had forced out the nomadic pastoralists. The landless farmers and war refugees were traditionally not livestock farmers and not used to the practice of transhumance on rangeland. Instead, they led a sedentary life on farms and set up a mixed farming operation of agriculture and animal husbandry. These migrants introduced an institutional structure for guiding resource use that was essentially different from the customary seasonal grazing as practised by nomads in Mongol-dominated territory (Dengkou County, Ejin, and Alxa Banners).

[17] N = 284, response rate is 98%.

[18] Village leader of Shangjijuan (oral communication, 1996).

Each village (often no more than a few households tied by kinship), clan head, or landlord had access to a certain area of pasture, in some cases officially bought from the state but generally accorded to them through customary rights. As the population expanded and grassland in the neighbourhood was ascribed to other villages by traditional rules, a custom of overlapped grazing emerged, called *chuanmu* by the Ningxia farmers. Since grassland at the time was vast and abundant, this method of resource use suited the ecological environment. Poorer farmers, endowed with less rangeland, were allowed to use pasture owned by other clans and landlords. The authority for delegating the grazing rights rested with the village elders, the clan heads, the individual owners, or, in exceptional cases, the ward head (or *baozhang*) of the *baojia* administrative tax and civil defence system. For example, the ward head was responsible for conflict resolution over the use of grassland and wells (right of way). Occasionally, temporary nomads—normally sedentary farmers—from neighbouring counties would come with their herds to graze on communal pasture. This was common practice during sustained droughts, yet seldom a problem for a village. In the case of agricultural reclamation, a sum of money had to be paid to the clan head or landlord who owned the rangeland.[19]

The People's Commune, however, was organized in such a way that it failed to create the necessary socio-economic and regulatory conditions that would allow individual users to pursue their own well-being without destroying the livelihood of future generations. Moreover, this failure occurred at a crucial time when the grasslands were becoming economically scarce due to expanding livestock and loss of arable land induced by political campaigns, such as the Great Leap Forward and the Great Proletarian Cultural Revolution.[20] This external change could not be adequately counterbalanced within the institutional structure of grassland management during the time of the people's communes. Instead, a pattern of resource use developed bearing all the traits of an open access regime, thus leading to the squandering of pastureland. Just as under the communes, the present attempt at privatization and parcelling of grassland under the pasture contract system fails to ensure the cooperation of grassland users. Therefore, the way grasslands have been used in collectivist times has persisted to the present, and the problem of free-riding remains unsolved.

[19] For a discussion of the history of grassland tenure in the Qing and Republican period, see Peter Ho, 'The Myth of Desertification at China's Northwestern Frontier (1929–1960)', *Modern China*, Vol. 26, No. 3 (2000), pp. 348–95. Most of the material about the traditional sedentary grazing system in Ningxia was derived from interviews with farmers over 60 years old and former landlords or their kin. One of the very few references that describe this grazing system is Ningxia Huizu Zizhiqu Nongyeting (ed.), 'Ningxia Huizu Zizhiqu Yanchixian Caoyuan Diaocha Baogao' ['Report of the Rangeland Survey in Yanchi County, Ningxia Hui Autonomous Region'], in Xumu Shouyi Xuehui (ed.), *1963 Huilun Wenji*, internal document (1964), p. 125.

[20] The statistics are provided in Peter Ho, 'Ownership and Control in Chinese Grassland Management: A Case Study of the Free-rider Problem in Pastoral Areas in Ningxia, China', in Eduard B. Vermeer, Frank Pieke, and Woei Lien Chong (eds.), *Cooperative and Collective in China's Rural Development: Between State and Private Interests* (New York: M. E. Sharpe, 1998) pp. 205–13.

At present, the Chinese government adheres to the idea that squandering of the resource can be avoided only through strengthening the pasture contract system (seen in terms of more and wider powers for the costly supervisory system that enforces the carrying capacities: the grassland police force) or, in some exceptional cases, by establishing national nature reserves guarded by special police forces. As the badly implemented contract system has already become the orthodox form of land tenure, it will not be easy to argue for the establishment of common property in China. The concepts of common property theories run counter to the principles of the pasture contract system. A common property regime is based on resource use and control by a community of users that can effectively exclude non-community members from using that particular resource. The current pasture contract system, however, always needs to rely on an external agency of control (the state) to ensure that the individual users do not free-ride and exceed the carrying capacities of the plots of grassland. In addition, whereas common property of grassland proposes flexible limits of pasture (that is, rotational grazing or even nomadic pastoralism)—thus making optimum use of the variability in rangeland production over time and space—the pasture contract system employs fixed boundaries (for example, through fencing) based on a 'proper use factor' or a maximum carrying capacity of the grassland.

From the above-mentioned points it does not follow that—theoretically—a more privatized form of land tenure, such as the pasture contract system, could not coexist with nomadic pastoralism. But there are several issues at stake. First, is privatization more cost-effective than a common property arrangement? In fact, the practice of the pasture contract system has proved that privatization is not a viable option for the arid and semi-arid regions where extensive livestock raising prevails. The reasons are the high transaction costs involved to make it effective, and the need to be mobile so as to spread the risk of drought and blizzards (*dzud* in Mongolian). Second, how high is the demand of the group of users on the resource? In the Chinese rural context, population pressure is often too great to allow for anything more than animal husbandry on a basis of subsistence. Privatized livestock farming with more economies of scale is only then possible when ample alternative employment opportunities are present. And third, what is the government-perceived development path for pastoralism? At present, the (local) authorities are still persisting in the sedentarization of nomads, which has led to a rapid decline of nomadic pastoralism and concentrated land degradation around the herders' settlements. We will touch on these issues in the discussion of the village case studies below.

The Yanchi Experiments

As a region for experiments with alternative tenure arrangements, Ningxia might be equally important for animal husbandry as Yunnan Province is for forestry. In the 1980s, local attempts have been undertaken in Ningxia to establish corporate management systems with the village as the basic unit of use and control. These attempts were mainly made in Yanchi County, located in the steppe-desert region in the north-east of the autonomous region (see also Figure 4). Due to increasing problems of desertification, Yanchi frequently experimented with new grazing practices, sometimes based on principles of traditional Mongol range management. In the early 1960s, Yanchi began grazing experiments in an attempt to solve overgrazing and stimulate more sustainable grassland use.[21] Unfortunately, these were seriously interrupted by the sociopolitical upheaval of the Cultural Revolution. But the experimentation was resumed as the economic reforms gained momentum in the early 1980s.

The interesting aspects of the Yanchi grazing practices are twofold. First, it is a local initiative aimed at introducing a new management form in a sedentary livestock farming system quite unlike that of nomadic Mongol herders. Second, the system was uniformly introduced in the entire county, in rich and poor regions alike. Together, these factors make Yanchi a challenging region to conduct a comparative study of the viability and the institutional dynamics of such village range management systems. By relying on concepts from theories of common property resource management and collective action,[22] I will attempt to answer a series of questions focusing on the impact of the newly introduced institutional structure for range management on the existing grazing practices. One can wonder how a sedentary livestock farming system reacted to the imposition of a new institutional management structure encouraging rotational grazing, as opposed to the past free-for-all grazing. Moreover, did the system indeed offer sufficient incentives for collective action on the part of the pastoralists, thus stimulating sustainable livestock farming? Were the outcomes of these methods of range management the same for the various regions in Yanchi? And how valuable are the Yanchi experiences for the rest of China?

This chapter has been written on the basis of qualitative in-depth interviews and a quantitative survey of 284 farm households carried out in twenty villages in four counties.[23] The village case studies draw from two sample villages (Xiawangzhuang and Shangjijuan) both located in the

[21] Zhizhong Lei, Guo Gang, Yang Hongchun, and Mo Dayan, 'Ningxia Huizu Zizhiqu Yanchixian Caoyuan Diqu Mumin Liyong Caodi Fangfa de Diaocha Yanjiu' ['Research of Methods of Grassland Utilization of Nomads of Grazing Areas in Ningxia Hui Autonomous Region'], in *Ningxia Huizu Zizhiqu 1963 Caoyuan Yanjiu Baogao Xuanbian* [A Selection of Grassland Research Reports of Ningxia Hui Autonomous Region], internal document (Yinchuan: Ningxia Huizu Zizhiqu Nongyeting Xumuju, 1964); and Hongchun Yang, 'Ningxia Huizu Zizhiqu Caodi Ruogan Tedian Ji Qi Liyong' ['Some Special Traits of Grassland in Ningxia Hui Autonomous Region and Its Utilization'], in Xumu Shouyi Xuehui (ed.), *1963 Huilun Wenji* [Abstracts of the Discussion Meeting of 1963] Internal Document (Yinchuan: Xumu Shouyi Xuehui,1964).

[22] See also Wade, 'The Management of Common Property Resources', pp. 95–106; Oakerson, 'Analyzing the Commons'; and Elinor Ostrom, *Governing the Commons: The Evolution of Institutions for Collective Action* (Cambridge: Cambridge University Press, 1990).

[23] The villages are Shangyuan, Xiamaguan, Xigouzi, and Guankou in Tongxin County; Xiawangzhuang, Shangwangzhuang, Ma'erzhuang, Guankou, and Shangjijuan in Yanchi County; Qianwa, Liwa, Xintang, Xiaoshigou, Lanyuan, and Guanting in Guyuan County; Changcheng, Shanzhuang, Xiaosi, Niuzui, and Chenzhuang in Pengyang County.

arid, desert-steppe region of Yanchi with an annual precipitation of 200–250mm. The population in Yanchi is predominantly Han with only 3 per cent belonging to the Muslim Hui. The county has 13 per cent of the total area of pasture in Ningxia; 84 per cent of the county is grassland (of which 85 per cent—473,400ha—is ranked as usable pasture). Making up 55 per cent of total agricultural output, animal husbandry is the main agricultural activity in Yanchi.[24]

A Tale of Two Villages

When you ask any official of the Ningxia Provincial Department of Animal Husbandry how grasslands are managed and used, he will not fail to mention the merits of the pasture contract system. Were you to travel two administrative levels lower in the bureaucracy and pose the same question to someone working at the Yanchi County Bureau of Animal Husbandry, you would hear quite a different story. The official might not only be more critical, at times even cynical, about the pasture contract system, but he will also talk about village-based range management. And indeed, a brief tour around Yanchi confirms that all villages have one or more range guards, employed and paid by the village community, who watch over a plot of pasture closed off during a certain time of the year. Furthermore, the plot that is closed off can differ over time, depending on the condition of the grassland vegetation, the plot in the worst condition being closed off first. Often, with a tinge of pride, the county officials talk about this management system as an alternative to the pasture contracts.

Since the early 1960s, Yanchi has been a region for grassland management experiments in Ningxia. However, the early experiments with rotational grazing by fencing and appointing range guards were not very successful. It proved to be difficult to manage and supervise the fenced area as it was too extensive (1,300ha in total). It frequently happened that barbed wire was stolen, or the fence pushed over, so that sheep and goats could still be pastured in the restricted area. Furthermore, it is said that the guards were not always diligent in patrolling the area, as they received a low salary.

With the support of the Yanchi Party Committee and the Ningxia Science and Technology Commission, a new project was launched in 1987. The project was mainly technical, including research on such topics as the grazing behaviour of sheep, water-saving techniques, and agro-forestry practices. A spin-off of this project was the establishment of an institutional structure for rotational grazing. The project started in Sidunzi Natural Village in which, based on the relatively negative experiences of the earlier experiments, a much smaller area of only 25ha was fenced in.

[24] Ningxia Tongjiju (ed.), *Ningxia Tongji Nianjian 1994* [Ningxia Statistical Yearbook] (Yinchuan: Ningxia Renmin Chubanshe, 1994), pp. 84, 265; Zhongguo Ziran Ziyuan Congshu Bianyi Weiyuanhui (ed.), *Zhongguo Ziran Ziyuan Congshu: Ningxia Juan* (Beijing: Zhongguo Huanjing Kexue Chubanshe, 1995), p. 205; and Ningxia Caochang Zhibei Ziyuan Diaochadui, *Ningxia Caochang Ziyuan Diaocha Baogao*, Neibu Ziliao [Research Report of Rangeland Resources in Ningxia, restricted] (Yinchuan: Xumuju, 1985), p. 132.

The area was divided into four smaller areas, three of which were in alternating use over four months, while one was improved and closed off for pasturing for the entire year. The more mobile and traditional overlapped grazing between villages (which was delegitimized during the period of the communes and had actually developed into a situation of free-riding) was no longer allowed on the fenced pasture, and each farm household received a grazing permit that included a map showing the area open for pasturing. Furthermore, the sheep numbers per household were restricted on the basis of stocking rates determined for the fenced-in grassland. In general, the number of sheep and goats per person was limited to three, calculated for a total of the whole village. But there were no sanctions if the village raised more ruminants than stipulated and the quota did not seem to have very much effect. For the supervision of the grassland, a range guard was appointed from among the villagers, and was paid by the natural village itself.[25]

Soon after the project had been launched in Sidunzi village, demonstration meetings were held for village leaders of the neighbouring villages. The new range management system gradually spread to other townships in Yanchi. As this management system was adopted by other villages over time, it lost much of the initial scientific rigour employed in Sidunzi village. The range management system that evolved in later years evinces many characteristics of what in academic literature is referred to as a 'common property regime'. But is the Yanchi model a true common property regime? Did it offer more incentives to the livestock farmers to cooperate rather than to free-ride than the previous situation of open access? Let us examine in a little more detail the Yanchi model in two villages to provide some answers to these questions.

The Old Project Area: Xiawangzhuang Village

Village introduction. Xiawangzhuang village is one of the six natural villages belonging to Sidunzi Administrative Village, which in part falls under the jurisdiction of Chengjiao Township. Xiawangzhuang is located about 1km south of Sidunzi village, where the experimentation with common property arrangements started. Due to irrigation, the village belongs to the richest regions of Yanchi County, and has an average annual net per capita income of 1,365 RMB (the county average is 669 RMB).[26] There are over 500 inhabitants—all Han Chinese—and the village was divided into three villagers' groups (*zu*) at the end of the 1980s: a northern, middle, and southern villagers' group, each headed by a village leader. The head of the middle group is simultaneously the village leader of Xiawangzhuang.[27]

[25] Yanchi Caodi Nongye Xitong Yanjiu Ketizu (ed.), *Ningxia Yanchi Caodi Nongye Xitong Yanjiu* [Research on Grassland Agricultural Systems of Yanchi, Ningxia] (Lanzhou: Gansu Kexue Jishu Chubanshe, 1992), pp. 8–9, 55–6.

[26] Figures for 1996, when one US dollar was worth about eight RMB.

[27] This is a rather confusing situation. Xiawangzhuang does not legally exist as a natural village, because this term does not appear in law. As Xiawangzhuang was divided into three smaller villagers' groups, which is an official legal category, it can be either an

The village has about 125ha agricultural land, of which approximately 70ha is irrigated land. The availability of irrigation (twenty-one wells) has enabled the village to cultivate cash crops, such as linseed, sunflower, aubergine, and other vegetables. In this township, income from livestock products (mutton, hides, and cashmere)[28] accounts for approximately 19 per cent of the total farm income, the bulk of which is made up by agriculture (69 per cent) and sidelines (11 per cent).[29] Agricultural products are generally sold in the county seat, only 12km away, which can be easily reached by a noisy and shaky local 'taxi-brousse'. The total number of sheep and goats in the village is around 1,800. The average number of sheep and goats per household is lower (twenty-one sheep per household) than in Shangjijuan Village in Ma'erzhuang Township, which is discussed below.[30] The greater part of the village grasslands (650ha in total) are situated at the southern side of the village (a smaller portion lies to the north). The southern village pasture is enclosed by hills, in front of which lies a pocket of desert. To the east of the village pasture is the grassland belonging to Sidunzi village; to the west, that of Shangwangzhuang village. The average amount of pasture per person is about 1.3ha (0.4ha per animal). Furthermore, there are fodder bases covering over 120ha, planted with alfalfa (Medicago sativa, or *zihua muxu*).

The main problems of this village as voiced by the peasants are (in order of decreasing importance): (*a*) lagging grain production due to the high price of fertilizer; (*b*) a receding ground water level, as a result of excessive irrigation; and (*c*) desertification, causing a decrease in livestock productivity. This subjective ranking of the problems in this village suggests that animal husbandry is less important than agriculture.

The common property regime: the leaders. The leaders of the southern, middle, and northern villagers' group stand for election when the need is felt by the villagers, sometimes once a year, sometimes less frequently. The present leaders have been in office for several years in a row, two of them actually since the middle of the 1980s. All three village leaders said they would like to resign, as they find their tasks burdensome, but found it difficult to do so because the villagers thought they had good relations with the bureaucracy and were able to secure funds on occasion from which the entire village benefited.

The management and control of the village pasture rests with the three village group leaders. Depending on the condition of a certain plot of pasture, they decide whether to close it to grazing and when it may be used again. The villagers are normally not consulted on these matters. Formerly,

administrative village (meaning that it is no longer under the jurisdiction of Sidunzi) or a villagers' group with the northern, southern, and middle villagers' groups being equal in status. However, the way farmers refer to it suggests that the villagers' group is seen as a smaller unit than the natural village.

[28] Sheep and goats in Ningxia are not held for milk production.

[29] All figures for Chengjiao Township are derived from a survey of 413 farm households in 43 natural villages, carried out by the Ningxia Academy of Social Sciences in 1995.

[30] $N = 81$, mean $= 21.8$, and standard deviation $= 11.5$.

the grassland management station discussed with the village group leaders which plots to assign for closure, which would simultaneously be improved through additional and aerial sowing of grass seeds. However, budgetary constraints on the grassland stations have forced them to give up these activities entirely, and the condition of the pasture has been deteriorating ever since.

The three village leaders have the right to appoint and dismiss rangers, who are responsible for watching the closed pasture. If the ranger does not live up to his tasks, part of his salary is withheld, and in some cases he can even be fined. But such a situation has not occurred over the past five years. Smaller decisions, pertaining to the kind of penalty imposed on violators of the grassland regulations, are usually taken by the rangers themselves.

The ranger. In Xiawangzhuang there are two rangers: one to watch over the closed pasture, the other to guard the alfalfa fodder bases on the northern side of the village. The farmers have to pay 3 RMB per sheep or goat to a fund from which the rangers are paid. Guarding the grassland yields a salary of 120 RMB per month; the task of watching the fodder bases pays 80 RMB a month. For this money the rangers are expected to work full-time, from 8 a.m. to 8 p.m., every day in the week. The person guarding the range was a former team leader in the 1970s; he has been a ranger for over five years.

The boundaries of the grassland. Since 1986, the villagers have started to close off grassland after the village leader had seen the promising results of rotational grazing at a demonstration meeting in Sidunzi village. In the beginning farmers opposed closing off pasture, saying that grassland was 'common property' (they meant 'open access') and 'pasture should be open to all'. However, as farmers faced increasing difficulties in finding good grazing areas for their flock, a favourable climate was created for a stricter regulation of grassland use. The findings of Pennarz are similar. Based on research in Sichuan Province and pastoral areas in Qinghai, she observed a more even distribution of resources, stricter land use regulation, and a stronger commitment to work for common interests in regions where land was scarce (with high population pressure) than in regions where it was abundant.[31] On the relationship between the demand on the resource and the dynamics of the management regime, Wade wrote, 'the greater the demands (up to a limit) and the more vital the resource for survival, the greater the chances of success'.[32] However, this is by no means the only factor influencing the viability of a common property regime.

According to the village leader of Xiawangzhuang, rotational grazing had started to work well by the beginning of the 1990s. Since 1994, four plots of grassland (approximately 300ha) have been closed off from use during most of the year. The boundaries of the pastures are quite clear. Hedges of Siberian pea trees (*Caragana korshinskii*, or *ningtiao*) separate

[31] Johanna Pennarz, *Collective Land Ownership and Sustainable Agriculture: Perspectives on the Diversity of Land User Rights in China*, Room Document No. 2, Workshop on Agricultural Policies in China, OECD Headquarters (12–13 December 1996), p. 6.

[32] Wade, 'The Management of Common Property Resources', p. 104.

the village pastures from those of neighbouring villages. The pea tree is a drought-resistant thorn bush, whose roots consolidate the soil and whose leaves can be used as animal feed. Unlike Shangjijuan village, which is dealt with below, the boundaries of closed pasture are marked not by fences but low earth mounds spaced at intervals of approximately 300m. The area is easy to oversee, although the closed plots are very dispersed (2–3km between each plot). Standing on a hill, one can easily see anyone entering the restricted area. Offenders are generally people from outside the village, as herders from the village itself feel it is in their own interest to stay away from the closed pastures. The alfalfa fodder bases are even easier to watch, as the area is very limited. The fodder area is contracted to farm households, each individual plot delimited by means of small earth banks.

Rules of allocation: who gets what and when? Controlled grazing plots are open for grazing during the period of gestation and birth of lambs (winter and spring). They are generally closed off in March. Depending on the vegetational situation (variety and density of palatable plants), the three village group leaders decide which plot is closed to grazing. The present plots indeed have more abundant vegetation, a result of aerial sowing by the Department of Animal Husbandry and the county grassland management station. In principle, every household is entitled to use the controlled grazing plots as intensively as is needed, regardless of the number of animals owned. Pasture that is not closed off can be used at will by the herders of the village and of neighbouring villages. However, the overlapped grazing with other villages takes place only occasionally, and has diminished since rotational grazing has been established as a management system over the county. It is important to note that there are two land tenure systems operating simultaneously: the common property regime, with restricted grazing rights on the controlled grazing plots, and a system of open access rights for herders within and outside the village on all other grassland. This is quite different from the ideal typical common property regime as discussed by authors such as Daniel Bromley, Elinor Ostrom, and Ronald Oakerson.[33]

The fodder bases are opened for use twice, during the traditional 'Arrival of Summer' (*xiazhi*, or the Chinese tenth solar term which occurs around June) and the 'White Dew' (*bailu*, fifteenth solar term around September). After each household has cut the alfalfa in its contract plot, the area is closed again. Each person in the village has an average amount of fodder area of 0.08ha.

Rules on membership. Only those who are born within the village are entitled to use the village pastures. The smallest social unit to which the villagers feel themselves attached in terms of the common property regime is the natural village. The community of Xiawangzhuang does not easily

[33] Bromley, *Making the Commons Work*; Ostrom, *Governing the Commons*; Oakerson, 'Analyzing the Commons'.

accept immigrants from other villages. When a former immigrant was asked whether someone from a neighbouring village could live here, he replied simply 'impossible'. During the twentieth century, there were only three instances in the history of Xiawangzhuang when people migrated to this village. The earliest immigrants were a family from Hebei that moved to Xiawangzhuang during the Second World War. At the time of the Cultural Revolution one family fled, but was allowed to return and was allotted a new plot of land. The most recent migrants were a couple of families that obtained permission to settle in the 1980s, because they could bring in girls at a time when marriageable women were scarce.

Rules on input. Up to 1991, the township forestry station gave a subsidy of 6 RMB for each mu that was planted with pea tree. Together with the financial contribution of 3 RMB per animal per household, this was channelled into a fund out of which the ranger's salary was paid. Furthermore, the seeds of the Siberian pea trees were collected annually, partly resown and partly sold at a price of 3 RMB per kilo to the forestry station. The revenues from this were also put into a collective grassland fund. For the planting of pea tree, the village hires farmers with sowing machines and tractors. They are paid 4 RMB per mu of grassland sown. Their payment also comes from the grassland fund. At present, pea tree is no longer planted collectively by the village. The peasants say it is no longer necessary as the plants have survived quite well; another reason may be that the forestry station no longer provides additional seeds. In addition to the forestry station, the county grassland management station used to provide the farmers with seeds of palatable shrubs such as milk-vetch (*Astralagus adsurgens*, or *shadawang* in Chinese) and cock's head (*Hedysarum scoparium*, or *huabang*). However, since 1993 the grassland management station has stopped providing plant seeds because of financial constraints. This has led to a gradual deterioration in the quality of the restricted plots of grassland.

The fodder bases were established in the late 1980s, and need to be resown once every two or three years. The alfalfa seeds are still provided free by the Yanchi Science and Technology Commission and the township grassland management station. After the alfalfa has sprouted, members of the two aforementioned organizations will ascertain whether the plants have been planted according to their instructions. When the area has been approved, the farmers do not have to pay for the seeds. If the fodder base does not meet the requirements, farmers have to pay 6 RMB per kilo of seed. 'More expensive than grain', as a farmer remarked dryly.

Punishing the offender. The village has stipulated that anyone who ventures into restricted pasture can be fined by the ranger an amount varying from 50 to 100 RMB. In more serious cases, the ranger can decide to confiscate a few sheep. Should the offender not pay his fine, then the animals will not be returned. In case of minor offences, the transgressor is generally given a scolding. People from the village itself are rarely fined, but the village leader will always be informed of the offence. If an offence is really serious, the village leader can decide to make known to the entire village, but this rarely happens. In addition to his salary, the ranger may also keep the money from the fines. In the eyes of the villagers the ranger has 'contracted' the task of guarding the grassland. In the entire village there are no more than ten herders. Only two of them dared to pasture in the closed area in 1995. In the same year, herders from other villages grazed their flock in the restricted area five to six times.

The outcomes. According to the majority of the peasants, there are insufficient good grazing areas, and degradation due to overgrazing is still increasing. A shift in grazing pressure has been observed from the restricted grazing area to open access grassland. On the open access grassland, the vegetation of grass and bushes has virtually vanished and been replaced by the unpalatable dog's bone (*Cynanchum komarovii*, or *laoguatou*).

Despite this, the overall rating of the common property regime by the peasants is undoubtedly positive. Compared with the period before the common property regime was established, free-riding within the village rarely occurs. The willingness of peasants to abide by the rules is striking compared with the situation in the Yunwushan nature reserve in Guyuan County (on the Loess Plateau in south Ningxia). The grassland there has been fenced in, and is open only during certain periods of the year when farmers are allowed to gather forage. There have been no attempts to devolve responsibility for the management of the reserve to village communities. The sole method of control is a fully-fledged police force to guard the area of approximately 2,300ha. Free-riding is the dominant grazing strategy of the farmers in the Yunwushan nature reserve.[34]

Farmers are strongly committed to the common property regime, for several reasons. First, the natural resource is relatively small, easy to oversee, and well demarcated. The distance between the resource and the village is minimal, which allows the ranger to reach the range early and to leave his post late in the day, thus exercising control over the resource during the greater part of the day. Free-riders who want to break the rules are easily detected, increasing resource users' confidence that abiding by the regulations will serve their common interests. Moreover, due to the relatively high grazing pressure on the pasture many believe that collective action is the best course.

Second, the group of users is quite small, which limits the transaction costs of communication and decision-making. There are most likely no more than thirty hired herders in the neighbourhood. Herding in Yanchi is always done jointly, several families hiring one person who herds collective flocks of sometimes over 200 animals. In return, the herders are paid about 18 RMB per year per animal. The ten or so herders of Xiawangzhuang belong to a village community that is sufficiently small to allow for social control of their behaviour. Social control is guided through

[34] For more details see Ho, 'Ownership and Control in Chinese Rangeland Management', pp. 213, 215.

an elaborate set of rules pertaining to the boundaries of the resource, allocation, membership, input, and punishment.

Finally, the common property regime is supported by local authorities, who have managed to penetrate the village community and to establish and monitor a management system run by the village itself. Moreover, the local authorities provide the farmers with a variety of services ranging from the provision of seeds for forage plants to veterinary services. We do see, however, that halting the provision of plant seeds has a direct effect on the quality of the grazing areas.

On the other hand, the power of the local state is effectively counterbalanced through the leverage of the village leaders. These leaders have the power to make claims for the village population, and have managed to secure certain state projects beneficial to the village. The village organization offers a forum in which common problems pertaining to resource use can be discussed. It is important to note that local authorities did not attempt to establish a new institutional structure to guide the common property regime, but relied on the existing village leaders, who have already been in office for a considerable time. All this sounds very positive, but we should not forget that the grasslands in Xiawangzhuang are still very much under stress. One may wonder how long the common property regime in Xiawangzhuang can last given the pressure of persisting grassland degradation. Another village just 45km to the south-west offers a glimpse of what might be Xiawangzhuang's gloomy future.

Shangjijuan Village: Living on the Edge

Village introduction. Shangjijuan village—located 1km north-east from Ma'erzhuang Township—is a hamlet that could appear in one of Gabriel Garcia Marquèz's novels if it were not in China. The twenty or so mud houses, with a total population of 125 Han Chinese, developed from the settlement of the Shang family. They moved to this remote area in the early 1920s in search of suitable pasture. At the time, the founder of the village raised over a thousand sheep and boasted that he owned several hundred hectares of pasture. Shangjijuan village (literally, Pen of the Shang Clan) has changed names as often as a double agent. During the 1950s, it was named Shangjijuan Brigade and encompassed five villages. At the height of the Cultural Revolution, the name Shangjijuan was considered too feudal and was changed into Yuqiang village (Wall of Rain). Today, the village has entered the registers under the double name of Yuqiang Administrative Village, Shangjijuan Natural Village.

The contrast with Xiawangzhuang could not be greater, although the ecological conditions are comparable. With an average annual per capita net income of 498 RMB (a figure derived from the township statistics), Shangjijuan is much poorer. The village is completely dependent on rainfed, subsistence agriculture. The cultivated crops include corn, common millet, and buckwheat. The main source of revenues for farmers is extensive livestock farming (57 per cent of total income), whereas agriculture accounts for only a minor part (25 per cent). The average sheep equivalent[35] per household is almost three times higher than for Xiawangzhuang, where pasture per person is over eight times higher (10.5ha as opposed to 1.3ha in Xiawangzhuang). The total number of sheep and goats is around 1,500. Wool and cashmere are no longer sold to the township supply and marketing cooperative, but collected by itinerant merchants.

The greatest problem of the village is the destruction of grassland through digging for medicinal herbs, which is done mainly by farmers from outside the township. Ma'erzhuang Township is one of the areas in Yanchi County where liquorice root (*Glycyrrhiza uralensis* or *gancao*) grows in abundance. This herb is both a blessing and a curse for the village. Liquorice not only makes good fodder, it is also used in traditional Chinese medicine. For the ordinary Dutchman it is quite important as well, as he could not imagine his beloved 'dubbel zoute drop' (a very salty kind of candy) without the extract of liquorice root. The collecting of liquorice root can provide an average farming family with a considerable amount of extra cash in a short time, during the season as much as 800–900 RMB.[36] The liquorice is sold to the township supply and marketing cooperative, where it is also processed for export to other provinces. Unfortunately, liquorice root is not that easy to obtain. It has very long roots, and to collect it deep holes have to be dug in the grassland, which cause considerable wind erosion. Over the past few years, farmers in regions where liquorice root grows have seen their homes and fields gradually covered by sand dunes that literally 'move into their villages'.

According to official statistics, the purchased amount of liquorice has risen dramatically. The amount of state procurement of liquorice was 754 tons in the 1950s, 1,265 tons in the 1960s, 2,816 tons in the 1970s, and 3,300 tons in the 1980s. The year 1993, when the state monopoly on liquorice was lifted, saw a record of over 4,000 tons purchased, of which 3,080 tons were purchased by the Yanchi Medicine Factory alone.[37] Since then, the liquorice market has been booming, with serious consequences for the grassland resources. It is said that in Yanchi County 80,000ha of grassland has become desertified because of the liquorice digging. The digging also enhances the frequency and intensity of sandstorms. In May 1993 a sandstorm raged over Xinjiang, Inner Mongolia, Gansu, and Ningxia. One of the biggest storms for decades, it left 85 people dead and 264 injured, while 120,000 head of livestock were killed or lost. The total damage was estimated at more than 500 million RMB.[38] The problem of grassland destruction through the collection of medicinal herbs is not

[35] For this chapter I have employed the conversion coefficients to standardize livestock numbers used by Longworth and Williamson, that is, 1.00 for sheep and 0.82 for goats (Longworth and Williamson, *China's Pastoral Region*, p. 24). The figures for the structure of rural income and sheep equivalents were derived from my own survey of ninety-eight farm households in Yanchi County (forty-eight in Ma'erzhuang Township).

[36] Figure from the survey of ninety-eight farm households in Yanchi.

[37] Ningxia Nongye Kanchadui (ed.), *Yanchi Shamohua Tudi Zonghe Zhengzhi Shiyan: 1991–1995* [Experiment for Integrated Desert Control in Yanchi: 1991–1995] (internal report, 1996), p. 189.

[38] See: Yan Wu, 'Ren bu zi zhi, Tian zhi Ren' ['If Man Cannot Control, He will be Governed by Heaven'] *Nongmin Ribao* (23 June 1993), p. 1.

confined to Ningxia. In fact, farmers from Ningxia and Gansu have frequently been reported engaging in the illegal digging of sea grape (*Ephedra distachya*) and black moss (*Nostoc flagelliforme*) in neighbouring Inner Mongolia.[39]

Violent clashes have taken place between those digging for liquorice root and those trying to protect their ground. Battles involving the deaths of several farmers have escalated in recent years, with hundreds of diggers from neighbouring counties pouring into Yanchi in search of the precious root. As the diggers are often poor Muslim Hui farmers from neighbouring counties, the clashes have an unmistakably ethnic and religious undertone as well. The ethnic character of the conflicts has severely limited the government's scope for political manoeuvring. In dealing with the matter, the government of the autonomous region has to move very cautiously in order to avoid offending either the Hui population it is supposed to represent or the Han, who might easily feel 'sacrificed' to the need to preserve the religious and political autonomy of the Hui. Attempts have been made to cultivate liquorice, but the cultivated plants have a much lower percentage of the active healing property than their wild counterparts. Scientific experiments with genetic engineering have been carried out, but the results have not been very encouraging. This means that there is not yet any alternative to digging for liquorice root in grassland. The seriousness of the problem prompted the central government to proclaim a total ban on the exploitation and sale of liquorice and black moss in 2000.

The common property regime: a sketch. As in Xiawangzhuang, a common property regime has been established in Shangjijuan at the instigation of local authorities. The management structure is very similar to that of Xiawangzhuang, with a certain part of the village pasture closed off from use, and a ranger hired by the village to watch over it. This particular village was lucky since as much as 400ha of grassland, located close to the village, was fenced in 1992 with financial support of a Hong Kong-based NGO.[40] The practice of rotational grazing started as a small area marked with earth mounds (30ha) in the 1980s. The area used to be heavily desertified, and pasturing was strictly prohibited from 1980 to 1990. After the vegetation had recovered, the village leader decided to open it for use to all farmers on an equal basis for specific periods. In the beginning of the project many farmers opposed rotational grazing, but because the restricted area was small they finally accepted it. The area was gradually expanded as the acceptance of the system grew. Today, the restricted pasture is open for use twice a year, during spring and winter (see Figure 5). During these periods farmers are allowed to pasture their flock for around forty-five days.

The ranger in this village is hired in the same way as in Xiawangzhuang, with every farmer contributing a share to his salary on the basis of the number of sheep and goats owned. In neighbouring villages the system is different as the task of guarding grassland rotates among the farmers, who

[39] Cui Liwei, 'Caoyuan de Jienan' ['Rangeland Disaster'], *Fazhi Ribao* [Legal Daily] (14 July 1997), p. 6.

[40] The NGO is called World Vision (*shijie xuanminghui*).

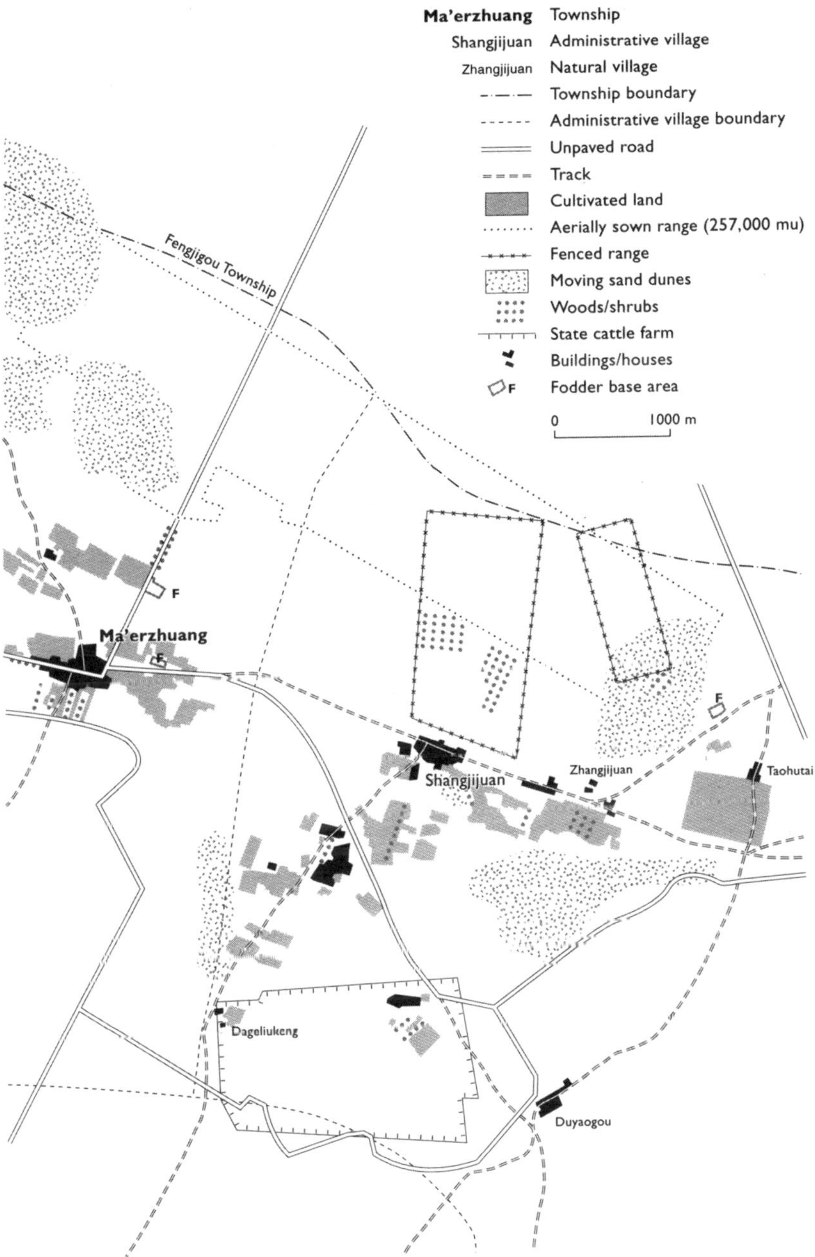

Figure 5: **Map of grassland around Shangjijuan village.**

Note: This map was drawn on the basis of an official map of Ma'erzhuang Township. Unfortunately, a similar map could not be derived for Xiawangzhuang village due to the lack of cooperation of the township authorities.

Source: Author.

each contribute one day's patrolling for each ten sheep (or goats) their household owns. The ranger said that the most frequent offences include (*a*) digging for liquorice root; (*b*) cutting fodder outside the stipulated periods, for which fines are imposed ranging from 100 to 500 RMB; and (*c*) illegal pasturing in the fenced-off area. In general, farmers are quite satisfied with the system of rotational grazing. Free-riders within and from outside the village who illegally pasture in restricted areas are not very common. As in Xiawangzhuang village, farmers say that overlapped grazing has greatly diminished. As for the digging for liquorice by the villagers themselves, arrangements have been made that are enforced by the ranger. The farmers allowed to dig for liquorice in the fenced area for only eight to ten days in March and October.

The Battle over Resources: Digging for Herbs

As noted above, the liquorice, which grows in abundance in Shangjijuan village, attracts farmers from far and wide, leading to serious desertification. In 1996, the harvest of millet and sorghum in Shangjijuan was completely destroyed by moving sand-dunes. The village is surrounded by pockets of desert, while a large sand-dune has even moved into the main street.[41]

Each year during the slack season, feelings run high as farmers from neighbouring townships and counties start digging for liquorice root on the pastures of Ma'erzhuang Township. For Shangjijuan village, relations are bad especially with adjoining Fengjigou Township, aggravated by a lingering boundary dispute about the right of way (see also Fig. 3).[42] Since 1992, several serious conflicts have occurred in Ma'erzhuang Township. After skirmishes over digging for liquorice root took place on 29 March, 30 April, and 1 May 1995, the prefectural police arrested almost a hundred people, including all local-level cadres at the village and township level of Ma'erzhuang and Fengjigou. Among those arrested, seventeen were released on bail, one was placed under house arrest, three were convicted, while two escaped and went underground. The convicted included the township party secretary of Ma'erzhuang, several members of village party branches, cadres of the villagers' committees, and other lower-level officials (see the Annexe to this chapter reproducing leaflets).[43]

In May 1996, violence broke out again as over five hundred Hui Muslims from Tongxin County forced their way into the pastures of Ye'erzhuang village (7km west of Shangjijuan). The digging for liquorice root ended in a raid on Ye'erzhuang. As one eyewitness recounted: 'Armed with cudgels and sticks we marched forward to stop them. But there were too many of them. In the meantime, they had surrounded our village with tractors.

[41] However, the large dune in the main street is not always seen in a negative way. Says one farmer: 'When we are tired after having tilled the land, we like to sit on the dune, enjoying the cool breeze in the evenings.'

[42] The dispute was finally settled in court, which ruled in favour of Shangjijuan village. The verdict was proclaimed in document no. 1992/124 of the Yanchi County Government.

[43] Ma'erzhuang Xiang Cunmin Weiyuanhui, *Guanyu Ma'erzhuang Xiang Shehui Zhi'an Jushi E'hua de Qingkuang Fanying* [A Reflection of the Decline of Public Order in Ma'erzhuang Township] Parts I and II, unpublished leaflet (Ma'erzhuang, 13 May 1996).

Hundreds of Hui rushed into the village, beat up anyone who dared to come near them, smashed our furniture, stole our TV sets and then escaped from the scene.'

The police and the grassland police[44] are completely powerless when conflicts erupt on such a scale. Most villages have therefore organized their own militia to patrol the village pastures. Shangjijuan village has no vigilantes of its own, but the village leader says the village does not need a vigilante patrol: 'If I find anyone digging illegally, all I have to do is to yell, and all the villagers will rush to protect their land. That is how the situation is: farmers have become so worked up that they are ready to fight.'

The Reach of the Commons

The evidence suggests that the common property regimes in both Shangjijuan and Xiawangzhuang provide enough incentives for collective action by the villagers. The good performance of these management systems is also reflected in the villagers' assessment of the effects of fencing. In the survey sample of ninety-eight households covering four natural villages in Yanchi County, the majority of the respondents (58 per cent) stated that fencing had an obvious positive effect on pasturing. The most-cited problem with the fencing was its high cost (66 per cent of respondents). Other problems and criticisms revealed by the survey included the idea that rangeland belongs to everybody and should be open to all (31 per cent) and the problem of illegal grazing by others (22 per cent). Difficulties in obtaining barbed wire (18 per cent) or fear of conflicts with neighbours (12 per cent) were least mentioned. Most farmers (91 per cent) would partly or fully fence in rangeland if they had the means.[45]

Desertification forms an integral part of life in these villages. According to farmers in Xiawangzhuang and Shangjijuan, neither over-grazing nor illegal cutting of fodder but the digging for liquorice root by people from outside the township is the real cause of desertification in the area. Many farmers feel that, because the rangeland is not theirs but state-owned, it is common property and thus open to everyone (86 per cent of respondents). Apart from the area that is fenced in, it is very difficult to exclude outsiders from digging for liquorice root in village pastures. The majority of farmers (57 per cent) also think that the boundaries of the village pastures may not be very clear to people from neighbouring villages.[46]

The common property regimes of these two villages seem to work remarkably well. One might have expected significant differences between the institutional dynamics of the common property regime in a relatively prosperous settlement such as Xiawangzhuang and that in the much poorer Shangjijuan village. Also, since Xiawangzhuang belongs to the early project area in which rotational grazing was introduced as an experiment, this village received more care and attention from the local authorities in

[44] A task force, specifically charged with the management and control of grasslands in China (see also Chapter 5, p. 146).

[45] Of the sample of ninety-eight farm households, all respondents answered this question.

[46] For all these questions: n = 98, response rate is 100%.

building up the common property regime than was the case in Shangjijuan village. Furthermore, as rangeland degradation in Shangjijuan has reached such alarming proportions because of the digging for liquorice root by farmers from outside the township, it would not have been surprising if farmers there were less committed to the common property regime than those of Xiawangzhuang. However, there are no indications that farmers in Shangjijuan are less dedicated to the regime because of external socio-economic pressure. Neither has this had a significant impact on the way the system works in the two villages.

There are several reasons for the success of the experiments with common property management in Xiawangzhuang and Shangjijuan. First of all, the closed rangeland used for rotational grazing in the villages in Yanchi County is small (generally 300–400ha) and is located in the vicinity of the village. This proximity allows rangers to be present at the range, and thus exercise control over the resource, for the greater part of the day. Boundaries are clear through fences, hedges, or the use of earth mounds. These factors facilitate the detection of rule-breaking free-riders, which in turn increases villagers' trust in the system and their willingness to abide by the rules. Farmers' recognition of the need for collective action is enhanced by the users' relatively high demand for the resource, which has already led to a certain degree of desertification.

Second, the group of users is small, which limits the transaction costs of communication and decision-making. In the majority of villages in Yanchi, herding is done in common with several families hiring one person to herd collective flocks of over 200 animals.[47] The number of herders per village is low, which allows behaviour to be easily supervised through social control within the village community. Permissible behaviour is prescribed through sets of social rules pertaining to the delimitation of the resource, allocation of resource use, membership, input, and punishment, as elaborated above for Xiawangzhuang.

Third, county and township authorities took great pains to establish and spread a corporate range management system. They supported and nurtured a management system that runs counter to the privatization aimed at by the pasture contracts. Moreover, there was no attempt to set up a new institutional structure to guide common property management: instead, local authorities relied on the existing village institutions to effectuate the range management system.

Finally, the village leaders play an important role in the management of the common property regime. They effectively counterbalance the power of the local authorities, with whom they maintain good relations, allowing

[47] The reason for this is that larger herds are easier to manage. Small flocks of sheep are quite difficult to herd. They 'are not happy in small groups, they spread and wander and join larger herds: they will not move predictably, in a body'. Gudrun Dahl and Anders Hjort, *Having Herds: Pastoral Herd Growth and Household Economy* (Stockholm: Department of Social Anthropology, University of Stockholm, 1976), p. 255. There is also a maximum size for sheep and goat herds. Based on research among the Kababish Arabs in Sudan, Asad states that the maximum flock size is 200 head irrespective of whether flocks are sheep only or mixed; if the flock consists entirely of goats, the maximum size is only twenty-five head. Asad, cited in Dahl and Hjort, *Having Herds*, p. 255.

them to secure funds and services for the farmers.[48] They have proved themselves capable managers of the common property regime, with sufficient authority and confidence to speak out and act on behalf of the villagers.

It is important to remember that the situation of livestock in Ningxia is quite different from that of traditional pastoral areas such as Inner Mongolia and Xinjiang. Livestock farming in Ningxia is settled and not (semi-) nomadic. Moreover, the grazing areas in Ningxia are smaller and located closer to the user groups than in the traditional pastoral regions. Nonetheless, the Yanchi experiments have proved that rangeland can be successfully managed by a village community on the basis of a property arrangement at low transaction costs.

In China, as in much of Africa, rangeland management on the basis of carrying capacities is often not viable, as it involves very high enforcement costs.[49] Given the implementation difficulties of the pasture contract system, which is based on the concept of carrying capacity, some scholars and officials within the Chinese Ministry of Agriculture have proposed that responsibility for management and control of rangelands should be vested in the collective, be it the administrative or the natural village, smaller traditional social groups such as the Mongolian *khot ail*, or even shareholding cooperatives. The Yanchi experiments are a valuable example of how this could be achieved.

Despite these positive results, however, the experiments with common property arrangements in Yanchi County also have their limits. Although villagers generally abide by the rules of the common property regime, desertification and rangeland degradation persist. The main cause of the degradation of grassland resources comes not from within but from *outside* the village. It is the exploitation of liquorice root by poor farmers from outside the township that causes such large-scale desertification. Poverty drives these farmers to look for additional and uncontrolled sources of revenue: the digging for liquorice root can provide most farmers with illegal, and thus non-taxed, extra income.

The Yanchi experiments painfully demonstrate the limits of natural resource management by the village community. When other users outside the village community value the natural resource differently, it is likely that the degradation of rangeland will continue regardless of the land

[48] There are many studies of the intermediary role of village-level cadres between the local state and the village. See also Elisabeth Croll, *From Heaven to Earth: Images and Experiences of Development in China* (London: Routledge, 1994) pp. 112–13; and Anita Chan, Richard Madsen, and Jonathan Unger, *Chen Village under Mao and Deng*, rev. edn (Berkeley: University of California Press, 1992) pp. 32–3.

[49] In the academic world there is also considerable criticism of carrying capacity as a leading principle in grassland management. Authors such as Leeuw, Bartels, Scoones, and Behnke have extensively written on this topic. See, for example, Gerrit B. Bartels, Brien E. Norton, and Gregory K. Perrier, 'The Applicability of the Carrying Capacity Concept to Africa: Comment on PDN Paper 29b by de Leeuw and Tothill', *Pastoral Development Network*, Paper No. 30e (London: Overseas Development Institute, 1990), and Roy H. Behnke, Ian Scoones, and Carol Kerven (eds.), *Range Ecology at Disequilibrium: New Models of Natural Variability and Pastoral Adaptation in African Savannas* (London: Overseas Development Institute, 1993).

tenure regime. We see clear evidence of this in the case of the regional conflicts over medicinal herbs. Particularly, destitute diggers of liquorice root will defy any law in the search for short-term gains to alleviate their poverty. Therefore, a common property regime is not a panacea. Perhaps this is one of the main lessons to be learnt from the Yanchi experiments: where the power of the common property regime stops, the space is opened for macroeconomic policies of poverty alleviation, such as the development of alternative income-generating activities and the physical and social infrastructure necessary to alleviate the pressure on rangelands.

Annexe: Two Leaflets

Translator's note: *The following two leaflets were handed out during farmers' protests against liquorice digging in Yinchuan on 18 May 1996. The leaflets were confiscated by the police.*

The first leaflet is incomplete and starts with the third (and last) page:

A Reflection of the Decline of Public Order in Ma'erzhuang Township (Part I)

. . . flustered and the masses have slept in the wild for three months long. Ten Party members and cadres endured hunger and have been on the run for seven months.

The catastrophe of 1995 had already passed and we hoped that the coming year would bring good times. But we did not expect that more disaster would befall us. In early spring 2,000–3,000 people came digging for liquorice root. Every day we asked for emergency aid and entreated the government to take forceful measures to stop [the digging]. Although the government took actions to prevent the digging, the diggers kept pouring in. On 11 May, over 500 people from Tongxin forced their way into Ye'erzhuang. A part of the masses of Ye'erzhuang persuaded them to stop, which angered the masses of Tongxin. Three hundred people with seventeen cars made a show of their strength and rushed into the village. When anyone came near them, they beat him up. They surrounded the houses, pounded the interior, and then ran away from the scene . . .

At this moment, these serious, daily conflicts have begun again all over the region. The government lacks force and cannot control the situation. The masses cannot control it either, because those who destroy are bold and assured, while those who protect themselves are severely punished when they oppose their suffering. Are we not the offspring of the Yellow Emperor? Why is China's law unable to protect the victims? When will our bitter days end?

We strongly demand:

1. the early release of the two people who were convicted because they tried to prevent outsiders from digging liquorice;
2. the severe punishment of the plunderers of 2 May 1995 and 11 May 1996, who have beaten, smashed, and looted;

3. the compensation of economic losses for the beating, smashing, and looting that happened two times;
4. the end to the destruction and return of peace to our homes.

The farmers of Ma'erzhuang Township, Yanchi County
13 May 1996

A Reflection of the Decline of Public Order in Ma'erzhuang Township (Part II)

The digging of liquorice root was prevented for five subsequent years, but since 1992 several massive fights have occurred. After incidents occurred on 29 March, 30 April, and 1 May 1995, the police of Yinnan Region have been involved in solving cases, while suspected township and village cadres, and nearly 100 people have been summoned to court, interrogated, investigated, taken into custody, and arrested. To date, seventeen people were released on bail, one person was placed under house arrest, three people were convicted, and two people escaped after their arrest. Among them are officials from the township party and government, the Village Party Branch, leaders and cadres from the villagers' committee, the County and Township People's Congress, and members of the Party and Youth League.

During this period, the entire township lived in confusion and terror. The grass roots organizations, including the Township Party Committee, the government, the Village Party Branch, and the villagers' committee, were paralysed for over five months. Cadres and the masses fled chaotically. During daytime they hid everywhere and at night they lived in the wild. When it rained or there was wind, the suffering was even more bitter. The situation resembles the war years, and people are flustered, while the atmosphere is tense. Approximately ten cadres and people went in hiding and endured hunger. Some were on the run for over seven months.

In 1995, agricultural production suffered severe losses in every respect, while the basic equipment was destroyed. This caused a shortage of feed for sheep and cattle in 1996 and a serious lack of grain for the farm households: some already have great difficulty in maintaining a livelihood. In particular, the relatives of those arrested or taken into custody for a long time can hardly maintain their living at present, because they could not harvest last year. To date, 4 per cent of the sheep raised in the entire township have died. It is the highest mortality for many years. The percentage of nursing sheep decreased by 30 per cent compared with last year.

The majority of cadres and the masses interrogated and arrested have also been beaten. One person's backbone was injured [literally, displaced], while two others suffered from serious internal injuries. Two people could not cope with the beating and insults during interrogation and attempted suicide. Relatives who wanted to visit and rescue them have spent countless sums of money to go to court, but you can only suppress your rage and keep your resentment to yourself.

In the early spring of 1996, flowers bloomed everywhere and all was full of life. Yet the region of Ma'erzhuang was densely covered with clouds of anxiety while people's hearts were filled with confusion and chaos. Since March, the hand tractors of those coming from outside to dig for liquorice increased from twenty, thirty, to over 100 (including tractors with three wheels). Moreover, the diggers increased from 300 to 400 to over 2,000. Cadres and masses from the county, township, village, and team urged the diggers several times to stop, but their impetus has become increasingly strong and their numbers only increased. Under this pressure, the local masses hardly have courage left to resist, nor do they have the ability to protect their resources and homes. They can only report and ask higher relevant bureaux for a solution as soon as possible. But to date there are hardly any measures or means, and the destruction continues, the losses get worse, there is no way to pasture the flocks, and the masses cannot live a normal life.

Every day, Ma'erzhuang, the Elixir of Life, endures trampling and destruction, and every day there are losses of several tens of thousands RMB. The masses resist the situation more and more, while their feeling of opposition grows increasingly stronger. The trust in the Party and the government is decreasing, and the rural work of the Party is more and more difficult to develop.

The masses bear doubt and misgivings about reality and they have no way to explain it.

1. It is hard for the masses to accept that a society of the rule of law and legislative norms is unjust. The majority of the masses are unyielding with regard to the implementation of law to protect homes, resources, and the ecological environment. But there are some malefactors who wantonly disturb the public order, destroy production, the ecological environment, and the grassland, and willfully beat, smash, and loot. They commit illegal actions time and again, while nobody dares to enforce the law upon them. For example, for the past five years people disruptively dig for liquorice in Ma'erzhuang, which caused the '2 May' incident when there was beating, smashing, and looting. Those who have organized and planned the crimes and the criminals who beat, smashed, and looted are still far beyond the reach of the law. The criminal elements that besieged and beat state officials and police have escaped the just punishment of the law.

   That even today, in the 1990s, such obvious illegal actions can receive protection from relevant bureaux is really hard for people to understand. If we go on like this for long, how can the grass roots organizations continue with their education to the masses of the rule of law? How can we control the law? How can we maintain social stability?
2. The disruptive digging for liquorice extends over a period of five years and can by no means be prohibited. This causes a serious burden to society. First, the masses do not understand the loss of control over public order by the Party and government, which weakens their judicial consciousness. Second, it increasingly hinders the work of grass roots cadres and organizations at all levels, and it

also frustrates work enthusiasm. Third, it undermines the trust, concentration, and centripetal force of the masses in the Party and the government. Fourth, it directly affects the implementation of rural policies and guidelines of the Party.

3. The worsening turbulence of the public order in local society, the intensifying long-term disturbance of social contradictions, will lead to even more serious consequences. The tolerance of the masses is limited. If we have to endure again what cannot be endured, bloody incidents more serious than before might happen, which will have an immeasurable impact on the social stability.

The farmers of Ma'erzhuang Township, Yanchi County

Summary and Concluding Observations: The Political Economy of Transition

Ownership as an Institution

Who owns China's land? This is the question that sparked my research years ago. There is no question as place- and time-specific yet as fundamental as the land ownership question. Land is essential to human existence. Probing into the question of land ownership directs the academic gaze towards cultural and temporal differences in the control over one of the basic means of production, and forces us to rethink what we know and compare that with what we do not know. Some scholars would retort: why focus on ownership while comparative sociological, legal, and anthropological research has demonstrated that the concept of ownership is bound in time and space? Did not Van Vollenhoven, the *éminence grise* of legal-anthropological studies, show through his ground-breaking work in the Dutch East Indies that the concept of a 'bundle of rights' more aptly describes the existing cultural and regional differences in the control over land?[1]

There are several compelling reasons why this research has taken land ownership as an object of study. First, in the transformation of ex-socialist and centrally planned economies into market-based economies, the institution of ownership is inextricably linked to the political economy of transition. One needs only to think of the political importance attached to the privatization of state assets as a means to rally social support in the former Soviet Union, or the sensitivity of free land sale in eastern and central European countries as some of them entered the European Union. The People's Republic of China is no different, but it has been extremely cautious in handling the institutional change of land ownership.

Second, economic reform and transition are predicated upon ideal-type societies featuring free markets protected by the rule of law, democratic and pluralist politics, and a dynamic civil society. Part and parcel of this idea is secure and private property safeguarded by the state. For some policy-makers and scholars this is tantamount to establishing ownership as an absolute and supreme right.[2] The Chinese government, however, is

[1] See also C. Van Vollenhoven, *Miskenningen van het Adatrecht* [Misunderstandings of Adat Law] (Leiden: Brill, 1909); H. W. J. Sonius, *Introduction to Aspects of Customary Land Law in Africa: As compared with some Indonesian Aspects* (Leiden: Universitaire Pers Leiden, 1963); and F. von Benda-Beckmann, *Property in Social Continuity: Continuity and Change in the Maintenance of Property Relationships through Time in Minangkabau, West Sumatra* (The Hague: M. Nijhoff, 1979).

[2] In spite of the civil law definition of ownership, the right of ownership in Western society is also restricted in many ways, and the owner cannot do with his property as he pleases. See also Govaert C. J. J. Van den Bergh, 'Property versus Ownership: Some Cursory Notes', in Joep Spiertz and Melanie G. Wiber (eds.), *The Role of Law in Natural Resource Management* (The Hague: VUGA, 1996), p. 172.

unlikely to institutionalize the private ownership of land resources in the foreseeable future. On the contrary, the tendency of national policies points to the development of land lease into 'lease into perpetuity' under the conditions of absolute ownership for the state and collective. Not only may such a project sound at odds with certain premises of neo-liberal economics, but its sheer scale as an example of institutional engineering is unprecedented in human history. It is why we must closely watch China's reforms of the land property rights structure.

Third, since land is one of the three basic means of production (along with labour and capital) its ownership is of direct ideological importance. In the ex-socialist countries land reform was generally the driving force that won the rural populace over to the Communist cause. With his promise to expropriate the landlords and rich peasants, Mao Zedong built up his power base in the rural areas, which eventually brought him victory over China. Decades after the Communist revolution, the issue of land ownership flies in like a bat from hell as governments struggle with the question what to do with ex-owners and their claims. In eastern Germany and Albania, for example, the issue of previous ownership stirred up old conflicts and reopened old wounds. China seems to have largely circumvented this problem by simply covering it up.

For these reasons, one of the most fruitful focal points for the study of institutional change in transition countries is ownership. Throughout this book we have seen how the state tries to shape and create institutions of land ownership, use, and management in order to guide and effect changes in the socio-economic environment. On the other hand, we have also seen how sometimes the socio-economic parameters actually dictate the structure of institutions. And, worse, we have seen how the state's failure to respond to shifting socio-economic parameters by creating the right institutions at the right time (or 'getting the institutions right') has led to the creation of what I termed 'empty institutions' featuring social conflict, environmental degradation, and the victimization of farmers. In such conditions, the newly created institution is merely a paper agreement or an empty shell with little effect on the behaviour of social actors. On the other hand, if the state is committed to creating 'credible institutions' that can gain sufficient trust from social actors, it is crucial that the right balance be struck in the complex interplay between institutions and socio-economic parameters—it is what determines the success or failure of the politics and economics of transition.

In this book, I have shown that during the reforms the Chinese state has at times deliberately refrained from creating and defining certain institutions: 'intentional institutional ambiguity'. These actions have been most pronounced in the stalling of the registration of rural land titles and the refusal to clear up the legal confusion surrounding collective ownership. Despite overt calls by delegates of the National People's Congress for a clear definition of collective ownership, the central government did not address this issue: *not* during the last revisions of the Constitution and the Land Administration Law; *not* in the newly proclaimed Rural Land Contracting Law; and, unfortunately, also probably *not* during the drafting of the new Property Law. I have argued that the 'intentional institutional ambiguity' upheld by the Chinese state is one of the main mechanisms that make the Household Contract Responsibility System for agricultural land (or cropland) tick: in other words, lends it credibility in the eyes of social actors.

In Chapter 1 we saw that, despite foreign observers' fear of dampened economic incentives as a result of tenure insecurity, cropland tenure is widely perceived as credible as the land reallocations are supported by the majority of farmers. This credibility points to the critical role that land plays in Chinese rural society today: that of a social security system rather than a transferable and marketable commodity. In a situation of limited alternative off-farm employment, the Chinese peasant is bound to his tiny plot of land as a basic means of livelihood. Frequent land reallocations in response to changes in household size guarantee that each member of the village collective has equal access to land resources. Under these conditions, it is the insecurity rather than the security of property rights that explains the high level of credibility that the tenure system enjoys. One might actually conclude that institutional credibility is a function of the degree to which insecurity of tenure provides security to social actors' expectations of egalitarian access to land. In this respect, the state-supported institutional ambiguity serves as the lubricant of a well-oiled machine.

Seen in this light, the government's unofficial stance towards the 1997 policy of '30 years no change' in the term of land lease shows its pragmatism in effecting institutional change. A Director General within the Ministry of Agriculture noted:

> The '30 years' no change' policy is not likely to work in the short run, because it is going to take decades before enough farmers have been transferred to other economic sectors. Only then will the population pressure on land be sufficiently brought down to allow secure lease rights. But of course we hope that the policy will already have some effect in controlling the frequency of land reallocations.[3]

Whereas in the past the Chinese government had enhanced tenure security as an end in itself, it now realizes that the degree of tenure security should be made dependent on the local socio-economic and demographic conditions.

It is important to note that intentional institutional ambiguity to date has also prevented the large-scale eruption of land-related grievances over ownership that ruptured transitional economies such as in east Germany, Poland and Kyrgyzstan.[4] Although, during the period of the communes, land ownership in China was vested in the team by party decree, the team, or

[3] Sheng Li (oral communication, 3 March 2002).

[4] This is shown, for example, in a recent case at the European Court for Human Rights in Strasbourg. In the final days of the German Democratic Republic, Prime Minister Hans Modrow ordained that full ownership be granted to the farmers of the former collectives (LPG) and their heirs. The German government of Helmut Kohl, however, reversed this measure in 1992. In response, around 70,000 former LPG members and their descendants filed a case at the European Court for Human Rights, which in January 2004 ruled that

natural village for that matter, did not exercise actual control over the land. In fact, in the name of economic development land was frequently illegally expropriated from the villages by higher administrative levels—the brigade, the commune, or the local state. Over time, however, considerable investments have been made in the land by the new (illegal) owner, thus establishing his customary right to the land. As a result, land cannot be simply returned to the original owner. If the team or natural village were to be reinstated in central state law as the principal owner of collective land, it would have the legal means to reclaim the land previously stolen from it. And that would lead to a renewed stream of ownership claims. In order to avoid widespread social conflict over land, the central government decided—with good reason—to leave collective land ownership undefined.

The ownership of state-owned land is as ambiguous as that of collective land. State-owned land faces a dual problem of definition. Like collective land, it was unclear which administrative level represented ownership: the central state, province, prefecture, or county. This situation was clarified with the passing of the revised Land Administration Law in 1998, when it was stipulated that the central state was the sole representative of state-owned land. However, the stipulation did not end the confusion over state land—certainly not in the case of state-owned natural resources. Shortly after the founding of the new Chinese republic, forest, grassland, and wasteland were nationalized. This land was not *terra nullius*, but has been inhabited for centuries by ethnic minorities and Chinese settler farmers. Their communities suddenly found themselves enclosed in state-owned territory. According to the current laws, forest, grassland, and wasteland can be considered collectively owned only if legal proof of it can be submitted. As we saw above, collective ownership is intentionally kept ambiguous by the central state. Therefore, ethnic minorities and former Chinese agricultural colonists can have little hope that their claims to land will be recognized. It remains to be seen whether the intentional institutional ambiguity over ownership will work as well for forest, grassland, and wasteland as it does for agricultural land. The legal cases reviewed in Chapter 2 are testimony to the complex situation of ex-ownership. From the cases we saw that intentional institutional ambiguity has provided the Chinese judiciary with a certain flexibility in dealing with the minefield of land ownership: rectifying forced land evictions and expropriations from the past, yet without sacrificing long-term economic interests. However, the cases also clearly demonstrated the potential sources of land-related conflicts. The question is whether these might not erupt in the long run as commercialization and urbanization increasingly pit former and new land owners against each other.

the decision by the Kohl administration was unlawful. In addition, the German government has been ordered to provide suitable financial redress to the victims of expropriation. At the time of writing, the German government is still studying the possibility of a higher appeal. Michel Kerres, 'Hof voor Mensenrechten: Onteigening in ex-DDR onrechtmatig' ['Court for Human Rights: Expropriation in former DDR unlawful'], *NCR Handelsblad* (23 January 2004), p. 5.

Critical Problems in Land Administration

The international community's initial reservations about China's experiments in the privatization of land use rights instead of ownership rights have been replaced by recognition and acclaim. The Household Contract Responsibility System started as a political compromise that could preserve the ideological principle of state land ownership, but has become one of the prime successes of the economic reforms. This success was based on the promotion of farmers' incentives by reinstating their managerial rights to land. It seems unlikely, however, that in the course of economic development land lease can continue unless the ownership question is resolved. As the basis of the Household Contract Responsibility System is unclear, there is no chance of further commercialization of land lease. And this will seriously impede rural economic development. There are clear indications that a critical moment has been reached and further delay in institutional reform in the land administration system will have grave consequences. In the chapters on grassland, forestry, and wasteland we saw that the ambiguous ownership structure leads to bad stewardship of the land or, in the long run, to the rise of impoverished, landless farmers. In 1996 it was estimated that environmental degradation, ranging from desertification to deforestation and salinization of land, affected around 83.2 million ha or 60 per cent of China's total arable area.[5] In addition, widespread losses of arable land arising from urban construction activities have been reported. The latter problem is a direct outcome of the ambiguity in collective land ownership. In the wealthier, coastal regions of China, cities have rapidly expanded into rural areas due to the lower value of agricultural land. As it is unclear which level of the collective is legally entitled to represent land ownership, corrupt local cadres have a powerful incentive to sell land that is not theirs. The clearest example of such dark practices was the dishonourable discharge in October 2003 of Tian Fengshan, Minister of Land Resources. Tian was charged with corruption and land theft during his term as governor of Heilongjiang Province from 1995 to 1999.[6] Over the years, many farmers have been faced with forced eviction from their land as entire villages have been sold for real estate development. It was estimated that over the period 1985–96 the total loss in arable land due to construction activities amounted to 1.3 million ha.[7] Since China has only one-third of the world country average of arable land, these losses also threaten China's food security.

Another issue that has brought land ownership to the fore is the need for integrated spatial and environmental planning. The Chinese countryside has witnessed rapid industrialization over recent decades. Most of these so-called township and village enterprises make use of outdated and highly

[5] *The Role of Sustainable Agriculture in China: Environmentally Sound Development*, Seventh Report for the Fifth Conference of the China Council for International Cooperation on Environment and Development (Shanghai: 23–5 September 2003), p. 10.

[6] See Garrie van Pinxteren, 'Chinese Minister Ontslagen' ['Chinese Minister Sacked'), *NCR Handelsblad* (23 October 2003), p. 4.

[7] Ministry of Agriculture, *China Agricultural Development Report* (Beijing: Nongye Chubanshe, 1997), p. 100.

polluting technologies. As a result, there has been a rapid rise in air and water pollution. The financial losses in crop reduction due to acid rain were estimated to range from 4.5 billion to 5 billion RMB in 1993, while the loss of forest areas amounted to 5 billion RMB. In the same year, the irrigation areas affected by polluted water rose to 15.73 million ha, which accounted for 16.5 per cent of total farmland and 36.57 per cent of the total available irrigation area.[8]

To effectively cope with this environmental challenge, it is critical that spatial and environmental planning is conducted in an integrated manner. However, the success of the land lease system also has a downside. Due to decollectivization the old commune system was replaced and land was subsequently leased to approximately 160 million family farming units.[9] This led to an extreme fragmentation in land and its management. With a doubling of the rural population over 1949–88, the average land per capita is today less than 0.08ha (as against 0.18ha in 1949).[10] The fragmentation in the control over land means that integrated spatial and environmental planning has become virtually impossible. For example, in the case of land expropriation for the construction of waste-water treatment facilities or the relocation of polluting industries to industrial parks, negotiations would have to be undertaken with a multitude of stakeholders. In addition, expropriation and relocation are unfeasible if the legal owner of the land is unknown. Effective spatial and environmental planning is, therefore, above all a matter of clarifying land ownership. And that means land registration.

Past practices of land registration demonstrate that the central government's fear of social conflict is not unfounded. Since the dismantling of the communes, various attempts have been made to register land titles. However, the need to clarify boundaries for land registration reignited disputes that had simmered for years in legal fuzziness. Social resistance was particularly fierce in the forest sector (see Chapter 4). In the first three years of forest registration, a total of 1.4 million cases were recorded—an annual average of 460,000. Provincial-level disputes posed a special problem.[11] For this purpose, a special mission for dispute resolution and reassessment of provincial administrative boundaries was organized in 1999 by the State Forestry Bureau and the Ministries of Land Resources and Civil Affairs (responsible for drawing administrative boundaries).[12]

[8] Fu-Chen Lo and Yu-qing Xing (eds.), *China's Sustainable Development Framework: Summary Report* (Tokyo: United Nations University Institute of Advanced Studies, 1999), pp. 19–21.

[9] Erwin M. Reisch, 'Land Reform Policy in China: Political Guidelines and Tendencies', in Eduard B. Vermeer (ed.), *From Peasant to Entrepreneur: Growth and Change in Rural China* (Wageningen: Pudoc, 1992), p. 15.

[10] The rural population rose from 541,670,000 in 1949 to 1,096,140,000 in 1988. See Xiaohua Zhang and Yu Li (eds.), *Zhongguo Tudi Guanli Shiwu Quanshu* [Practical Encyclopedia of China's Land Administration] (Beijing: Zhongguo Dadi Chubanshe, 1997), pp. 1414–15.

[11] State Forestry Bureau (ed.), China Forestry Yearbook 1949–1986 (Beijing: Zhongguo Linye Chubanshe, 1992; reprint of 1987), pp. 55, 480.

[12] *Ibid.*, p. 480; State Forestry Bureau (ed.), *China Forestry Yearbook 1999/2000* (Beijing: Zhongguo Linye Chubanshe, 1999/2000), p. 110.

Due to the large-scale eruption of ownership disputes, land registration in rural areas came to a full standstill during the mid-1990s. Most significantly, land registration stopped before the level of the natural village: the original owner of land during the collectivist period. The Chinese central government is aware that land registration can no longer be postponed, particularly so in the view of China's recent entry into the World Trade Organization (WTO). The first step on that road will be the clarification of land ownership. But that debate has only just begun.

Who Owns China's Land?

The land ownership debate in China is to date still sensitive not only because of the issue of ex-ownership. In addition, the debate touches on the foundations of the Chinese state and Communist ideology. The collapse of the Soviet Union in 1992 and the subsequent surge of privatization of state assets throughout the former eastern bloc countries also caused the ownership debate to flare up in China. Some politicians and scientists advocated outright privatization of land while others promoted a renewed nationalization. It is clear from the political debate today that the Chinese government will not abandon the principle of state and collectively owned land with the possibility of private lease. In this sense, the ownership structure envisaged is similar to the British system under which land is in name owned by the Crown but can be leased to legal persons.

The ownership debate in China currently focuses on the level of collective ownership: the natural village (legally termed the 'villagers' group') or the administrative village. Generally there are two camps in this debate: those who propose a continuation of the land ownership structure of the People's Communes by granting ownership to the natural village or villagers' group, and those who advocate disowning the natural village and raising the level of ownership to the administrative village. The first group is represented by two research groups within the Chinese Academy of Social Sciences and the China People's University,[13] which were commissioned in 1998 by the National People's Congress to draft the current Property Law. Their opponents consist of senior officials within the Ministry of Land Resources, the Ministry of Agriculture, and the State Bureau of Forestry, as well as some experts formerly involved in the drafting of the Land Administration Law. As the Director General quoted above stated: 'Granting ownership to the villagers' group will cause a great shock (*yinqi zhendong*). What that bunch of scientists from the Chinese Academy of Social Sciences has proposed does not fit reality, the research that they do is rather far removed from the actual situation.'[14] One may wonder why the choice of the level of collective land ownership is such a crucial one. In order to understand the drastic nature of what is proposed, one must closely examine the various arguments.

[13] The research group of the Legal Research Institute of the Chinese Academy of Social Sciences is headed by Liang Huixing; the other group of the Faculty of Law of the People's University is led by Wang Liming.

[14] Sheng Li (oral communication, 3 March 2002).

The arguments of those wishing to abolish the natural village (or villagers' group) as a basic unit of land ownership are threefold. Vesting ownership in the administrative village would greatly facilitate land registration and spatial planning. In 1998 there were 739,980 administrative villages as against almost 1.5 million natural villages.[15] The registration of titles of the natural villages would be extremely difficult because of the sheer number of cases and, more importantly, because it would direct renewed attention to historical claims to land. The official policy of the Ministry of Land Resources is to entirely circumvent the previous ownership question by reducing people's sense of ownership in different steps. For this reason, the law stipulates that land titles before Land Reform in the 1950s are invalid, thus blocking any claims that stem from a period when private and (ethnic) customary ownership still existed.[16] Denying the natural village the right to own land is no less than the next logical step in drawing attention away from ownership, this time by invalidating claims that might spring from illegal expropriations in the collective period. Greatly complicating the granting of ownership to the natural village is the fact that an unknown number of natural villages are equivalent to single clans or families. Ownership by the natural village would then be tantamount to granting family ownership, which would be politically unacceptable.

Second, it is argued that the current situation of the land lease system already confirms the relative unimportance of the natural village as a unit of land ownership. Under the Household Contract Responsibility System the administrative village (under the supervision of the township) usually acts as the formal lessor instead of the natural village. Wang Guanghua, the former Deputy Director General for Land Titling of the Ministry of Land Resources, remarked: 'The brigade or administrative village for that matter is already the land owner. We cannot revert to the past any more, the boundaries of the production team have been smashed for ages (*jiexian zao bei dapo*). Under the Household Contract System, the administrative village is the unit that issues the lease contract, and it is supervisor of the villagers' group.'[17] This official has a point, of course, as in over 60 per cent of land leases the administrative village acted as the lessor.[18] Moreover, the right to changes in the land lease contract is by law reserved to the administrative village.[19]

A final argument against land ownership by the natural village (or villagers' group) is institutional. The question is whether the natural

[15] National Bureau of Statistics, *China Statistical Yearbook 1999* (Beijing: Zhongguo Tongji Chubanshe, 1999), p. 379.

[16] Article 30, 1950 Land Reform Law, in Jianhong Sun (ed.), *Tudi Quanshu Shiwu Zhinan* [Practical Compass on Land Titles] (Beijing: Zhongguo Dadi Chubanshe, 1998), p. 111.

[17] Guanghua Wang (oral communication, 4 October 2001).

[18] The villagers' group accounted for 32.3%, the township for 1.1%, and other categories for 3%. See Huimin Wang, 'Dangqian Nongcun Tudi Chengbao Jingying Guanli de Xianzhuang ji Wenti' ['The Present Situation and Problems facing the Management and Administration of Rural Land Lease'], *Zhongguo Nongcun Guancha*, No. 5 (1998), p. 56.

[19] See article 14, Revised Land Administration Law in Weilian Fang (ed.), '*Zhonghua Renmin Gongheguo Tudi Guanlifa' Shiyong Jianghua* [A Practical Discussion of the 'Land Administration Law of the People's Republic of China'] (Beijing: Zhongguo Minzhu Fazhi Chubanshe, 1998), p. 209.

village would be capable of representing collective ownership if it were given the right to land ownership. In other words, can the natural village effectively represent the common ownership of its members—the farmers? It could successfully do so only if it possessed the institutions to exercise that right. And this is the crux of the matter: the natural village is not a self-governing unit, in contrast to the administrative village which has its own governing body, namely, the villagers' committee. The cadres of the administrative village are, at least in principle, democratically elected in present-day China. It is thus reasoned that the administrative village could better represent the interests of the members of the rural collective.

The drafters of the Property Law, however, reject these arguments, on several grounds—first, on grounds of basic human rights. During the collectivist period land was formally vested in the team or natural village. Therefore, a central government committed to the rule of law could not possibly all of a sudden confiscate the property of over 1.5 million villages and hand it over to a higher administrative level. Even if the natural village presently lacks an independent and transparent governing body, the natural village as a territorial, administrative, and social unit is a reality. It cannot just be brushed aside as irrelevant in matters of land administration. There would, in fact, be a great danger of an outburst of widespread social resistance if the government attempted to do so.

Valid as it is to question the natural village's ability to effectively represent the farmers' legal interests in land, it can also be asked whether the administrative village would perform any better. Due to rapid urbanization the value of land in the wealthier and coastal regions has risen steeply. From 1997 to 1998 the revenues from transferred land increased by 78.1 per cent, to 13.2 billion RMB.[20] With the increase in value, the number of illegal land transactions rose too. In 1995 there were 248,000 reported cases of illegal land transactions, of which 157,000 concerned unlawful occupation of land, 9,702 unapproved land transactions, and 27,640 illegal land sales.[21] With these mounting economic interests, vesting ownership in the administrative village might tempt local officials even more into selling off others' land to expanding cities.[22]

If we consider the ways the collective could properly represent the joint interests of its members, we touch on the collective's institutional foundations and on the issue of rural democracy.[23] In this respect, those drafting the new Property Law rightly remarked that 'the ownership of collective

[20] National Bureau of Statistics, *China Statistical Yearbook 1999*, p. 233.

[21] Zhang and Li (eds.), Practical Encyclopedia of China's Land Administration, p. 1490.

[22] As Jiang Xueqin writes: 'Illegal land confiscation—a result of highly ambiguous laws, lack of central monitoring and short-sighted greed—is now very pervasive . . . For the government in Beijing, it's also very worrying. Confiscation is the hottest issue in the countryside, and has sparked large-scale riots in southern Guangdong and Fujian provinces.' See Jiang Xueqin, 'Stealing the Land', *Far Eastern Economic Review* (7 February 2002), p. 57.

[23] Some of the recent issues involved are described in L. Diamond and R. H. Myers 'Elections and Democracy in Greater China', *The China Quarterly*, Vol. 162 (June 2000), pp. 365–86; and Zhenyao Wang, 'Villagers' Committees: the Basis for China's Democratization', in Eduard B. Vermeer, Frank N. Pieke, and Woei Lien Chong (eds.), *Cooperative and Collective in China's Rural Development: Between State and Private Interest* (New York: M. E. Sharpe, 1998).

property belongs by nature to the collective ownership of the working masses. The feature of common ownership of collective property can only be expressed through democratic management by the members of the collective who exercise [this] ownership through democratic procedures.'[24] It is a highly critical issue. One of the reasons why the villagers' group needs to be reinstated as the basic owner of land is that the villagers' committee of the administrative village—in varying degrees democratically elected—has to date been unable to protect the villagers' group's legal interests in land. Against this backdrop, the drafters of the new Property Law decided to make some critical choices in the formulation of the bill.

The Draft Property Law: Reinstating the Former Owner?

The most far-reaching clause for rural land ownership in the current version of the Property Law is article 135. It reads:

> Land owned by the rural collective is according to law owned by the villagers' group (*cunmin xiaozu*). Land which is already owned by the rural collective of the village or township (town) belongs to the ownership of the rural collective of the village or township (town). Collectively owned land that originally existed within cities should be owned by the collective organization (*jiti zuzhi*). Unclear titles to collective land should be determined as owned by the villagers' group.[25]

The importance of article 135 lies in the fact that it unequivocally reinstates the lowest collective level as the basic owner of land. In addition, it significantly strengthens this ownership by including the stipulation that, when titles to collective land are unclear, it should be owned by the villagers' group (or natural village). Article 135 also considers the recent developments sparked by urbanization, by determining that land originally belonging to the collective yet included in an urban area should still be owned by the collective. The legal experts involved in drafting the Property Law explain their motives for including this stipulation as follows:

> The current legislation has already formed three entities: collective ownership by the villagers' group, collective ownership by the villagers' committee, and collective ownership by the rural collective of the township (town). These three entities reflect to a certain extent the system of 'three-level ownership with the team as basis' which was formed after the people's communes were established in the 1960s in China. The rural reforms of the 1980s have not fundamentally denied the coexistence of these three types of land rights. Completely changing this property rights structure would not only be impossible to execute in practice, but would also result in the emergence of many conflicts that would be difficult to resolve.[26]

Although the proposed Property Law represents in certain respects a positive break with the past, it is remarkably silent about the question of communal, customary land rights. Interestingly, the draft does include separate sections on common ownership (*gongyou*) and ownership by

[24] See Liming Wang (ed.), *Zhongguo Wuquanfa Cao'an Jianyigao ji Shuoming* [Proposed Draft and Discussion of the China Property Law] (Beijing: Zhongguo Fazhi Chubanshe, 2001), pp. 283–4.

[25] *Ibid.*, pp. 35–6.

[26] *Ibid.*, p. 287.

social groups (*shehui tuanti*) and religious organizations (*zongjiao zuzhi*). However, it is uncertain whether such ownership also pertains to land, which is not listed under the property types of these ownership forms—particularly so, as collective ownership of land is listed as a special item within collective ownership.[27] This is highly disappointing, because alternative tenure regimes are critical in the management of marginal resources with slow economic returns, such as wasteland and grassland (see Chapter 6).

In addition, the matter of historical land claims that predate Land Reform is not taken up in the draft Property Law. Under the current legislation, land titles before Land Reform have no legal force. Ever since the proclamation of the Land Reform Law in 1950, this has been the guiding principle for the assessment of land titles. This principle has been reiterated time and again in important national laws, regulations, and legal interpretations up to this day. Yet, if the Chinese government and judiciary are to take seriously their task of dealing with the injustices of the past, when land holdings were anything but secure, this stipulation can no longer be maintained. In the course of ownership shifts, land has never been systematically registered. In addition, the only land permits allowed as legal evidence for title—issued, if at all, during Land Reform and the Four Fixes Movement in 1962—are absolutely insufficient to serve as a sound basis for land registration. For these reasons, all evidence that might be used to assess the title to land, even if dating from before the People's Republic, should be taken into account.

At the time of writing—late 2004—the draft version of the new Property Law is still under review by the National People's Congress. However, over two years after its submission to the NPC, the majority of politicians and experts still do not expect a final decision on collective ownership soon. It is a clear illustration of the sensitivity and complexity of land ownership in China today. An earlier proposal on exactly this issue was stranded during the revision of the Land Administration Law in 1998.[28] However, the socio-economic parameters back then were quite different from those of today, due to China's membership of the WTO. Under these changed conditions it is clear that the intentional institutional ambiguity adopted as official policy in the past can no longer be a solution. Under WTO regulations China will be forced to open up its market to foreign companies. As a result, Chinese farmers will face increased competition from abroad. An agricultural sector incapable of achieving greater economies of scale due to extreme land fragmentation is bound to lose out. In addition, if China is committed to a stable environment for foreign

[27] Articles 135, 159 and 161, *Ibid.*, pp. 35, 42–3.

[28] Although 'some delegates of the NPC Standing Committee remarked that it is unclear who represents the land ownership . . . of the farmers' collective', as the minutes of the NPC mention, the Land Administration Law did not clarify the issue. See Boyong Li, *Quanguo Renda Falü Weiyuanhui guanyu 'Zhonghua Renmin Gongheguo Tudi Guanlifa (Xiuding Cao'an)' Shenyi Jieguo de Baogao* [Report on the Results of the Review of the 'Land Administration Law of the People's Republic (Revised Draft) by the Law Committee of the National People's Congress], speech at the Fourth Session of the Standing Committee of the Ninth National People's Congress (24 August 1998), p. 3.

direct investment, land property rights must be secure and marketable. It is therefore a *conditio sine qua non* that an efficient market is established that allows for free transfer of land. An integral institutional requirement for such a market is a systematic registration of land titles starting with the basic owner—the villagers' group. But that hurdle has still to be taken. A senior official of the Ministry of Land Resources commented on this:

> Land titling should start from the smallest unit of ownership, which is the villagers' group, after which use rights can be registered. But presently it is like we have done it the other way around. The Household Contract Responsibility System first consolidated the individual's land use rights, while the ownership right of the villagers' group has not been registered at all (*genben meiyou dengji*)![29]

Few people today are aware of China's lack of a national land registry. The institutional engineering of a land registry involves the careful establishment of the 'right' institutions at the 'right' time with ample regard to regional variation and sources of social conflict. Only with sufficient caution can credible institutions be created that are capable of gaining the rural populace's trust and can lead to long-term sustained economic growth. The development of a cadastre involves a major restructuring of rural policies, laws, and state administration in line with current socio-economic and political conditions. Land plots need to be surveyed and their data stored in a transparent and effective information system. The complexity of the issues involved, including previous ownership, customary rights, and conflict resolution, implies that in-depth research will be imperative. Lastly, the sheer scale of the undertaking means substantive investments from the central government and international donors, such as the World Bank, the Asian Development Bank, and the United Nations. The task of land registration in the world's most populous country implies that land ownership will remain one of China's critical questions for decades to come.

[29] Ping He (oral communication, 28 February 2002). He Ping is head of the Department for Land Titling of the Directorate General for Land Titling of the Ministry of Land Resources.

Appendix A
Title of Land Ownership of Two Villages

Note: In all the appendices, editorial insertions are enclosed in square brackets. The land contracts are part of the author's collection of Chinese land contracts. However, for reasons of space only a small selection is included here. Each photo is preceded by the English translation of the document.

[Front page]

CERTIFICATE
BOUNDARIES OF LAND TITLE

Unit: [not filled in]

土 地 权 属 界 綫

认 可 书

单位__________

[First page]
Through on-site examination by personnel of both sides it has been confirmed that the boundaries of the land titles between Jianshe Village (Party A) and Fengshen Village (Party B) run from the point of convergence between the extended line from the southern large weir of the irrigation canal of Fengle Commune and the Fengji canal (3.4.5) to the point of convergence between the old Shenba irrigation canal and the Fengji canal (A.B)22. This [document] is to certify that the views are unanimous and there are no disputes.

(Party A)	(Official Stamp) Stamp of the Villagers' Committee
(Party B)	(Official Stamp) Stamp of the Villagers' Committee
(Person [charged with] Assessment of Party A's Boundaries)	[signature]
(Person [charged with] Assessment of Party B's Boundaries)	[signature]
(Leader of Party A)	[signature]
(Leader of Party B)	[signature]
(Participating Person from the Higher Level)	[signature]
(Examining person)	[signature]
	November 1991

建设村（甲方）与丰收村（乙方）

之间的土地权属界线，经双方人员在现地核对，确认自丰收五社渠南大渠子的延长线与丰济渠交汇处(3·4·5)拐点至白什巴渠与丰济渠交汇处(A·B)22拐点之间，意见一致，没有争议，特此为据。

（甲方）（单位公章）

（乙方）（单位公章）

（甲方指界人）[illegible]

（乙方指界人）张鲁

（甲方领导人）[illegible]

（乙方领导人）张鲁

（上级参加人员）[illegible]

（调查人员）[illegible]

91 年 11 月 日

[Second page]
Map of the Boundaries of the Land Titles
[Map]
Scale 1:20,000

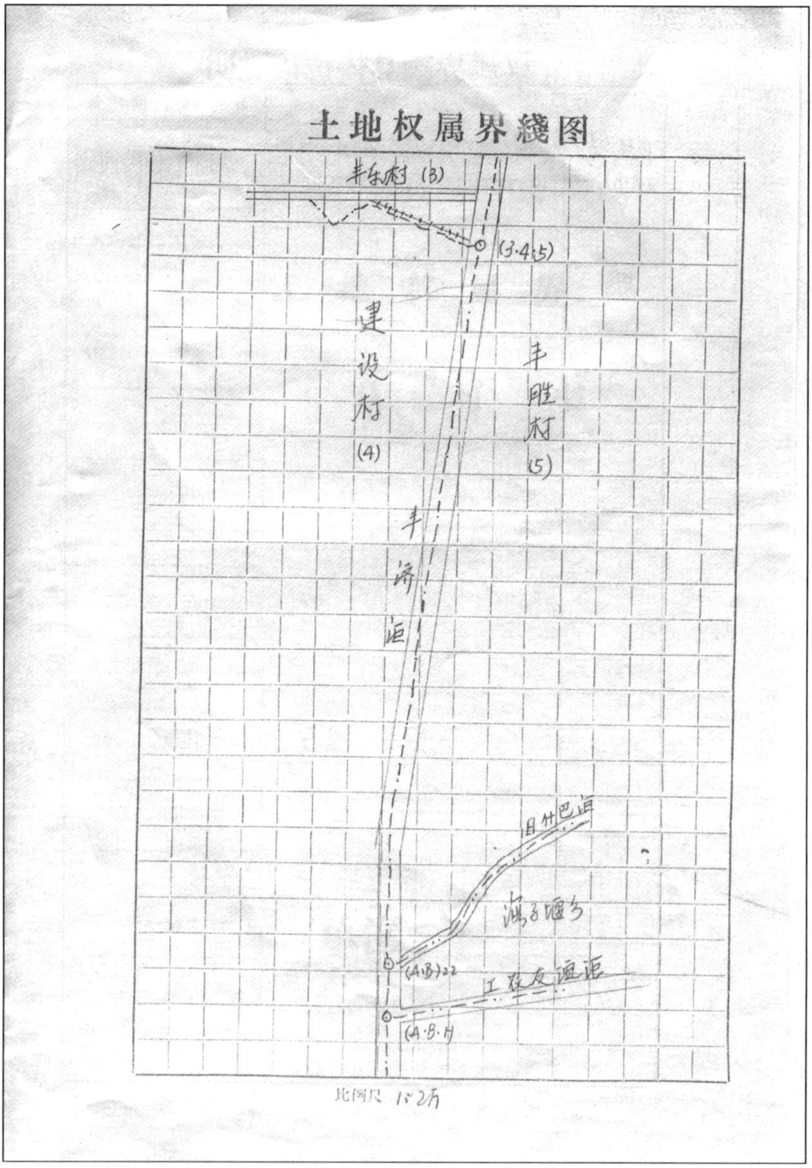

[Back page]

Explanation on the exact location of the boundaries of the titles

Number of points	Location of points	Location of boundaries
(3.4.5)	The point of convergence between the extended line from the southern large weir of the irrigation canal of Commune X and the Fengji canal[1]	The centre of the Fengji canal forms the boundary
(A.B)22	The point of convergence between the old Shenba irrigation canal and the Fengji canal	

[1] This is the one of the main irrigation canals that runs north of the county.

权属界綫具体位置說明

拐点号	拐点位置	界线位置
(3·4·5)	丰乐五社沟南大堤路延长线与丰济沟的交汇处	以丰济沟中心为界.
(A·B)22	旧什四沟与丰济沟的交汇处.	

Appendix B
Record of Land Dispute Between State Forest Farm and Village

[Front page]

CERTIFICATE
REASONS FOR THE LAND DISPUTE

Unit: [not filled in]

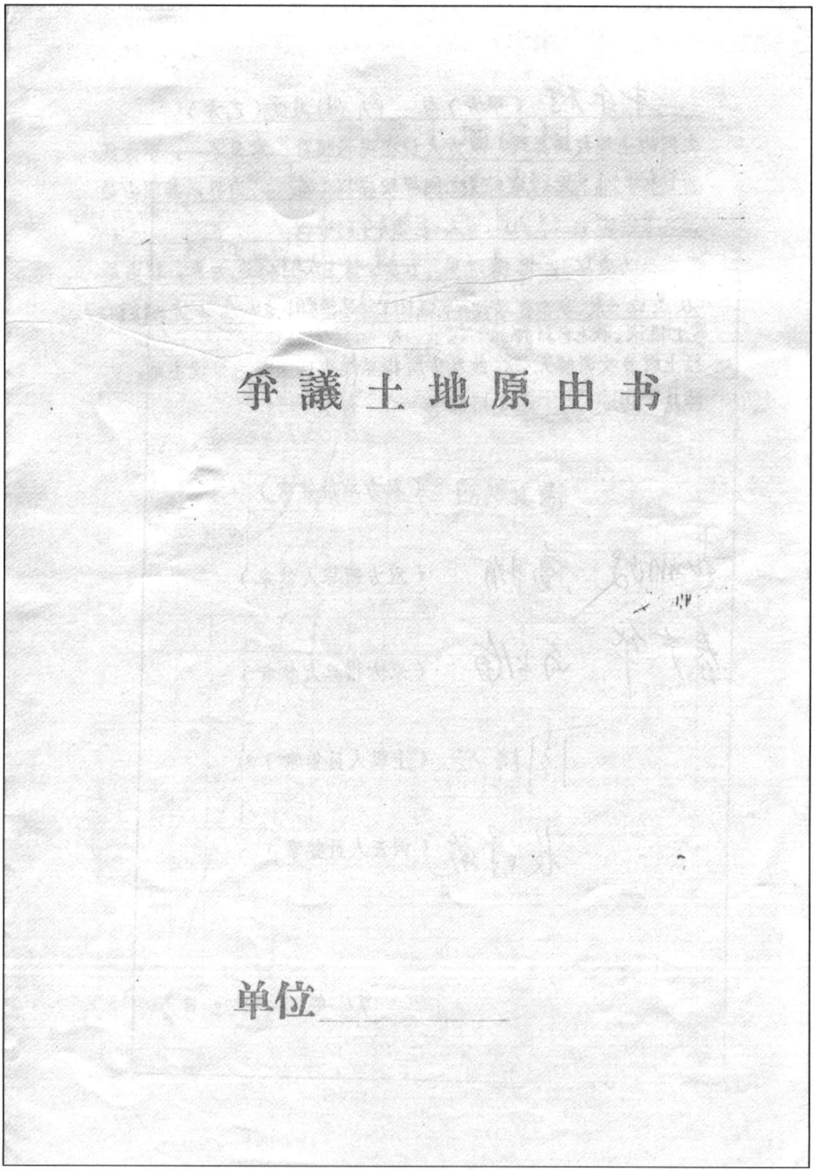

争議土地原由书

单位________

[First page]
Regarding the boundaries of land titles between Fengle Village and the Shelterbelt Forest Farm, on-site examination by personnel of both sides has shown that the views are not unanimous. Party A deems that between the Xinhua drainage canal and the point where the natural moat converges with the irrigation canal, the irrigation canal should be the boundary. The reason for this is that [the area] north of the canal is sandy wasteland and not desert. Party B deems that the moat north of the canal should be the boundary, because this area has always been regarded as the jurisdiction of the forest farm since its establishment. Furthermore, since 1982 repeated agreements have been signed with Fengle Village and the township government.

Repeated mediation by the higher level [authorities] has been in vain. For this reason the land in between the boundaries pointed out by both sides has been defined as contested land, for which this explanation.

(enclosed documents: ___ pieces)

(Official Stamps of Both Parties)
Stamp of the Villagers' Committee
[Stamp of the Shelterbelt Forest Farm is missing]

(Signatures of Leaders of Both Parties)
[two signatures]

(Signatures of Persons [charged with]
Assessment of Both Parties' Boundaries)
[two signatures]

(Signature of Participating
Person from the Higher Level)
[one signature]

(Signature of Examining person)
[one signature]

22 November 1991

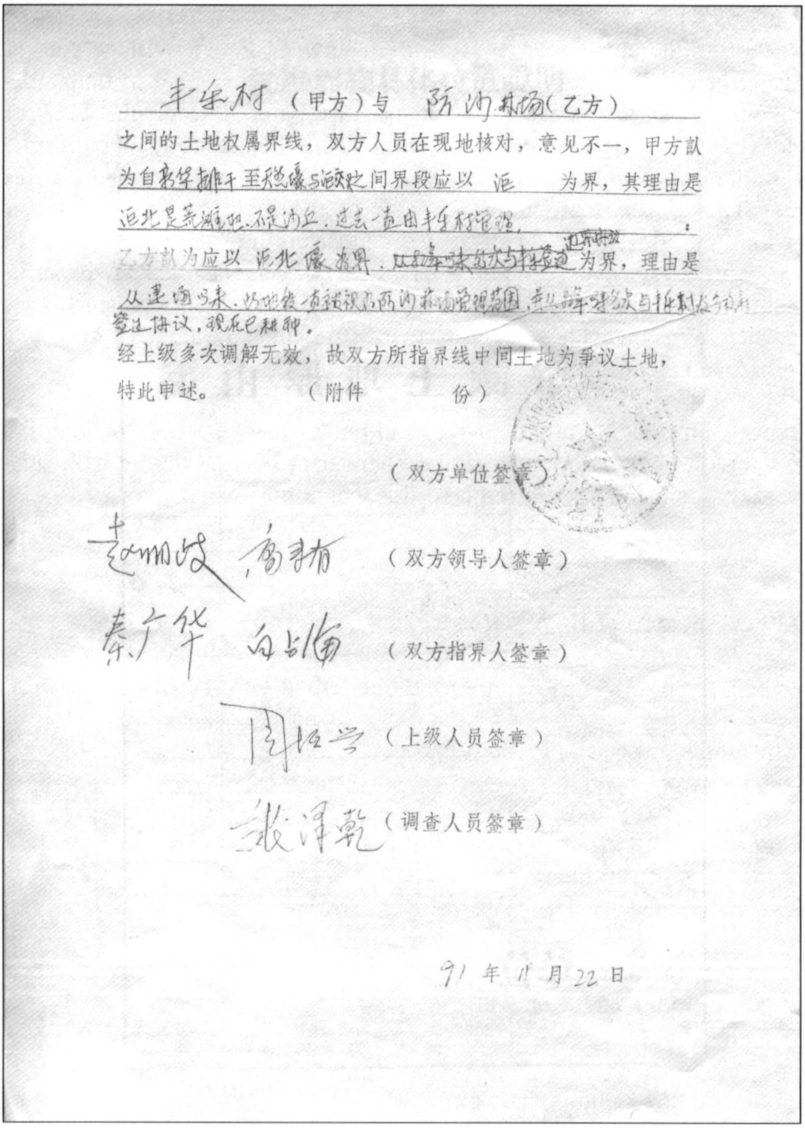

丰乐村（甲方）与 防沙林场（乙方）

之间的土地权属界线，双方人员在现地核对，意见不一，甲方認为自[illegible]至[illegible]之间界段应以 渠 为界，其理由是渠北是荒滩地、不是沙丘，过去一直由丰乐村管理，

乙方認为应以 渠北[illegible]为界，理由是从建场以来，[illegible]防沙林场管理范围，[illegible]协议，现在已耕种。

经上级多次调解无效，故双方所指界线中间土地为争议土地，

特此申述。（附件 份）

（双方单位签章）

（双方领导人签章）

（双方指界人签章）

（上级人员签章）

（调查人员签章）

91 年 11 月 22 日

[Second page]
Map of the Boundaries of the Land Titles
[Map]
[No scale]

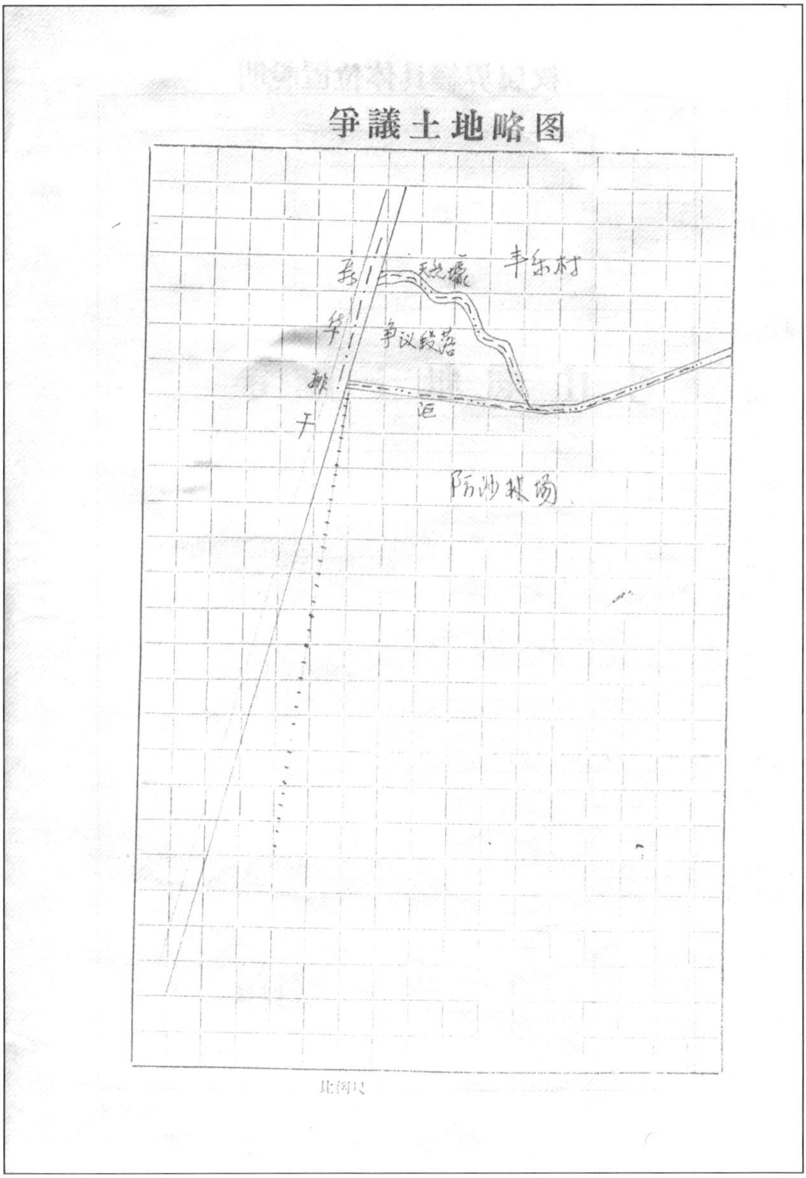

[Back page]

Explanation on the exact location
of the boundaries of the titles

Number of points	Location of points	Location of boundaries

[Table not filled in]

权属界綫具体位置說明

拐点号	拐点位置	界线位置

Appendix C
Title of Land Ownership of a Village School

[Front page]

CERTIFICATE
BOUNDARIES OF THE LAND TITLE

Unit: Primary Village School of Qianjin Village

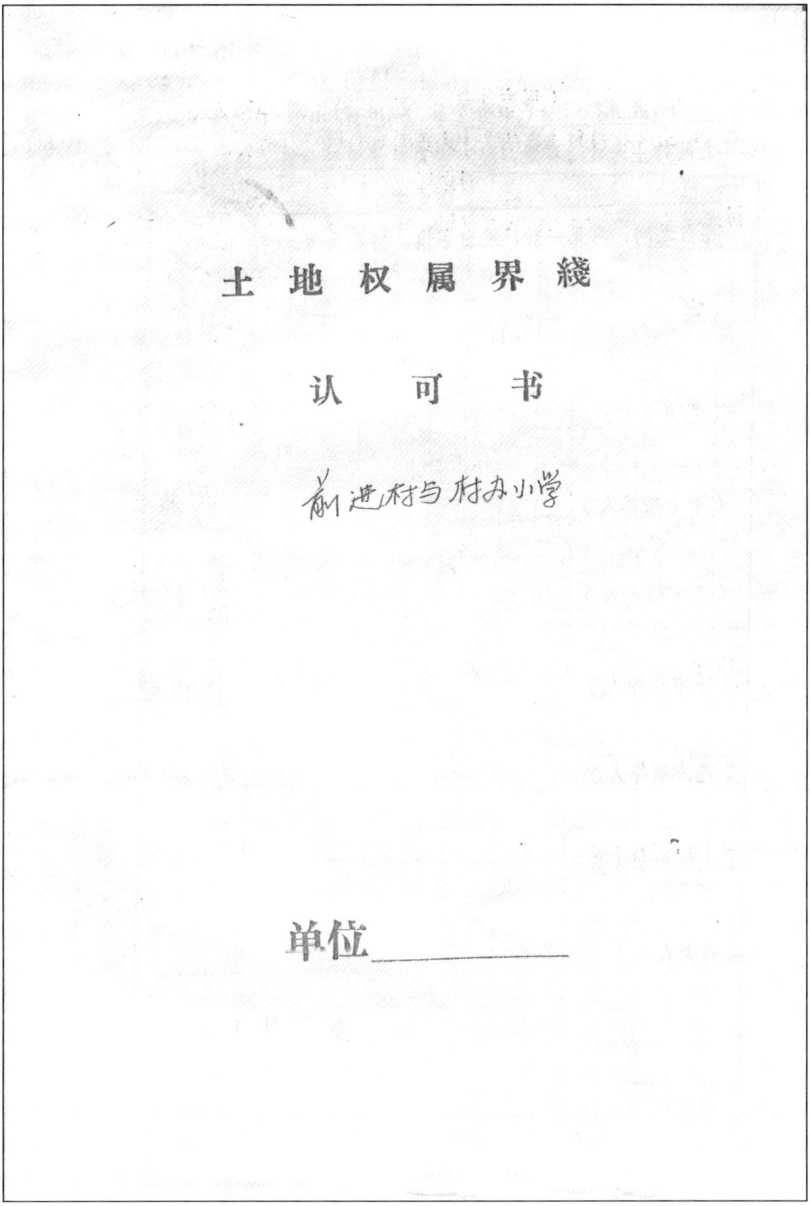

土 地 权 属 界 綫

认 可 书

前进村与村办小学

单位__________

[First page]
Through on-site examination by personnel of both sides it has been confirmed that the boundaries of the land titles between Village Qianjin Village (Party A) and the Village Primary School of Qianjin Village (Party B) run from point [not filled in] to point [not filled in]. This [document] is to certify that the views are unanimous and there are no disputes.

(Party A)	(Official Stamp) Stamp of the Villagers' Committee
(Party B)	(Official Stamp) Stamp of Village Primary School

(Person [charged with] Assessment of Party A's Boundaries)	[signature]
(Person [charged with] Assessment of Party B's Boundaries)	[signature]
(Leader of Party A)	[signature]
(Leader of Party B)	[signature]
(Participating Person from the Higher Level)	[signature]
(Examining person)	[unsigned]
	Year/Month/Day [not filled in]

前进村（甲方）与前进村小学（乙方）

之间的土地权属界线，经双方人员在现地核对，确认自

拐点至

拐点之间，意见一致，没有争议，特此为据。

（甲方）（单位公章）

（乙方）（单位公章）

（甲方指界人）[illegible]

（乙方指界人）赵福林

（甲方领导人）[illegible]

（乙方领导人）赵福林

（上级参加人员）[illegible]兰

（调查人员）

年 月 日

[Second page]
Map of the Boundaries of the Land Titles
[Grid map is empty]

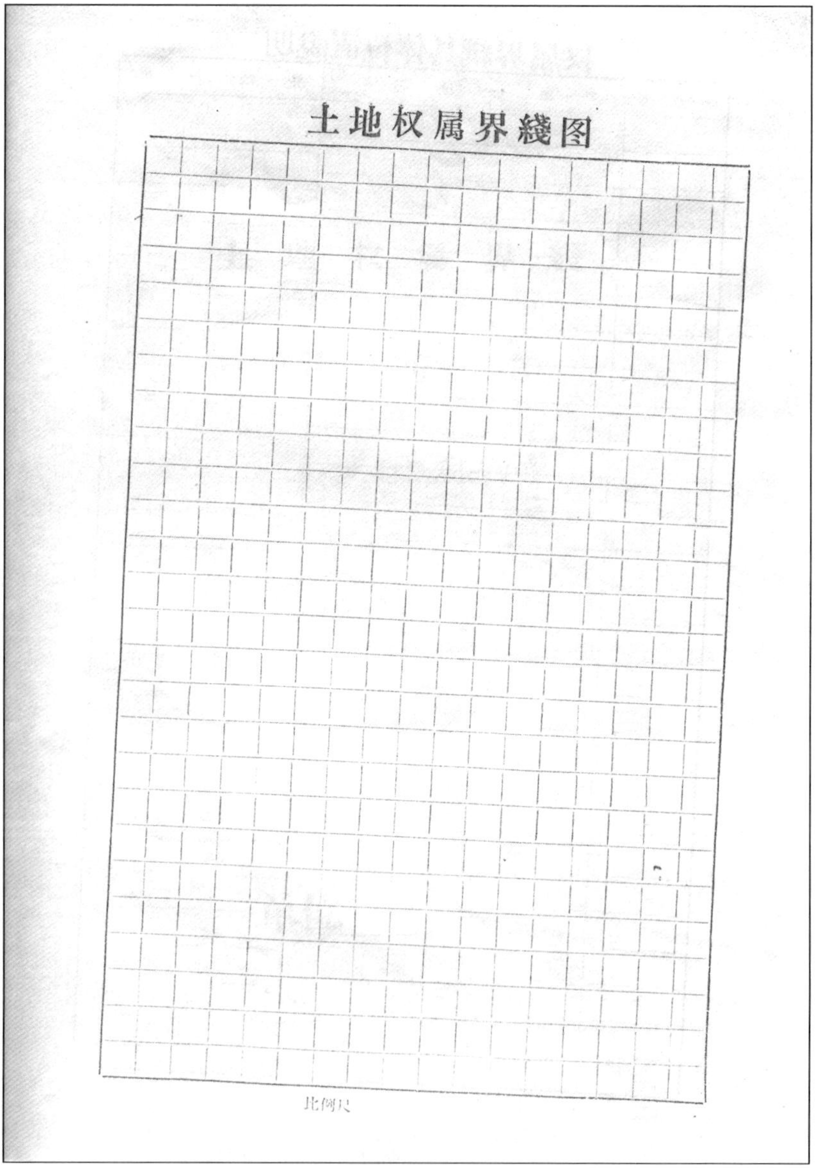
土地权属界綫图

比例尺

[Back page]

Explanation on the exact location
of the boundaries of the titles

Number of points	Location of points	Location of boundaries

[Table not filled in]

权属界綫具体位置説明

拐点号	拐点位置	界线位置

Appendix D
Title of Land Ownership of a Brick Kiln

[Front page]

CERTIFICATE
BOUNDARIES OF LAND TITLE

Unit: Privately-owned Brick Kiln of Qianjin Village

土 地 权 属 界 綫

认 可 书

前进村与村集体砖窑

单位________

[First page]
Through on-site examination by personnel of both sides it has been confirmed that the boundaries of the land titles between Qianjin Village (Party A) and the Privately-owned Brick Kiln of Qianjin Village (Party B) run from point [not filled in] to point [not filled in]. This [document] is to certify that the views are unanimous and there are no disputes.

(Party A)	(Official Stamp) Stamp of the Villagers' Committee
(Party B)	(Official Stamp) Stamp of Village Primary School
(Person [charged with] Assessment of Party A's Boundaries)	[signature]
(Person [charged with] Assessment of Party B's Boundaries)	[signature]
(Leader of Party A)	[signature]
(Leader of Party B)	[signature]
(Participating Person from the Higher Level)	[signature]
(Examining person)	[unsigned]
	Year/Month/Day [not filled in]

前进村（甲方）与 村办砖窑（乙方）

之间的土地权属界线，经双方人员在现地核对，确認自

拐点至

拐点之间，意见一致，没有争议，特此为据。

（甲方） （单位公章）

（乙方） （单位公章）

（甲方指界人） 贺栓

（乙方指界人） 贺玉亭

（甲方领导人） 张德旂

（乙方领导人） 贺玉亭

（上级参加人员） 周拉巴

（调查人员）

年 月 日

[Second page]
Map of the Boundaries of the Land Titles
[Grid map is empty]

土地权属界綫图

[Back page]

Explanation on the exact location
of the boundaries of the titles

Number of points	Location of points	Location of boundaries

[Table not filled in]

权属界綫具体位置説明

拐点号	拐点位置	界线位置

Appendix E
'Second Round' Land Lease for Household (copy for farmer)

[Front page]

Rural Collective Land Lease Certificate of Zhejiang Province

[First page]

Rural Collective Land Lease Certificate of Zhejiang Province

Rural Work Office of the Zhejiang People's Government
[Stamp of the Rural Work Office of the Zhejiang People's Government]

[Second page]

Rural and sub-urban land is owned by the collective, apart from land owned by the state as provided by law; housing sites, private plots of cropland and hilly land are owned by the collective.

—cited from the Constitution of the People's Republic of China, article 10, section 2

Civilians' and collectives' legal lease and management right of collective land and state-owned land in use by the collective is protected by law. The rights and duties of the lessee and lessor are stipulated in the lease contract according to the law.

—cited from the General Principles of Civil Law, article 8, section 2

The land lease certificate is the sole legal evidence of the right to lease land held by the obligee, and is protected by statutory law.

—cited from the Number 39 Document issued by the Secretariat of the Zhejiang People's Government in 1998

[Third page]

Rural land lease certificate of Zhejiang, number [. . .]

After examination and approval, this certificate is issued for the lease and management of land (agricultural fields) by the farm household according to the Notice of the Central Secretariat of the Chinese Communist Party and the Secretariat of the State Council on 'The Further Stabilization and Perfectioning of the Contract Relations of Rural Land'—Document Number 16 issued by the Secretariat of the Chinese Communist Party in 1997, as well as the related Several Suggestions of the Secretariat of the Provincial Party Committee and the Secretariat of the Provincial People's Government on 'Executing well the Second Round of Lease, and Stabilizing and Perfectioning the Household Contract Responsibility System'—Document Number 70 issued by the Secretariat of the Provincial Party Committee in 1997, in order to protect the legal interests of the lease of collective land by the farmer. This farm household enjoys the right to lease to the land enlisted in this contract for [. . .] years, starting from [. . .] year [. . .] month [. . .] day and ending on [. . .] year [. . .] month [. . .] day.

[. . .] year [. . .] month [. . .] day
[Stamp of the People's Government of Longquan City]

农村和城市郊区的土地，除由法律规定属于国家所有的以外，属于集体所有；宅基地和自留地、自留山，也属于集体所有。

——摘自《中华人民共和国宪法》第十条第二款

公民、集体依法对集体所有的或者国家所有由集体使用的土地的承包经营权，受法律保护。承包双方的权利和义务，依照法律由承包合同规定。

——摘自《中华人民共和国民法通则》第八十条第二款

土地承包权证是权利人拥有土地承包权的唯一合法凭证，受国家法律保护。

——摘自浙政办发(1998)39号

浙农包(　)字第　号

根据中共中央办公厅、国务院办公厅《关于进一步稳定和完善农村土地承包关系的通知》(中办发[1997]16号)和省委办公厅、省政府办公厅《关于搞好第二轮土地承包工作稳定完善家庭联产承包责任制的若干意见》(省委办[1997]70号)的有关规定，为了维护农民承包集体土地的合法权益，经审查核实，对农户承包经营的土地(大田)，核发此证。该农户对本证所列土地享有　年承包权，起止日期为　年　月　日至　年　月　日。

龙泉市人民政府

年　月　日

[Fourth page]

Lessee	Household head			Number of people in family		
	Family members	Relation	Surname and name		Relation	Surname and name
	Address	Township (town)		Village		Villagers' group
Full name of lessor						
Number of lease contract						
Contracted area		mu fen li hao				
of which	irrigated area	mu fen li hao				
		mu fen li hao				
		mu fen li hao				

[Fifth page]

REGISTRATION OF PLOTS OF CONTRACTED LAND

Name of plot	Area (mu)	Category	Location (boundaries)

Note: The area must be expressed to three decimal places, the same hereafter.

承包方	户主			人口	
	家庭成员	关系	姓名	关系	姓名
	地址	乡(镇)		村	组
发包方全称					
承包合同编号					
承包土地面积		亩	分	厘	毫
其中	水田	亩	分	厘	毫
		亩	分	厘	毫
		亩	分	厘	毫

1

承包土地地块登记

地块名称	面积（亩）	类别	座落（四至）

注：面积数应精确到小数点后三位，下同。

2

Appendix F
'Second Round' Land Lease for Household (copy for village committee)

[First page]

Form for the Approval of the Lease Right Certificate of Rural Collectives in Longquan City (Inventory per Household)

<table>
<tr><td rowspan="5">Lessee</td><td>Household head</td><td colspan="3">(Signature or stamp)</td><td>Number of people in family</td><td colspan="2"></td></tr>
<tr><td rowspan="3">Other family members</td><td colspan="2">Relation</td><td colspan="2">Surname and name</td><td colspan="2">Age</td></tr>
<tr><td></td><td></td><td></td><td></td><td></td><td></td></tr>
<tr><td></td><td></td><td></td><td></td><td></td><td></td></tr>
<tr><td>Address</td><td colspan="6">Township (town) Village Villagers' group</td></tr>
<tr><td colspan="2">Full name of lessor</td><td colspan="3"></td><td colspan="2">Number of lease contract</td><td></td></tr>
<tr><td colspan="2">Term of lease</td><td colspan="6">From year month day until year month day</td></tr>
<tr><td colspan="2">Contracted area</td><td colspan="6">mu fen li hao</td></tr>
<tr><td rowspan="2">Of which</td><td>irrigated area</td><td colspan="6">mu fen li hao</td></tr>
<tr><td>dryland</td><td colspan="6">mu fen li hao</td></tr>
<tr><td>Remarks by the village economic collective</td><td colspan="3">Signature and stamp of person in charge:
(stamp)
year month day</td><td>Remarks by the township or town government</td><td colspan="3">Signature and stamp of person in charge:
(stamp)
year month day</td></tr>
<tr><td>Examination and approval by responsible department at city level</td><td colspan="7">Signature and stamp of person in charge:
(stamp)
Year month day</td></tr>
<tr><td colspan="2">Signature of managing person</td><td colspan="2"></td><td colspan="2">Number of lease right certificate</td><td colspan="2"></td></tr>
</table>

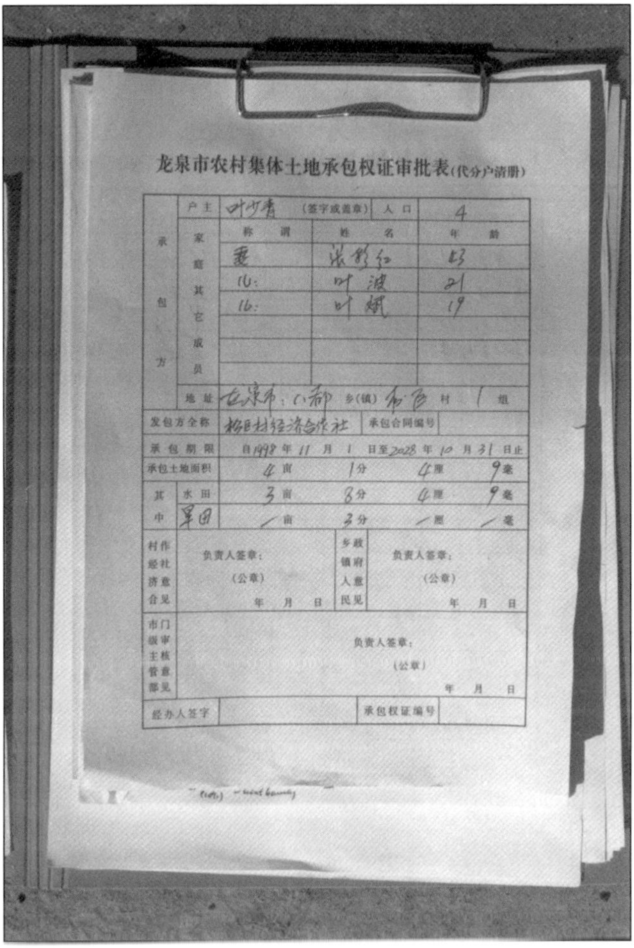

龙泉市农村集体土地承包权证审批表（代分户清册）

承包方	户主	叶少青（签字或盖章）	人口	4
	家庭其它成员	称谓	姓名	年龄
		妻	张彩红	
		儿	叶波	21
		儿	叶枫	19
	地址	龙泉市 乡(镇) 村 1 组		
发包方全称			承包合同编号	
承包期限		自 1998 年 11 月 1 日至 2028 年 10 月 31 日止		
承包土地面积		4 亩 1 分 4 厘 9 毫		
其中	水田	3 亩 8 分 4 厘 9 毫		
	旱田	/ 亩 3 分 / 厘 / 毫		
村经济合作社意见		负责人签章：（公章） 年 月 日	乡镇人民政府意见	负责人签章：（公章） 年 月 日
市级主管部门审核意见		负责人签章：（公章） 年 月 日		
经办人签字			承包权证编号	

[Second page]

REGISTRATION OF PLOTS OF CONTRACTED LAND

Name of plot	Category	Area (mu)	Yield	Location (boundaries)

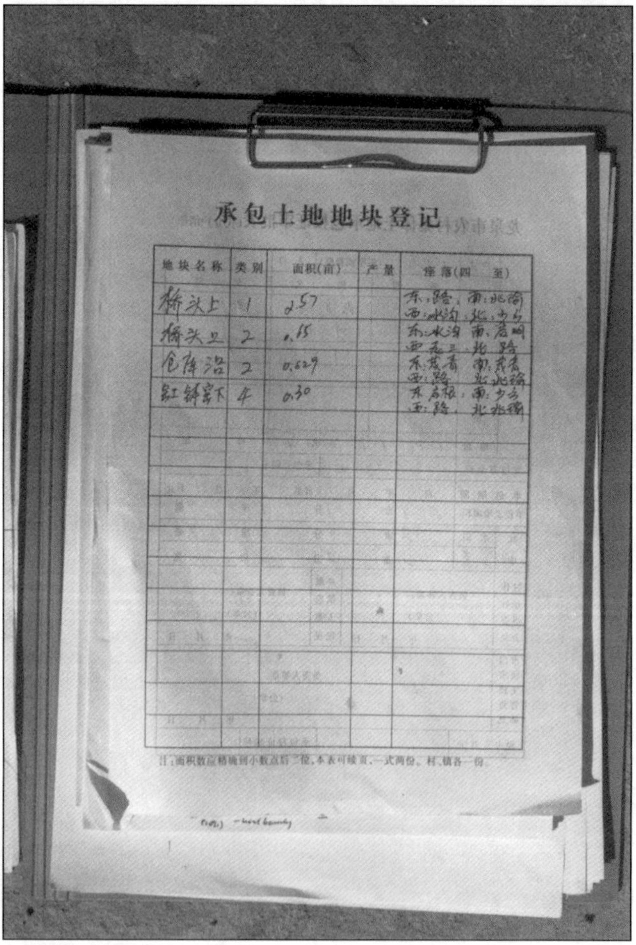

承包土地地块登记

地块名称	类别	面积(亩)	产量	座落(四至)
桥头上	1	2.57		东:路,南:北沟 西:水沟 北:[illegible]
桥头[illegible]	2	.55		东:水沟 南:[illegible] 西:[illegible] 北:路
[illegible]	2	0.629		东:[illegible] 南:[illegible] 西:路 北:[illegible]
[illegible]	4	0.30		东:[illegible] 南:[illegible] 西:路 北:[illegible]

注:面积数应精确到小数点后二位,本表可续页,一式两份,村、镇各一份

Appendix G
Contract of Mountain [Forest] Responsibility Land

Lease Contract for Responsibility Mountain <Complete> Forest of Longquan County Number 018461

Lessor: Xiaoyao Village First Team contracts four plots of collective mountain forest with a surface of 28.8 mu (enclosed table) to the farm household of Qiu Shunbao for management until 30 December 2032.

Lessee: Qiu Shunbao has to observe conscientiously the regulations of the lease, and must pay the collective fees according to the agreement and the higher level regulations.

Representative of the Lessor: Qiu Shunbao Lessee: Qiu Shunbao
Supervising unit:

[stamp of the
Village Committee
of Xiaoyao]
10 October 1990

Enclosed table

Name of mountain plot	area (mu)	Boundaries		Estimated volume of timber
		East	South	
		West	North	
		East	South	
		West	North	
		East	South	
		West	North	
		East	South	

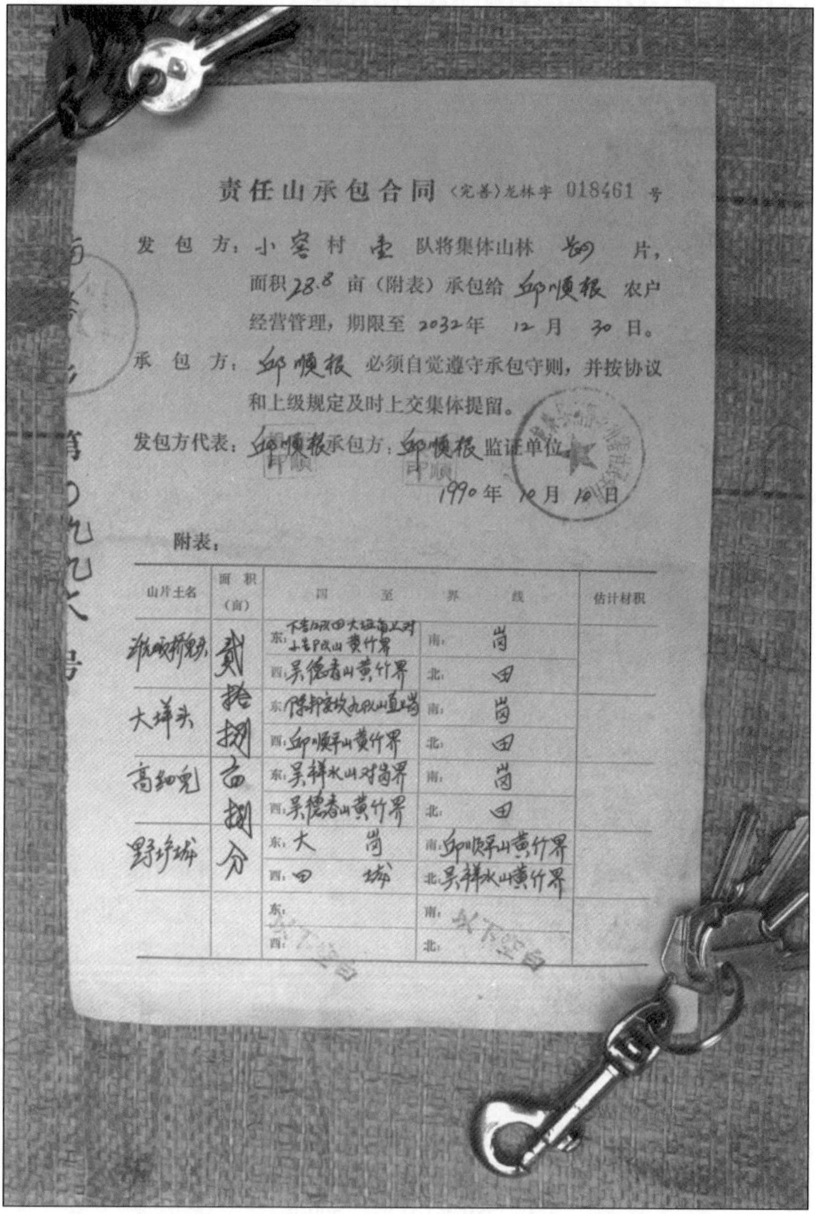

责任山承包合同 （完善）龙林字 018461 号

发包方：小客村 壹 队将集体山林 肆 片，
面积28.8 亩（附表）承包给 邱顺根 农户
经营管理，期限至 2032年 12 月 30 日。
承包方：邱顺根 必须自觉遵守承包守则，并按协议
和上级规定及时上交集体提留。
发包方代表：邱顺根 承包方：邱顺根 监证单位
1990年 10月 10日

附表：

山片土名	面积（亩）	四至界线		估计材积
[illegible]	贰拾捌亩捌分	东：下昔石坑田大坵旁上对上昔P坑山黄竹界	南：岗	
		西：吴德春山黄竹界	北：田	
大垟头		东：陈邦家坟丸坑山直端	南：岗	
		西：邱顺平山黄竹界	北：田	
高细儿		东：吴祥水山对岗界	南：岗	
		西：吴德春山黄竹界	北：田	
野猪坳		东：大 岗	南：邱顺平山黄竹界	
		西：田 坳	北：吴祥水山黄竹界	
		东：	南：	
		西：	北：	

Appendix H
Wasteland Contract of Changcheng Village

Changcheng Administrative Village,
Chengyang Township, Pengyang County

AFFORESTATION CONTRACT FOR 'FOUR WASTELANDS' SUITABLE FOR FOREST

In order to stimulate farmers' incentives to use and develop afforestation on the 'Four Wastelands' suitable for forest, this 'Afforestation Contract For "Four Wastelands" Suitable For Forest' has been specifically concluded, according to the spirit of the Rural Meetings of the entire region and the consultations between Changcheng Village, Chengyang Township (hereafter: Party A) and Villager [Cui Yan], from [Bai Miao] Team, Changcheng Village, Chengyang Township (hereafter: Party B), to facilitate mutual compliance.

I) Content, Area and Location of the Auction

Party A has auctioned the use rights to the 'Four Wastelands' suitable for forest for [area in mu] land, to party B for the use of afforestation (for the category of land, and boundaries refer to the table attached).

II) Term of use, and term of re-vegetation[1] and grassland construction

The term of use is 50 years (calculated from the day the contract is signed), inheritance, transfer and rent are permitted, the term of re-vegetation and grassland construction is one year (the end of 1994).

III) Management of the 'Four Wastelands' suitable for forest

1) Party B has the right to use, management and usufruct to the 'Four Wastelands' suitable for forest.
2) The afforestation of the 'Four Wastelands' suitable for forest should adhere to the principle of 'suited to the soil, suited to trees', and should be implemented by engineering management, namely planning according to the engineering project; construction design according to the planning; check and approve according to the construction scheme.

IV) Rights and Duties of Party A and B

1) The 'Four Wastelands' use right bought by Party B is protected by law, no person has the right to change or infringe on it.

[1] The term *zaolin* is translated as 'afforestation', while *lühua* has been translated as 'vegetate'. The term *zaizhi* has been rendered as 'planting'.

2) Party A will provide Party B with saplings necessary for afforestation for one time.
3) At regular intervals, Party A will inspect and approve the entire plot, the management and protection, and the planting by Party B. If norms have not been met, corresponding punishment will be given.
4) Party B has to use the 'Four Wastelands' suitable for forest for afforestation and is not permitted to use it for other purposes.
5) Party B must fulfil its afforestation duties in time, and the survival rate[2] [of the saplings] has to be above 70 per cent.
6) Party B will strictly control the nursery stock provided by Party A, the nursery stock that is not up to the standard will be rejected, while Party B will be required to provide new nursery stock that meets the standards.
7) Party B has to plant and level the land according to the planning design and demands (standards are attached).
8) One can only proceed to fell the trees that have grown to full size after reporting to the Forestry Bureau for investigation and approval.

[2] The term here is *shenghuolü*, which is less demanding than *baocunlü*.

拍卖宜林"四荒地"造林合同

为了调动广大农民开发利用宜林"四荒地"造林的积极性，根据全区农村会议精神，城阳乡长城村（简称甲方）和城阳乡长城村 白庙 队村民 [illegible] （简称乙方）协商，特订立本拍卖宜林"四荒地"使用权造林合同，以便双方共同遵守。

一、拍卖的内容、面积和地点

甲方将 亩宜林"四荒地"使用权拍卖给乙方用于造林（地貌类别、四址界线附表于后）。

二、使用期限及绿化期限

使用期限为五十年（从签订合同之日起计算）、允许继承、转让、租赁，绿化期为一年（1994年底）。

三、拍卖的宜林"四荒地"的管理

1、拍卖的宜林"四荒地"由乙方使用、管理、受益。

2、拍卖的宜林"四荒地"造林坚持适地适树的原则，实行工程管理，即按工程项目规划；按规划设计施工；按施工方案验收。

四、甲、乙双方的权利和义务

1、乙方所买的"四荒地"使用权受法律保护，任何人无权变更和强占。

2、甲方一次性提供给乙方造林所需的合格适用树苗。

3、甲方定期检查、验收乙方整地、栽植、营护情况，对达不到标准的给以必要的处罚。

4、乙方对拍卖的宜林"四荒地"必须用于造林，不许改作他用。

5、乙方必须按期完成造林绿化任务，成活率必须在70%以上。

6、乙方对甲方提供的苗木进行严格验收，对不合格苗木拒绝接收，并要求甲方重新提供合格苗木。

7、乙方必须按规划设计要求进行整地、栽植（标准附后）。

8、树木成材以后需要采伐利用的必须报经林业局审批后方可进行。

五、奖罚

1、对按时完成绿化任务，质重全优的给予物质奖励。

2、没有按期完成造林绿化任务的，每亩收缴延误绿化费10元，未绿化部分收缴甲方重新拍卖给造林积极的户，但不退还原拍卖费。

3、整地达不到设计标准的每亩罚款1—5元。

4、栽植达不到标准的罚款5—10元。

V) Rewards and Punishments

1) Rewards and awards will be given if the re-vegetation duties have been fulfilled in time and the quality is good on all points.
2) If the re-vegetation and afforestation duties have not been fulfilled in time, a fee for the losses incurred by the delay in planting duties of 10 RMB per mu will be levied, the portion that has not been afforested will be taken back and auctioned again to households that are active in afforestation, whereas the original auction fee will not be returned.
3) If the levelling of land does not meet the designed standards, a fine of 1–5 RMB per mu will be imposed.
4) If the planting does not meet the standards a fine of 5–10 RMB will be imposed.
5) If the survival rate does not meet the standards (except for natural disasters beyond control), a fine of 10–20 RMB per mu will be imposed. In addition, it will be required to replant. A fine of 20–40 RMB per mu will be imposed on those who do not replant.
6) Apart from levying a fee for the losses incurred by the delay in planting duties on those who reclaim and plant other agricultural crops on the 'Four Wastelands' suitable for forest, indiscriminately build houses, and cause soil erosion, punishment will also be given according to the 'Soil and Water Conservation Measures'.
7) If Party A has not provided the nursery stock in time, influencing the timely completion of the planting, then Party A must compensate the losses of Party B.

VI) There are two copies of this contract; Party A and B both hold one copy. [The contract] is in effect since the date of signing.

Party A: The Village Committee of Changcheng Village	Stamp [Village Committee of Changcheng Village, Chengyang Township, Pengyang County]
Party B: Farmer [not filled in] of Team [not filled in] of Changcheng Village	Stamp
Date	28 March 1994

Standards for land levelling and planting:

Stripping fields and counter erosion hills: must be 1.2–2m wide, with a distance of 4m between the strips. Counter erosion ditches with an angle of 15° must be constructed on the fields, which have to be ploughed 30cm deep. Both sides of the field must be level in order to prevent water runoff. Every 5m a small earth dyke has to be constructed.

Fish ponds: must be 80 × 80cm, 50cm deep, in the form of a winnow, the layout in the form of the character '[*pin*]', with 3m in between the ponds, and 3m in between the rows.

Planting: the roots must be unfolded and tightly fit [in the soil], the branches must be straight, the upper [part] must be open[3] and the lower [part] must be solid, the rows between the trees must be regular and ordered, and the saplings must be planted in ten cm of soil.

Designation of the plot	Land category	Area	Boundaries
		9	

[3] I have rendered *xu* (void, empty) as 'open', referring to the necessity of open space for the tree top to develop freely.

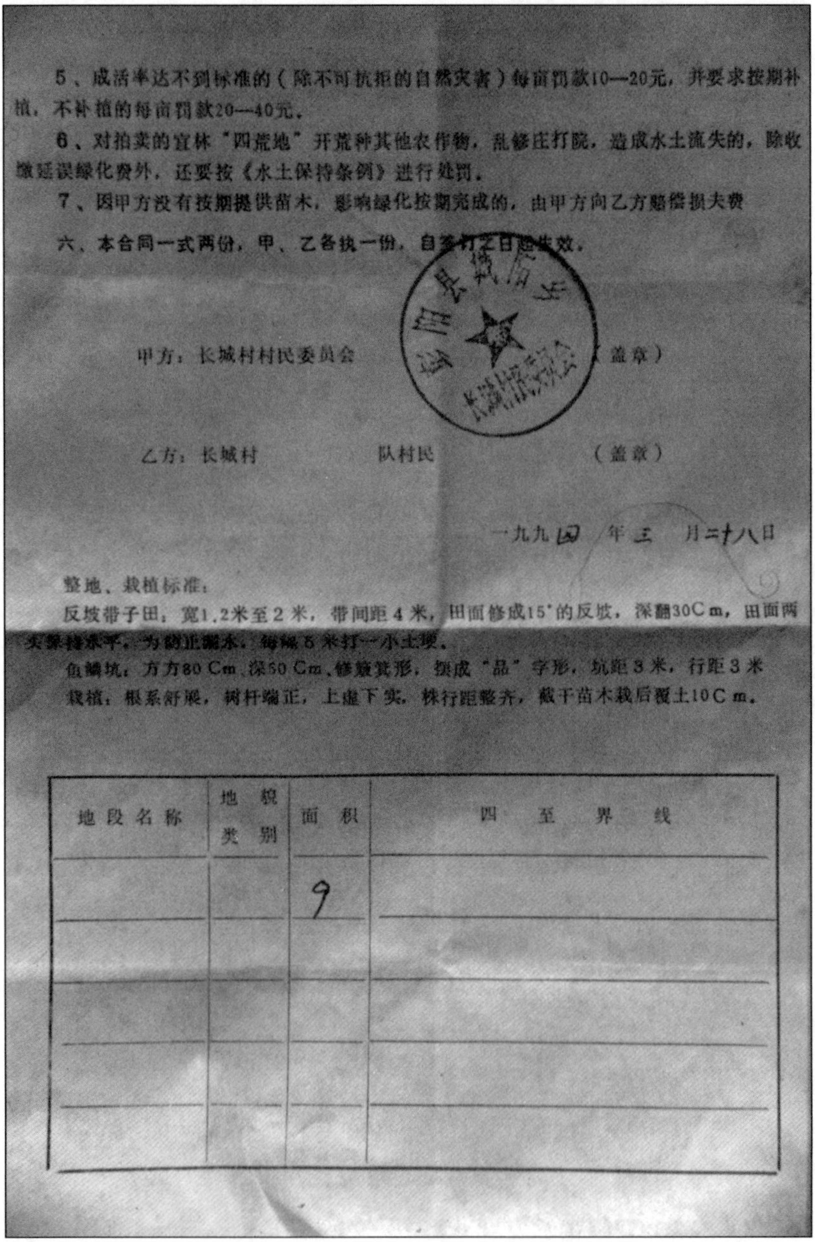

5、成活率达不到标准的（除不可抗拒的自然灾害）每亩罚款10—20元，并要求按期补植，不补植的每亩罚款20—40元。

6、对拍卖的宜林"四荒地"开荒种其他农作物，乱修庄打院，造成水土流失的，除收缴延误绿化费外，还要按《水土保持条例》进行处罚。

7、因甲方没有按期提供苗木，影响绿化按期完成的，由甲方向乙方赔偿损失费

六、本合同一式两份，甲、乙各执一份，自签订之日起生效。

甲方：长城村村民委员会 （盖章）

乙方：长城村 队村民 （盖章）

一九九四 年三 月二十八日

整地、栽植标准：

反坡带子田：宽1.2米至2米，带间距4米，田面修成15°的反坡，深翻30Cm，田面两头保持水平，为防止漏水，每隔5米打一小土埂。

鱼鳞坑：方方80 Cm、深50 Cm、修簸箕形，摆成"品"字形，坑距3米，行距3米

栽植：根系舒展，树杆端正，上虚下实，株行距整齐，截干苗木栽后覆土10Cm。

地段名称	地貌类别	面积	四至界线
		9	

Appendix I
Wasteland Contract of Guanting Village

Guanting Administrative Village
Guanting Township, Guyuan County

CONTRACT OF THE FOUR WASTELANDS AUCTION
OF GUANTING TOWNSHIP[1]

In order to develop and use the Four Wastelands resources, to deal properly with the control of gullies, to improve the ecological environment, and [? most likely: 'to step up grassland'] construction, the Four Wastelands Auction is executed—according to Party Document No. 13/1994 issued by the County Party Committee, and [? most likely: 'the Guyuan Prefectural Party Committee'].

Party A: According to the spirit of the policy, Qianwa village has sold 12 mu of wasteland, with a land price of 4 RMB per mu (in total: 48 RMB) to Hai Qing, for the development and use of planting trees and grass. During the period of use, both parties are not allowed to end the contract without legitimate reasons.

Party B: Hai Qing has come to an agreement with the village to buy from Party A, 12 mu—in the east bounded by Nanmao, in the south bounded by Menxujun [?], in the east bounded by the limits of Liwa, and in the north bounded by the limits of Lühua [?]—for the use of planting trees and grass. This is in effect since the date of signing the contract. The period of use is 50 years. During the period of land use, the user of the land is not allowed to change its utilization. His use is protected by law. No work unit, or individual is allowed to infringe on it.

Signature of the Representative of Party A	Stamp [Guanting Village Committee, Guanting Township, Guyuan County]
Signature of Party B	Stamp Hai Qing
Supervising Authority	Stamp [Guanting Township Government, Guyuan County]
Date	14 July 1994

[1] Handwritten copy, hence the several unreadable sections.

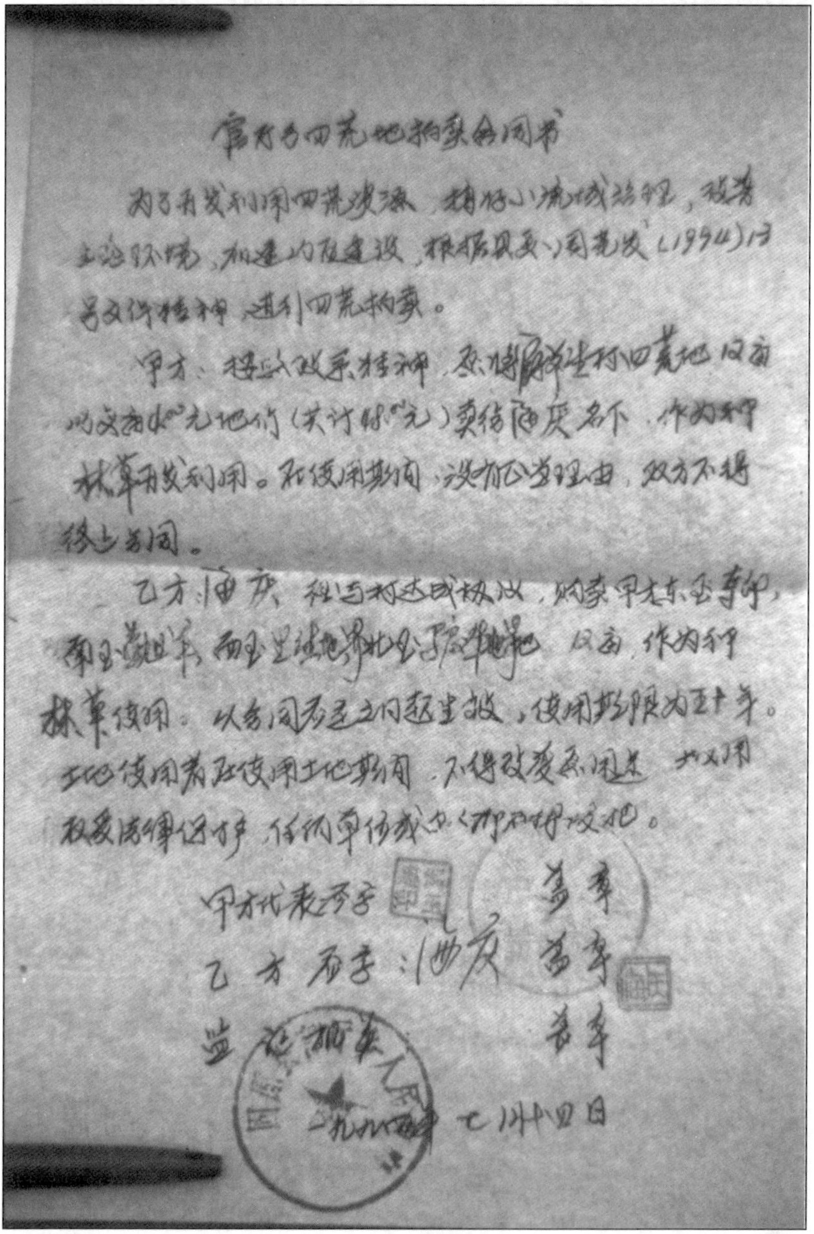

官厅乡四荒地拍卖合同书

为了开发利用四荒资源，搞好小流域治理，改善生态环境，加速山区建设，根据[illegible]发（1994）13号文件精神，进行四荒拍卖。

甲方：按照政策精神，[illegible]官厅村四荒地[illegible]亩，以每亩[illegible]元地价（共计[illegible]元）卖给[illegible]庆名下，作为种林草开发利用。在使用期间，没有正当理由，双方不得终止合同。

乙方：[illegible]庆，经与村达成协议，购买甲方东至[illegible]，南至[illegible]，西至[illegible]，北至[illegible] [illegible]亩，作为种林草使用。从合同签定之日起生效，使用期限为五十年。土地使用者在使用土地期间，不得改变原用途，其[illegible]权受法律保护，任何单位或个人不得[illegible]。

甲方代表签字 [illegible] 签章

乙方签字：[illegible]庆 签章

监证机关 [illegible] 签章

一九九[illegible]年七月十四日

Appendix J
Hand-Written Contract of Village Land Transfer to a Company

Table for Rent of Arable Land from Concerned Farm Households of Qingtian Village by the Vegetable Development Shareholding Limited Company of Longquan City							
Name and surname	Villagers' group	Area in mu	Original grain yield	Name and surname	Villagers' group	Area in mu	Original grain yield

[The column 'Villagers' group' is not filled in, instead this column contains the farmers' name stamps or fingerprints. The column 'Original grain yield' has not been filled in at all]

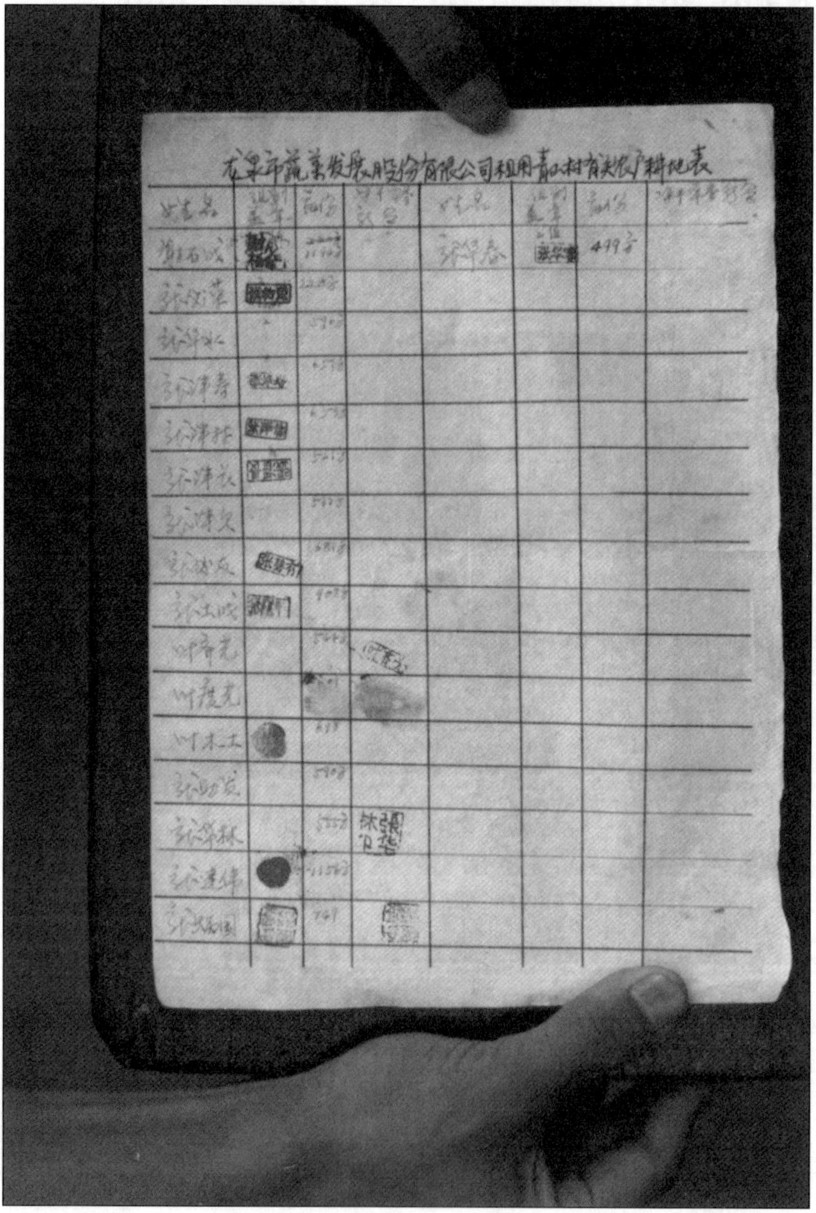

Appendix K
Hand-Written Pasture Boundary Agreement (no map included)

Boundaries and Area of the Pasture of Shangyuan Village

The northern border with Weizhou Township:
From the north wall of the cattle pen of Gaoshugouwan at the foot of the Luoshan Mountains, then 400m into the small moat stretching in the northeastern direction. Afterwards, from the moat to the east along the north wall of the Lala pen, into the south-eastern direction until the crossing of the 1063 footpath along the Yongqing Temple of Shangyuan (in the middle of the footpath of the Yongqing Temple of Shangyuan is a crossing with the footpath to Zhoujiayao).

[etcetera, etcetera, no full translation is given here]

Shangyuan Village
[Stamp of the Village Committee of Shangyuan Village]
20 September 1985

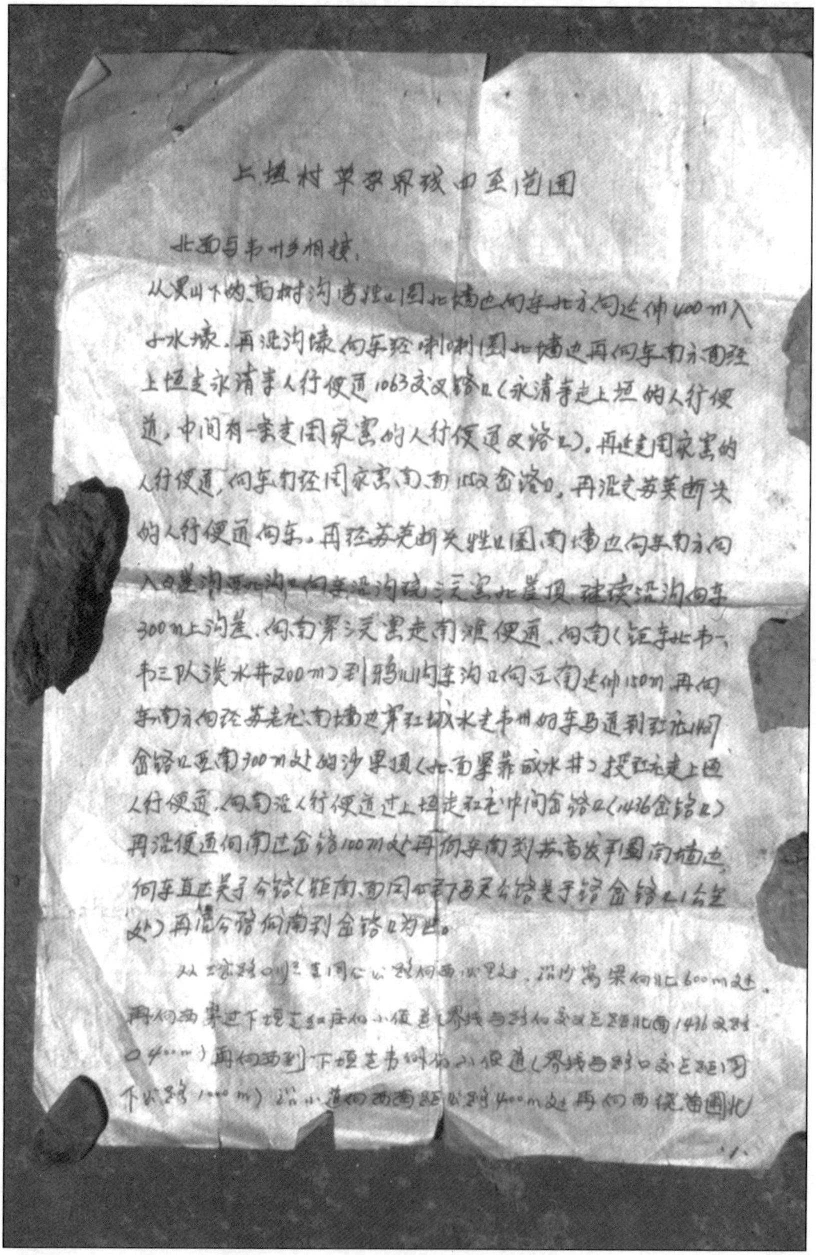

上垣村草场界线四至范围

北面与韦州乡相接，

从罗山下的[illegible]树沟[illegible]园北墙边向东北方向延伸600m入小水壕。再沿沟壕向东经[illegible]园北墙边再向东南方向经上垣走永清寺人行便道1063交叉路口（永清寺走上垣的人行便道，中间有一条走周家窑的人行便道交叉路口）。再沿走周家窑的人行便道，向东南经周家窑南[illegible]1052交叉路口，再沿走苏英断头的人行便道向东。再经苏英断头[illegible]园南墙边向东南方向入白崖沟[illegible]沟口向东沿沟[illegible]三窑北崖顶，继续沿沟向东300m上沟崖，向南穿三窑走南[illegible]便道，向南（距韦北韦一、韦三队淡水井200m）到鸦儿沟东沟口向正南延伸150m再向东南方向经苏老[illegible]南墙边穿红城水走韦州的车马道到红[illegible]交叉路口正南300m处的沙梁顶（北面[illegible]咸水井）按红[illegible]走上垣人行便道，向南沿人行便道过上垣走红[illegible]中间交叉路口（1436交叉路口）再沿便道向南过交叉路口100m处再向东南到[illegible]园南墙边，向东直达[illegible]交叉路口（[illegible]）再[illegible]向南到交叉路口为止。

从[illegible]向北600m处，再向西[illegible]下垣[illegible]（[illegible]1436[illegible]400m）再向西到下垣[illegible]小便道（[illegible]1000m）沿小道向西[illegible]400m处再向西[illegible]北

·1·

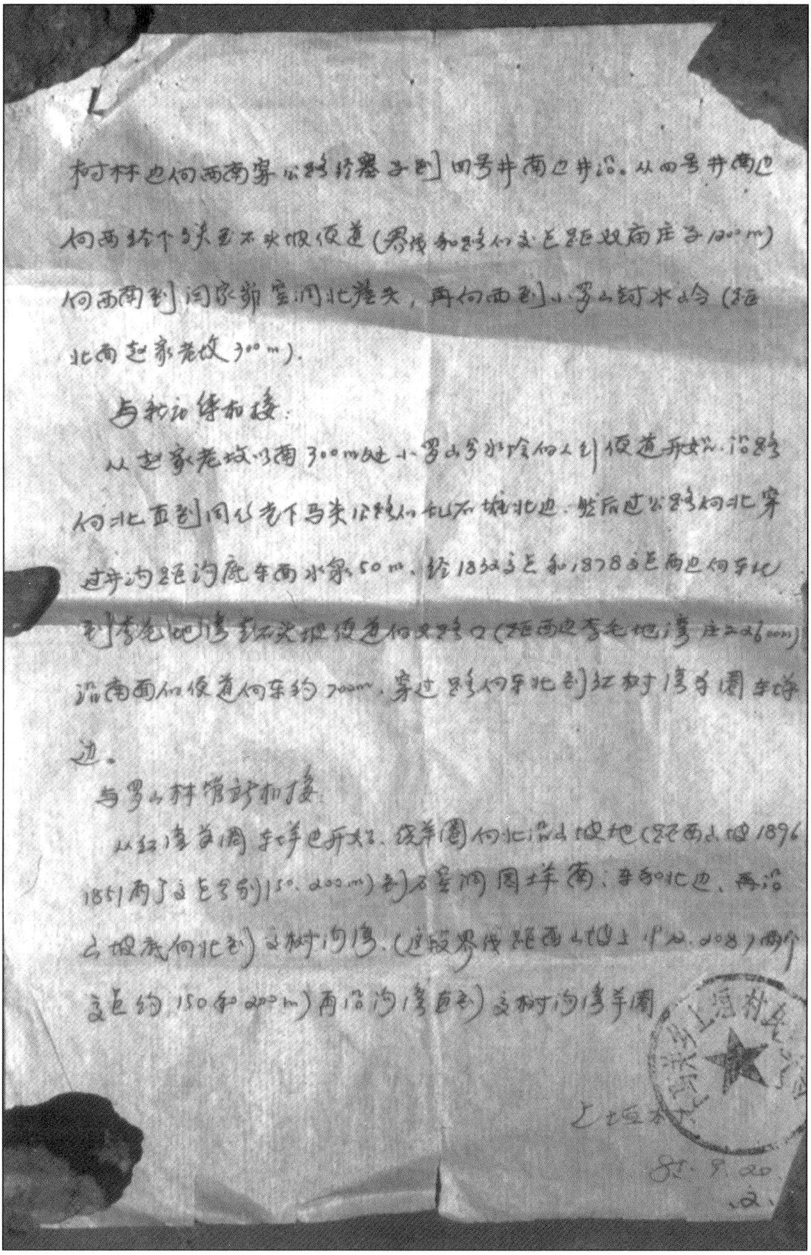

村林边向西南穿公路经塞子到四号井南边井沿。从四号井南边
向西经下[illegible]头至不[illegible]坡便道(界线和路的交点距[illegible]庄子1200m)
向西南到闫家[illegible]窑涧北[illegible],再向西到小罗山[illegible]水岭(距
北面赵家老坟300m)。

与[illegible]相接:

从赵家老坟以南300m处小罗山分水岭[illegible]到便道开始,沿路
向北直到闫[illegible]老下马尖公路[illegible]北边,然后过公路向北穿
过[illegible]沟距沟底东西水泉50m,经18[illegible]点和1878点西边向东北
到李老[illegible]湾[illegible]坡便道的交路口(距西边李老[illegible]湾庄2260m)
沿南面的便道向东约700m,穿过路向东北到红树湾羊圈东墙
边。

与罗山林管站相接:

从红湾羊圈东墙边开始,经羊圈向北沿山坡地(距西山坡1896
1851两个交点分别150、200m)到石窑涧[illegible]南、东和北边,再沿
山坡底向北到红树沟湾,(这段界线距西山坡上1896、2008)两个
交点约150和200m)再沿沟湾直到红树沟湾羊圈。

上垣村[illegible]

85.9.20

[illegible]

Appendix L
Pasture Use Contract for a Village

Note: The following contract was issued to Shangjijuan Production Team as a legal person by the Yanchi County People's Government.

[Front page]

NINGXIA HUI AUTONOMOUS REGION
TEMPORARY PASTURE USE CONTRACT

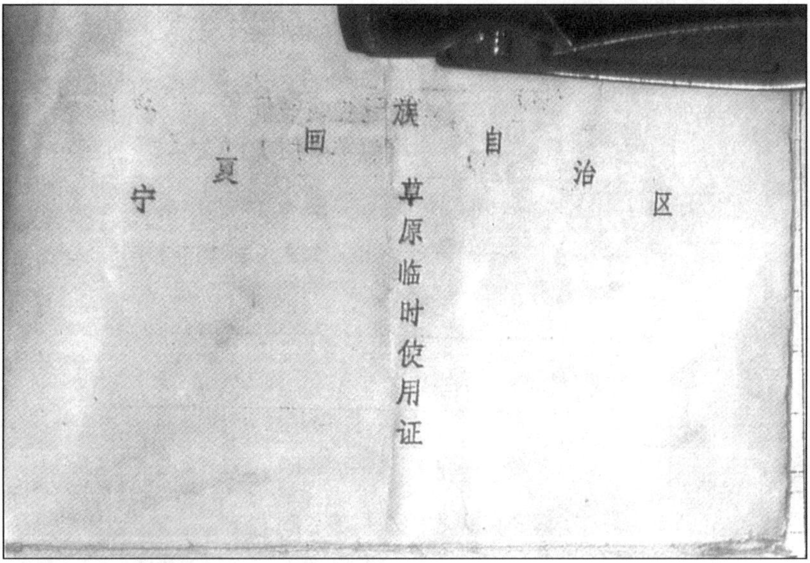

[First page]

Explanation

1. The grassland allocated for long-term use cannot be leased or sold.
2. The using unit must determine suitable stocking rates for the grassland in long-term use, according to the annual grass production. It is not permitted to overstock. The trespasser is punished according to relevant rules and the situation.
3. The unit holding this permit has the obligation to rationally use, protect and construct the grassland.
4. The unit which holds use rights to the grassland allocated for long-term use can lease grassland to households and joint households in order to establish the grassland production responsibility system.[1]

[1] This article seems to contradict article 1. Although not stipulated as such, article 1 implies that the collective can lease grassland on condition that it is not leased to households outside the village.

5. If grassland allocated for long-term use is seriously degraded as a result of misuse or mismanagement, the situation shall be dealt with according to township grassland management regulations.
6. This permit is uniformly printed by the autonomous region and distributed by each county.
7. The section 'remarks' can be used to specify matters such as grassland protection and construction.
8. This permit must be properly kept and should not be lost. Loss of the permit must be reported and is dealt with according to the situation.

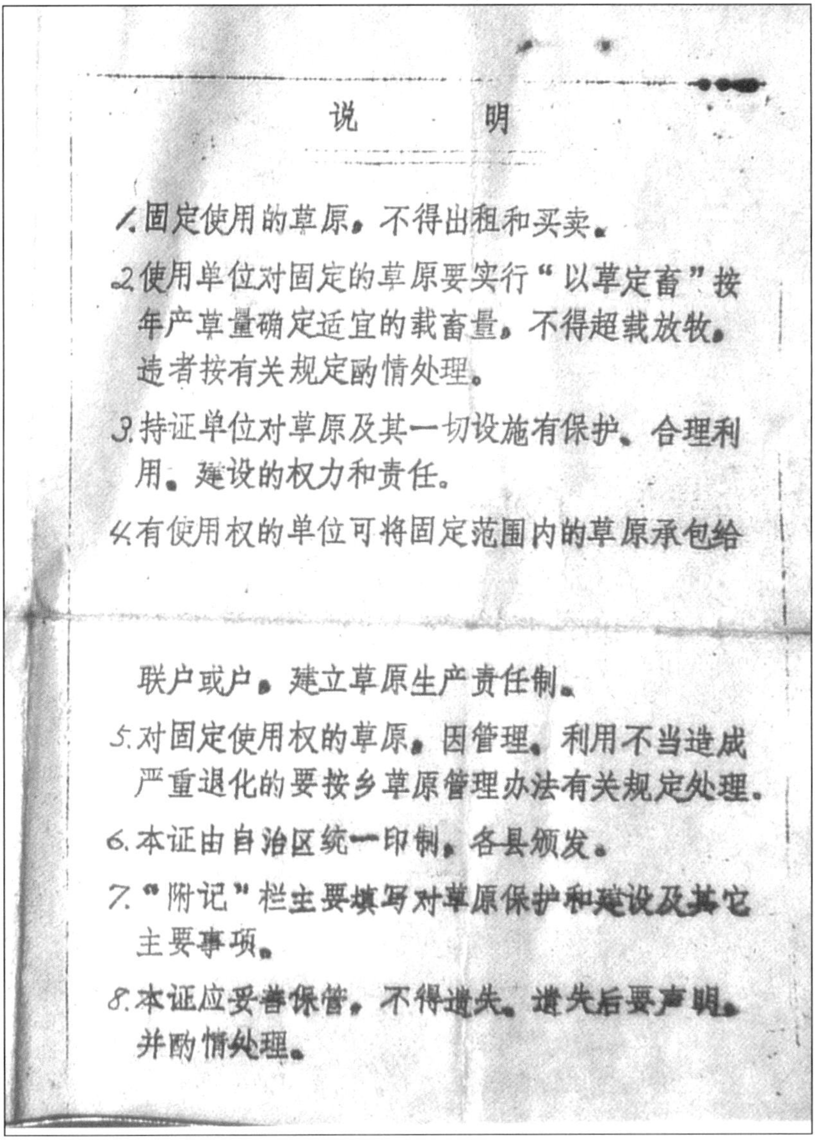

说　明

1.固定使用的草原，不得出租和买卖。

2.使用单位对固定的草原要实行“以草定畜”按年产草量确定适宜的载畜量，不得超载放牧。违者按有关规定酌情处理。

3.持证单位对草原及其一切设施有保护、合理利用、建设的权力和责任。

4.有使用权的单位可将固定范围内的草原承包给联户或户，建立草原生产责任制。

5.对固定使用权的草原，因管理、利用不当造成严重退化的要按乡草原管理办法有关规定处理。

6.本证由自治区统一印制，各县颁发。

7.“附记”栏主要填写对草原保护和建设及其它主要事项。

8.本证应妥善保管，不得遗失。遗失后要声明，并酌情处理。

[Second page]

Position of grassland	Boundaries
East	From the well in the back towards the northeast until marker stone 1462 of Shahui, then towards the west until marker stone 1463 of Gushantang, towards the southeast until Huzidong, towards the southwest until Huzidong, towards the southwest until Wanghuaqing, and in the southwest with the boundary of Yuqiang Team as the standard
West	
South	
North	

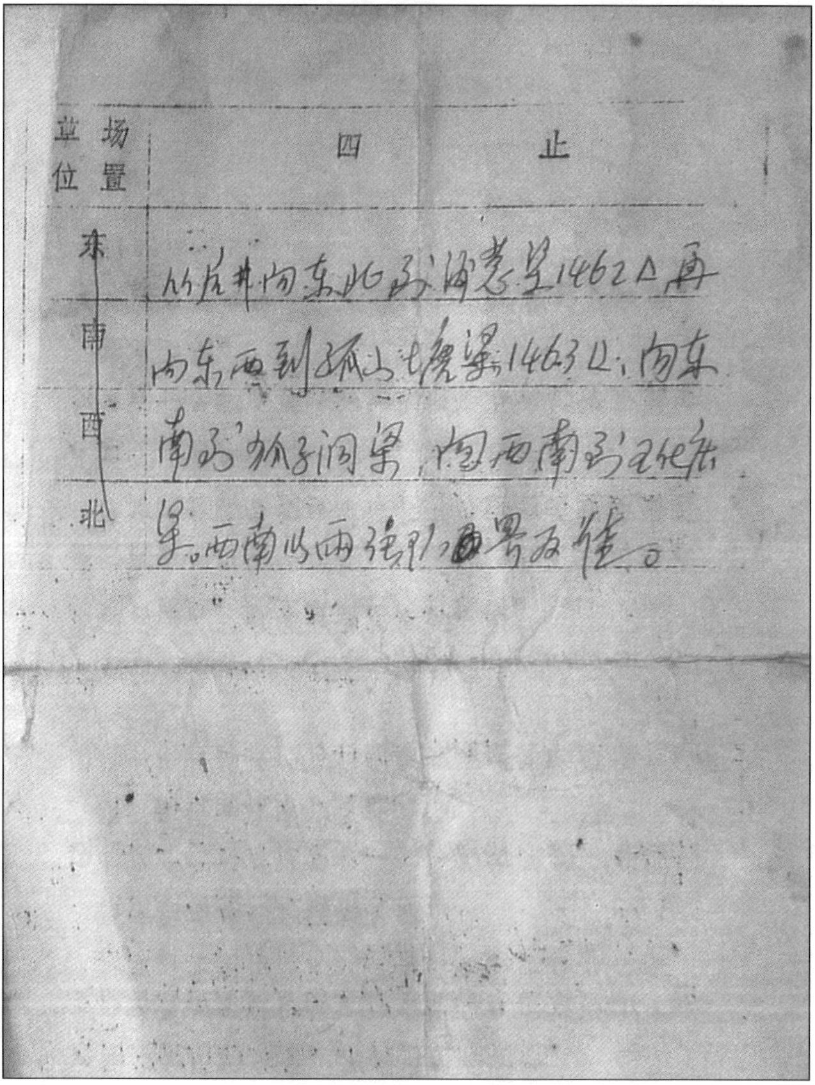

草场位置	四止
东	
南	
西	
北	

[Fourth page]

Usage	Area (in mu)	Stocking rate (in sheep equivalent)	Present construction facilities[2]
Herding	23087.5		

Remarks

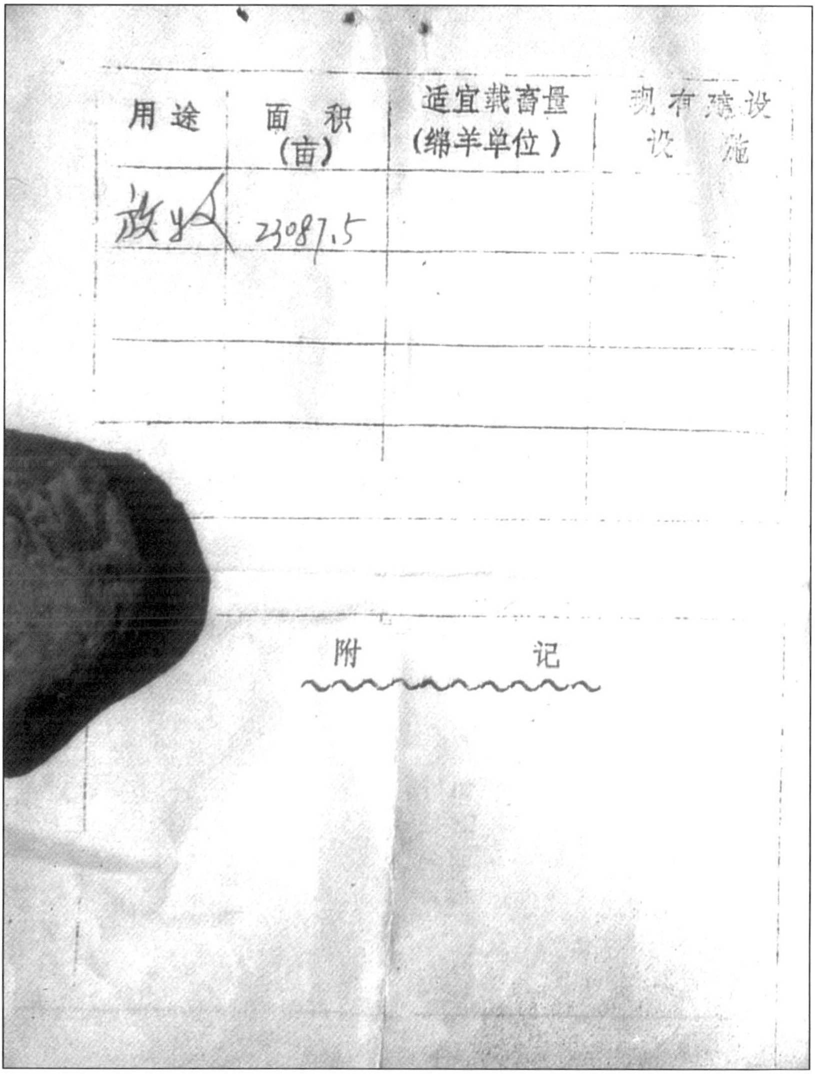

用途	面积(亩)	适宜载畜量(绵羊单位)	现有建设设施
放牧	23087.5		

附记

[2] It is not clear what is meant by this term, but it probably refers to shelter belts and soil and water conservation measures.

[Fifth page]

The Ningxia Hui Autonomous Region, Pasture Use Contract (temporary), number [not filled in]

The grassland as specified in the contract can be used by:

Shangjijuan Production Team, Yuqiang Village, Ma'erzhuang Township

The contract is issued by the following unit:

Seal of the Yanchi County People's Government

Date: 1 February 1984

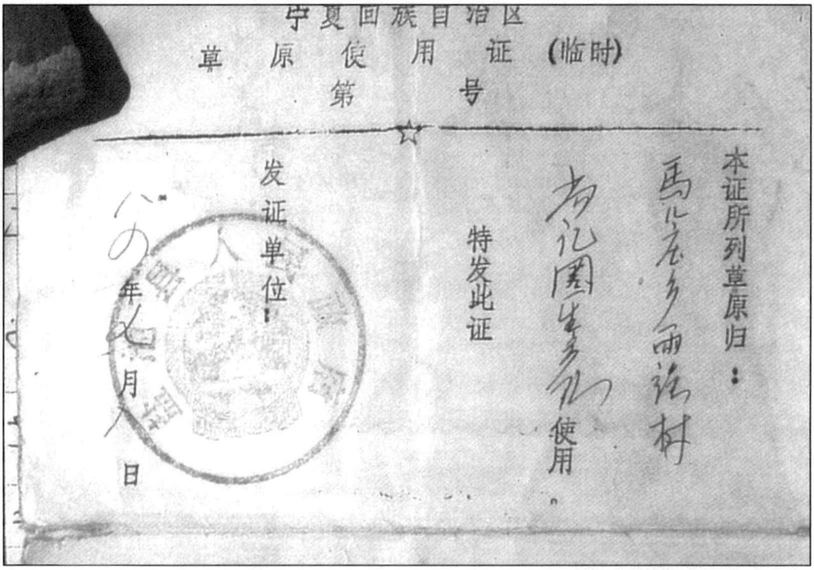

宁夏回族自治区
草 原 使 用 证 (临时)
第 号

本证所列草原归：
使用
特发此证
发证单位：
年 月 日

Appendix M
Pasture Use Contract for a Household

Note: The following contract was issued by Ma'erzhuang Township to an individual farmer in Shangjijuan Village

[Front page]

PASTURE LEASE AND USE CONTRACT

Economic Work Section of the Yanchi County Party Committee

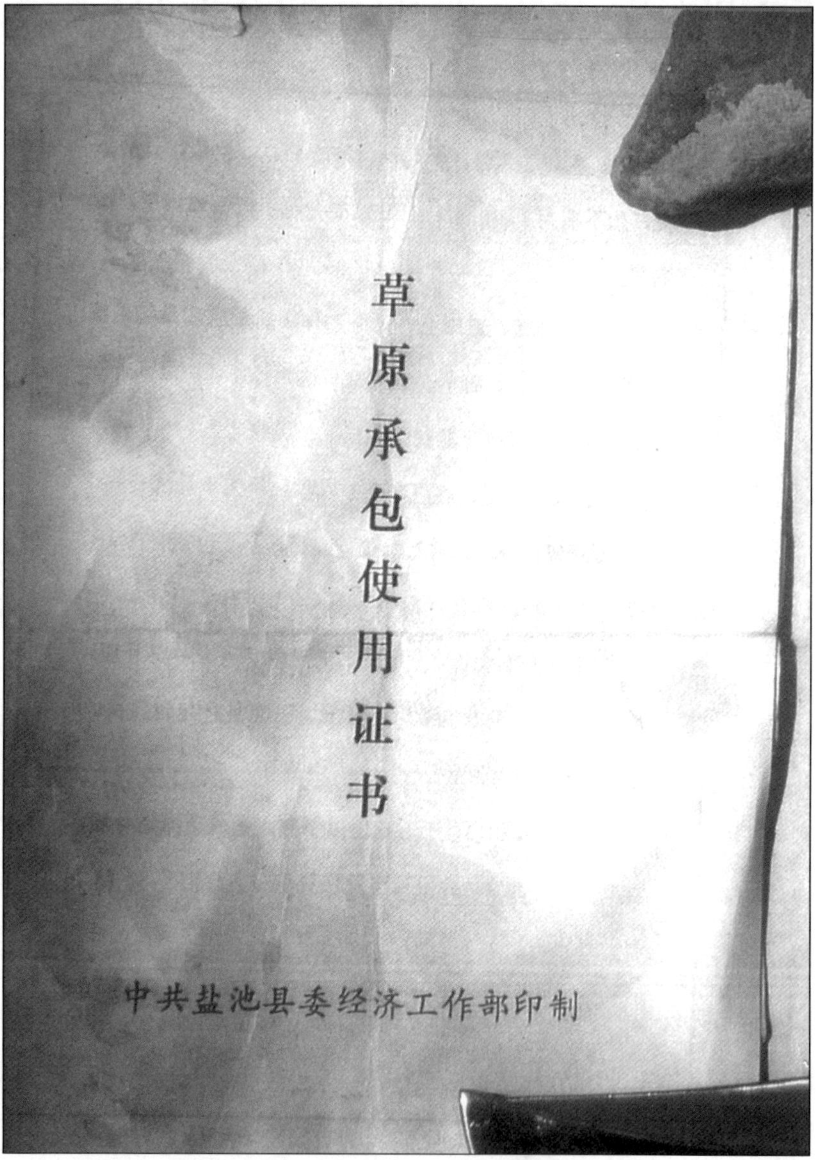
草原承包使用证书

中共盐池县委经济工作部印制

[First and second pages]

1. The person who leases also uses, manages, and constructs grassland for the long term, but is not allowed to sublease or sell it. Those without permission are not allowed to build houses and brick grotto dwellings [on the leased land].
2. If grassland is leased, it is strictly forbidden to practise overlapped grazing, to cross boundaries in order to collect liquorice root, wild herbs, or to water livestock. Recent cases of illegal overlapped grazing must be reported to a higher administrative level depending on the jurisdiction.
3. Planning of grassland use must be coordinated. Grassland construction shall be combined with the management per household (per contracting unit). Shelterbelts and artificial grassland (including resown area) originally present on the grassland must be protected and managed by the using unit. If these are damaged, a penalty shall be imposed depending on the situation.
4. It is strictly forbidden to dig for herbal roots, to collect fodder, or to reclaim grassland. Those who dig and collect are fined 30–50 RMB per offence. Those who reclaim and cultivate are fined 100 RMB per mu, and are required to afforest and replant the area within a given term.
5. If management and construction are inadequate or usage is inappropriate causing grassland degradation, a grassland compensation fee is imposed. Furthermore, the offender is required to restore the vegetation within a given term on penalty of revocation of the use right to grassland.
6. Stocking rates shall be enforced. If overstocking occurs, a grassland management fee of 10 RMB per sheep is imposed.

Grassland usage	Boundaries				Length	Width	Area (mu)	Construction tasks
	E	W	S	N				
	Boundary of Shangjijuan	Boundary of Shang[jijuan] and Ye'erzhuang	Boundary with Er	Boundary with Feng[jigou]	1600	250	600	

Issuing unit: Ma'erzhuang Township People's Government

Supervising unit: Yuqiang Administrative Village Committee

Leasing and using household: Shang Zhong

Time: 30 August 1987

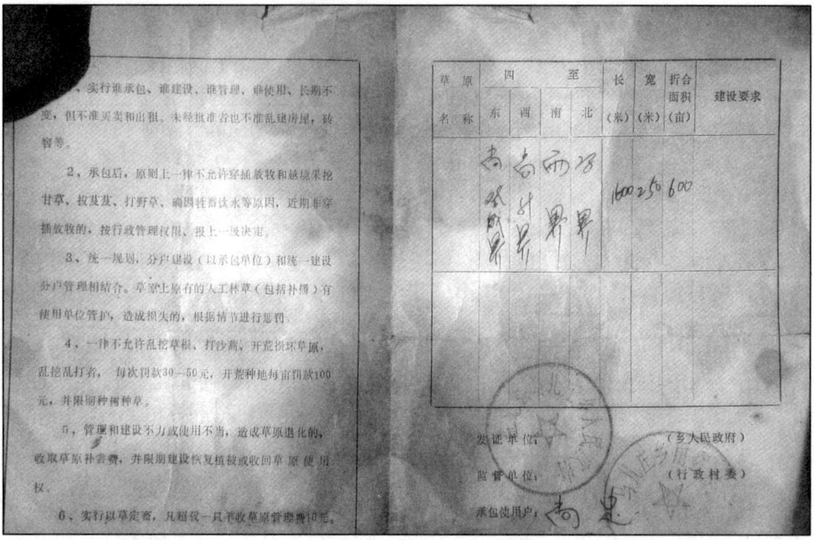

、实行谁承包、谁建设、谁管理、谁使用、长期不变，但不准买卖和出租。未经批准者也不准乱建房屋，砖窑等。

2、承包后，原则上一律不允许穿插放牧和越境采挖甘草、挖发菜、打野草、确因牲畜饮水等原因，近期非穿插放牧的，按行政管理权限、报上一级决定。

3、统一规划，分户建设（以承包单位）和统一建设分户管理相结合。草原上原有的人工林草（包括补播）有使用单位管护，造成损失的，根据情节进行惩罚。

4、一律不允许乱挖草根、打沙蒿，开荒损坏草原，乱挖乱打者，每次罚款30—50元，开荒种地每亩罚款100元，并限期种树种草。

5、管理和建设不力或使用不当，造成草原退化的，收取草原补尝费，并限期建设恢复植被或收回草原使用权。

6、实行以草定畜，凡超牧一只羊收草原管理费10元。

草原名称	四至				长（米）	宽（米）	折合面积（亩）	建设要求
	东	西	南	北				
	[illegible]	[illegible]	[illegible]	[illegible]	1600	250	600	

发证单位：（乡人民政府）

监督单位：（行政村委）

承包使用户：[illegible]

Bibliography

Note: For laws and regulations, the bibliography only provides the book or edited volume in which these were included and not their full reference as cited in the text.

Ai, Yunhang, 'Jiakuai "Sihuang" Ziyuan Kaifa de Zhongyao Tujing' ['Speed up the Important Means to Develop "Four Wastelands" Resources'], *Zhongguo Nongcun Jingji* [Rural Economy of China], No. 11 (1995), pp. 42–7.

Anonymous, *The Role of Sustainable Agriculture in China: Environmentally Sound Development*, Seventh Report for the Fifth Conference of the China Council for International Cooperation on Environment and Development (Shanghai: 23–5 September 2003).

Ash, Robert and Richard L. Edmonds, 'China's Land Resources, Environment and Agricultural Production', *The China Quarterly*, No. 156 (December 1998), pp. 836–79.

Ba, Tu and Lin Tai, *Zhongguo Caoyuan Xumuye Jingji Fazhan Gailun* [General Discussion of China's Economic Development of Animal Husbandry and Pastoralism] (Beijing: Minzu Chubanshe, 1993).

Can, Liu, (ed.), *Shequ Linye Fazhan yu Xiaochu Pinkun de Zhidu ji Anli Yanjiu* [Case Studies in Community Forestry Development and Poverty Alleviation] (Beijing: Zhongguo Nongye Keji Chubanshe, 2000).

Chen, Jiyuan (ed.), *Zhongguo Nongcun Shehui Jingji Bianqian: 1949–1989* [Socio-economic Change in China's Countryside: 1949–1989] (Taiyuan: Shanxi Jingji Chubanshe, 1993).

Chen, Su, 'Tudi Chengbao Jingying Wuquanhua yu Nongdi Shiyongquan Zhidu de Queli' ['Changing the Contract Right to Land into a Real Right and the Establishment of a System for Agricultural Land User Rights'], *Zhongguo Faxue*, Vol. 3 (1996), p. 89.

Cheng, Yuk-shing and Shu-ki Tsang, 'Agricultural Land Reform in a Mixed System: The Chinese Experience of 1984–1994', *China Information*, Vol. 10, Nos. 3–4 (Winter 1995/Spring 1996), pp. 44–54.

Cui, Liwei, 'Caoyuan de Jienan' ['Rangeland Disaster'], *Fazhi Ribao* [Legal Daily] (14 July 1997), p. 6.

Cunmin Weiyuanhui, Changcheng (ed.), *Changchengcun Yilin 'Sihuangdi' Paimai Zhili Qingkuang Jianjie* [A Short Introduction to the Control and Auction of 'Four Wastelands' suitable to Forestry of Changcheng Village] (28 September 1994).

Deng, Ke ,'Tudi Neng Baozhang Nongmin Shenme?' ['What can Land Guarantee for the Farmer?'], *Nanfang Zhoumo* (14 June 2001), p. 3.

Dong, Zhiyong (ed.), *Dangdai Zhongguo de Linye* [Forestry in Contemporary China] (Beijing: Zhongguo Shehui Kexue Chubanshe, 1985), p. 114.

Du, Shouhu, 'Wo Guo Tudi Zhidu you yici Da Geming' ['Another Revolution in the Land System of China'], in Shouhu Du and Xiaomin Guo, *'Sihuang' Ziyuan Liuzhuan: Lilun, Zhengce, Shijian* [The Circulation of 'the Four Wastelands' Resources: Theory, Policy and Practice] (Beijing: Dabaike Quanshu Chubanshe, 2000), p. 6.

Editorial Committee for Party Literature (ed.), *Selected Works of Deng Xiaoping (1975–1982)* (Beijing: Foreign Languages Press, 1984).

Fagui Xuanbian Bianxiezu, Difangxing (ed.), *Difangxing Fagui Xuanbian* [A Compilation of Local Laws and Regulations] (Beijing: Zhongguo Jingji Chubanshe, 1991).

Fang, Weilan (ed.), *Zhonghua Renmin Gongheguo Tudi Guanlifa' Shiyong Jianghua* [A Practical Discussion of the 'Land Administration Law of the People's Republic of China'] (Beijing: Zhongguo Minzhu Fazhi Chubanshe, 1998).

Food and Agriculture Organization (FAO) (ed.), *China Forestry Report* (Rome: FAO, 1998), p. 1.

Gao, Guiying, 'Yisilanjiao yu Ningxia Funü Wenti' ['The Issue of Women in Ningxia and Islam'], *Huizu Yanjiu* [Research on the Hui], No. 2 (1995), p. 57.

Guanting Xiang Renmin Zhengfu, *Guanyu Zhizhi, Zhili luan kai Shanhuang Gongzuo de Anpai Yijian* [Suggestions for the Arrangement of Work concerning the Prevention and Control of the indiscriminate Reclamation of Barren Mountains], Government Document No. 1996/24.

Guojia Tongjiju (ed.), *Zhongguo Tongji Nianjian 1994* [China Statistical Yearbook 1994] (Beijing: Zhongguo Tongji Chubanshe, 1994).

Hanstad, Tim and Ping Li, 'Land Reform in the People's Republic of China: Auctioning Rights to Wasteland', *Loyola of Los Angeles: International and Comparative Law Journal*, Vol. 19, No. 3 (1997), p. 548–554.

Ho, Peter (ed.), *Developmental Dilemmas: Land Reform, and Institutional Change in China* (London and New York: Routledge, 2005).

Ho, Peter, 'China's Rangelands under Stress: A Comparative Study of Pasture Commons in the Ningxia Hui Autonomous Region', *Development and Change*, Vol. 31, No. 2 (March 2000), pp. 385–412.

Ho, Peter, 'Mao's War Against Nature? The Environmental Impact of the Grain-first Campaign in China', *The China Journal*, No. 50 (July 2003), pp. 37–59.

Ho, Peter, 'Ownership and Control in Chinese Grassland Management: A Case Study of the Free-rider Problem in Pastoral Areas in Ningxia, China', in Eduard B. Vermeer, Frank Pieke, and Woei Lien Chong (eds.), *Cooperative and Collective in China's Rural Development: Between State and Private Interests* (New York: M.E. Sharpe, 1998), pp. 205–13.

Ho, Peter, 'The Clash over State and Collective Property: The Making of the Grassland Law', *The China Quarterly*, Vol. 161 (March 2000), pp. 227–50.

Ho, Peter, 'The Myth of Desertification at China's Northwestern Frontier (1929–1960)', *Modern China*, Vol. 26, No. 3 (2000), pp. 348–95.

Hu, Cunzhi, (ed.), *Tudi Dengji Lilun yu Fangfa* [Theory and Methods of Land Registration], Vol. I (Beijing: Zhongguo Nongye Chubanshe, 1998).

Hu, Kangsheng (ed.), *Zhonghua Renmin Gongheguo Nongcun Tudi Chengbaofa Shiyi* [Legal Interpretation of the Rural Land Contracting Law of the People's Republic of China] (Beijing: Falü Chubanshe, 2002).

Hu, Wei, 'Household Land Tenure Reform in China: Its Impact on Farming Land Use and Agro-Environment', *Land Use Policy*, Vol. 14, No. 3 (1997), pp. 175–86.

Huang, Guangming, 'Xin Tudi Geming' ['The New Land Revolution'], *Nanfang Zhoumo* (14 June 2001), pp. 1–2.

Huang, Xiangmou, 'Shenhua Shanqu Nongcun Gaige de yige xin Luzi: Hechi Diqu Paimai "Wuhuang" Shiyongquan de Diaocha' ['A New Road for the Deepening of the Rural Reforms: Research of the Auction of the "Five Wastelands" in Hechi Prefecture'], *Guangxi Minzu Yanjiu* [Guangxi Ethnic Studies], No. 1 (1996), pp. 23–6.

Huang, Zuhui and Yinyin Chen, 'Nongdi Chanquan Jieguo he Wo Guo de Jiating Nongye' ['The Structure of Property Rights of Agricultural Land and China's Household Agriculture'], *Nongye Jingji Wenti*, No. 5 (1998), p. 19.

Hung-yee Chen, Albert, *An Introduction to the Legal System of the People's Republic of China* (Hong Kong: Butterworths Asia, 1992).

Inner Mongolia Law Institute of Social Academy of Sciences (ed.), *A Collection of Selected Translations of the Inner Mongolia Autonomous Region Local Legal Regulations* (Hohhot: Neimenggu Renmin Chubanshe, 2000).

Jiang, Xueqin, 'Stealing the Land', *Far Eastern Economic Review* (7 February 2002), p. 57.

Jihua Weiyuanhui Guotudiqusi, Guojia (ed.), *Zhonghua Renmin Gongheguo Guotu Fagui Huibian: 1988–1996* [Compilation of Regulations on State Land of the People's Republic of China: 1988–1996] (Beijing: Zhongguo Jihua Chubanshe, 1996).

Kung, Kai-sing James, and Shouying Liu, 'Farmers' Preferences regarding Ownership and Land Tenure in Post-Mao China: Unexpected Evidence from Eight Counties', *The China Journal*, No. 38 (July 1997), pp. 33–64.

Kuomingtang, Kung-fei 'Nung-ts'un Jen-min Kung-she Kung-tsuo T'iao-li' Hsiu-cheng Ts'ao-an ['Revised Draft of "The Work Regulations for the Rural People's Communes" by the Communist Bandits'] (Taipei: unpublished, 1965), article 17, collection of Library of Sinological Institute, Leiden University.

Law Implementation Inspection Group (ed.), *Zhongwai Hezuo Jinqingyuan Fengchanlin (Zhicai) Jidi Youxian Gongsi de Youguan Qingkuang* [Situation of the Sino-Foreign Cooperative Fengchanlin (Paper) Base Company Ltd. of Jinqingyuan], presented at the 28th Session of the Standing Committee of the Eighth National People's Congress (31 October 1997).

Lei, Zhizhong, Guo Gang, Yang Hongchun, and Mo Dayan, 'Ningxia Huizu Zizhiqu Yanchixian Caoyuan Diqu Mumin Liyong Caodi Fangfa de Diaocha Yanjiu' ['Research of Methods of Grassland Utilization of Nomads of Grazing Areas in Ningxia Hui Autonomous Region'], in *Ningxia Huizu Zizhiqu 1963 Caoyuan Yanjiu Baogao Xuanbian* [A Selection of Grassland Research Reports of Ningxia Hui Autonomous Region], internal document (Yinchuan: Ningxia Huizu Zizhiqu Nongyeting Xumuju, 1964).

Li, Boyong, *Quanguo Renda Falü Weiyuanhui guanyu 'Zhonghua Renmin Gongheguo Tudi Guanlifa (Xiuding Cao'an)' Shenyi Jieguo de Baogao* [Report on the Results of the Review of the 'Land Administration Law of the People's Republic (Revised Draft)' by the Law Committee of the National People's Congress], Speech at the 4th Session of the Standing Committee of the 9th National People's Congress, 24 August 1998, p. 3.

Li, Changjian and Jipang Yang (eds.), *Zhongguo Linye Wushinian: 1949–1999* [Fifty Years of Forestry in China] (Beijing: Zhongguo Linye Chubanshe, 1999).

Li, Sheng, ' "Sihuang" Shiyongquan Paimai zhong de Falü Wenti' ['Legal Issues of the Auction of Use Rights of the "Four Wastelands" '], *Nongye Jingji Wenti* [Problems of Agricultural Economy], No. 4 (1995), p. 30.

Li, Yongmin, Zhiquan Bai, and Shiling Li, 'Lüliang Diqu Paimai "Sihuang" de Zuofa yu Xiaoguo' ['Methods and Results of the "Four Wastelands" Auctions in Lüliang Prefecture'], *Zhongguo Nongcun Wenti* [Rural Economy of China], No. 5 (1994), pp. 27–9.

Li, Yuan (ed.), *Zhonghua_Renmin Gongheguo Tudi Guanlifa Shiyi* [An Interpretation of the Land Management Law of the People's Republic of China] (Beijing, Falü Chubanshe, 1998).

Li, Yutang, *Caoye: Fuquo Qiangmin de Xinxing Chanye* [Pastoralism: The Newly Established Industry to Strengthen the People and Enrich the Country] (Yinchuan: Ningxia Renmin Chubanshe, 1994).

Lin, Jianqing, *Quanguo Renda Falü Weiyuanhui Dui 'Zhonghua Renmin Gongheguo Tudi Guanlifa Xiuzheng'an (Cao'an)' de Shenyi Jieguo de Baogao* [Report on the Results of the Review of the 'Revised Amendment of the Land Administration Law of the People's Republic (Draft)' by the Law Committee of the National People's Congress], Speech at the 5th Session of the Standing Committee of the 7th National People's Congress, 23 December 1988, p. 1.

Liu, Dachang, 'Tenure and Management of Non-State Forests in China since 1950: A Historical Review', *Environmental History*, Vol. 6, No. 2 (2001), pp. 240–49.

Liu, Jen-Kai, 'The Main National Leadership of the PRC', *China Aktuell* (July 1998), pp. 2–5.

Liu, Jinzao, *Qingchao Xuwenxian Tongkao* [A Continued Encyclopedia of Documents of the Qing dynasty] (Shanghai: Shanghai Commercial Press, 1936 reprint of 1921 edition), p. 1904.

Liu, Shouying, Michael R. Carter and Yang Yao, 'Dimensions and Diversity of Property Rights in Rural China: Dilemmas on the Road to Further Reform', *World Development*, Vol. 26, No. 10 (1998), pp. 1789–806.

Liu, Xinhua (ed.), Xin Tudi Guanlifa Quanshu [Encyclopedia of the New Land Administration Law], Vols. I and II (Beijing: Zhongguo Wujia Chubanshe, 1998).

Lo, Fu-Chen, and Yu-qing Xing (eds.), *China's Sustainable Development Framework: Summary Report* (Tokyo: United Nations University Institute of Advanced Studies, 1999).

Lu, Qiangzhi (ed.), *Xibu Da Kaifa Zhinan* [Compass of the Great Development of the West] (Beijing: Zhongguo Shehui Chubanshe, 2000).

Lu, Renyong, Zhongli Wu, and Zhuang Xu, *Ningxia Lishi Dilikao* [A Historical Geography of Ningxia] (Yinchuan: Ningxia Renmin Chubanshe, 1993).

Ma, Kewei (ed.), *Tudi Dacidian* [The Great Dictionary on Land] (Changchun: Changchun Chubanshe, 1991).

Ma, Qibin and Wenbin Chen (eds.), *Zhongguo Gongchandang Zhizheng Sishi Nian* [Forty Years of Chinese Communist Party Rule] (Beijing: Zhonggong Dangshi Chubanshe, 1989).

Ma'erzhuang Xiang Cunmin Weiyuanhui, *Guanyu Ma'erzhuang Xiang Shehui Zhi'an Jushi E'hua de Qingkuang Fanying* [A Reflection of the Decline of Public Order in Ma'erzhuang Township] Parts I and II, unpublished leaflet (Ma'erzhuang, 13 May 1996).

Mao, Zedong, 'The Foolish Old Man who Removed the Mountains', 11 June 1945, reprinted in: *Selected Works of Mao Tse-Tung*, Vol. 3 (Beijing: Foreign Languages Press, 1977).

Mao, Zedong, *Nongken* [Agricultural Reclamation], No. 6 (1966), p. 44

Ministry of Agriculture, *China Agricultural Development Report* (Beijing: Nongye Chubanshe, 1997).

National Bureau of Statistics (ed.), *China Statistical Yearbook 2003* (Beijing: Zhongguo Tongji Chubanshe, 2003).

National Bureau of Statistics, *China Statistical Yearbook* (China Statistical Press, Beijing, 1999).

National People's Congress, *Zhonghua Renmin Gongheguo Senlinfa* [Forest Law of the People's Republic of China] (Beijing: Fazhi Chubanshe, 1999).

Neimeng Xingzheng Quhua Bianjie Lingdao Xiaozu (ed.), *Xingzheng Quhua, Tiaochu Bianjie Zhengyi Wenjian Xuanbian* [A Compilation of Documents on the Handling of Boundary Disputes and Administrative Divisions] (Hohhot: Restricted Circulation, 30 August 1990).

Ningxia Caochang Zhibei Ziyuan Diaochadui, *Ningxia Caochang Ziyuan Diaocha Baogao*, Neibu Ziliao [Research Report of Rangeland Resources in Ningxia, restricted] (Yinchuan: Xumuju, 1985).

Ningxia Huizu Zizhiqu Nongyeting (ed.), 'Ningxia Huizu Zizhiqu Yanchixian Caoyuan Diaocha Baogao' ['Report of the Rangeland Survey in Yanchi County, Ningxia Hui Autonomous Region'], in Xumu Shouyi Xuehui (ed.), *1963 Huilun Wenji*, internal document (1964).

Ningxia Nongye Hezuo Jingji Shiliao Bianxiezu (ed.), *Ningxia Hezuo Jingji Shiliao* [Historical Material of the Cooperative Economy of Ningxia], Vol. I (Yinchuan: Ningxia Renmin Chubanshe, 1988).

Ningxia Nongye Hezuo Jingji Shiliao Bianxiezu (ed.), *Ningxia Nongye Hezuo Jingji Shiliao* [Historical Material of the Collective Agricultural Economy of Ningxia], Vol. 1 (Yinchuan: Ningxia Renmin Chubanshe, 1988).

Ningxia Nongye Kancha Shejiyuan (ed.), 'Ningxia Zhibei Quhuatu' ['Regional Planning Map of Vegetation in Ningxia'], in *Ningxia Zhibei* [The Vegetation of Ningxia] (Yinchuan: Ningxia Renmin Chubanshe, 1988).

Ningxia Nongye Kanchadui (ed.), *Yanchi Shamohua Tudi Zonghe Zhengzhi Shiyan: 1991–1995* [Experiment for Integrated Desert Control in Yanchi: 1991–1995] (internal report, 1996).

Ningxia People's Congress, 'Ningxia Huizu Zizhiqu Caoyuan Guanli Tiaoli' ['Grassland Management Regulations of the Ningxia Hui Autonomous Region'], article 10, *Ningxia Ribao* [Ningxia Daily] (29 December 1994), p. 3.

Ningxia Tongjiju (ed.), *Ningxia Tongji Nianjian 1994* [Ningxia Statistical Yearbook] (Yinchuan: Ningxia Renmin Chubanshe, 1994).

Nongcun Guding Guanchadian Bangongshi (ed.), *Quanguo Nongcun Jingji Dianxing Diaocha Shuju Huibian, 1986–1990* [A Compilation of Data from the National Rural Survey, 1986–1990] (Beijing: Zhonggong Zhongyang Dangxiao Chubanshe, 1992), p. 329, 437.

Nongye Zhengce Tigai Faguisi (ed.), *Nongyefa Quanshu* [A Complete Edition of Agricultural Laws] (Beijing: Zhongguo Nongye Chubanshe, 1994).

Pengyang Xian Linyeju (ed.), *Changcheng Cun Paimai Yilin 'Sihuangdi' Shiyongquan de Zuofa* [The Methods of the Auction of Use Rights to 'Four Wastelands' suitable for Forestry by Changcheng Village] (28 January 1994).

Pengyang Xian Renmin Zhengfu, *Guanyu Yifa Jiaqiang Linmu Guanli, Zhizhi Daofa Huangshan de Tonggao* [Proclamation Concerning the Strengthening of Forest Management according to the Law and the Prevention of Illegal Felling at Waste Mountains], 1 August 1994.

Pengyang Xian Renmin Zhengfu, *Guanyu Yinfa 'Yilin "Sihuang" de Paimai, Chengbao, Lühua Shixing Yijian' de Tongzhi* [Concerning the Distributed Notice 'Remarks on the Implementation of the Auction, Contracting and Afforestation of the "Four Wastelands" '], Government Document No. 1994/8 (1 March 1994).

Renda Fazhi Gongzuo Weiyuanhui (RFGW) (ed.), *Zhonghua Renmin Gongheguo Tudi Guanlifa Shiyi* [An Interpretation of the Land Administration Law of the People's Republic of China] (Beijing: Falü Chubanshe, 1998).

Selden, Mark, and Aiguo Lu, 'The Reform of Landownership and the Political Economy of Contemporary China', in Mark Selden (ed.), *The Political Economy of Chinese Development* (Armonk, NY: M. E. Sharpe: 1993).

Shi, Wenzheng, *Caoyuan yu Caoye de Fazhi Jianshe Yanjiu* [Research of the Construction of a Judicial System for Rangeland and Pastoralism] (Hohhot: Neimenggu Daxue Chubanshe, 1996), pp. 37–8, 43.

Smil, Vaclav, 'China's Agricultural Land', *The China Quarterly*, No. 158 (June 1999), pp. 414–29.

State Council (ed.), *Guowuyuan Pizhuan Linyebu, Minzhengbu deng Bumen guanyu Tiaochu Shengji Shanlinquan Jiufen Wenti de Baogao de Tongzhi* [Notice approved and circulated by the State Council on the Report of the Ministry of Forestry, Ministry of Civil Affairs, and other Ministries regarding the Arbitration of Provincial Mountain and Forest Rights Disputes], Document No. 95 (17 July 1984), p. 1.

State Forestry Bureau (ed.), *'98 Hongshui Jujiao Senlin* [The 1998 Floods: Focusing on Forests] (Beijing: Zhongguo Linye Chubanshe, 1999), pp. 1–2.

State Forestry Bureau (ed.), *China Forestry Yearbook 1949–1986* (Beijing: Zhongguo Linye Chubanshe, 1992, reprint of 1987), p. 55, 476, 480.

State Forestry Bureau (ed.), *China Forestry Yearbook 1998*, (Beijing: Zhongguo Linye Chubanshe, 1998).

State Forestry Bureau (ed.), *China Forestry Yearbook 1999/2000* (Beijing: Zhongguo Linye Chubanshe, 1999/2000).

State Forestry Bureau (ed.), *Zhongguo Linye Tongji Zhibiao Jieshi* [Explanation on the Indicators of China's Forest Statistics] (Beijing: Zhongguo Linye Chubanshe, 2000).

State Statistical Bureau (ed.), *Zhongguo Tongji Nianjian 1997* [China Statistical Yearbook 1997] (Beijing: Zhongguo Tongji Chubanshe, 1997).

Sun, Jianhong (ed.), *Tudi Quanshu Shiwu Zhinan* [Practical Compass on Land Titles] (Beijing, Zhongguo Dadi Chubanshe: 1998), p. 99, 107, 109, 111, 131, 282–93.

Tang, Hongqian, and Shougu Du (eds.), *Lindi, Linmu Quanshu yu Shehui Linye* [Property Rights of Forestland and Trees and Social Forestry] (Chengdu: Chengdu Keji Daxue Chubanshe, 1995).

Walker, Anthony, *Land, Property and Construction in the PRC* (Hong Kong: Hong Kong University Press, 1991).

Wang, Cunxue, Xiangcong Ma, Mingchuan Huang, and Sheng Li, 'Nongye Falü Tixi Jianshe Jiben Wenti' ['Fundamental Problems on the Construction of a Legal System for Agriculture'], *Faxue Yanjiu*, Vol. 18, No. 6 (1996), p. 72.

Wang, Han, and Jingming Yao, 'Neiwubu Jigou ji Zhineng' ['The Functions and Structure of the Ministry of Internal Affairs'], *Zhongguo Minzheng*, No. 1 (1999), p. 35.

Wang, Huimin, 'Dangqian Nongcun Tudi Chengbao Jingying Guanli de Xianzhuang ji Wenti' ['The Present Situation and Problems facing the Management and Administration of Rural Land Lease'], *Zhongguo Nongcun Guancha*, No. 5 (1998), pp. 56–7.

Wang, Kuilong, Shang Lisheng, and Zhang Xiuzhi (eds.), *Heilongjiangsheng Shishi 'Zhonghua Renmin Gongheguo Caoyuanfa' Tiaoli Yiyi* [An Interpretation of the Grassland Regulations of Heilongjiang according to the 'National Grassland Law'] (Harbin: Heilongjiang Renda Nonglin Bangongshi, internal publication, 1994).

Wang, Liming (ed.), *Zhongguo Wuquanfa Cao'an Jianyigao ji Shuoming* [Proposed Draft and Discussion of the China Property Law] (Beijing: Zhongguo Fazhi Chubanshe, 2001).

Wang, Wenxue, 'Paimai "Sihuang" Zhishan Zhifu—Shanxi Sheng Pinkun Shanqu Paimai "Sihuang" Shiyongquan de Shijian yu Sikao' ['Auctioning

"Four Wastelands": Harness the Mountains, Extend Wealth—Reflections and Practice on the Auction of Use Rights to the "Four Wastelands" in the Poor Mountainous Area of Shanxi Province'], *Nongye Jingji Wenti* [Problems of Agricultural Economy], No. 8 (1994), p. 21.

Wang, Xiyu, 'Huangshan Kaifa Zhili Zhong de Zhidu, Zhengce he Nonghu Xingwei—Shanxi Sheng Lüliang Diqu Paimai "Sihuangdi" Ge'an Yanjiu' ['System, Policy and Behaviour of Rural Households within the Control and Development of Barren Mountains—A Case Study of the Auction of "Four Wastelands" in Lüliang Prefecture in Shanxi Province'], *Zhongguo Nongcun Jingji* [Rural Economy of China], No. 11 (1994), pp. 4–5.

Wu, Fuqing, and Kangtai Cao (eds.), *Zhonghua Renmin Gongheguo Senlinfa Shiyi* [An Interpretation of the Forest Law of the People's Republic of China] (Beijing: Falü Chubanshe, 1998).

Wu, Yan, 'Ren bu zi zhi, Tian zhi Ren' ['If Man Cannot Control, He will be Governed by Heaven'] *Nongmin Ribao* (23 June 1993), p. 1.

Wu, Ziping and Alan W. Kirke, 'An Assessment of Some Key Chinese Agricultural Statistics', *China Information*, Vol. 9, No. 1 (Summer 1994), p. 42–76.

Xiang, Hongyi (ed.), Tudi Quequan Shiyong Shouce [A Practical Manual for the Assessment of Land Title] (Beijing: Zhongguo Dadi Chubanshe, 1996), p. 110.

Xiang, Zhongyang, 'Guanyu "Zhonghua Renmin Gongheguo Tudi Guanlifa (Cao'an)" de Shuoming' [Explanation on the 'Land Administration Law of the People's Republic of China'], speech at the 15th Session of the Standing Committee of the 6th National People's Congress, 15 March 1986, p. 2.

Xiong, Datong (ed.), *Zhongguo Jindai Linyeshi* [A History of Forestry in Modern China] (Beijing: Zhongguo Linye Chubanshe, 1989).

Xu, Feng, 'Gufen Hezuo yu Nongye Tudi Zhidu Gaige' ['Shareholding Cooperatives and the Reform of the Agricultural Land System'], *Nongye Jingji Wenti*, No. 5 (1998), p. 22.

Yanchi Caodi Nongye Xitong Yanjiu Ketizu (ed.), *Ningxia Yanchi Caodi Nongye Xitong Yanjiu* [Research on Grassland Agricultural Systems of Yanchi, Ningxia] (Lanzhou: Gansu Kexue Jishu Chubanshe, 1992).

Yang, Hongchun, 'Ningxia Huizu Zizhiqu Caodi Ruogan Tedian Ji Qi Liyong' ['Some Special Traits of Grassland in Ningxia Hui Autonomous Region and Its Utilization'], in Xumu Shouyi Xuehui (ed.), *1963 Huilun Wenji* [Abstracts of the Discussion Meeting of 1963] Internal Document (Yinchuan: Xumu Shouyi Xuehui, 1964).

Yang, Hongkui, 'Contract Dispute of Taiwanese Hou Ren Shou accusing Liu Yi of transferring Contract Management Rights over Hilly Lands owned by the Countryside Collective Economic Organization', *China Law*, Vol. 18, No. 1 (March 1999), pp. 89–90.

Yang, Wenzhi and Cunzu Yu (eds.), *Huangtu Gaoyuan Quyu Zhili yu Pingjia* [Evaluation and Control of the Loess Plateau Region] (Beijing: Kexue Chubanshe, 1992).

Yin, Runsheng, 'Forestry and the Environment in China: The Current Situation and Strategic Choices', *World Development*, Vol. 26, No. 12 (1998), p. 2159.

Yuan, Xiang (ed.), *Zhongguo Nianjian Di Yi Hui* [China Yearbook No. 1] (Shanghai: Commercial Press Ltd., 1924).

Zhan, Jianli, Caoyuanchu and Caoyuan (ed.), ' "Caoyuanfa" Zhishi Jiangzuo' ['Intellectual Discussion about the Grassland Law'], *Xinjiang Xumuye: Zengkan* [Animal Husbandry in Xinjiang: Special Issue] (1995), p. 40.

Zhang, Lei, and Hongxiang Wang (eds.), *Zhongguo Linye Falü Shiyong Shouce* [A Practical Manual for China's Forestry Laws] (Beijing: Zhongguo Linye Chubanshe, 2000).

Zhang, Linxiu, Jikun Huang, and Scott Rozelle, *Land Management, Tenure and Ownership Policies: Land Policy and Land Use in China*, Workshop on Agricultural Policies in China (OECD Headquarters, 12–13 December 1996, restricted).

Zhang, Peichang, Guofan Shao, Guang Zhao, Dennis C. Le Master, George R. Parker, John B. Dunning Jr, and Qinglin Li, 'China's Forest Policy for the 21st Century', *Science*, Vol. 288 (23 June 2000), pp. 2135–6.

Zhang, Shuchen, 'Guanyu "Sihuang" Paimai de Diaocha yu Sikao' ['Research and Reflections about the Auction of the "Four Wastelands" '], *Jingji, Shehui* [Economy, Society], No. 2 (1997), pp. 49–52.

Zhang, Xiaohua and Yu Li (eds.), *Zhongguo Tudi Guanli Shiwu Quanshu* [Practical Encyclopedia of China's Land Administration] (Beijing: Zhongguo Dadi Chubanshe, 1997), pp. 1414–15.

Zhang, Yaoqi, 'Costs of Plans vs Costs of Markets: Reforms in China's State-Owned Forest Management', *Development Policy Review*, Vol. 18 (2000), p. 291.

Zhang, Yaoqi, Guangcui Dai, Heyu Huang, Fanwen Kong, Zhiwei Tian, Xuan Wang, and Lei Zhang, 'The Forest Sector in China: Towards a Market Economy', in Matti Palo and Jussi Uusivuori (eds.), *World Forests, Society and Environment* (London: Kluwer Academic Publishers, 1999).

Zhang, Yaoqi, Jussi Uusivuori, and Jari Kuuluvainen, 'Impacts of Economic Reforms on Rural Forestry in China', *Forest Policy and Economics*, No. 1 (2000), p. 27.

Zhonggong Guyuan Diqu Weiyuanhui Bangongshi (ed.), *Guyuan Diqu Nongcun Gongzuo Huiyi Cailiao Huibian* [Proceedings of the Rural Work Meeting of Guyuan Prefecture] (January 1994), p. 6.

Zhonggong Guyuan Diwei (ed.), *Guanyu Yinfa Diwei Shuji Rui Cunzhang, Xingshu Fuzhuanyuan Tai Weimin Zai Paimai 'Sihuangdi' Xianchang Huiyi Shang Jianghua de Tongzhi* [Notice of the Speech delivered at the Occasion of the Auction of the 'Four Wastelands' by Prefectural Party Secretary Rui Cunzhang and Deputy Prefect Tai Weimin], Party Document No. 1994/28, p. 3.

Zhonggong Guyuan Diwei (ed.), *Guyuan Xingzheng Gongshu Guanyu Paimai 'Sihuangdi' Shiyongquan Ruogan Zhengce Guiding* [Some Policy Regulations concerning the Auction of Use Rights to the 'Four Wastelands'—the Guyuan Communist Party Committee and the Administrative Office], Party Document No. 1994/20 (1994).

Zhonggong Guyuan Diwei Nonggongbu (ed.), *Nanbu Fangkai Wenjian Xuanbian* [A Selection of Documents on the Opening Up of the South] (restricted, 1994).

Zhonggong Zhongyang Bangongting (ed.), Zhonggong Zhongyang Bangongting, Guowuyuan Bangongting guanyu Jinyibu Wending he Wanshan Nongcun Tudi Chengbao Guanxi de Tongzhi [Notice by the Central Secretariat of the CCP and the Secretariat of the State Council on the Further Stabilization and Perfectioning of the Contract Relations of Rural Land], No. 16 (1997).

Zhongguo Falü Chubanshe (ed.), *Zhonghua Renmin Gongheguo Cunmin Weiyuanhui Zuzhifa* [The Organic Law on the Villagers' Committee of the People's Republic of China], 4 November 1998 (Beijing: Zhongguo Falü Chubanshe, 1998).

Zhongguo Falü Chubanshe (ed.), *Zhonghua Renmin Gongheguo Xianfa* [The Constitution of the People's Republic of China, 4 December 1982] (Beijing: Zhongguo Falü Chubanshe, 1999).

Zhongguo Falü Nianjian Bianji Weiyuanhui (ed.), *Zhongguo Falü Nianjian 1997* [China Legal Yearbook 1997] (Beijing: Zhongguo Falü Nianjianshe, 1997).

Zhongguo Renmin Jiefangjun Guofang Daxue Dangshi Yanjiushi (ZRJGDDY) (ed.), *Zhonggong Dangshi Jiaoxue Cankao Ziliao* [Reference and Educational Material on the History of the CCP], Vol. 23 (Beijing: Guofang Daxue Chubanshe, 1986).

Zhongguo Renmin Jiefangjun Guofang Daxue Dangshi Yanjiushi (ed.), Zhonggong Dangshi Jiaoxue Cankao Ziliao [Reference and Educational Material on the History of the CCP], Vol. 23 (Beijing: Guofang Daxue Chubanshe, 1986).

Zhongguo Renmin Jiefangjun Guofang Daxue Dangshi Yanjiushi (ed.), *Zhonggong Dangshi Jiaoxue Cankao Ziliao* [Reference and Educational Material on the History of the Chinese Communist Party], Vol. 24 (Beijing: Guofang Daxue Chubanshe, 1986).

Zhongguo Renmin Jiefangjun Guofang Daxue Dangshi Yanjiushi (ZRJGDDY) (ed.), *Zhonggong Dangshi Jiaoxue Cankao Ziliao* [Reference and Teaching Material for the History of the CCP], Vol. 23 (Beijing: Guofang Daxue Chubanshe, 1986).

Zhongguo Tudi Guanli Zonglan Bianji Weiyuanhui (ZTGZBW) (ed.), Zhongguo Tudi Guanli Zonglan [An Overview of Land Management in China] (Beijing: Falü Chubanshe, 1992), pp. 68–71.

Zhongguo Ziran Ziyuan Congshu Bianyi Weiyuanhui (ed.), *Zhongguo Ziran Ziyuan Congshu: Ningxia Juan* [Encyclopaedia of China's Natural Resources: Ningxia Volume] (Beijing: Zhongguo Huanjing Kexue Chubanshe, 1995).

Zhongguo Ziran Ziyuan Congshu Bianyi Weiyuanhui (ed.), *Zhongguo Ziran Ziyuan Congshu: Ningxia Juan* (Beijing: Zhongguo Huanjing Kexue Chubanshe, 1995).

Zhou, Qiren, *Zhongguo he Suoyouquan Guanxi de Bianhua* [Changes of the Relationship between the State and Ownership] Nos. 1 and 2, Rural Institutions Research Group of the State Council (Beijing: Rural Development Research Centre, 1993).

Zhuang, Xueying, 'Rehabilitation and Development of Forest on Degraded Hills of Hong Kong', *Forest Ecology and Management*, No. 99 (1997), pp. 197–201.

Zizhiqu Dangwei, 'Guanqie Zhixing Zhonggong Zhongyang (1985) 1 Hao Wenjian de Shixiang Zhengce Guiding' ['Ten Policy Regulations concerning the Implementation of Document No. 1 (1985) of the Communist Party and Central Government'], reprint, *Ningxia Daily* (5 April 1985), in Ningxia Nongye Hezuo Jingji Shiliao Bianxiezu (ed.), *Historical Material of the Collective Agricultural Economy of Ningxia*, Vol. 2 (1988), p. 819.

Zuo, Ting, 'Shehui Linye Shijian zhong Zhidu Fangmian de Ruogan Wenti' ['Some Issues Regarding the System of the Practice of Social Forestry'], *Zhongguo Nongcun Jingji*, Vol. 179, No. 11 (1999), pp. 19–24.

Index